Space Sirens, Scien
and Princesses

Space Sirens, Scientists and Princesses

The Portrayal of Women in Science Fiction Cinema

DEAN CONRAD

McFarland & Company, Inc., Publishers

Jefferson, North Carolina

ISBN (print) 978-1-4766-6927-4
ISBN (ebook) 978-1-4766-3271-1

LIBRARY OF CONGRESS CATALOGUING DATA ARE AVAILABLE

BRITISH LIBRARY CATALOGUING DATA ARE AVAILABLE

Front cover: (left to right) A replica of the Maria robot from the 1927 film
Metropolis (Science Museum, London); Jane Fonda as the title character from
the 1968 film *Barbarella* (Paramount Pictures/Photofest); Alicia Vikander
as Ava from the 2015 film *Ex Machina* (Universal Pictures/Photofest)

Printed in the United States of America

McFarland & Company, Inc., Publishers
  Box 611, Jefferson, North Carolina 28640
    www.mcfarlandpub.com

To Lynne, with love.
I'm sorry I couldn't include
This Is Spinal Tap. Maybe next time.

xxx

TABLE OF CONTENTS

ACKNOWLEDGMENTS

Back in 1993, my dear friend Tim Hatcher bought me my first laptop computer, so that I could write my first book during my year away in Pittsburgh, Pennsylvania. It was quite a machine: chunky and heavy, with a monochrome display and a 100-megabyte hard drive. Tim considered it a gift, but I intended to reimburse him from of the proceeds of that book. As it turns out, he was closer to the truth. Again. It is the unerring support and the regular acts of kindness, generosity and forgiveness of friends and family over many years that have enabled me to continue doing what I do. They should be recognized here, so my heartfelt thanks go to Mum and Dave, Jim and Gillie, Sarah and Roy, Irene and Barry, Chris and Louise, Geography Tim, Theatre Tim and of course Lynne. Always there when I need them.

Special thanks specific to this book must start with Lynne; I couldn't have done it, or many other things, without her sacrifice and support. John Streets trawled through every page of the manuscript, except this one, and kept me supplied with feedback and interesting snippets from the daily newspapers. I am grateful for his sterling efforts (although I must confess that I didn't always get around to reading the cricket reports). Thanks also to Jason Gould for his supportive and incisive comments, especially on the early chapters; they have been greatly appreciated. My friend and Japanese teacher Sayuri-san kept me sane with non–science fiction conversation during the bulk of the writing, so to her I say, ありがとうございました。

Additional thanks are due to those scholars, critics and commentators who have responded to my e-mailed requests and questions. Most of them have been quoted and referenced in the main text in some way; all of them contributed more than I have had space to include. For their time, support and generous spirit, my appreciation goes to John Clute, Christine Cornea, Glen Donnar, Matthew Wilhelm Kapell, Jane Killick, Marie Lathers, Penny Montalvan, Lynne

Magowan, Laura Mulvey, Bonnie Noonan, Simone Odino, Ace G. Pilkington, Olga A. Pilkington and Jay (J.P.) Telotte.

Finally, I would like to recognize John Wesley Harris, whose death in 2008 robbed me of a mentor, an advocate and a friend. All those trips to the cinema were not entirely wasted, John!

PREFACE
Invisible Man

This book has been busting to get out of me since I completed my Ph.D. on the subject almost 20 years ago. Back then, the publishers that I contacted didn't seem to want to take women in science fiction films seriously—or at least not my thoughts on them. Populist imprints saw the work as too academic, while university presses were not convinced that it was academic enough. Twenty years on, the landscape of genre cinema study has changed, as the field of cultural studies has blossomed—especially in the U.S. However, prejudices and detractors remain. My recent attempts to develop a television documentary series exploring this subject were met time and again with the same response from broadcast commissioners and editors: "It's too niche." By which they must mean that the representation of roughly half the population within the most popular cinema genre of the day is "too niche." The battle for credibility is not over.

But prejudice cuts all ways. I have one acquaintance—a lifelong science fiction literature reader—who continues to scoff at the idea that the genre's movie output might merit any serious analysis or discussion. He seems to have forgotten that his favored form has fought hard against negative perceptions created by the pulp novels, magazines and comic books that popularized "Scientifiction" in the early decades of the 20th century. He may not think that those early forms merit study either; he's certainly unlikely to endorse the popular cultural notion that "if anything is worth talking about, then everything is."

While I was researching in 1993/4 for my first attempt at a book, *Star Wars: The Genesis of a Legend*, I was quizzed by a former school friend, and another detractor: "Why are you bothering with that old film? Why aren't you writing a book on *Jurassic Park*?" Why indeed? After all, it was clear that *Star Wars* was going to disappear without a trace. My next detractor appeared in the form of a senior lecturer when I came to select my Ph.D. research topic. "Your thesis will have to work extra hard to convince people that this is worthy of a doctorate," he warned. "Shakespeare would be an easier sell." The advice was well-intentioned, but it seemed ironic coming from a scholar in the field of drama, a related subject not long out of its own battles for recognition by the academic community. Happily, my enlightened examiners had my back. Professor Neil Sinyard had written a book on Nicolas Roeg (and corrected the misspelling of the film director's name in my thesis) and Professor Edward James was, and remains, a respected science fiction expert. They were rigorous, but ultimately well-selected by my supervisor, the late and much-missed John Harris—for years my cinema-companion on trips to see the latest science fiction release.

My earliest science fiction cinema memory is of standing in line outside my local ABC in Colchester, England, waiting to see *Star Wars*. That must have been early 1978, when I was almost eight years old. My next memory is of rushing home to see a documentary about it, broadcast by one of only three television stations that we had in the UK in those days. We had no recording devices, so if a program was missed, it was gone, until the repeat. I remember feeling gloomy at the realization that we would have to wait maybe five years for *Star Wars* to be shown on television. I had become a fan.

In those days, boys like me didn't really think much about the role of women outside the home environment, much less their representation in science fiction cinema. It must have seemed natural that Princess Leia was a damsel-in-distress, and not unnatural that Aunt Beru was just about the only other woman in the film—and spent most of her time preparing food. Five years and two *Star Wars* movies later, the situation hadn't changed very much. I had not been old enough to see *Alien* at the cinema, so I didn't yet realize that women in science fiction films didn't have to lounge around in gold bikinis, waiting to be rescued.

It wasn't until I was introduced to feminism at the age of fifteen that I began to think about these things, and it wasn't until I reached university at the age of twenty that I began to write about them. By then, I could see that Princess Leia was a female stereotype drawn from myth and fairytale, and not necessarily representative of the strong, independent figure that modern women wanted to see—and be. I wrote as much in that first *Star Wars* book. Later, when I came to research for my Ph.D., "an assessment of the development of the female in commercial science fiction film," I was able to place Leia into context, but I still didn't really appreciate her key contribution to the profile of women in the genre. Twenty years, a few publications and two aortic valve replacements later, I consider her to be crucial. What's more, I have changed my mind about the significance, or otherwise, of quite a few female roles—sometimes shifting my opinion 180 degrees. Perspective is essential to understanding history.

While I was writing my doctoral thesis all those years ago, I was challenged by the brilliant Dr. Nike Imoru to state what I—a man—could bring to the study of women in science fiction cinema. "Objectivity," I mused, a response received with more grace than perhaps it deserved. I'm older now; maybe no wiser, but certainly more battle-worn. Scars bring their own wisdom and so I realize that objectivity is impossible. I try not to let being a man affect my analysis, but it will. Science fiction cinema has been skewed by more than a century of patriarchal perspectives, so there is no reason to think that I'm immune. As a result, I may well be guilty of exaggerating the importance of my favorite films (because I'm a little in love with Helen Benson) and of underplaying the importance of my least favorites (because I think that *The Hunger Games* movies are a little over-rated). Science fiction seems to generate fan allegiances like no other genre. We all have our favorite characters, films, performers and directors; they populate and inform our own narratives for the genre and, ultimately, our perspectives on it. That, basically, is my excuse for missing your favorite character, film, performer or director. This is my book, these are my perspectives and—after some time spent observing women in science fiction films—this is what I think. I like to imagine that this "post-feminist" age allows my contribution to be nothing more and nothing less than anyone else's. Who knows? But you have been warned.

INTRODUCTION
Captive Women

Why, I guess you don't know everything
about women yet.—*Princess Leia*

We seem to be living through a golden era for women in science fiction cinema. Some of the genre's most acclaimed recent hits—*Gravity* (2013), *Ex Machina* (2015), *Arrival* (2016)—focus on female characters; the huge success of the fantasy film *Wonder Woman* (2017) appears to have encouraged DC franchise producers to develop a *Batgirl* project; *Star Trek Beyond* (2016) has finally given that franchise a *bona fide* female action character; the biggest industry property of them all has replaced Luke and Han with Rey and Jyn; and even the mainstay of machismo, Mad Max, relinquished his spot to a woman in *Fury Road* (2015). For now, that is. After all, we have been here before.

One of the recurring themes of the present work is the oscillating fortunes of female characters in the genre. Evolution and revolution across one hundred and twenty or so years of science fiction cinema have brought golden ages and dark phases. The practical, resourceful protagonist roles taken by women before the First World War reverted largely to male roles when peace returned, leaving women to tend their professional husbands and fathers as they had before. In 1929, Gerda Maurus played the impressive Friede Velten in *Frau im Mond*, just before the widespread adoption of sound-on-film made this stunning, silent classic obsolete overnight. Voiceless Friede was stranded, but she was not alone: female characters stagnated for the next twenty years. Tradition, convention and stereotype took charge until the intervention of another war gave women a chance to show what they could do once again. And so the cycles continued. The female scientists who emerged after the Second World War were held back

5

by 1950s' notions of domesticity and motherhood; feminist advances in the 1960s were stifled by a technological backlash in the '70s; the strong women of the 1980s were becoming monstrous and sidelined by the middle of the '90s; and into the new millennium, an uncertain future eased female representation back towards the past once again.

No film genre takes more time, effort and money to produce than science fiction, especially in the 21st century with the increasing reliance on dense digital spectacle. Add to this an industry that has always tried to take as few risks as possible with its expensive product and the result is the "imaginative conservatism" to which the genre will always return at times of stress. When war, recession, industry upheaval, government legislation and new technologies threaten, science fiction retreats—and female roles suffer. What follows attempts to make sense of a genre that can present women as sexy robots, killer queens, feisty princesses, naked aliens, omnipotent computers, warriors, astronauts, scientists, mothers, lovers, stewardesses and so much more. It explores and exposes the many and varied female roles in what has become the most popular, visually arresting and commercially lucrative cinema genre.

Histories

This is a cinema history. It is not a work of cultural, critical, film or feminist theory—although its does drift into all of those fields in places. The aim of this book is to present a full-length survey of female representation across the entire history of science fiction cinema. It tries to place as many relevant movies as possible in chronological order, and then to find connections between characters, narratives and themes across time. The objective has been to observe patterns and trends, not to propose über-theory. The Filmography spans the period 1895 to 2018 and lists more than 650 science fiction films; that seems a lot, but some sources suggest that this accounts for around 6 percent of feature releases during that period.[1] All that this book can ever hope to do, then, is offer a broad-brush overview of a vast and expanding subject; however, given that this is the first book-length survey of its type, perhaps that is all it needs to do.

Of course, there are numerous other contributions to this field and associated subjects, many of which have been leaned on by this one. Early general histories of science fiction cinema, such as John Baxter's 1970 study *Science Fiction in the Cinema*, tend not to isolate men and women; their job was one of introduction to the subject, the films and the themes. Phil Hardy's *Aurum Film Encyclopedia: Science Fiction* (incorporating the work of Walt Lee, Denis Gifford,

Anthony Masters, Paul Taylor, Paul Willerman and Kim Newman) has been an invaluable reference volume, setting films from 1895 to 1995 in context— and often, helpfully, commenting on their female characters. It has become more common now for surveys of film to include sections that are dedicated to gender representation. For example, Christine Cornea's 2007 book *Science Fiction Cinema: Between Fantasy and Reality* offers many perceptive insights into "the masculine subject" and "the feminine subject," especially in the films of the 1980s and '90s. Bonnie Noonan appears to be working through the eras book-by-book, using her personal recollections as a starting point for *Women Scientists in Fifties Science Fiction Films*, before moving on to a critical study of *Gender in Science Fiction Films, 1964–1979*. In *Space Oddities: Women in Outer Space in Popular Film and Culture, 1960–2000*, Marie Lathers makes some valuable connections between modes and methods of female representation across media. Space and the stories that are told about it are, of course, central to the study of science fiction cinema.

Books that focus on specific movies can offer useful insights, although one leader in this field, the *BFI Classics* series, does seem to have concentrated more on the "men and machines" end of the genre. Elsewhere, Ximena Gallardo C. and C. Jason Smith's examination of Sigourney Weaver's journey through the first four *Alien* films, *Alien Woman: The Making of Lt. Ellen Ripley*, is a good example of a book-length single character study, but these are relatively rare. A little more common are book chapters focusing on specific aspects of female representation, such as Steve Chibnall's *Alien Women: The Politics of Sexual Difference in British SF Pulp Cinema*. More common still are journal papers and magazine articles. In recent years, the British Film Institute's monthly magazine *Sight & Sound* has included features on female directors and women in silents, Westerns and World War II movies, but its best barometer for the plight of women in science fiction films remains, for now, Kim Newman's film reviews. It is no surprise that the internet is now the easiest place to find information about female characters; however, it can also be the hardest place to find reliable information. Simone Odino's website devoted to *2001: A Space Odyssey*— *2001Italia.it*—includes the fascinating research piece *Who's that girl? (actress-spotting in ['2001: a space odyssey'])*, but it sits amid countless online lists that are often entertaining, but add very little to the serious study of women in the genre. Wise words from film and science fiction specialist J.P. Telotte arrived by e-mail during the preparation of this book: "the problem, as you've probably already encountered, is where/how to stop." Indeed.

The present work offers more detail than some of these commentaries, but it cannot hope to penetrate the depths reached by others. Instead, it goes long, encompassing thirteen decades of female representation in science fiction cinema. Navigating a path through the insights already out there, as well as the films themselves, has contributed to the fun and frustrations of writing this book.

Herstories

Many film fans, critics and commentators point to Ridley Scott's 1979 film *Alien* as a significant movie in the development of women in science fiction cinema, and so it is. Some regard it as the most significant movie, with respect to female roles, in the genre's history. This is harder to quantify. At the time of *Alien*'s release, reviewers seemed more interested in its art direction and creature design than in Sigourney Weaver's lone female survivor, Ripley. It was a similar situation for Linda Hamilton's portrayal of Sarah Connor in *The Terminator* (1984)—another popular candidate for "most significant movie." She attracted less contemporary critical interest than the appearance of Arnold Schwarzenegger in what was his breakthrough genre film. The significance of *Alien* and *The Terminator* has been bolstered by retrospective projection, which began to occur in earnest after their first sequels: *Aliens* (1986) and *Terminator 2: Judgment Day* (1991). This is not to say that those first films were not important, of course they were. Without *Alien*, there would have been no *Aliens*, but the second film is where Ripley's character really begins to develop. Without *The Terminator*, James Cameron and Gale Anne Hurd might not have brought their talents to bear on *Aliens* and Ripley may not then have had the impact that she did. What is more, this director and producer team would not have had the budget to make *Terminator 2: Judgment Day* in the way that they did—and this is where Connor's character has most impact. Ripley and Connor undoubtedly went on to influence the roles that followed, through the warrior women of the late 1980s and into the '90s, past the kick-boxing babes of the early 2000s and onto the competent female characters of the current decade. But this chain of events did not begin in 1979.

Alien might not have been made if *Star Wars* had not been such a massive success in 1977. Princess Leia has the fight of the feminists, but her feet are firmly in feminine, fairytale traditions and the Saturday morning serial *Flash Gordon* (1936). George Lucas was also inspired by the grand vision of *2001: A Space Odyssey* and the merchandizing of *Planet of the Apes*, two 1968 films that offer very different roles for women. The female ape, Dr. Zira, can be linked back via Pierre Boulle's 1963 novel to the women of science who emerged on screen during the Space Age of the 1950s; the most accomplished of these also went into space in films like *Rocketship X-M* (1950). They were not the first;

the influences go further back. In 1929, Fritz Lang had included a female astronaut in the title of his silent film, *Frau im Mond*, a high-water mark in the genre's focus on female protagonists. Eponymous women had been pioneered by the 1912 film *Freezing Auntie*, and, as so often, Georges Méliès had got in early with active females in *A Trip to the Moon* (1902). There is little doubt that he would have seen potential in the attractive young women who feature in the single-scene science ditties made at the end of the 19th century—films like *X-Rays* (1897), in which an X-ray machine is used to spy on a courting couple (albeit as skeletons!).

If an historical overview has any value, it is in showing that nothing exists in isolation. It is difficult, if not impossible, to quantify precisely the influence of any single movie or role, but if an attempt is to be made, films and characters need first to be placed in context—in relation to each other, to the wider cinema industry and to the world in which they all sit. Only when the history is charted is it possible even to suggest connections and propose theories. This book is the result of an attempt to navigate that history.

Definitions

Vexed questions concerning the nature of science fiction have been debated for some time and will continue to be for some time to come. There is not enough space here to do justice to a subject that could fill an entire separate book. Despite the likelihood that arguments will never be settled to the satisfaction of all,[2] there is still an expectation that a survey such as this will offer a definition of the genre; however, in *Where No Man Has Gone Before: Women and Science Fiction*, Lucie Armitt argues that "to define something before one starts is immediately to constrain it, to imprison it within a label in relation to which all innovation becomes deviation."[3]

That sounds reasonable, but it also opens up the potential for all cinema to be science fiction. Indeed, it could be argued that this was true for its earliest days: medium and genre were interchangeable. People on screen in 1895 did not need to perform the impossible; the mere fact of their performance seemed impossible. To the spectator, this artistic revolution brought a kind of magic. The magic was, of course, underpinned by science and technology, but if, as Arthur C. Clarke once noted, "any sufficiently advanced technology is indistinguishable from magic," then this particular revolution was a science fiction one—or at least a fantasy one. When film critic and historian David Robinson describes the pioneers of cinema as a "collection of scholars and showmen, instrument makers and conjurors, adventurers and impresarios, charlatans and visionaries,"[4] he might equally be referring to any number of science fiction filmmakers, from Georges Méliès through Eugen Schüfftan and John Dykstra to James Cameron. Whether it is the mute, monochrome tricks of early nitrate pioneers or the 3-D, VR conjuring of the current CGI wizards, science fiction is part of the DNA of cinema.

Of course, to say that all cinema today is science fiction—when most audiences are sophisticated enough to see through the magic—would, perhaps, be pushing the point; besides, it is not entirely helpful to the reader. John Brosnan offers one possible solution to this conundrum in his entertaining 1991 history, *The Primal Screen*. Answering potential complaints about his omission of the 1933 classic *King Kong*, he states: "it's definitely fantasy, not sf (well, it is in my book)."[5] This comment is allied to Norman Spinrad's witty conclusion that "science fiction is anything published as science fiction."[6] These responses are not entirely helpful either; nor are they entirely serious, but they do lead to a serious point, highlighted by Andrew Tudor: "We are caught in a circle which first requires that the films are isolated, for which purposes a criterion is necessary, but the criterion is, in turn, meant to emerge from the empirically established common characteristics of the films."[7]

Science fiction will always be a matter for argument. For some, there will be no essential difference between the giant gorilla King Kong and the various oversized creatures who rampaged through the 1950s in films such as *Them!* and *Gojira* (both 1954). To others, the crucial difference is that the latter become monstrous as a result of nuclear activity; they are metaphors for the dangers of an atomic age. King Kong's size is not explained, which may be why Brosnan has confined that film to fantasy. He may be applying one of the most useful descriptions of science fiction—and the one that underpins the majority of inclusions in this volume—the "explicable novum":

> ...some new element, something that distinguishes the fiction from reality as presently constituted. A novum could be a vampire or a colonised planet. The sub-set that is sf insists that the novum be explicable in terms that adhere to conventionally formulated natural law; the remainder, fantasy, has no such requirement.[8]

Peter Nicholls' simple approach provides limits, but it also liberates the genre from the oppressive dictates of those who would seek to confine it too much; however, it is not perfect. Time travel is a potential problem because, according to Einstein, it is impossible. If it is accepted as possible for the purposes of the narrative, is it enough that *Back to the Future* (1985) explains it using the Flux Capacitor? Is that device enough of an "explicable novum"? And what of *Peggy Sue Got Married* (1986) and *The Time Traveler's Wife* (2009), which offer no McGuffin gadget at all? When *Star Trek* technical expert Michael Okuda came to explain the science behind the transporter technology in *Star Trek: The Next Generation*, he diligently took account of Heisenberg's uncertainty principle by inventing "Heisenberg compensators."[9] When asked by a fan at a conference how they work, Okuda replied, "Very well, thanks." It is all he could do for his particular "explicable novum."

A one-minute film in which a pig is turned instantaneously into sausages by means of a wooden box (see: *La Charcuterie mécanique*, 1895) might not be considered as part of the genre today; however, to discard a fiction once the science has caught up is dangerous. That would eliminate a good number of space travel films, along with some computer narratives and every attempt to exploit X-rays during cinema's silent period. Very quickly, attempts to delineate the genre get bogged down. This is perhaps why Edward James prefers to describe science fiction as a "bundle of perceptions."[10]

In order to make sense of the genre's scope for his 1977 *Visual Encyclopedia of Science Fiction*, Brian Ash divides it into a series of "thematics"—genre subcategories that begin to interrogate James' bundle. His list is worth reproducing here:

> Space and Star Drives, Exploration and Colonies, Biologies and Environments, Warfare and Weaponry, Galactic Empires, Future and Alternative Histories, Utopias and Nightmares, Cataclysms and Dooms, Lost and Parallel Worlds, Time and Nth Dimensions, Technologies and Artefacts, Cities and Cultures, Robots and Androids, Computers and Cybernetics, Mutants and Symbiotes, Telepathy, Psionics and ESP, Sex and Taboos, Religion and Myths, Inner Space.[11]

As James suggests, perception is key. Coupled with Ash's comprehensive list, it is a reminder that each facet of the genre carries a different significance, and one that changes according to who or what it is applied to—and who does the applying. This, rather than a neat definition, is crucial to an understanding of female representation in science fiction cinema.

Language

For the most part, "female representation" in this book means "women's roles and characters," but not always. The aim has been to cast the net as wide as possible, which means taking account of gendered examples of animated dolls (*Coppélia: la poupée animée*, 1900), goddesses (*Le Voyage dans la Lune*, 1902), robots (*The Perfect Woman*, 1949), apes (*Planet of the Apes*, 1968), furniture (*A Clockwork Orange*, 1971), monsters (*Alien*, 1979), spaceships (*Battle Beyond the Stars*, 1980), computers (*2010*, 1984), Klingons (*Star Trek VI: The Undiscovered Country*, 1991), personifications of love (*The Fifth Element*, 1997), children (*War for the Planet of the Apes*, 2017), and any other category that fits into what Denis Gifford calls the genre's "things, its and aliens."[12]

The use of language presents many further potential pitfalls, which could also be the subject of a whole other book. Qualitative terms like "progressive" and "regressive" have been avoided as far as possible, because they are too loaded, not least by the question "from whose perspective?" Helen Benson in the 1951 film *The Day the Earth Stood Still* saves the world, but her social and professional roles as mother and secretary tie her to a traditional representation that was actively used to hold women back in the 1950s. In the movie's 2008 remake, Benson is a Princeton professor, but she does not get to save the world. Is this "progressive" or "regressive"?

"Feminist" and "feminism" are also loaded terms whose meaning alters with perspective. This study cannot be a feminist reading of science fiction film for many reasons, not least because it could never do justice to the fractured and multi-faceted nature of feminisms over time. This text draws attention to specific standpoints as they become relevant to the discussion (for example, Lizzie Borden's 1983 Marxist Feminist experiment, *Born in Flames*, discussed in Chapter V); however, an attempt to encompass multiple feminist perspectives would inevitably take the focus off the history. That book is left to others. In the meantime, for feminist readings of *Alien*, for example, the reader is directed to James H. Kavanagh's and Judith Newton's essays in Annette Kuhn's invaluable 1990 collection, *Alien Zone: Cultural Theory and Contemporary Science Fiction Cinema*,[13] and for a wide range of other materials, begin with *Femspec*, the feminist journal dedicated to science fiction and fantasy genres across multiple disciplines.[14]

Finally, the term "actress" is increasingly regarded as diminutive, pejorative and unnecessarily discriminatory, so the word has not been used outside quoted material. The terms "female actor" and "male actor" feel a little clumsy, so the intention was to use just "actor" and to add "male" only when that alternative identification became necessary. As it transpires, neither has been required throughout the text. The focus has remained firmly on the historical survey.

Chapters

The obvious way to approach an historical survey is to present the facts in chronological order; however, as Brian Ash shows above, the themes of science fiction are so iconic and evocative that it is tempting instead to let them guide the framework. The problem with this approach is that it can soon become confusing. A chapter on "robots" (from *An Animated Doll*, 1900 to *Ex Machina*, 2015), followed by a return to the beginning for a chapter on "mothers" (from *An Over-Incubated Baby*, 1901 to *Arrival*, 2016), would illuminate those themes, but it could well also obscure the general development of female representation across the genre over time. A compromise is necessary. This work runs in chronological order, era-by-era, picking up themes as they become prominent with respect to women within the genre. The text then refers backward to earlier films and forward to later films in order to add context and to support any argument being made. For example, the discussion about cognition in Chapter VI comes at a time when artificial intelligences were increasingly being presented as female. This does not suggest that women did no thinking before 1980; it means that their new roles as robots, computers and computer users shaped their development in the genre going forward.

Chapters are not divided rigidly by decade. This is partly because some decades, such as the 1930s, would yield very short chapters. It is mainly to give a sense of where the important watershed points occur: the beginning of the sound era; the end of World War II; the upheavals of the sixties; the impact of George Lucas; the end of Ripley; and start of the new millennium.

Chapter I examines the foundations of the genre as they emerged during the silent period, 1895–1929. Many recognizable female roles—robots, mothers, mediators—appeared during this time, but emphasis is placed for now on the basic female functions within the narrative, along with her relationship with male characters. Absence, token presence and support for men (especially during World War I) are representations that will follow female characters through the entire history of science fiction cinema.

Chapter II picks up the baton at the beginning of the sound era, when women were largely confined to convention again—losing the gains made after World War I and through the 1920s. Female roles were fairly static during the 1930s and '40s, as the genre consolidated its audience and its aesthetics. Therefore, the opportunity is taken here to discuss central elements of female representation: sex and sexuality, along with some of the theory that underpins their use in the genre. Science fiction's unique ability to enable men to portray their fantasies remains crucial to the way women are presented in these films, so theories and observations discussed in this chapter create a foundation for the rest of the book.

Chapter III recognizes the effect that emerging post–World War II sciences and technologies had on the genre—and their impact on female representation. The Atomic Age, the Space Race and the Cold War would each play a part in women's development as professionals, especially within the sciences. It was a period of oscillating fortunes, though, as female characters bumped against the "glass ceiling" that protected roles reserved for men. In the 1950s' battles for identity there was an expectation that women would return to traditional domestic roles in support of "us" against "them."

Chapter IV bridges the gap between the period of exponential growth experienced by American science fiction cinema in the 1950s and the worldwide genre explosion that came in the wake of *Star Wars*. This is a period of two halves: the shifting sixties are characterized by sexual and social revolutions and the move to color film; the seventies witnessed a retreat toward serious tales about "men and machines." Between these two decades sits a watershed year for the genre: 1968.

Chapter V begins with the release of *Star Wars* in 1977 and charts its impact on the genre's female roles. This period would develop into the golden era for female representation, as characters not only took the lead, but, crucially, drove the narratives and made decisions in their own heroes' journeys. Through the second half of the 1980s and most of the '90s, some female characters developed a "masculinity" and robustness that continue to affect the genre today. The machismo has largely disappeared, leaving the tough "femininity" that had underpinned the role of Princess Leia back in 1977.

Chapter VI begins by returning to the 1980s to examine the familiar elements of female representation that had continued to run alongside the radical female character revolution. These were the elements of tradition and stereotype that would begin to return once the genre became tired of its "masculinized" women. But female representation had come too far to allow a return entirely to convention. The result was a mixed-bag of characters, as the genre reached a postmodern phase—and the world approached the new millennium.

Chapter VII brings this history up to date with a reflection on cinema's widespread adoption of digital technologies. The millennium began uneasily for women, as the genre reverted again to telling stories about "men and machines"; however, enough influence from the golden era had trickled down to keep female roles ticking over. The huge success of *Avatar* in 2009 placed women close to the center of commercial science fiction narratives once again and kick-started a new revolution. It was one that has now brought female characters to prominence in some of the biggest genre franchises of all.

Finally, an appendix provides short commentaries on fifty or so films that may prove useful to anyone interested in the history of female representation in science fiction cinema.

I

SCIENCE FICTION
Silents and the Establishment
of Female Roles

At the beginning of 1895, projected moving pictures had yet to be unveiled to the public. By the turn of the 20th century, the clamor for this quirky, novel entertainment had become so great that an entire new industry had blossomed, with individuals and companies making and distributing thousands of movies around the world. These typically 1- to 3-minute silent pieces offer a window onto the societies of that world: their fashions, what made them laugh, what made them return to the cinema for more, their grasp of new science and technology, and, central to this history, their treatment of women. It is easy for the modern viewer to scoff at early examples of an emerging genre: a bucket of liquid-electricity thrown over a mother-in-law to stop her nagging is, after all, both silly science and moderate misogyny. However, these are the roots of science fiction cinema, and the genre's fruits have never really fallen far from that tree.

———— ∞ ————

Stereotypical Foundations

It was suggested in the Introduction that all cinema in the earliest years of the medium was essentially science fiction. That is, the creation and consumption of the moving image was a scientific marvel—a wonder in and of itself. Indeed, those very early movies barely even concern themselves with a story; instead, their "Brilliant and interesting Scenes absolutely true to life in PRECISION, PROPORTION AND MOTION"[1] seem to exist merely to document the arrival and fidelity of the technology. Arguments about the first story film and the first "real" science fiction movie belong (and are offered) else-where.[2] In order to cut to the chase, this text follows Phil Hardy and his *Aurum Film Encyclopedia: Science Fiction*, which, more than twenty years after its latest edition, is still the best reference work in the field—to 1995. In his survey, Hardy takes a step back from the vexed questions of genre definition, and allows the simple narrative spectacle of the early "trick films"[3] to guide his choice for the first science fiction film.

TRICK FILMS

La Charcuterie mécanique was produced in 1895 in France by pioneers of cinema technology, the Lumière Brothers. In this one-minute, silent, black and white film, a butcher and three other men heave a live pig into a large wooden box. Moments later, assisted by the magic of cinema, the beast appears at the other end as bacon, sausages, pork chops and so forth. The butcher passes the goods to his male assistant, while three other men tend the steam-powered machine. There are no women in this "first" science fiction film. This witty piece was so successful that it prompted a number of embellished alternatives by other filmmakers looking to cash-in on its commercial potential. George A. Smith's 1897 British version, *Making Sausages*, is advertised in a trade catalog with the following description: "Four men cooks at work in the kitchen. Live cats and dogs are put into the machine and come out as sausages."[4] No female characters are listed for this early science fiction picture either. The household pets theme was picked up again in 1901 for The Edison Company's *Fun in a Butcher Shop*, whose catalog entry includes the description: "Two enterprising Dutchmen are at work at their sausage mill. A constant stream of boys and men are coming into the sausage factory...."[5] A casting policy appears to be emerging in these films.

The concept of cinema sausages was clearly profitable enough for film-makers to continue making variations on the theme for around a decade. As late as 1904, Edison's company was still pedaling the basic concept in its 4-minute film, *Dog Factory*. This is a particularly gruesome version, in which the "Patent Dog Transformator" turns clients' unwanted dogs into strings of sausages, which the male butcher hangs on pegs labeled, "pointer," "terrier," "setter" and so forth. The conceptual development here is that the butcher's machine can turn the sausages back into dogs. The important narrative devel-opment from the perspective of female representation is that two of the cus-tomers who arrive for their "while you wait" dog are women. After nine years, the mechanical butcher theme has introduced female characters to the story.

It is fair to say that factors such as rudimentary distribution networks and the reluctance to waste a good idea did mean that content development in cinema's early period was slow in many areas. Even so, this short history of the early sausage movies does offer an opportunity to analyze developments in female roles specifically. As noted above, to begin with, there were no female roles. Even Frenchwoman Alice Guy Blaché, identified by Ally Acker and others as "the first woman film director in history"[6] (and so is, by extension, science fiction cinema's first female director) presents exclusively male butchers in her curious 1900 "cats-turned-into-hats" version, *Chapellerie et charcuterie mécanique*. The earliest appearances by women in these earliest films appears to be as onlookers, watching men doing things, such as making sausages.

Her promotion, by 1904, from female bystander to one of those customers for Edison's *Dog Factory* may be progress, but even here we can see preconceptions in play to restrict that progress. The first woman to arrive at the dog shop chooses a string of dachshund sausages that are duly turned back into a live dog. But this one is too feisty and the woman can't cope with it, so back into the transformator it goes. The butcher then makes a terrier: this dog is far more docile and the woman leaves the shop happy. The salesman does not want to make the same mistake twice, so the second female customer is presented with a small, cute puppy, which she immediately picks up and takes away.

It is, of course, important to recognize the dangers of over-analysis here, especially given the unsophisticated nature of this 4-minute, silent, black and white movie. At a number of points, the players acknowledge the camera, as they might well have been used to doing with their live theater audiences. These actions exemplify the naïve, even amateurish, nature of the set-up, less than a decade into the Cinema Age. Indeed, amid *Dog Factory*'s frenetic, largely-improvised, pacing and pointing, it is not always clear who is choosing the dogs and who has the dogs chosen for them, which is an important consideration for those wishing to establish who has agency in this scenario. The line of creative intention is not as clear as it may appear to be in contemporary, scripted movies (which have, in their turn, become subjects for over-analysis). Dangers aside, one simple message of this rudimentary movie seems clear: women are best suited to small, submissive dogs.

Female customers in *Dog Factory* are one thing, but—leaving Freudian analysis aside for now—a far more significant revelation resides in the early sausage factory movie series as a whole. It is one that will come to resonate through the history of science fiction cinema, up to and including those contemporary, scripted movies. The significant point is this: there are no female butchers here.

It is tempting now to explore parallels between the sausage machines of these early movies and the sausage factory nature of contemporary science fiction cinema; however, this task will be saved for Chapter VII. Of more use at this early stage is the potential for those first films to reveal something significant about female representation in the genre as a whole. To this end, it is useful to glean a series of generalized observations from the specifics of female role development in the string of sausage factory movies, 1895–1904:

a. She is absent
b. She is a narrative bystander or token presence
c. She supports the male characters
d. Her roles are restricted by tradition
e. Her reactions are governed by stereotype

These observations may look familiar, even to those not acquainted with very early period of science fiction cinema. The extent to which they underpin female representation through the entire 120 years of the genre will be tested by the history explored throughout this text. Drawn, as it is, from the earliest science fiction movies, the above list helps for now to define a base-line for discussion about female roles. But will this prove to be a point of departure: a launch-pad for steady development; or will it become a millstone: a restrictive series of default conditions?

Reflections of the Male Self

In 1926, journalist Terry Ramsaye published *A Million and One Nights: A History of the Motion Picture Through 1925*. It is an entertaining and fascinating glimpse at cinema's early days, offered by a man who was close by. Like the films themselves, Ramsaye's text provides the 21st century reader with an invaluable—albeit mediated—perspective on another world and time. Before describing the birth of the movie industry, Ramsaye describes "the prehistory of the screen,"[7] during which "man" sought constantly to fulfill "his" wish to represent "himself" pictorially. For Ramsaye, the motion picture's unparalleled ability for realistic reproduction made it "the Prayer Wheel of the Wish."[8] And by inference, if not by explicit definition, that wish was male: "The ego of man makes him want to know himself."[9]

Ramsaye's text is very male-centered throughout. This is partly a result of his writing in the 1920s, when the pronouns "he," "him" and "his" took prominence in the description of action and ownership. "Man" himself repre-sented "humankind" in a way that is disappearing from contemporary history books; however, that memory does remain, and will prove important to the representation of women. It is there in the famous first words spoken by Neil

Armstrong as he stepped onto the surface of the Moon: "That's one small step for man, one giant leap for mankind." It is a sentiment that has strong science fiction echoes too, perhaps most famously in Captain Kirk's *Star Trek* credit-sequence voice-over: "to boldly go where no man has gone before."

Even NASA, responding to a more enlightened age, has published suggestions that Armstrong actually meant to say (or indeed did say), "one small step for (a) man...,"[10] and Kirk's line has long been replaced with "where no *one* has gone before...."[11] But the oft-replayed 1960s originals cannot easily be erased. They are a reminder not only of a patriarchal—male-centered—society that once was, but of the male control that still exists. Men dominate Ramsaye's eighty-one chapter titles, a fact that in turn reflects the new art form's patriarchal early period. Moving pictures offered their male innovators an ego-trip: an unrivalled opportunity to project themselves to the world; or as Ramsaye rather flamboyantly puts it:

> That ego is the very soul of both the arts and the sciences. Man in his own profession and his own recreation. The chief of his desires, the keenest of his wishes, the greatest of his recreations is the business of re-creating himself biologically and his emotional adventures in memory and its art forms.[12]

It is important to note that cinema's pioneers did not necessarily prioritize the medium's potential for artistic expression. Intellectual, scientific and technological curiosity were high on the agenda,[13] which is still reflected today in the aims and awards of the *Academy of Motion Picture Arts and Sciences*. Moreover, it was the potential for financial exploitation that turned a technological wonder into an industry. The art developed later. In the meantime, screen entrepreneurs reasoned that what they showed on the screen would need to appeal to an audience; to do that, it would need to "re-create" them in their world—a patriarchal world. The reason that those first sausage machine films contain only men is not necessarily that women are not considered capable, or even that they are not considered necessary; it is largely because they are *not considered*. This basic patriarchal notion helps to define the first default condition for science fiction cinema:

a. Men do things.

It is never easy to be certain about the content of movies which exist now only as catalog entries and fragments, however, female characters do appear to be entirely absent from the earliest experimental science fiction films. Leading players are easier to identify, so we can be more certain that there is nothing prominent for female players in period that is otherwise remarkably imaginative and prescient *vis-à-vis* the genre to come. *Frankenstein* is evoked in the French film, *Chirugien Americain* (1897), in which a male beggar is given new body parts by a doctor. In the same year, robots are hinted at in *Gugesse et l'Automate*, and the consequences of a radical, new discovery is explored by male scientists in the British film, *X-Rays* (1897). A male astronomer imagines space travel in *La Lune à un Metre* (1898); giant insects plague a Frenchman in *Un Bot Lit* (1899) and an American man in *A Jersey Skeeter* (1900); and flying technology is introduced in the technically innovative movie, *A la Conquête de l'Air* (1901). Thus, in cinema's first five years, many of the themes that would become stalwarts of the science fiction genre were introduced with barely a nod to female representation. The notion that a genre concept might be tested on men, and by men, before women are exposed to it will be visited more than once as this history unfolds.

Female absence itself will also become a recurring theme. It is one not confined just to the films, as written histories and commentaries too have, for whatever reason, avoided reference to female representation. Perhaps the most unexpected of these is Vivian Sobchack's now classic 1980 survey of science fiction cinema, *The Limits of Infinity* (updated and expanded in 1988 as *Screening Space: The American Science Fiction Film*), which virtually ignores the specific place of women in the genre. This was rectified to a degree by Sobchack's 1995 essay, "The Virginity of Astronauts: Sex and the Science Fiction Film," but her early omission remains surprising.

Also surprising is Adilifu Nama's analysis of the 1968 movie *Planet of the Apes* in his 2008 text, *Black Space: Imagining Race in Science Fiction Film*. Here, Nama mentions four astronauts traveling at the beginning of the film, and then the three "spacemen" who survive the journey. Missing from his account is the fact that the deceased astronaut—Lt. Stewart, played by Dianne Stanley—is female. It may seem a small point to highlight, after all Stanley's role is so tiny that many commentators leave Stewart unidentified or indeed ignore the role completely[14]; she is not even listed in the film's original credit roll. However, *Black Space* is about the effect of hegemonies—dominant powers—on content and representation in science fiction cinema. In a text in which "the historical structured absence of black people"[15] is an important, recurring theme, Nama has chosen to reference the fourth-astronaut role, but not its (her) gender.

There is surely no malice in these omissions, just other priorities in play. Sobchack's focus is science fiction films in general and Nama's is racial representation in the genre. Marie Lathers would more naturally be expected to notice Stewart's death, and her gender, with a book entitled *Space Oddities: Women and Outer Space in Popular Film and Culture, 1960–2000*,[16] which she does. Perhaps other commentaries, and the films they encompass, are instead merely further examples of what feminism and film academic Constance Penley identifies in *NASA/Trek: Popular Science and Sex in America* as an "ambivalence

... toward the idea of women in space."[17] Zooming out on this idea reveals a rather more challenging earlier text, in which French feminist theorists Hélène Cixous and Catherine Clément suggest that this "ambivalence" is the result of a male dominance of everything—a "philosophical, social and cultural phallocentrism" ... "which certainly means that she is not thought, that she does not enter into the oppositions, that she does not make a couple with the father (who makes a couple with the son)."[18]

In short, patriarchy is not about women, so don't expect the films created within a patriarchal environment to be about women either. Indeed, that father/son dynamic will become very important to science fiction cinema, not least in the early chapters of the *Star Wars* saga.

Absence is in itself a statement; it is engineered by other controlling forces, as Nama points out in Chapter 1 of *Black Space*, entitled "Structured Absence and Token Presence." Nama argues that the non-appearance of black characters can be as damaging as their inclusion in subservient roles (in his case: maids, chauffeurs, porters and butlers), because it normalizes that particular treatment. The potential is there for female roles too, a point that will be returned to in Chapter VII's discussion about the 2015 film *Ex Machina*. Repeated representation—or removal—leads to stereotypes and conventions, which have a way of creating expectations, which in turn develop an air of normality from which film studios can be reluctant to deviate.

It is now to the second part of Nama's useful first chapter title that this history turns, as it searches for female presence in the genre films of the late 19th and early 20th centuries. The women onlookers in Edwardian hats mentioned above may well be the first female performers in science fiction movies. That is unlikely to be proven, but it is certainly true that the role is indicative of the primary on-screen employment for women during cinema's first twenty years. It also helps to expand the genre's default condition to:

b. Men do things; women watch them (sometimes from off-screen).

A good example of this passive female participation in male activity is the 1906 classic produced by British cinema pioneer Robert W. Paul. *The Motorist* is a 3-minute film, famous in genre circles for its fantasy car journey over the Moon and around the rings of Saturn.[19] Five women appear in this movie: four bystanders and the passenger of the car driven by the man of the title. This is fairly typical of the period, but things were beginning to change. *The Motorist* was to be Paul's last science fiction film. Like other inventors who had engineered and developed the technology of cinema—such as Thomas Edison in America and the Lumière brothers in France—Paul would not keep up with the race to develop ever more sophisticated screen content.

As science fiction's one-minute ditties became longer, they could no longer rely on simple tricks and novelty narratives typified by the 1901 film *The Elixir of Life*, in which an old man drinks a potion and transforms into a young man. Any number of female bystanders could be added to this picture to create an observant chorus, but the basic premise is unlikely to sustain for more than an additional minute or so. As the playwrights of Greece had discovered two and a half thousand years earlier, the lone protagonist player eventually needs a deuteragonist foil, someone to play against—perhaps even a woman...

Narrative Traditions

There can be little doubt that this next stage in the development of female representation in science fiction film was advanced by the work of Georges Méliès. Indeed, the French writer, producer and director—as well as leading player in many of his 500-plus films—is identified by Terry Ramsaye as the savior of an art form that was already flagging by the turn of the 20th century:

> ...the motion picture industry fell into decline in the United States. The screen had nothing to say. The novelty of pictures that moved was gone, Authorship was lacking. The potentialities of the screen art were as pigment on the palette with no artist to transfer them to canvas.
> Then magic came to the rescue.[20]

Whether or not Méliès, the magician-cum-filmmaker, actually saved the whole cinema industry is debatable. It is certainly true, however, that his science fiction and fantasy movies were hugely influential; this was demonstrated not least by the number of filmmakers who copied his ideas and plagiarized his work. In his turn, Méliès leaned on existing genre works such as those of Jules Verne and H.G. Wells to create pictures that were ahead of their time. His most reproduced image—the Moon's face with a spaceship embedded in his eye—remains an icon, not only of science fiction film, but of cinema's silent era in general. Viewed today, Méliès work may seem less than revolutionary in its depiction of women; however, built on existing narrative traditions, the roles he created were to have a lasting effect on the genre.

HER VOYAGE BEGINS

Méliès' 1902 film *Le Voyage dans la Lune* has often been called the world's first science fiction cinema epic—and for good reason. Firstly, this was the longest genre film to date. Quoted timings range between 13 and 21 minutes, depending on various factors,[21] but even the lowest estimate puts it way beyond the standard 1- or 2-minute pieces of the day. More significant to this history is the "epic" nature of Méliès' special effects, artistic ambition and narrative scope—which offered potential for a range of female representations. For this reason, it is worth taking a detailed look here at the content of this first epic film, known in English as *A Trip to the Moon.*

Scene 1: Twenty male science academy members, dressed not unlike wizards, are meeting to discuss their plans for a trip to the Moon. The spectator's point-of-view is created by a single, fixed camera, elevated in what would be the stalls of a live theater. The scenery is painted on a series of flats and backdrops, augmented with treads and rostra. As with the majority of Méliès' cinema work, this movie is essentially a filmed theater performance, with cross-fades between scenes. Female representation in this first scene comprises three bemused clerks seated behind desks, watching the men gesticulate wildly about their plans, plus six assistants, dressed as pages, who bring telescopes in for the male scientists. Six further page-girls enter with changes of clothes for the male academics at the end of the sequence. Following a female-free scene in a rocket workshop, the twelve women re-appear dressed in a combination of bathing costume and sailor's uniform. They help the male scientists into their capsule, which they then push into the giant space-gun that will fire the men at the moon. A male sailor lights the fuse and the scientists are away, cheered and waved off by the bathing sailor girls.

Having arrived and clambered out onto the Moon's surface in their top hats and frock coats, the male astronauts settle down for a nap. While they are asleep, the men are visited by six female stars—faces poking through the stage backdrop—and three nymph-like figures, headed by their spiritual leader, played by music hall singer Bluette Bernon.[22] These women, sometimes identified by

Women supporting men doing things. Performers from the *Corps de Ballet du Châtelet,* and Bluette Bernon as Selene, goddess of the Moon, in *Le Voyage dans la Lune* (1902).

commentators as the goddess of the Moon, Selene, and her "Selenites,"[23] sprinkle glittery snow on the sleeping men to wake them; it soon transpires that the visitors are in danger: the Moon is also inhabited by grotesque male creatures, who capture the astronauts. They are taken underground into the presence of the creatures' king, who is attended by five elegant, passive females. The human travelers attack and kill the king and escape back to their capsule, which they heave over a cliff. Assisted by gravity, the men then fall to Earth for a safe landing in the ocean; a steam-ship tows them to dry land; the twelve bathing sailor girls cart and escort the capsule to the town square; and a mixed-gender local crowd celebrates the return of the conquering male lunar heroes. *Finis*.

Naïve though this science fiction narrative now seems, in terms of female involvement, it represented a departure from the regular pre–1902 fare. Georges Méliès' creative strengths as a filmmaker leaned heavily on his theater experience. Indeed, longer versions of *Le Voyage dans la Lune* include a dance interlude midway through, featuring the *Corps de Ballet du Châtelet*. It was natural to Méliès for a dramatic presentation to feature a female chorus; and judging by the number of times the filmmaker employed them, audiences agreed. Two years later, stars from the famous *Folies Bergère* appeared as pretty Parisiennes in *Le Raid Paris à Monte Carlo en deux heures*. The *Corps de Ballet du Châtelet* had already featured in his 1899 version of the fairytale, *Cinderella and the Glass Slipper* and Méliès employed them again for his 1903 fantasy picture, *Le Royaume des Fées* and for his 1907, 18-minute, exaggerated reworking of the Jules Verne classic *Deux Cent Milles Lieues sous les mers ou le Cauchemar du pêcheur*. In this latter film the dancers appear as semi-clad sea nymphs!

Georges Méliès was clearly not averse to the charms of an attractive chorus line, but he was also a practical storyteller. While the importance of their sexual allure is not insignificant (and will play a greater part in Chapter II's discussions), Méliès' women go beyond mere set decoration and bystanders; instead they are employed within his narrative. In the case of *Le Voyage dans la Lune*, the dancers double as the servants, sailors and Selenites who are essential to help the men on their way. In this respect, Méliès' movies neatly illustrate the next element in the list describing female representation in science fiction cinema:

c. Men do things; women assist them.

EXTENSIONS TO THE MALE SELF

The cinema, as Ramsaye points out, offered its early artists unparalleled access to tools for self re-creation. Male domination of moving pictures inevitably led to a screen celebration of the male Self in action; and women—equally inevitably—were added to the men's creative toolbox. To feminist academics Lorraine Gamman and Margaret Marshment, this dynamic and its *raison d'être* remain simple: "Men act; women are acted upon. This is patriarchy."[24]

There have been many psycho-social studies into the notion of the Self (me) and the Other (everyone else): Jacques Lacan's "mirror stage," Gustav Jung's "archetypes" and Eric Berne's "transactional analysis," to name but three, all have something to offer the analyst hoping to make sense of cinema's characters and their interactions. These general theories would easily fill a complete other book, so for brevity and focus, this specific study will draw on useful summaries offered by psychologist Edward Sampson in *Celebrating the Other: A Dialogic Account of Human Nature*. In his text, Sampson provides theoretical underpinnings that can be applied to the treatment of women by men in science fiction cinema. For example, building on Sigmund Freud's "instinct" and "interpersonal" theories, which place the individual *in conflict* and *in concert* with society respectively,[25] Sampson highlights the work of French sociologist Marcel Mauss, who describes two recognizable aspects of the Self:

1. *Moi* (the self-contained, monologic individual)
2. *Personne* (the individual as a member of an ordered-collective)[26]

Emphasizing a single-voiced ("monologic"), self-celebration, the concept of *moi* presents itself in science fiction cinema most obviously—though not exclusively—through the absence of the female; however, very few of the genre's films beyond the first five years actually feature no women at all. Instead, when the men—the largely "self-contained" drivers of their own narrative— accept assistance from female characters they become members of the "ordered-collective" that describes the *personne*. Of course, there are no extra points here for guessing who does the ordering of collectives in patriarchal society and cinema. Women are granted membership of a hierarchy that serves men through social positioning.[27] In short, men represent Self and women represent Other.

Once again, Sampson simplifies matters by offering a clear and instructive division between aspects of what he describes as the "social Other":

1. The Western project Other (socially constructed as useful)
2. The Hegelian Other (to be destroyed)[28]

The Hegelian Other will be looked at again in Chapter VI. For now, it is Sampson's Western project Other that helps to describe and explain the female bystanders, assistants and helpers already identified as a feature of early science fiction cinema.

According to Sampson, the Western project Other is the product of religious, philosophical, cultural, economic and scientific communities throughout

Western history. All of these communities have been contrived and constructed primarily by educated, white males, and crucially, "the objects of their construction have been defined as all that the dominant group is not." So, the Other is a part of the Self. That is, the female is an extension to the male Self:

> Every construction has its dominant group—the constructors—and its others, those who are constructed...
> ...the dominant groups have given priority to their own experiences and their places in the world and have constructed *serviceable* others.[29]

Sampson borrows the phrase "serviceable others" from Pulitzer- and Nobel-Prize–winning writer Toni Morrison, who uses it to describe the role of African Americans, "whose constructed characteristics were essential ... to the definition of the white–American character."[30] In a similar fashion, the female roles of early science fiction cinema became necessary in order to define the male roles. For example, the importance of the male scientists-cum-travelers in *Le Voyage dans la Lune* is reinforced by the women who run around after them. In this case, the women validate the men's pomposity. The extent to which this axiom sustains generally for the entire history of science fiction cinema remains to be seen. For now, it is useful to take a closer look at the subtle nuances of this simple dynamic as it applies to the genre's foundation films. For this exercise, "men do things; women assist them" can be divided into three distinct parts:

c.i. Men do things; women assist them—passively.

c.ii. Men do things; women assist them—practically.

c.iii. Men do things; women assist them—actively.

The first of these has been seen before. Passive assistance can be found in the social and domestic stereotype roles that litter science fiction cinema. These are the servants, daughters, wives, pedestrians, passengers and customers who appear in the background to make the scene and the position of the (male) protagonist more convincing. They are "extras."

The second can be explained by expanding the description of the 1906 film *The Motorist* mentioned above. It was suggested there that the female passenger in this film is a bystander to the male action. This is largely true, but not entirely. While most of the film sees her sitting passively in the passenger's seat, while the man drives them on their incredible journey, there is a moment towards the beginning of the narrative when she reacts to a policeman who has jumped onto the hood. She pushes him off (and under the wheels of) the car, allowing the journey to continue. This switch from passive to practical assistance may seem subtle, even insignificant, but female roles in science fiction cinema develop slowly, and this is still the very early period when the woman's *raison d'être* is to support the man in his scenario. This position as secondary to the male can also be seen reflected in the earliest films to include female characters in their titles: *The Doll Maker's Daughter* (1906) and *When the Man in the Moon Seeks a Wife* (1908). Women appear to have arrived in these stories, but both titles identify the female character as object, rather than subject. She may now be integral, but it is still not yet her plot; it is the men who do the making and the seeking.

When those very early "trick films" gave way to pictures boasting a degree of real science, the men continued to do the making and seeking, while women continued to assist them. A period of wide-ranging scientific and technological developments was reflected in films such as the very early *Les Rayons Roentgens* (1897), one of the many pictures that capitalized on the discovery of X-rays, and the later *The Motor Car of the Future* (1911), part of a trend to reflect this age of new inventions. Also reflected was a degree of cynicism and ignorance, as scientists and inventors were ridiculed in what might be called a period of "silly science films."

Electricity and its partner, magnetism, were explored and exploited in Spain, France, Britain and America with *El Hotel Eléctrico* (1905), *La Cuisine Magnétique* (1908), *Galvanic Fluid* (1908) and *The Electric Servant* (1909) respectively. Filmmakers were having fun with the new sciences: the distilled electrical fluid in *Liquid Electricity* (1907) promotes energy, while *The Magnetic Squirt* features a liquid which forces the squirtee to do the bidding of the squirter. The general tone of these early science fiction films can be seen in the revealingly titled, *The Inventions of an Idiot* (1909) and *Scroggins Goes in for Chemistry and Discovers a Marvelous Powder* (1911)—assisted by his young bride, Mrs. Scroggins.

The ridicule during this period of silliness is not reserved for the (male) scientists alone. Often it is the mothers, lovers, mistresses, maids and brides— passive bystanders in earlier scenarios—who now become the butts of these new science-based jokes. This is the time when daughters and nieces were beginning to interact practically with their scientist, inventor, politician and professional fathers and husbands, which they would continue to do in *Rescued in Mid-Air* (1906), *Pawns of Mars* (1915), *The Comet's Comeback* (1916), *Beneath the Sea* (1915) and *Wake Up!* (1914). This growing prominence also increased their chances of becoming foils for the filmmakers' jokes. Much of this humor relies on the depiction of nagging women: in the 1907 U.S. film *The Hair Restorer*, a jealous wife plucks out her husband's scientifically re-grown hair when she notices the amorous effect it has on their maid. And the nagging wife appears to be universal: in 1909, she appears in the British film *Invisibility*, and in the French film *The Elixir of Strength*, in which a "hen-pecked" husband and father uses a "brute strength" potion to become master of the women in his house. French women receive further violent attention in the 1911 movie *Vers l'Immortalitié*, in which social overcrowding problems are caused by a new immortality potion. The suggested solution is to kill off all mothers-in-law!

CONQUEST OF THE (FEMALE) OTHER

This trend for misogyny under the cloak of humor is clearly a product of the "silly science films" of the time, but it also hints at a deeper resentment. A development in male fears about things to come can be seen in two films which share the same concept, but supply quite different narrative outcomes. In the 1910 British film, *Freezing Mixture*, the scientific fluid of the title is used to immobilize (and so silence) a nagging aunt, much to the delight of her husband and the housemaid. Two years later, an American version includes the aunt in its title—and so signals a key shift in emphasis. In *Freezing Auntie* (1912), the woman discovers the plot against her just in time to substitute water for the freezing fluid. Then, feigning a frozen posture, she waits for her chance to take revenge on her assailants. In what appears to be the first science fiction film to include a woman as the subject of its title,[31] the men have, for once, become the objects. What is more, the joke is on them.

The active assistant role embodied in Georges Méliès' Goddess Selene had been an important departure, away from the merely passive, or even the practical helper, roles traditionally given to women. She is a woman with agency—that is: the power to make her own decisions. In *Le Voyage dans la Lune* she decided to help the men; in *The Hair Restorer*, that agency had been used by a jealous wife to regain her husband; in *Freezing Auntie* the men are thwarted, pursued and punished. It is perhaps no coincidence that this 6-minute movie was written by a woman: Marion Brooks. It is an early example of a trend for science fiction films that would reflect male fears about real-world developments that were bubbling under the surface of society. Even old-guard producers were getting in on this act.

A la Conquête du Pôle, released in 1912, ten years after *Le Voyage dans la Lune*, is described by Hardy as "the longest of the, by now, old-fashioned fantasies of Georges Méliès."[32] The cinema that he did so much to develop was moving on artistically, technically and psychologically. The French magician-turned-filmmaker may have been a master purveyor of traditional fantasy, but he was not noted as a commentator on the contemporary, real world; however, he did have one last trick up his sleeve. Before closing the curtain on Méliès' science fiction film career, it is worth taking a look this 1912 film and its attempts to understand and incorporate revolutionary social changes with which women were threatening to re-shape his world. The film is known in English as *The Conquest of the Pole.*

Scene 1: Once again, this Méliès movie opens with a gathering of male scientists to discuss an ambitious trip; this time it is a competition to reach the North Pole by powered flying machine—the new, revolutionary mode of transport. In contrast to this, the director's old, static camera is again situated in the stalls, and the familiar page-girls and female assistants supply practical support for the men. It feels very familiar, until the male scientists' meeting is disturbed by a group of women carrying signs in French, reading such things as, "Down with men" and "We want to go to the Pole." Then an inter-title screen-caption appears, explaining that "a delegation of suffragettes interrupts the important work of the Academy." The female interlopers are chased away into the corridor, where the next scene finds their rotund leader conducting a meeting—rallying her radical troops.

After another familiar scene in a factory where other women are employed sewing canvas for the airplane's wings, the voyage is ready. The lead suffragist[33] is also ready. Following a failed attempt to disrupt the North Pole Race leaving ceremony by forcing her way onboard the men's flying machine, she hitches a ride on the side of a hot-air balloon owned by a rival male group. After a few seconds, the large woman is shaken off the basket, falls a few hundred feet, lands on a spike atop a church spire, and explodes (like a balloon). Méliès' message at this point is simple: the "crazy suffragette" leader has met her just fate, allowing the wacky race to the pole to continue for the many teams of magnificent men in their flying machines.

It is the academicians from the opening scene who win the race, after being guided by helpful star maidens who form the constellations that lead the men to the North Pole. The explorers crash-land and are then attacked by a giant creature that lives at the pole. It is at this stage that Méliès' narrative takes its most surprising turn: the now-desperate men are rescued in a dirigible piloted by a woman! The scene is short and it may be that the woman—dressed in an over-sized fur coat and hat—is supposed to be playing a man, but the effect on the audience is surely the same. This is a human woman saving men from peril. A scene of celebration for the returning heroes closes the film; the strange female figure does not appear again. *Finis.*

While there are many similarities between *Le Voyage dans la Lune* and *A la Conquête du Pôle*, it is clear that Georges Méliès was also grappling with a changing world. It was a world that the 51-year-old veteran of over 500 films was not best placed to understand—or to represent. On reflection, it is fair to suggest that Méliès liked women. He liked to include them in his films. Whether he appreciated their needs is a different question. His need to take the line of

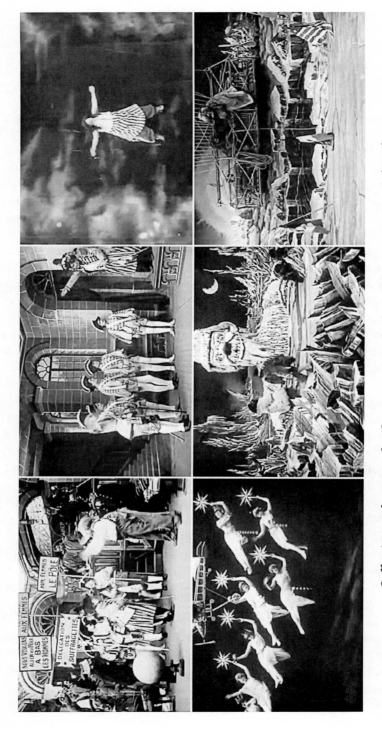

Suffragists are lampooned and a woman saves the day in *A la conquête du pôle* (1912).

least resistance by ridiculing the female suffragists in *A la conquête du pôle* is an example of a lazy misogyny, not uncommon to the period. Even Alice Guy Blaché had taken an easy, comedic route by predicting an alternative world of tyrannical women and effeminate men in her marginal genre film, *Les résultats du féminisme* (1906). Méliès did not have to use a woman in the climactic rescue scene of *A la Conquête du Pôle*; one of his male extras could easily have taken the role. Modest and ambiguous it may be, but this simple on-screen appearance was a clear departure from the norm in 1912. More significantly, it signaled a future of flux for female characters.

But this was a future that Méliès would have no part in. His strongest screen women were drawn from fairytale traditions, which a mere decade later would already appear to Terry Ramsaye as dated and "grotesque."[34] The old-guard with its staged fantasies had created a legacy, but it would now take a new generation of filmmakers to build on that legacy to develop distinctive science fiction ethics, aesthetics and conventions. Along with this would come a new(ish) breed of female character.

Genre Inventions

By the turn of the 20th century, women across the Western world were pushing for social and political change. The women of New Zealand had won the vote in 1893, followed by the white women of Australia in 1902. In the Scandinavian nations of Finland, Denmark and Norway, women had gained degrees of suffrage by 1906, 1908 and 1913 respectively. Although it would take the effects of a world war and a revolution to bring much of the rest of Europe, Canada, America and Russia into line, the writing seemed to be on the wall for men-only politics in the new century.

A la Conquête du Pôle may have been a little dated as art, but Méliès' response to the female suffragists was shared by a science fiction community that was able to package its ridicule in a unique way. The years running up to the First World War witnessed a brief, but important, trend for films that imagine future societies in which women have not only gained the vote, but have taken over. Combining the cynical attitudes aired in the "silly science" films with a more modern genre approach, these films take their opportunity to mock and question female ambition and aspiration. The 1911 French film *One Hundred Years After* imagines a New York City of 2011, controlled by "tall, lithe maidens wearing silk top-hats and knickerbockers," while the men are "undersized creatures wearing feathers in their hats, and skirts"[35]; women also dominate future societies in the 1914 American movies *In the Year 2014* and *Percy Pimpernickel, Soubrette*, in which various depictions of chaos, effeminate men

and social disharmony are, as Hardy points out, "evidently intended as propaganda against female suffrage."[36]

Representing the present through an imagined future while clinging on
to the past was quite a balancing act, but it is one that has become familiar to
science fiction cinema. It has sustained the *Star Trek* franchise for years. Female
suffrage may not have received a sympathetic airing in the pre-war years, but
developing gender- and world-politics meant that it was becoming increasingly
harder for the burgeoning genre to ignore women.

HONORABLE MENTIONS

The effect of "The Great War" of 1914 to 1918 on female roles in Britain
is notable. In a nation so close to mainland Europe, fear of invasion was a primary preoccupation. Women are placed in dire peril in the 1914 film *An Englishman's Home*, which imagines an invasion by Germans; however, in the same
year, three further fear-of-invasion movies place women in much more active
roles. In *If England Were Invaded*, a foreign invasion is thwarted by a band of
locals, aided by an heroic female Post Office worker, and in *Wake Up!*, a daughter recovers stolen plans that would have revealed the nation's defenses to the
enemy. In *England's Menace*, a brave young woman goes further: she intercepts
a wireless message destined for a spy in their midst, evades the enemy agent,
and then races her father's motorcycle to Downing Street to get the news of
the imminent invasion to the Prime Minister. England is saved. The strength
and effectiveness of the female role in *England's Menace* may have been influenced by the fact that she was played by the director's wife, Edna Flugrath;
however, it is clear from this series of British pre-war propaganda films that
women in general were seen as potentially important to the defense of the
realm. On one hand, this was a call to action for the women of Britain; on the
other hand, here was a warning to the potential invader: "Don't mess with us—
even our women will out-smart you!"

As so often, however, modern ideas were being combined with more conservative values in a time of change. Following this line, a traditional damsel-
in-distress approach was added to galvanize the people of Britain in *Wake Up!*,
which duly features a scene depicting the murder of three girls. By the time
Victory and Peace came to be made in 1918, real women had been killed, injured
or placed in danger all over Europe. The central character in this late fear-of-
invasion film is a nurse who saves a British army officer, and is then herself captured. There can be little doubt that this story was inspired by the fate of the
real British nurse Edith Cavell, who was executed by the Germans in Belgium
in 1915 for her role in saving allied soldiers.[37]

Real women off-screen were making their mark on screenplays, which is where most female contributions can be found before the 21st century. However, according to Lizzie Francke in *Script Girls: Women Screenwriters in Hollywood*, writing was not generally recognized as a discrete art by the industry until around 1912.[38] Julia Crawford Ivers, then, may be the first identifiable female science fiction screenwriter for her 1916 U.S. film *The Intrigue*, a battle of the sexes, in which warring factions are led by a Baron and a Countess, the latter played by Lenore Ulric. Other early women screenwriters may never be traced, but it is likely that more existed, for as Mollie Gregory states in *Women Who Run the Show*, "not since the days of silent movies (1910–28) have women worked in any real numbers in the industry."[39]

The Intrigue was made the year before America entered the war, but it was surely inspired by talk of joining the conflict. In the absence of fears about direct invasion, however, the American industry seems to have had an ambiguous attitude towards the on-screen trend for strong, active female characters. This is perhaps best exemplified by the 14-part scientific detective chapter-play series, *The Exploits of Elaine* in 1914, followed by ten weekly episodes of *The New Exploits of Elaine* in 1915. Judging purely by the prominence of the female character—the title role, played by the Pearl White, doing all of her own stunts—it would seem that female representation in the U.S. was moving apace. However, the crime-busting science in these series is led by the male detective, Craig Kennedy, while increasingly contrived plots place Elaine in deep, and then deeper, peril—as a damsel-in-distress to be rescued by Kennedy with his gadgets. The title of a previous Pearl White chapter series, *The Perils of Pauline* (1914), might had given a clue about where the Elaine series would lead; indeed, the title of her third and final 12-chapter series leaves little doubt: *The Romance of Elaine* (1915).

As so often with women in science fiction cinema, the progression was not linear. Gains made here are lost over there, as the industry gives with one hand, gets nervous about the change, and so takes back with the other hand. It is this tendency for the genre to return to traditional representation again and again that the leads to the next observation drawn initially from those early sausage factory films:

   d. (despite their potential) Women's roles are restricted by tradition.

During World War I, cinema's influential pre-war nations—France, Germany and Britain—lost power to the U.S.,[40] whose own industry had largely migrated away from the commercial chaos of New York to the sunny seclusion of California. Hollywood had started on its journey to become the center of the commercial cinema world. As the movie moguls settled into an industry mentality, and Europe recovered from the devastations of war, the movies matured. And as a more distinct and serious approach to science fiction also began to emerge, developments in female representation would be forced to strike a balance between tradition and imagination—yet another compromise that would persist for the next 100 or so years.

An early example of this compromise can be seen in *Himmelskibet*, a serious Danish film produced in 1917, while the carnage of World War I was unfolding 600 miles or so to the south-west of Copenhagen. Reflecting the Danes' neutral wartime position,[41] *Himmelskibet*—released in the U.S. as *A Trip to Mars*—takes a tale and title made familiar by Méliès and gives it a pacifist twist. Men from Earth at a time of war travel to Mars, where they discover a society in harmony with itself, led by a male high priest. This is a place of Wagnerian mythology, where unattainable nymphs offer the "dance of chastity" to hopeful lovers who whisper coyly under the "tree of longing." It all stands in stark contrast to the movie's depiction of Earth, with its drinking, gambling and general debauchery. When the Earthmen export violence to Mars by shooting a bird

A Martian mediator marries her Earthman and "space opera" is born. Gunnar Tolnæs as Captain Planetaros and Lilly Jacobson as Marya in *Himmelskibet* (1917).

and a Martian, the killers are taken to be tried in the "Hall of Judgment." It is here where the film's central female figure makes her mark, not only on this narrative, but also on the history of women in the genre.

The high priest's daughter, Marya, pleads with her father not to harm the Earthmen and then volunteers to speak on their behalf at the trial. Her mediation succeeds. She then falls in love with the first officer and takes him to a garden of glowing flowers, not unlike one to which Neytiri introduces Sully in *Avatar* (2009). The Martian and human are married, before returning to Earth with the rest of the men. Intelligent, composed and sensitive, Marya is now considered a talisman by the human crew, who remain calm when their ship is hit by an electrical storm: the men are content that "there will be no trouble where she is." In the final sequence of the film, the Martian Marya's powers of mediation are presented as the great new hope for a lasting, peaceful civilization on Earth.

At 97 minutes, *Himmelskibet* was the longest science fiction feature to date, which may have contributed to Hardy's description of it as "the film that marked the beginning of the space opera sub-genre...."[42] It also marks a watershed point for the role of women. While it retains many of the melodramatic flourishes of earlier films, it also explores some of the psychology of space travel and the notion that the genre might be used to deliver a socio-political message. *Himmelskibet* signaled the arrival of a more ambitious, more sophisticated genre with epic intentions. Whether its female characters would break free of tradition and stereotype would be another matter; after all, this was not the last time the genre would see the female mediator.

Epic Intentions

In her 1991 essay *Between the Boys and Their Toys*, Susan Thomas identifies the female mediator as a significant role in science fiction cinema. Thomas' primary subject is one of the genre's most famous roles, in a film whose art design still stands as a beacon to science fiction cinema's vaulting ambition: Maria in *Metropolis*. The monumental sets of Fritz Lang's 1927 silent epic frame a society in which thousands of subterranean workers are condemned to a life of drudgery and misery, while above ground, a handful of rich capitalists enjoys lives of ease and luxury, eating the fruits of the workers' labors. As a poor nursery worker, tending the children of the bourgeoisie, Maria, played by Brigitte Helm, experiences both of these worlds. She sees iniquity in the inequality and, importantly, resolves to do something to address the imbalance.

Thomas points out that Maria serves as an essential conduit between two patriarchal worlds, symbolizing "the heart as a mediator between the labouring classes and the ruling elite."[43] Men had also dominated the Earth and Mars of *Himmelskibet*, and the real England and Germany that sealed the fate of the caring nurse in *Victory and Peace*. Thomas then takes her observations in a specific direction, exploring much later films, such as *TRON* (1982) and *Short Circuit* (1986), in which women mediate between men and their technology. However, a purer form of the mediator figure, one closer to the traditions of Marya and Maria, also runs through science fiction cinema. In her most notable appearances, she mediates between Earthmen and a Christ-like space traveler in *The Day the Earth Stood Still* (1951), between man and ape in *Planet of the Apes* (1968), and between men and the alien in *Starman* (1984). Any doubts that this female type would endure into the 21st century were surely cast aside by Amy Adams' acclaimed performance as the intelligent, calm and sensitive Dr. Louise Banks in *Arrival* (2016).

It can surely be no coincidence that Maria and Marya share their names with the Virgin Mary, whose mediation between Man and God is a quintessential example of this female type in the Western tradition. It is a very strong point of cultural contact; it is also, however, a narrative shortcut that helps to ensure that:

e. Women's (re)actions are governed by stereotype.

It is not clear whether Lang's wife, writer Thea von Harbou, was aware of *Himmelskibet* and Marya when she created Maria for *Metropolis*. It is, however, likely she and her husband were aware of the 1924 Soviet film, *Aelita* (or *Aelita: Queen of Mars*), another landmark in science fiction film design and female presence. *Aelita* shares plot and character elements with *Himmelskibet* and *Metropolis*, but it also contains a warning about what happens when women's actions drift away from expectation—or stereotype.

Aelita, played by Yuliya Solntseva, may be Queen of Mars, but control there is exercised by men, leaving the frustrated puppet-ruler to spend her days flitting around the movie's beautiful, constructivist sets, and gazing at Earth through a televisor device. Through this, she spies, and falls in love with, an Earthman, who, after a long and ponderous sequence set in Moscow, visits Mars. When the visitor gets into trouble, Aelita mediates on his behalf. She then helps him to release Mars' subterranean workers from their life of drudgery and misery. Her actions sound noble; however, unlike Marya and Maria, Aelita is not an altruistic mediator. She intercedes for her own ends: she wants the Earthman for herself and she wants to wrest control of her society from the men who rule it. But almost as soon as she achieves both of these aims, she is punished for her ambitions. Moments after her proclamation, "From now on, I alone will reign and rule," she falls (or is she pushed?) to her death, not unlike the suffragist who falls (or was she pushed?) from the hot-air balloon in *A la Conquête du Pôle*.

As a queen from elsewhere, Aelita reinstates a science fiction line that can be traced back through *The Automatic Motorist* (1911) and *Voyage autour d'une étoile* (1907) to *Voyage of the Arctic* (1903), with its Queen of the Polar Regions. Further back are the many ambitious queens of fairytale, theater and mythology: and as in *Snow White*, *Macbeth* and *Medea*, science fiction queens are often punished for their ambitions. They do not fall into line with Toni Morrison's "serviceable Other," borrowed by Sampson, above, to describe characters who are constructed to support and service the (male) Self. This unwanted, nonconforming female figure is a fly in the ointment; she is "The Hegelian Other" that needs to be destroyed in order to maintain a normal functioning (patriarchal) society. This is a science fiction cinema society.[44]

Aelita links the nagging wives and female suffragists of earlier pictures with the glamorous, despotic genre queens who would follow, including: Zsa Zsa Gabor's Talleah, Queen of Venus in *Queen of Outer Space* (1958), Anita Pallenberg's Great Tyrant in *Barbarella* (1968) and Alice Krige's Borg Queen in *Star Trek: First Contact* (1996). All are powerful; all are destroyed, in a genre that repeatedly allows women to take two steps forward before pulling them at least one step back.

As science fiction epics, *Himmelskibet*, *Aelita* and *Metropolis* are indicative of a genre with grand ambitions. As vehicles for memorable female characters, they paved the way for another iconic Lang/Harbou role that neatly encapsulates the position of women in science fiction cinema at the close of the silent era: *Frau im Mond*, released in 1929. This is an elegantly designed, beautifully acted film, with impeccable scientific advisors and a title that places its lead female front-and-center amid the action. However, it is also a ponderously shot, over-long melodrama, with a poor script and a prominent female character whose potential is largely wasted. In short, *Frau im Mond* can be used define female representation in the silent period.

Despite its title, the film is actually a tale about a rich man who is forced by a sinister man to convince his male industrialist friend to help him fly to the Moon—accompanied by an old male professor, a stowaway boy and the industrialist's fiancée, Friede, played by Gerda Maurus. Taking the order of narrative significance into account, the film might easily have been called, *Vier Männer, eine Frau und ein Junge im Mond*. The original title is of course important to this study because seventeen years after the 6-minute "silly science" film *Freezing Auntie* had broken the ice, the notion of a female lead was being used—as it had been in *Aelita*—to sell an expensive epic. Indeed, the mere notion of a strong-minded woman who travels to the Moon is, itself, far removed from the gentle Goddess Selene discovered there during *Le Voyage dans la Lune* a decade before. Friede is an independent-minded woman who states her opinion, saves the spaceship from the sinister Mr. Turner and makes a grand sacrifice in the finale to confirm her place as the "woman in the Moon." However, it is the men throughout who pull the strings. Women in *Frau im Mond* act as they are expected to act. On Earth, Friede is the passive, love interest caught in a triangle between her fiancé and his friend. In space, she assists the men with practical help. On the Moon, her primary role is to intercede regularly between the arguing men in her love triangle. Finally, and most significantly, she conducts the lottery that decides which of the men will have to remain on the moon. Doing this with her eyes closed, she takes the role of impartial female mediator, already familiar to science fiction cinema.

    Frau im Mond was released in English-speaking territories as *Woman in the Moon* and *Girl in the Moon*, titles which highlight this central female role. It was also released as *By Rocket to the Moon*. These alternative titles betray a

A promising role, but the rest is silence. Gerda Maurus, as the striking Friede Velten, mediates between Gustav von Wangenheim (left) as Ingenieur Windegger and Willy Fritsch as Wolf Helius in *Frau im Mond* (1929).

dichotomy shared by the film itself. While clearly framed throughout as a beautiful, feminine figure, Friede also wears men's clothing for her trip. This includes a tie, which has inevitably been described, alongside the big cigar smoked by the film's token female villain, as being "associated with phallic symbols" that "seem to reflect that the women are participating in what is resolutely a man's world."[45] The words "seem to reflect" are not necessary here. Freudian sexual allusions aside, it is absolutely clear that Friede is in a man's world, whether it is the one she left on Earth or the one she chooses for herself on the Moon. Like the English language titles, her true role is ambiguous and uncertain. On balance, *Frau im Mond* deserves its place as a landmark film in this history, if only for its promise of a glorious future for women in space. It remains an iconic film with an iconic role, but one that never quite delivers on its promise.

Through thirty-five years of considerable evolution in the genre, female representation within it had clearly developed; however, the genre's status as a patriarchal domain remained intact. While women had reached a point where they were now doing things, their actions remained stubbornly consistent with expectation. To paraphrase Lorraine Gamman and Margaret Marshment: Men do things; women are things. This is science fiction cinema.[46]

It is tempting to dismiss the earliest movies of any genre as naïve and unsophisticated, but the seeds are sewn in these first years. Absence, tradition, stereotype, invention and convention will all continue to play their part in female representation as the history of science fiction cinema unfolds. At the end of the 19th century, the Lumière Brothers could hardly have imagined the dominant position that their medium, and indeed the genre, would command at the beginning of the 21st century. What they and others did foresee, however, was the huge commercial potential of moving pictures. And so began the struggles to control the means and methods of producing the golden eggs. Male control had already restricted science fiction cinema's female characters; now, as the cost of production increased, ancient desires would threaten to confine women further. The stage was set for the creation of the most pervasive female roles in science fiction cinema; if only men could just imagine…

II

SCIENCE FANTASY
Sound, Technology and the
Service of Male Desires

Storytellers had been augmenting reality long before the arrival of science fiction, whose literary exponents were in turn bending natural laws long before the arrival of motion pictures. Now it was the turn of the filmmakers. The technologies of the new medium, coupled with the trappings of a burgeoning genre, presented man with an unparalleled opportunity to fulfill his most enduring, but elusive, desire: to create woman. Gods and mothers were replaced by pictures and sound in the quest for perfection—not just a grotesque *Frankenstein* chimera, but a culmination of millennia of heterosexual male fantasies. Writers, directors and producers were offered a choice: allow the imagination to fly to unimagined philosophical heights, or chase base desires towards visceral gratification. The resulting lovers, robots and mothers neatly embody science fiction cinema's enduring mission to have its cake and eat it too. As one old saying goes: expect "a lady in the parlor, a cook in the kitchen and a wench in the bedroom."

Creative Contradictions

For the first three-and-a-half (silent) decades of cinema's existence, filmmakers had been experimenting wildly with concepts, narrative techniques, technological approaches, and more. It was quickly realized that "fantastic films," to borrow Walt Lee's term,[1] more than any other, allowed these storytellers to portray just about anything. Just as important was their realization that audiences would accept just about anything that could be explained rationally by the narrative. Indeed, by the 1920s, science fiction cinema, with its proven ability to imagine new worlds, new histories, new environments, new technologies, new species, even new sciences, seems to offer the optimist a hope of new societies and new ideologies—and by extension, some imaginative and experimental approaches to the representation of women. But comparing hopes with observations exposes this genre's central creative contradiction: What science fiction cinema is *able* show is not always the same as what science fiction cinema is *willing* to show.

This chapter follows science fiction cinema as it negotiated the 1930s from the advent of sound to the beginning of World War II. Despite a few prominent examples, however, female roles were rather thin on the ground, leading to a period of limited development. Reasons for this will become clearer as the chapter progresses. The opportunity is taken therefore to discuss some of the theories that underpin elements of representation that run from the 19th century to the 21st century—taking in examples from all points on that timeline. These are the conventions that were established in Chapter I and will appear numerous times as this book progresses through the 20th century. Many of them were consolidated into genre stereotypes in the 1930s.

The influence of male control on female characters has already been established, underpinned by Ramsaye's 1926 observation that cinema supports Man in "the business of re-creating himself biologically"; however, male egos are not the only issue here. Patriarchy may define science fiction cinema's prevailing condition, but the oscillating fortunes of female characters—a recurring theme of this history—are shaped by more dominant external factors and challenges too. This was no less true of the late 1920s, as science fiction women rode the patriarchal wave towards perhaps the greatest challenge faced by the film industry to date: the arrival of sound.

SOUND

Although "talking pictures" were initially considered to be just another of cinema's fads or gimmicks, by the end of 1928, it had become apparent from audience reaction that the new format would endure. The days of the silent movie—despite the best efforts and accompanying artistry of the theater organist—were numbered. By 1929, some science fiction projects already in production had been converted to sound, or had sound segments inserted, in order to protect investments already made. In that year, the British film *High Treason* and the American, Jules Verne adaptation *The Mysterious Island* appeared in both silent and sound versions.

As early as 1930, silent science fiction cinema had all but disappeared, leaving movies such as the 1929 classic *Frau im Mond*, discussed at the close of Chapter I, somewhat isolated by events. Had Gerda Maurus' Friede not been silenced by this accident of history, *Frau im Mond* might have endured as a dependable beacon of female representation in science fiction cinema. Instead, it remains on the cusp of greatness, another example of the "two steps forward, one step back" feature that characterizes female representation through the history of the genre. Poor timing is not necessarily the fault of patriarchy, but it is also worth considering whether *Woman in the Moon* would have been made at all—at least with such a prominent female character—if Fritz Lang had been required to work within the confines of the new sound formats. His first "talkies," *M* (1931) and *The Testament of Dr. Mabuse* (1933), are, after all, aggressively male-focused.

The 1929 American movie, *Midstream*, written by Bernice Boon, Frances Guihan and Fanny Hatton, is one of those silent productions that were partially converted with inserted sound segments. In order to maximize the movie's impact—and perhaps to capitalize on the huge, breakthrough success of *The Jazz Singer*, barely two years earlier—a number of these inserts are singing sequences. In 1930, the British film *Elstree Calling* challenged the populist entertainments of yesterday: theater, and tomorrow: television, with a series of music hall and vaudeville-style sketches, framed as a near-future live TV broadcast. Without doubt, the most ambitious of these early science fiction musical experiments is the 1930 U.S. production, *Just Imagine*. If for nothing else, David Butler's film is worth watching for its depictions of Mars and a future New York City.[2] These are clearly influenced by the sets of the silent movies *Aelita: Queen of Mars* (1924) and *Metropolis* (1927), but in their turn, they surely provided inspiration for the art direction on the British Film *Things to Come* six years later, and perhaps even the cityscapes of and future-visions of *Blade Runner* in 1982. The technological predictions of *Just Imagine*, both real-world and fantasy, are important to this history of female representation because, while this is clearly an ambitious film with its eye on the future, it also keeps its feet firmly in the past.

Just Imagine opens with a grandiose, 1930 voice-over introducing images of New York City, 1880, which include three men and a woman whizzing past on a 4-seater bicycle. The audience is then invited to "just imagine" the same location one-hundred years later. In 1980, the cycling woman has been replaced by Maureen O'Sullivan as LN-18, piloting a hybrid car/plane/helicopter, which again pre-echoes *Blade Runner*, or even the flying cars of Coruscant in *Star Wars: Episode II—Attack of the Clones* (2002). In *Just Imagine*'s future, women and men initially appear to be equal, albeit equally oppressed by an overbearing,

Visions of a future that sounds like the past. Maureen O'Sullivan as LN-18 and John Garrick as J-21 in the science fiction musical *Just Imagine* (1930).

homogenizing society that replaces names with gender-neutral numbers, such as LN-18, J-21, Z-4 and the familiar sounding RT-42. The notion that society has changed inspires the first of the movie's songs: the male J-21, who is in love with O'Sullivan's LN-18, hankers for an "old-fashioned girl" with the charm his grandmother had.

During J-21's song, his friend, MT-42, imagines a series of ironic vignettes showing women of the 1930s having fun: one is making cocktails, another is seduced by a man, and a third is rocking a cradle with her foot while smiling, smoking and reading a book entitled "Ex-Wife." The sequence creates a sense of women blessed with new-found freedoms—in both 1930 and 1980. This notion is echoed in a later scene in which a man and woman agree to have a child; they select a boy and moments later collect their new baby from a vending machine. This is an egalitarian future. Or so it first seems.

It does not take long for *Just Imagine* to reveal itself as a proto-fascist 1930 vision of 1980, in which the laws of society are bent towards the pursuit of convention and tradition. Glimpses of what could be are quickly replaced by representation that leans heavily on stereotype—for both men and women. It is not clear if this is meant as warning in the light of political changes brewing in contemporary Europe, or a comment on social changes in America itself. Evidence from the film would suggest that it is more the latter.

Central to the narrative is a version of a classic love triangle tale. LN-18 is being wooed by two men: J-21, whom she loves, and MT-3, whom she doesn't. In this future, marriage partners are chosen in courts of law where formal applications, filed by male suitors, are considered. In this case, a male judge decides that MT-3 is the most worthy potential husband, and so LN-21 is given to him against her will. Her only hope is J-21's legal appeal; he has four months to distinguish himself by doing something noteworthy. This is where an already old, silent, science fiction cinema stalwart comes in. An aged scientist, Z-4, has built a space-plane, which requires a pilot for a trip to Mars. J-21 happens to be a pilot. With nothing now to lose, he embarks on the risky adventure, taking with him his friend MT-42 and the film's comedy character, Single-0, a man from 1930 who has been brought back to life in one of the film's science fiction sub-plots.

Despite its pretensions to modernity, *Just Imagine* uses its science fiction trappings to support traditional representation. The result is a series of tropes—characters, plots, ideas and themes—already familiar to the genre. These include: an academy dominated by men-of-science, supported by female technicians; men in most of the positions of power and influence; an evil queen (of Mars), destroyed for her ambition; a central male narrative, reflecting male desires, dilemmas and derring-do; and women subject to the whims of their fathers and fiancés. In short, *Just Imagine*'s egalitarian promise is quickly and consistently broken by genre and narrative clichés. In reality, however, this creative contradiction is not surprising; it is merely part of a process by which science fiction cinema has always balanced elements in a bid to ensure success—or at least, to avoid failure.

BALANCE

When science fiction introduces a new idea, it runs the risk of alienating its audience. Even when a film adheres to Peter Nicholls' requirement for an "explicable novum"[3]—where the new science element is explained within the fiction—some screen time must still be spent convincing a potentially skeptical audience that the concept is feasible. As French film theorist and critic Christian Metz points out, genres support this with "a genre logic": "a set of ground rules which have been laid down at the outset ... and within which they are perfectly coherent."[4]

Sequels reinforce this notion of established rules, meaning that *Jurassic World* (2015), for example, does not need to re-visit the explanation about dinosaur DNA in the blood of mosquitoes preserved in amber that was required by *Jurassic Park* (1993). The concept is taken as read, along with the direction of the plot and the familiar characters, including: greedy corporation man, untamed-but-decent male action hero, and two-dimensional, career-obsessed woman, played by Bryce Dallas Howard. By offering very little that is new, *Jurassic World* reduces the risk of alienating its audience.

Before the establishment of its genre codes and the appearance of its sequels, science fiction cinema reduced that risk by using characters and plots which had their roots in mythology, theater, literature and other traditional narrative forms—as well as society itself. Many of the forms of female representation highlighted in Chapter I are part of that process. If the audience recognizes and accepts elements of the story as "normal," it is easier to slip in other more radical, "abnormal" elements. At its most basic level, this science fiction balancing act takes four forms:

1. Narrative balance: between concepts, plots and characters
2. Intra-character balance: within a single role
3. Inter-character balance: between multiple roles
4. Format balance: between the narrative and screen technologies

In the first instance, a radical concept might be balanced by an established plot, or an abnormal plot could be countered by recognizable characters, and so forth. In the case of *Just Imagine*, the trip to Mars had been established in science fiction cinema for two-and-a-half decades and the love triangle had been a staple of drama for two-and-a-half millennia. Together, they create a "narrative balance" that helps to offset the strangeness of a scenario in which people have numbers instead of names. The characters themselves are not strange. Indeed, the beautiful, patient, gentle, largely passive female lead, LN-18, is a type that would be reprised by Maureen O'Sullivan many more times, including: as Jane Parker to Johnny Weissmuller's Tarzan in six movies from 1932 to 1942, and as Jane Bennet in the 1940 adaptation of Jane Austen's perennial favorite, *Pride and Prejudice*. It is because LN-18 is an established type that the audience can accept her piloting of the flying vehicle at the beginning of *Just Imagine*. What might be seen initially as an abnormal action is quickly countered with an assurance that LN-18 is the film's love interest, and soon after this, J-21's song reassures the audience that she is potentially an "old-fashioned girl." This "intra-character" balancing will become more complex as science fiction films become more sophisticated; that will be discussed further in Chapter V, where the concept reaches its apogee with the waitress-cum-warrior, Sarah Connor, in *The Terminator* (1984).

A clear example of the more blunt tool of "inter-character" balancing in *Just Imagine* can be found when J-21, MT-42 and Single-0 reach Mars. Here the men are greeted by the benign Queen Loo-Loo, played with relish by Joyzelle Joyner; however, they quickly discover that everyone on Mars has a doppelgänger, including Queen Loo-Loo, whose evil counterpart Queen Boo-Boo (also played by Joyner) attempts to kill the visitors. Clearly taking a Freudian id versus super-ego—animal instinct versus social restraint—dynamic as a model, this is a rather crude example of "inter-character" balancing; however, it is far from unique. It had been seen in 1927 when the human Maria stood in contrast to the robot Maria in *Metropolis*, and it appears eighty-seven years later in *Divergent* (2014), whose entire female-focused plot hinges on the concept of interacting and diverse character traits. In her history of science fiction cinema, Christine Cornea draws attention to the notion of female "doubling," especially in *film noir*, in which the *femme fatal*—the fatal woman—is "frequently juxtaposed or twinned with another female character."[5] Cornea transfers this character forward to science fiction films, including *Eve of Destruction* (1991). Connections are never easy to prove, but this *Just Imagine* example suggests a filmic model that pre-dates the *film noir* archetype.

The first three categories in the "balance" list above deal with internal narrative elements; the fourth is slightly different: it takes account of science fiction cinema's natural appetite for new screen technologies and techniques, and of the effect that this focus can have on the originality of the fiction. It is not just the earliest "trick films" that seem to exist merely to document the arrival and fidelity of the technology; science fiction cinema's 13 decades are littered with examples of this phenomenon. Eugen Schüfftan's visual effects for *Metropolis* (1927) are impressive, but H.G. Wells called it "quite the silliest film"[6]; in *Forbidden Planet* (1956), Disney animation and CinemaScope are deployed for a simplified re-telling[7] of Shakespeare's *The Tempest*; the Dykstraflex Camera revolutionized the battle sequences in the simple, space fairytale, *Star Wars* (1977); and major advances in 3-D digital presentation support *Avatar*'s successful 2009 re-visit of a story familiar from *Broken Arrow* (1950), *Dances with Wolves* (1990), *Pocahontas* (1995) and others. This focus on screen technology also affects women's roles. Each of the central female characters in these technical *tours de force* is drawn from conventional stories: they are pure, princess-like figures who mediate between safe elements of a home environment and dangerous external forces—and they are eventually rescued by men.

The need to use familiar narrative elements in order to balance new format elements is magnified by the introduction of technical innovations. Sound-on-film is an example of this; *Just Imagine* is an early result. New cinema technology is expensive. Add to this the fact that sound arrived around the time of the

Wall Street Crash, established itself during the Great Depression, and required the upgrading of thousands of cinema buildings, and it becomes understandable that production companies would take measures to protect their investments. That is, where possible to reduce the risk of alienating their audiences. Finding a safe, winning formula and then repeating it—or returning to it—becomes more important as the business of making, distributing and exhibiting movies becomes more expensive. What Upton Sinclair describes in 1933 as "the panic that was going to prostrate the financial world at the end of October, 1929"[8] affected even his subject, the film mogul William Fox. It is not surprising then that the period saw a reduction in the number of smaller producers and a further consolidation of the industry towards a 1930s conservatism—demonstrated by the Fox Pictures movie *Just Imagine*. Science fiction cinema was still a realm of imagination, but an industry dictum began to emerge: as the influence of the accountant increases, the freedoms afforded to the artist generally decrease. This holds true today.

Despite the impressive, creative minds of men, and a few women, the science fiction cinema that emerged from the silent years lacked focus and discipline. Creative contradictions persisted through the 1930s, a period in which the genre's cinema as a whole, according to Hardy, lacked "steady development or process of clarification."[9] The result included a series of bit roles for women in a collection of genre-hybrid films: The 1933 German moral satire, *Ein Unsichtbarer geht durch die Stadt*, features a mercenary girlfriend for the invisible man of the title. Gene Autry, the singing cowboy, is the focus of the first science fiction Western, *The Phantom Empire*, a 1935 chapter serial. In the same year, *The Big Broadcast of 1936*, features Bing Crosby in another television-themed vehicle for a series of variety acts. This film does offer a female baddie: a countess who kidnaps radio stars with ambitions to break in to television; however, this is a comedy turn for Lyda Roberti. Normal service is resumed for this series with *The Big Broadcast of 1938*, which features female dancers and showcases the comedy talents of W.C. Fields and Bob Hope.

The precarious finances of the period will have played their part in this creative mélange; however, a three-hundred-year-old observation by Shakespeare hints at a further contributing factor: "peace is nothing, but to rust iron, increase tailors, and breed ballad-makers."[10] Perhaps then the creative energies of science fiction cinema would be galvanized by another war.

FURY

The uneasy period before the Second World War predictably saw many science fiction filmmakers target a more serious approach—just as they had done before World War I. Aviation and weaponry were, once again, popular themes. The aircraft-destroying kappa-ray gun, with which *Code of the Air* ushered out the silent period in 1928, was picked up again *Ghost Patrol* (1936), another Western hybrid, this time featuring a cowboy detective. In *Charlie Chan at the Olympics* (1937), the much-loved Chinese detective's attempts to track down a robotic plane lead him to the infamous 1936 Berlin Games, presided over by Adolf Hitler. In the same year, the Nazi dictator was the inspiration for the villain of *Bílá Nemoc*, an adaptation of Karel Čapek's play by the same name, translated as *The White Disease* or *Skeleton on Horseback*. Science fiction cinema was now flexing its political and social muscles.

It is notable, however, that the number of women involved in these prewar stories is not as great as it had been in the run-up to the First World War. This may be the result of "narrative balancing," or perhaps because most genre films were now made far from Europe. Whatever the reason, women do not save their homelands from imminent invasion quite so often. They do, however, have a presence. An early example is the 1933 U.S. film, *Men Just Fight*, in which a mother heads a peace campaign that attempts to avert the impending war. She fails even to stop her own son fighting, and the movie concludes with an air raid over New York City in 1940. As the title might suggest, the film takes a sympathetic attitude towards pacifists, an unusual stance at a time when pacifism was often equated with communism. Indeed, in the patriotically macho, 1937 British film *Bulldog Drummond at Bay*—whose plot is very similar to *Charlie Chan at the Olympics*—Dorothy Mackill plays a secret service agent who helps to infiltrate a group of pacifists who are attempting to steal the plans for the nation's new super-weapon: a robotic plane. American respect for British women of this type is celebrated in the same year with Paramount Pictures' *The Girl from Scotland Yard*, in which Karen Morley plays a plucky heroine who attempts to thwart a madman's plans to destroy Britain with his airplane-mounted death-ray. It is notable that the writers, Doris Anderson and Dore Schary, do ensure that Morley's British heroine is eventually rescued by a square-jawed, male, American hero, which is either commercial expediency, a nod to the traditions of the genre, or prediction of real-world things to come. Released in 1936, amid the multi-genre mélange noted above, *Things to Come* is William Cameron Menzies' visualization of H.G. Wells' 1933 prediction about war and social-evolution, *The Shape of Things to Come*. After 100 years of war and social turmoil, the female fate is eventually to join the bland, unisex ranks of a male-controlled "Everytown" of 2036. A woman does join a space mission, but equality is only surface deep in this new society—just as it is in *Just Imagine*, with which it also shares its impressive futuristic city sets.

By and large, female roles in this jittery pre-war period balance the creativity of the genre with a traditional representation that is perhaps best characterized by the women who support male derring-do in the serialized "boys' own" adventures, *Flash Gordon* (1936), *Buck Rogers* (1939) and *Dick Tracy's G-Men* (1939). The number of damsels-in-distress during this time is relatively small; however, the number of women who raise their heads above the parapet is very small. A notable exception to the relatively flavorless female presence for this period comes in the form of Brigitte Helm as the evil Queen Antinea in *Die Herrin von Atlantis* (1932), but this is, in many ways, a relic of the silent period. Intriguing also is another U.S. genre musical, *It's Great to Be Alive*, a rare example for the inter-war period of a direct reference to women's suffrage. These aggressive approaches to male power are unusual at this time; however, responses to male fears about what women might achieve if they pressed too hard took many other forms—not least the more subtle propaganda presented in that first science fiction musical: *Just Imagine*. As noted above, this movie opens with a veneer of equality, but quickly reveals a more traditional sublayer. At its core, however, it is not merely conservative; it is actively nasty.

Below the frivolous, musical surface is a misogynist undercurrent, which includes attempts to silence women. These intentions are telegraphed early, when the male MT-42 identifies a female official through a security viewfinder; his friend, J-21, responds with "How I hate these modern women." The tone, if not the sentiment, is at odds with the misty-eyed offering of his "old-fashioned girl" song a few minutes later. The female official is a census-taker, played by Vera Lewis: an aging, stern, joyless figure, who becomes the butt of a male joke. Indeed, *Just Imagine* makes and takes many opportunities to mock women for their drive and ambition. Women are visible and active in this 1980, but it is the men who have a firm grip on society. The result includes the patriarchal marriage laws mentioned above; a "modern" backless dress that shows its wearer naked down to and including her buttocks; a male-only drinking club; and the sinister domestic control of LN-18 by the fiancé forced on her by the law courts.

The anti-female sentiment reaches its height with the identical twins who rule Mars: Queen Loo-Loo and Queen Boo-Boo. The first is benign, but vacuous, the second is evil and ambitious; together they preside over a dysfunctional system that stands in contrast to the efficient bureaucracy of the male-controlled Earth—an idea borrowed from anti-female-suffrage films of the silent period, such as 1914's *In the Year 2014* and *Percy Pimpernickel, Soubrette*. To be fair to the makers of *Just Imagine*, their intention may have been to suggest that neither of the political systems presented here is ideal; however, the movie's reckless attitude to gender politics tends to obscure this message. In reality, the film does not merely reject modernity in the "honest" manner of the comedy suffragist films of the silent period, or even of the titillating theme presented in *It's Great to Be Alive*; nor is it a merely an example of a movie that balances its unfamiliar features with traditional elements. Instead, this is a magnification of conservative, patriarchal ideals, in which female opinions are denigrated, modern women are domesticated, and powerful women are—as with the suffragist leader in *A la Conquête du Pôle* (1912)—eventually destroyed.

In his 1993 *Sight and Sound* article, *Trouble Ahead*, Michael Moorcock sounds a note of optimism for the genre: "My main hope is that human beings, aided by new technology and scientific theory, will develop a system of ethics and morals on which we can base any future democracy, future business practices, and future social programmes."[11]

Back in the 1930s, the "sophisticated ethic," identified by Michael Moorcock as needed by the genre to "deal with the profound changes in our daily and political lives," seemed a long way off. Rather than meeting its considerable potential to promote this ethic, science fiction cinema was producing magnifications of current prevailing morals and ideologies.

This is not entirely surprising during a decade that began with the uncertainties of the sound-on-film revolution and ended with the uncertainties of world war. The genre always retreats towards its patriarchal underpinnings at times of stress, so it is also unsurprising that the female roles that did emerge reinforce those traditions and conventions. Patriarchal underpinnings meant that, by the 1930s, much of science fiction had mutated into science fantasy— a genre bent towards the service of male whims and desires. It is worth taking some time out here to examine some of those predilections.

Fantastic Sex

Perhaps the most obvious manifestation of heterosexual male desire in science fiction cinema is the abundance of female flesh on display. *Just Imagine* has its fair share of this—from the backless dress noted above, through a semi-dressed woman "caught" on a tele-viewer, to the silver-bikini-clad dancers in its MGM-style musical numbers. However, objectification of women did not begin in 1930, nor was it unique to science fiction cinema. Back in 1897, genre pioneer Georges Méliès produced one of the earliest adult movies, *Après le Bal*, a 1-minute non-genre piece in which a woman returning from a ball is helped to undress by her maid, before taking a standing bath, naked in a tin tub. In reality, the water is sand and the woman is wearing a bathing suit that matches the color of her skin, but Méliès' intention is clear: pornographic stimulation.

Writer Jason Gould observes that the generalized observations about female role development identified at the beginning Chapter I might, with a few tweaks, "almost serve as a description of pornography (She is absent [in all but body])"[12]; however, sex acts themselves are relatively rare in science fiction cinema. Given the genre's potential to make manifest the male imagination, this is perhaps surprising. Gould continues, pointing to a possible reason:

> Those early films made me consider how similar they are in nature to pornography—the thrill of seeing something slightly blasphemous or illicit (the transformed animal), the incredibly basic, contrived or non-existent storyline, and of course their attitude toward women.

The suggestion seems to be that science fiction cinema is a realm of such rich and varied stimuli that sex—or at least the rarefied sex offered by pornography—is unnecessary. Instead, challenging ideas and concepts ensure that its audience gets its thrills elsewhere. This notion will be tested when the genre's attitude towards biological reproduction is discussed later. In 1930s' science fiction cinema, sexual acts, for whatever reason, were not on the agenda; however, the female form most definitely was—and had been for a while. In fact, this was starting to feel like a "look-but-don't-touch" genre.

Aesthetic allure, a model for many predatory queens to follow. Brigitte Helm as Antinea in *Die Herrin von Atlantis* (1932).

Pleasurable Looking

Looking and seeing are central to Christian Metz's influential essay, *The Imaginary Signifier*, which explains cinema's powerful effect by suggesting that a movie's meaning is created in the unconscious mind of the viewer. To support this idea, Metz links cinema-going with psychoanalysis, most notably the work of Jacques Lacan and his "mirror stage" development—the point at which a child begins to understand the idea of Self.[13] For Metz, the notion that "that person in the mirror is me!" is connected in the mind with "that person on the screen is me!" Lacan connects the discovery of the Self to what he calls the "symbolic order": the power structures and symbols that make up cultures and societies. Of course, this is linked to the patriarchy discussed in Chapter I. Indeed, to Lacan, the "symbolic order" is regulated by what he calls the "name of the father,"[14] which ensures that the male child develops an awareness of his powerful position within this structure, and the female child is reminded of her weak position. As was clear by the 1930s, science fiction cinema is very adept at creating weak positions for women—and then reminding them of this. Lacan's "name of the father" would find perhaps its most literal reflection in the central relationships of the first seven *Star Wars* films. To Metz, movies are more pleasurable for those who see themselves reflected on the screen. In order to succeed, survive and self-perpetuate, then, commercial cinema must ensure that the spectator is "maintained in his credulousness by the perfect organization of the machinery."[15] Once again, this links to patriarchy and to the male control of cinema.

Pleasure is central to Laura Mulvey's much-quoted essay, *Visual Pleasure and Narrative Cinema*, which links psychoanalysis and film with feminism. Mulvey echoes words written by Terry Ramsaye in 1926 in her statement that "the cinema satisfies a primordial wish for pleasurable looking."[16] Mulvey's essay agrees firmly with the idea, "developed through narcissism,"[17] that cinema favors the male viewer. He identifies with the male characters on screen—they are the subjects of the narrative—and he sees the female characters as objects. Women's place as supports, serviceable Others and objects within men's stories was established in Chapter I, and channeled through Gamman and Marshment's useful description: "Men act; women are acted upon. This is patriarchy."[18] However, Mulvey's essay introduces another layer. It adds the notion that women are included in male narratives as erotic objects, to be looked at. The is the "scopophilic" gaze that "arises from pleasure in using another person as an object of sexual stimulation through sight."[19] To paraphrase Gamman and Marshment: "men gaze; women are gazed upon. This is scopophilia." Of course, the idea that men like looking at women is not a new one, as Ramsaye notes in his history of film:

For eons the picture on the wall could only say "bear" and "woman." Now endowed with motion it can say "There goes the bear," and more joyously still "Here comes the woman." The yearnings of Adam Og and his friend Ug can now be satisfied, and Eva Egg may have her career.[20]

Ramsaye is not describing a feminist attitude here. Eva Egg's career is not professional; instead, it is defined by the desires of Og and Ug. It is scopophilic. That is a feminist notion, and one that is applied forcibly by academic and social critic, Camille Paglia in her 1990 book, *Sexual Personae.* Here she argues that idealized forms of the female (and male) image in many forms of art have reinforced a male offensive position:

Man, the sexual conceptualizer and projector, has ruled art because art is his Apollonian response toward and away from woman. A sex object is something to aim at. The eye is Apollo's arrow following the arc of transcendence I saw in male urination and ejaculation....[21]

Laura Mulvey's particular point is that cinema offers the perfect medium for this mechanism because of its unique ability—unlike, say, theater—to shift the emphasis of the look.[22] The film director can force the viewer to see, or not to see. Mulvey is unequivocal about the impact of this.

The study of women in film has broadened considerably since the publication of Mulvey's ground-breaking work, which inevitably stirred debate. Central to the challenges have been questions about whether the gaze is always male. In *Afterthoughts on "Visual Pleasure and Narrative cinema,"* Mulvey defends her apparent disregard for the female spectator, stating that she was "interested in the relationship between the image of women on the screen and the "masculinisation" of the spectator position, regardless of the actual sex (or possible deviance) of any real live movie-goer."[23] The current work might also be charged with ignoring sexual difference through its focus—despite a few notable exceptions, including Lizzie Borden's *Born in Flames* (1983) and Hilary Brougher's *The Sticky Fingers of Time* (1997)—on the heterosexual male viewer. Until there are more counter-examples, this text must reflect the generally recognized "masculinized" nature of the traditional science fiction film, the apogee of what Mulvey identifies as patriarchy's "favorite cinematic form—illusionistic narrative film."[24]

Despite its issues, Mulvey's work remains instructive to a survey of female representation in science fiction cinema because this is a particularly masculinized genre within an historically masculinized medium reflecting an undoubtedly masculinized society. It is perhaps unsurprising then that examples of "scopophilia" are abundant within it. Such is Mulvey's enthusiasm for her idea that it is worth applying it direct to science fiction cinema. Consider the following question:

Can a female character in a science fiction film—whatever else her function within the narrative—avoid being an object of heterosexual male desire?

Although female roles undoubtedly stagnated during the 1930s and '40s, science fiction cinema did bolster its position by developing a recognizable aesthetic. Many of the forms and features of the genre in the 21st century originate from this period. And many of the expectations about women represented a consolidation of conventions that originated through the silent period. In short, women have always been the subject of pleasurable looking in science fiction cinema...

Sexualized Beings

As noted, Georges Méliès regularly employed chorus dancers, largely in supporting roles, for his silent, melodramatic, fantasy narratives. Building on this theme, female appearances in the science fiction movies of the period are notable for their particular interest in young girls. The 1899 film *The X-Ray Mirror* features a girl at a mirror, trying on a hat; her reflection changes to the image of a ballet dancer, and then she faints. This 2-minute piece clearly capitalizes on the new science of X-rays to showcase its cinematic tricks; whether the girl is included as visual lure, or merely as a (fainting) narrative convenience, is not clear. The alternative title of the 1906 film *How to Make Time Fly* is clearer: *The Girl That Made Time Fly* offers more clues about what filmmakers considered might attract an audience. This 5-minute picture features a girl who disrupts time by manipulating a clock[25]—possibly the first example of time travel in cinema. Once again, Terry Ramsaye is instructive in the practical thinking of filmmakers in the early years of the 20th century, as he describes a Mutoscope director being presented with box office receipts from a film arcade:

U.S. Battleship at Sea, $0.25; Joseph Jefferson in Rip's Sleep, $0.43; Ballet Dancer, $1.05; Girl Climbing Apple Tree, $3.65 ... "Then," he said, "I think we had better have some more of the Girl-Climbing-Apple-Tree kind."
The production policy of the motion picture was ordained forever in that decision.[26]

Both the 1908 movie *When the Man in the Moon Seeks a Wife* and the 1912 film *The Electric Leg* involve heroes who accidentally stumble into dormitories full of school girls. In 1908, *The Airship* (or *100 Years Hence*) featured a Jewish man flirting with a semi-clad mermaid. By 1910, the French had pushed this form of titillation as far as to include an impromptu visit to a girl in her bath in *Burglary by Airship*. The British, during this pre–World War I period, appear to have avoided overt sexual objectification; however, this does not stop their films exploiting female beauty and presenting notions of aesthetic perfection.

In the 1909 film *Electric Transformations*, a male professor is teaching a group of young women in his laboratory. He has a device that can change objects, which he demonstrates by changing his female cook's head to resemble his. She is not pleased. She is happy, however, when the professor gives her another new head, this time resembling the prettiest girl in the class. Perhaps more problematic to the modern mind is the representation of aesthetic perfection offered by the 1907 U.S. movie *Dr. Skinnum*, in which the physician of the title promises to cure various physical "defects." A three-foot tall woman enters his scientific device and is stretched to become six foot. Her clothes, of course have not stretched, giving the filmmakers an opportunity for further titillation.

These early movies feel like experiments in what would later be called "exploitation quickies"; that is, films made cheaply and quickly to take advantage of one element, with little regard to overall production quality. In many ways, much of cinema's early output meets this description; however, these titillating genre films reveal an additional trend. Narrative components were being used as an excuse to present girls and semi-naked women on screen. Méliès' *Après le Bal*, feels like pornography because nudity is its *raison d'être*. However, pornography and sexual exploitation develop from separate sources.[27] Pornography has an agenda of its own; recognizable as a discrete genre, it employs its own codes, including subject matter, object fetishism, camera angles, and form, to meet the needs of its predominantly-male audience.[28] Science fiction lends itself to the presentation of pornography, but it remains merely a backdrop to a more seductive collection of impulses. The semi-naked mermaid might well be *The Airship*'s ultimate reason to be, but she is dressed in something else: science fiction.

The permissive spirit of that mermaid found its way into many of the genre's portrayals of female aliens. They began with exotic queens of unexplored regions on Earth, and developed further in 1932 and 1949 through the cruel sexual appetite of the fabled Queen of Atlantis in *Die Herrin von Atlantis* and *Siren of Atlantis*. The early queen figure quickly moved to the Moon and Mars, and from there, sexualized female aliens eventually populated many regions of space and time—ultimately finding perhaps their most overt reflection in *Species* (1995), their most rarefied form in the art design of *Alien* (1979) and a bit of both in the hybrid creation of *Splice* (2009).

Back when wider society was less permissive, the alien-ness of female science fiction characters seems to have legitimized their sexualization: that is, it allowed them to be shown doing things that they might not be permitted to do as humans. In many ways these sexual substitutes carry on the tradition of the Classical nude in public art: a liberal attitude to sexuality within a conservative setting. As military historian John Streets has pointed out, the *tableaux vivants*, or "living statues," of London's famous Windmill Theatre are another 1930s' example of this phenomenon.[29] In 1932, British theatre censorship rules held that moving nudes on stage were "obscene," but stationary nudes were accepted—like the Classical statue—as art. The result was naked women in a series of frozen stage scenes, portraying popular themes and characters— including mermaids. It seems that the sexual nature of the female performers was acceptable if they were dehumanized—like the bronzes and marbles of antiquity. The Windmill Theatre had its *tableaux vivants*; science fiction has its alien proxies.

All of this would appear to add some fuel to the notion that science fiction cinema is a site of creative contradictions. It has been noted that the genre's technologies and techniques present huge potential for pleasurable male viewing. This potential is increased again by the appearance of aliens and other proxies as excuses for sexualized representation. Science fiction cinema quickly became particularly proficient in what Laura Mulvey calls cinema's "skilled and satisfying manipulation of visual pleasure."[30] Men have of course remained in control of its production. Despite all of this pleasurable looking, science fiction is not an overtly pornographic genre; rather it seems to suffer from a "sexual inertia." As Jason Gould suggests above, the genre's tropes and trappings often seem to serve as replacements for sexual activity. And so the contradiction has been escalated to a creative conundrum: does science fiction sell sex or does sex sell science fiction?

BEING SEXUAL

Gould's comments above point to the idea that the trappings of science fiction can provide the genre with its own surrogates for sex. Evidence from the genre's recent output suggests that there may be something in this idea. Indeed, Vivian Sobchack explores the notion in her revealingly titled 1995 essay, "The Virginity of Astronauts: Sex and the Science Fiction Film": "Biological sexuality and women are often absent from science fiction film narratives, and when they do turn up they tend to be disaffiliated from each other, stripped of their cultural significance as a semiotic relation, carefully separated from each other..."[31]

Perhaps partly to justify the absence of women from her earlier book, *The Limits of Infinity*, Sobchack goes on to explain in detail why this absence occurs, some of which approaches Gould's surrogacy idea from a male repression angle: "one representation comes to stand for many" allowing "the shifting of impulses from one pathway to another."[32] There is evidence, however, that science fiction cinema in its teen years did in fact experiment with its sexuality.

In the 1912 U.S. film *How Patrick's Eyes Were Opened*, a man uses a TV-phone to catch his lover in the arms of other men. The concept of female promiscuity touched on in this 10-minute film was taken much further in the 1916 film *Without a Soul*. Alternatively titled *Lola*, it details the exploits of a beautiful woman who is resurrected by her father, and then casually ruins the lives of men who are sexually attracted to her. Danish filmmakers are seeking to contrast the depravity of Earth with an idyllic Mars when they include women in a scene of drunken debauchery in the 1917 film *Himmelskibet*, which features in Chapter I. The odd conceit of the 1917 Austrian film *A Tryton* sees the sea-monster of the title fall in love with a pretty woman—and then buy her from her husband! However, the woman's consequent promiscuity torments the creature and he lets her go.

The relatively "clean" world of suggested extramarital affairs and promiscuity bumps up against a more visceral, biological sex in 1918 with two versions of the 1911 Hanns Heinz Ewer novel, *Alraune*. She is the beautiful woman born to a prostitute mother who has been artificially inseminated using semen scooped from the ground beneath a hanged man. Various versions show Alraune growing up to be sexy, seductive and revengeful. In publicity descriptions of the Austrian-Hungarian version, the prostitute is apparently penetrated, and inseminated, directly by a mandrake root, although "it is questionable whether the film was in fact ever made."[33] It may be that such graphic sex was deemed to be taking the "Girl-Climbing-Apple-Tree" strategy too far; however, there is certainly still a trend towards the exploration of sexual themes as science fiction cinema enters the 1920s. Female sexuality is drawn into the 1920 version of *Dr. Jekyll and Mr. Hyde*, featuring a notable performance by the acclaimed American stage star John Barrymore. At least the sixth film adaptation of Robert Louis Stevenson's 1886 novella, this incarnation explores English Victorian world of private fantasy and sexual repression. Female roles are only hinted at in the novel, but here they include an innocent love interest for Dr. Jekyll, a vampish sex interest for Mr. Hyde and scenes in a seedy basement club.

The exploration of sexual themes continued the following year with *Sinners in Silk* and its examination of incest. The theme of inescapable generic lineage that had affected Alraune returns in the 1924 film *Orlacs Haende*, based on the Maurice Renard novel, *Les Mains d'Orlac*, in which a piano player's severed hands are replaced by those of a murderer. The hands have a mind of their own. This film version has been noted for the sexual violence towards women during the telling of its story. Phil Hardy, whose *Aurum Film Encyclopedia: Science Fiction* entries regularly highlight the fortunes of women in the genre, is particularly vocal on this point: "The misogyny of the film, a feature of so many of these fantasy films ... has become far harder to take now but it also provides a far more direct and obvious clue to the minds that generate these kinds of scenarios."[34]

The reader might be forgiven for wondering if Hardy considers the minds of modern filmmakers to be much the same, merely harder to fathom. Back when films were beginning to talk, two remakes of *Alraune* ensured that these scenarios continued to be placed before audiences. The erotically charged 1928 silent version flirts with the idea of incest introduced in *Sinners in Silk*, and reflects this in the alternative title, *Unholy Love*. Its second alternative title, *Daughter of Destiny*, is exaggerated to *Daughter of Evil* for a 1930 sound version, starring Brigitte Helm; she appears in a poster that leaves little doubt that this film is being sold on female promiscuity.

All of this points to the 1920s as being a decade when science fiction cinema became sexually mature—or, rather, promiscuous. It was using its unique narrative tools to explore male sexual fantasy through female sexual desire; however, this would be short-lived. In the late 1920s, Hollywood saw potential commercial damage in a public backlash against exploitation films across the industry—not only in science fiction. The result of this fear was self-censorship. Coupled with this, sound technology, as noted above, made films more expensive to produce, and so the risks associated with upsetting the audience were greater. A few more sexually-charged science fiction films were made, including: *Die Herrin von Atlantis* (1932); a remake of *Orlacs Haende* called *Mad Love* in 1935; and an eroticized version of the legend of *The Golem*, also in 1935. However, little in the way of overt sex made it past 1934 and the introduction of the Production Code Administration, which required every movie exhibited in the U.S. to hold a certificate to show that it followed the guidelines of the industry's own Production Code. This, of course also affected decisions made by non–American filmmakers wanting to distribute their films in the U.S. Science fiction's sexual awakening was on hold.

So, the genre came out of its early period well able to show sex, but no longer willing to go all the way; however, women remained pawns in a sort of male dance around the subject. As with the statues at The Windmill Theatre, sex was used for titillation, not recreation—and certainly not procreation. It is a tradition that continues to hold, or at least it still did in 1995, according to Vivian Sobchack: "The virginal astronauts of the science fiction film ... signify a conquering, potent, masculine and autonomous technology which values production over reproduction, which creates rather than procreates in a seeming immaculate conception and a metaphorically autocratic caesarean birth."[35]

Even if self-censorship and risk aversion had not stepped in, it is possible

Safe sex for the post–Production Code cinema of the 1930s. W.C. Fields as Santa being pulled by (from left) Marie Burton, Eleanor Counts, Eleanor Keaton, and Gwen Kenyon in the future-looking variety piece *The Big Broadcast of 1938* (1938).

that the sexual experiments of the 1920s would have come to a natural end. Their focus on female sexuality ran against the self-reflective, patriarchal nature of the genre. After all, once Narcissus had seen his own image, he was not interested in making love to anyone else; and once Prometheus had seen fire, he wanted it for his own creative purposes. For science fiction cinema, procreation and recreation may have withered on the vine, but during the 1930s, re-creation was alive and kicking.

Frankenstein Syndrome

Modern science fiction is a female creation. This is the implication of author and historian Brian Aldiss's argument[36] that the genre's first published novel was Mary Wollstonecraft Shelley's 1818 work, *Frankenstein; or, the Modern*

Prometheus.[37] Others disagree, including Adam Roberts, whose impressive *History of Science Fiction* makes a good case for Johann Kepler's 1634 text, *Somnium.*[38] Despite Kepler's work featuring a voyage to the moon—a staple of cinema's silent period—few surely would deny *Frankenstein*'s greater impact on the film genre. Roberts agrees: "this tale has a good claim to the title of 'most influential nineteenth-century novel,' and its presence in subsequent SF cannot be denied."[39]

Indeed, filmmakers have been inspired by Shelley's story on many occasions. Georges Méliès, once again, started the ball rolling with his 1897, 2-minute *Chirurgien Americain,* in which the surgeon of the title brings a tramp back to life. Apparent adaptations have ranged from James Whale's classic 1931 version featuring Boris Karloff as the monster, through the comedy of *Abbott and Costello Meet Frankenstein* (1948), to Hammer Films' *The Horror of Frankenstein* (1970), with the monster played by David Prowse—the man behind the mask of Darth Vader. In 1966, two monsters fight through Tokyo in the Japanese, *Furankenshutain no kaijū: Sanda Tai Gaira,* and a descendant of Baron Frankenstein appears in the Mexico-based exploitation quickie, *Jesse James Meets Frankenstein's Daughter.* The 1965 film *Frankenstein Meets the Space Monster* has nothing to do with the original story, whereas *Mary Shelley's Frankenstein,* Kenneth Branagh's 1994 version, co-written for the screen by Steph Lady, aims to be faithful to the 1818 text. There are many, many more examples. The online database at IMDb.com lists well over 100 films with *Frankenstein* in their titles, a number which does not include the many other films which leave their inspiration almost anonymous, including *Sammy's Automaton* (1914), *Flick* (1967) and *Splice* (2009).

The huge impact that Mary Shelley's *Frankenstein* has had on science fiction cinema could be due to her vagueness about how the creature is brought to life. This has, after all, allowed creative filmmakers to fill in narrative gaps, taking the story from gothic horror to comedy to Western to science fiction and back again. The more likely reason for the success of Shelley's story, however, is the power of its connection to primal desires and fears about life and death. Citing the work of Erasmus Darwin, Brian Aldiss states that "the enduring concept of *Frankenstein* rests on the quasi-evolutionary idea that God is remote or absent from creation: man therefore is free to create his own sublife."[40] In other words, he is able to extend his Self. Reflecting on this idea in *Feminist Futures,* Anne Cranny-Francis suggests that science fiction itself was born with the "automatization of the first man-made man."[41] Given the evidence offered by the genre so far, it is not surprising that male filmmakers would attempt to bend this power to their own ends.

BRIDES OF FRANKENSTEIN

In 1935, James Whale followed his 1931 classic *Frankenstein* with *Bride of Frankenstein*. For its first sixty minutes, this is largely a re-run of the second half of the first film, with Karloff's monster being chased around by characters with German names and clipped English accents. In the final fifteen minutes, however, an icon of cinema emerges. Shrouded in white, with knife cuts criss-crossing her throat, her piled-up, black hair shot through with a bolt of white, Elsa Lanchester stands as the female embodiment of Shelley's monster. But something else has changed: this is now very much a male creation.

In *Bride of Frankenstein*'s opening vignette, Lanchester also plays Mary Shelley herself, on an imagined stormy evening at the Swiss Villa Diodati in 1816, the place and time that the original *Frankenstein* novel was supposedly written. In this attempt to legitimize the new story about to unfold by suggesting that it might too have come from the mind of the original author, Lanches-

An icon of science fiction and Gothic horror is created. Elsa Lanchester as The Monster's Mate and Colin Clive as her creator, Henry Frankenstein, in *Bride of Frankenstein* (1935).

ter's Shelley offers a moral insight: "My purpose was to write a moral lesson: the punishment that befell a mortal man who dared to emulate God."

This theme is picked up in the film proper, where a clear distinction is made between female morals and male ambitions. In a dramatic conversation with his fiancée, creator of the original monster, Baron Frankenstein, reveals the extent of his ambition:

> I dreamed of being the first to give to the world the secret that God is so jealous of. The formula for life. Think of the power to create a man. And I did. I did it! I created a man. And who knows? In time I could have trained him to do my will. I could have bred a race. I might even have found the secret of eternal life.

In many ways, this speech encapsulates the male creative drive in science fiction cinema: there is the irony of the man telling the woman that he is the first to create life; the arrogance to assume that the creation will do his bidding; and finally, the ambition to live forever. It is no accident that one of the most enduring myths of the cinema should echo the success of cinema itself. When photographs were new, they were a marvel, but soon stationary figures were not enough. Someone said, "make them move," and they did move. But that was not enough either. Someone wanted them to be projected, large on a screen; then directors made them do things and writers made them be things. Others tinted the figures; yet more made them speak and sing, but this was not enough either. It never will be enough. Science fiction offers the cinema-goer the best hope to see God; *Frankenstein* offers the science fiction filmmaker his (and sometimes her) best chance to be God.

While film variations and adaptations of the original *Frankenstein* may skew and dilute the novel's narrative, the power and agency remains essentially with its female creator: Mary Wollstonecraft Shelley. This is woman creating man creating man. *Bride of Frankenstein* changes that dynamic, by placing power and agency in the hands of its male creator: James Whale. This is man creating man creating woman. As the sinister scientist, Dr. Pretorius explains to an initially skeptical Baron Frankenstein, this is the next stage in their journey to become gods:

> DR. PRETORIUS: Male and female created He them. "Be fruitful and multiply." Create a race, a man-made race upon the face of the earth. Why not?
>
> HENRY FRANKENSTEIN: I daren't! I daren't even think of such a thing.
>
> DR. PRETORIUS: Our mad dream is only half realized. Alone, you have created a man. Now, together, we will create his mate.
>
> DR. PRETORIUS: You mean...?
>
> DR. PRETORIUS: Yes. A woman. That should be really interesting.

The woman that they create is, inevitably, beautiful, unlike Boris Karloff's male monster of 1931, whom Lanchester's bride rejects as a grotesque—and is then destroyed for doing so. She is an example of the need, identified by Mulvey, for pleasurable (male) looking; she is not, however, a sexualized creature. This thread is picked up in later versions, including *Frankenstein Created Woman* (1966), in which *Playboy* magazine centerfold model, Susan Denberg,[42] seduces and kills three men after being given the life-force of her murdered (male) lover. That particular sexual dynamic may be worth exploring elsewhere; it is only necessary to note here that sexualized brides of Frankenstein are relatively rare. Her primary role is to show not only that man can become a god, but more importantly, that he can replace woman in the eyes of God. It is a fantasy that dominates science fiction cinema—and finds an outlet in one of the defining pillars of the genre: robots.

ROBOTS

The most famous female robot in science fiction cinema appears in Fritz Lang's 1927 epic, *Metropolis*, the film he made alongside his screenwriter wife, Thea von Harbou, two years before they made *Frau im Mond*. Described by J.P. Telotte in *Replications: A Robotic History of the Science Fiction Film* as the "centerpiece" of "the Seductive Text of *Metropolis*,"[43] this robot is the most enduring image of the film. Indeed, it has good claim to be the most enduring image of all science fiction cinema; however, left unexplained, "seductive" might be confusing. The robot design is seductive: sleek and stylish, with a late 1920s functional Art Deco elegance, this is the beautiful figure that inspired conceptual artist Ralph McQuarrie's designs for C-3PO in *Star Wars*. However, unlike many of the memorable and successful male robots of science fiction cinema— Gort, Robby, Huey, Dewey and Louie, R2-D2, Maximillian, Johnny 5 and even RoboCop[44]—the *Metropolis* robot only becomes useful to men when she has been given human form. From this point, she takes on three roles that characterize gynoids—female androids—in science fiction cinema:

1. Surrogate Sex
2. Scopophilia
3. Subjugation

The mad, male scientist of *Metropolis*, Rotwang, has created a robot that can take the form of any individual, who will then follow his commands. Maria, the mild-mannered mediator, is kidnapped and her form given to the robot. The transformation from robot to gynoid happens in a dramatic sequence that would later inspire James Whale's animation of the creations in *Frankenstein* and *Bride of Frankenstein*. What follows is an overt sexualization of Maria, as she performs an extremely provocative dance, almost-naked, for men at a

The duplicity of science fiction characters. Brigitte Helm as the "robot vamp" in human form and as the virginal mediator Maria in *Metropolis* (1927).

nightclub. As with the sexy aliens mentioned above, the science fiction trappings become an excuse for this sexual activity, resulting in an illogical narrative leap that is highlighted in critic Pauline Kael's description of the "robot vamp's bizarre, lewd wink" as one of the film's "oddities that defy analysis."[45] The psychoanalyst might suggest something additional happening here. The fact that it is the proxy of the chaste Maria who engages in the sexual activity triggered by the science fiction element, means that when she is returned to "normal" towards the end of the film, she bears no guilt for her actions. When the robot relinquishes her form, Maria re-emerges as the virginal, human heroine; it is an example of "intra-character balancing" that means that science fiction cinema can, once again, have its cake and eat it too.

This type of overt narrative-based sexualization of the gynoid will later be taken to uncomfortable extremes for the 1987 film *Cherry 2000* (discussed further in Chapter VI); however, it is worth noting that this type of exploitation—in which the notion of sex with the disposable female robot is central to the plot—is rare in science fiction cinema. Instead, the genre, again, favors a "look-but-don't-touch" ethos, allowing robots to serve as agents for a rarefied form of the scopophilia mentioned by Laura Mulvey. Adam Roberts highlights the enduring appeal of this to science fiction cinema when he describes the genre's invitation to men "to fantasise about worlds in which women as beautiful as Sean Young [Rachael in *Blade Runner* (1982)] can be purchased from an android store."[46]

Once again, it is a young girl who provides the initial inspiration for these female robots. She is taken from E.T.A. Hoffmann's novel, *Die Puppe* (1816), a tale about a mechanical doll that comes to life, popularized by Délibes' 1870 ballet *Coppélia*, which had in turn taken its inspiration from Edmond Audrian's opera *La Poupée*. Georges Méliès' two-minute film in 1900, *Coppélia: la poupée animée*, was followed by a number of science fiction versions including: *The Doll Maker's Daughter* (1906), *The Mechanical Statue and the Ingenious Servant* (1907), *The Inventor's Secret* (1911), *Hoffmanns Erzählungen* (1923). The theme was taken up again, in 1966, for the American/Spanish children's film, *Dr. Coppelius*; however, the robotic female is noticeably absent—in any of its forms—from science fiction cinema between the coming of sound and the coming of war. It seems that *Bride of Frankenstein* represents the primary development of this thread for this period. It also reveals a trend in female representation for a period described by Phil Hardy as being "in turmoil,"[47] one in which the genre was somewhat losing its way.

The robots of the genre are often linked back to Karel Čapek's *R.U.R.* (*Rossum's Universal Robots*), a 1920 play about an army of worker drones— slaves. Born within the patriarchally ordered film industry, male and female creations—in their various forms—support Lacan's notion of the "name of the father," and they carry the values of the "symbolic order." In short: because men create these women, they feel entitled to own and subjugate—or control—them. Occasionally women object, as in *The Bride*, a 1985 blend of *Bride of Frankenstein* and *Pygmalion*. Picking up the reigns of the 1935 film before the death of the female creature, Sting, as Baron Frankenstein, begins with noble plans for his creation: "I might make the New Woman, Clavell. Independent, free, as bold and as proud as a man. A women equal to ourselves."

As Steve Jenkins points out in his *Monthly Film Bulletin* review of *The Bride*, in the end Jennifer Beals' Eva (a popular name for the genre's created women, along with Eve and Ava[48]) "simply serves as the object of more of Sting's Byron-by-numbers malevolence"[49]; although she does also have something to say about that: "You can do what you like! You can take apart the body you put together, and you can take away the life you gave me, but you cannot have me. Not ever. Not even if you murder me and raise me up a thousand thousand times, you cannot have me."

The Bride represents an interesting turnabout. The death of the male creator rather than the created female in this film puts a temporary stop on the genre's relentless quest to grant more potential power to men. But it is short-lived. In this quest, male sights are set firmly on the most powerful, but elusive, role of all: The Mother.

Name of the Mother

Motherhood is the single most popular—or perhaps pervasive—female characteristic in science fiction cinema. Mother could easily have a chapter of her own in this study, except that her appearance is so regular that she cannot easily be corralled in one section. Mother Nature figures support the emerging genre in Chapter I; men attempt to become mothers in Chapter II; her "domestic normality" grounds the genre through Chapter III; motherhood is central to the genre's most celebrated female roles, as covered in Chapter V; she becomes the monstrous alien in Chapter VI; and she underpins the many modern changes charted in Chapter VII. For 120 years, mother's domestic role has served as a gyroscope, stabilizing the unsettling and unnerving nature of the science fiction as it has spun off in all directions. She is there in the 1-minute 1901 skit, *An Over-Incubated Baby*, and she is still there in 2016 for the acclaimed movie, *Arrival*. It is clear that she will be back many times in this text; for now, it is useful to take a brief look the cultural processes that underpin the mother in science fiction cinema.

The role of the mother has been central to the process by which the genre balances familiar and unfamiliar elements in order to aid what poet Samuel Taylor Coleridge calls "that willing suspension of disbelief."[50] The use of women as "ordinary" mothers supports the extraordinary exploits of the male; and the "ordinariness" of motherhood balances the extraordinariness of female exploits—when women do get to take part. It could be argued then that defining a woman as a mother is an attempt to keep her in her place—to root her in stereotype; however, therein lies a dichotomy. Mothers are far from ordinary. They do things that men cannot: they create life.

According to Camille Paglia, men's jealousy of women shows itself in the earliest stories:

> The book of Genesis is a male declaration of independence from the ancient mother-cults. Its challenge to nature, so sexist to modern ears, marks one of the crucial moments in western history ... It remade the world by male dynasty, cancelling the power of mothers.[51]

While science fiction cinema has leaned on mothers' prominent presences in myth, literature and drama to secure itself culturally, the genre has routinely attempted to cancel the power of mothers by skewing her biological role. Vivian Sobchack's work on biological sex in "The Virginity of Astronauts" is mentioned above, and Barbara Creed's argument that man's desire to "become woman" and eliminate the threat of the archaic mother[52] will be discussed when monstrous horror figures come to prominence in Chapter VI. Back in the 1930s, man's fear of the past was dressed up as a preoccupation with the future. *Frankenstein* had given man hope that he might project himself not only onto society, but also into that future; the trappings of science fiction are built on this "challenge to nature." The ultimate hope appears to be that quintessential female role of the mother might be usurped—if enough attempts are made.

As well as the baby vending machine described earlier, the 1930 musical

Just Imagine adds the notion of "incubator babies" through MT-42's joke that his parents were "General Electric." In 1901, the comic potential of male-controlled motherhood was explored briefly in the *An Over-Incubated Baby*, in which an infant is turned instantly into an old man when Professor Bakum's machine goes wrong. A more serious approach to the business of child-creation technology opens the 1976 film *Logan's Run*, in which child-rearing has been automated and conception has been sanitized. Once again, characters with numbers for names predict a motherless future for society:

FRANCIS-7: Do you know who his seed-mother was?
LOGAN-5: Of course not. I'm curious, not sick!

In 1933, three years after the release of *Just Imagine*, the U.S. movie *It's Great to be Alive* explored the notion of the fatherless future. Another genre musical, this is described by Phil Hardy as "one of the strangest ... excesses in the history of Science Fiction film,"[53] which is quite a claim for a genre such as this. In the not-too-distant future, all but one of the world's male population has been killed off by a virus, "masculinitis." The remaining women attempt to create an artificial man, in order to save the human race, but they fail, leaving the single surviving man expected to re-populate the world by natural means. He refuses. It is difficult to be certain about the intentions of a film that is all but impossible to view currently[54]; however, it is hard to get away from the notion that this male-produced movie is taking its opportunity to point out that "womankind" cannot function alone—without men. Despite this, science fiction cinema is replete with examples of attempts by men to function alone—without women. In fact, Single-0, the resurrected male visitor from the past in *Just Imagine* hints at that as an ultimate aim: "So, women are still causing trouble? You would think in fifty years they could have found a good substitute for them."

Of course, women are too important to science fiction cinema to be removed altogether. It is tempting, though, to link the 1930s birth-control ambitions with political aims and eugenics movements of the period. Judy Wajcman reveals more deeply rooted and longer lasting real-world examples of male attempts to control reproductive technologies in *Feminism Confronts Technology*. In a chapter called "Reproductive Technology: Delivered into Men's Hands" she explores the effect of the patriarchal technologies in "enabling male domination of woman and nature."[55] As the present work unfolds, more movie examples will reveal the genre's unique position to respond to the uneasy and complex relationship between men and mothers, including social and political attempts to control women who retain the ability to give birth in films such as *The Handmaid's Tale* (1990) and *Children of Men* (2006)—male adaptations of novels written by women. As the ultimate reflection of the "Frankenstein syndrome," motherhood adds another item to science fiction cinema's collection of creative contradictions: men cannot let their mothers go, but nor will they let them be.

———— ∞ ————

In many ways 1930 to 1945 was a lost period for women in science fiction cinema. Development within the genre had already slowed down after the early silent era of massive expansion, and now sound and censorship had dampened creativity. New themes and concepts were rare, few of the movies endured, and the way seems to have been lost somewhat. But change was happening elsewhere, as the swirling dust of a fractured film industry coalesced to consolidate power in the studios. Locked in wary orbits around each other, these massive bodies produced science fiction more recognizable for its style and elegance than its ideas and risk. With this safe approach, the male power-base would become more entrenched, creating themes that would endure. However, this would prove to be the calm before the storm. Science fiction was about to enter a period of post-war conflict: a golden age of huge productivity and influence— and of conservatism. Women's roles were set, once again, to be re-drawn, as they always are when worlds collide....

III

Science Fact
Peace and the Emergence
of Female Professionals

When the soldiers of World War One had come home, destined to return to jobs that their wives, sisters and mothers had been holding down for years, it had been hard for them to claim that theirs was exclusively "men's work." This notion would go on to win women some respect and voting rights around the world. When the scientists of World War Two returned home, their new, innovative approaches to technology and human knowledge were destined to permeate science fiction cinema. The Space Race was in its starting blocks, medicine was on the march, and computers were becoming an exciting reality. Armed once more with practical wartime experience, women were ready to ride this new wave. Early gains were hard wrought in the face of conservatism and domesticity, but slowly and surely, they made their marks professionally in the brave new world of 1950s science. From science comes knowledge, and knowledge is power. The genie was well-and-truly out of her bottle now.

—⟨∞⟩—

Social Earth

The 1950s is generally recognized as a golden age for science fiction cinema, especially in America. During the Second World War, U.S. studios had consolidated gains made during the Great War, leading to a further domination of the industry and the genre. Evidence of this can be seen in Phil Hardy's 1991 *Aurum Film Encyclopedia: Science Fiction*, where the number of entries rises from 53 international productions in the 1940s to 218 in the following decade; 70

percent of these 1950s films are U.S. productions, followed by 12 percent British, and then about 4.5 percent coming from both France and an emergent Japan. These numbers are not exact, as information is being unearthed and added to databases all the time, but given that Hardy and his own source of inspiration, Walt Lee's *Reference Guide to Fantastic Films*,[1] identify movies with the greatest distribution and impact on English-speaking territories, they still offer a valuable picture of the science fiction movie scene. It is inevitable then that much of this chapter, and the history beyond, will reference films from the United States.

America had approached World War II with an emphasis on weekly chapter serials portraying all–American heroes, including Flash Gordon, Buck Rogers and the technical-gadget wielding detective, Dick Tracy. The roles played by women in these formulaic tales of male exploits had all been seen before, as had many of the female characters in the superhero movies that also gained popularity through the war. The likes of *Batman* (1943) and *Captain America* (1944) no doubt provided patriotic escapism in the years around the war, but despite Dorothy Short's strong heroine figure in *Captain Midnight* (1942), and the arrival of Lois Lane in the form of Noel Neill in the hugely profitable 1948 *Superman* chapter series, this was a very fallow period for female characters. Like the 1930s, the '40s offered very little in the way of innovation; indeed, it is fair to say that this decade, with its increasingly masculine personifications of nationhood, was the worst so far from the perspective of those seeking interesting and meaningful roles for women.

As the post–1940s genre shook off the comic-book and radio-based action heroes, it also reduced its reliance on the literary sources that had propped up science fiction films in earlier decades. Literature did retain some influence in the form of films such as *Mysterious Island* (1951), another remake of *Alraune* (1952), *Abbott and Costello Meet Dr. Jekyll and Mr. Hyde* (1953), *20,000 Leagues Under the Sea* (1954), plus a British version of George Orwell's *1984* in 1956; however, the golden age is notable for its original screenplays, presenting a new (arguably more serious) kind of science fiction film. Surely this fresh approach had the potential to present a new kind of science fiction cinema woman too— one not bound by literary stereotypes and genre traditions.

Small Steps Forward

Rudolph Mate's 1951 science fiction classic *When Worlds Collide* had an immediate impact on the genre by being one of the its earliest color movies— and certainly its highest profile example.[2] Twelve minutes into the film, however, there is a more subtle indication of a direction of movement for the genre, as science, cinema and society regained their footing after the Second World War.

The film opens in a South African observatory, where an astronomer has made a discovery: Earth is in the path of the star Bellus and is about to be destroyed. The observation data is flown to America by pilot-courier, David Randall, to be checked by leading astronomer, Professor Cole Hendron. However, it is Hendron's daughter, Joyce, played by Barbara Rush, who feeds the data into the "differential analyzer," a state-of-the-art arrangement of spinning metal rods and chattering cogs that resembles a cross between a bedstead and Babbage's Difference Engine.[3] To modern eyes, this machine looks ludicrously dated: a throwback to the pre-war analogue calculating machines, soon to be made redundant by the commercialization of electronic computers. For now, however, this was cutting-edge, even futuristic, technology. Cutting-edge is, of course, the life-blood of science fiction cinema, and the makers of *When Worlds Collide* wanted to show it off. To emphasize the coming revolution, it is Joyce Hendron who analyzes and interprets the data, and it is this female scientist who confirms the South African observations. The worlds will indeed collide. The sequence seems quaint now, but it is difficult to overestimate the importance of the images, around the 12-minute mark, of Hendron sitting at the differential analyzer's output plotter, monitoring the graphs, actively checking the calculations against her slide-rule and noting the results in her journal. This woman is no passive receiver who regurgitates information; she is a mathematician, crunching critical data using the most advanced technology available in 1951. Writer Jason Gould has suggested that Hendron's active function here may have been intended as a recognition of the crucial roles that real women had played during the war as code breakers and experimental-computer operators[4]; for the genre, it was certainly an indication of things to come.

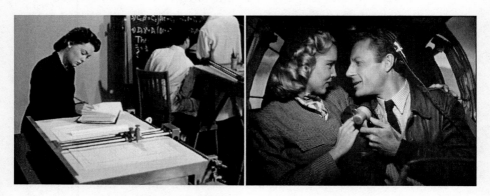

New world meets old. Barbara Rush as mathematician Joyce Hendron at the differential analyzer, and Kasey Rogers with Richard Derr in *When Worlds Collide* (1951).

When Worlds Collide takes a very different tack from its 1930 French predecessor, *La Fin du Monde*, in which the imminent destruction of Earth by an approaching comet triggers a series of orgies, which "were filmed with a flair for the erotic."[5] Instead, this 1951 version of the concept characterizes a decade of conservative values—especially in the U.S.—that help to create the foundations for what Constance Penley calls "our hoariest and seemingly most sexless genre."[6] Penley is referring largely to graphic sex and intercourse. Sex in the form of objectification and what Laura Mulvey identifies as "scopophilia" has never really deserted the genre. Indeed, this takes on a rather British flavor for the suggestive and titillating 1949 film, *The Perfect Woman*. With its feet firmly in the past, on paths cut by the likes of *Coppélia* and other sexualized dolls and robots discussed in Chapter II, this film involves what genre historians and reviewers John Clute and Peter Nicholls describe as "underwear fetishism and a sauciness quite close to the rim of what the period regarded as decent."[7] The perfect woman of the title is Penelope Belman, played by Patricia Roc, who takes the place of a lifelike female robot—a gynoid—that has been created by her scientist uncle, Professor Belman. The male characters' ignorance of the fact that the robot is actually a real woman presents opportunity for the kind of semi-clad comedy that must have influenced the British *Carry On* film series. John Baxter develops this thread in his 1970 book, *Science Fiction in the Cinema*, an early overview of the genre: in *The Perfect Woman*, he notes, "efforts with the corpse-like robot only involve them in a variety of obscene poses which, had the Principles been nude, would have graced any set of French postcards."[8] Compared with the colored, calm, clinical approach of *When Worlds Collide*, two years later, *The Perfect Woman*'s black and white bawdiness already seems dated. It is tempting then to see the turn into the 1950s as heralding a cut-off point for these silly forays into sexual exploitation—at least for Americans. But of course, revolutions do not always happen overnight.

A scene in Jack Arnold's 1953 U.S. science fiction film classic *It Came from Outer Space* finds two women and a policeman in a sheriff's office. The distressed older woman is reporting the disappearance of her husband. The younger woman, June, played by Kathleen Hughes, has nothing to say or do, until the end of the scene when she stands, pans her breasts in an arc close to camera lens, and exits. Seen on television, this action makes little sense until it is remembered that *It Came from Outer Space* was originally released in 3-D. It then becomes clear that June, like so many genre elements before and after her, exists to document the arrival and fidelity of the cinema technology—and, presumably, to enhance critical (male) reception of the film. In many ways, the future had arrived in the 1950s; however, it still brought with it the scopophilia discussed in Chapter II and the patriarchal drive introduced in Chapter I.

The patriarchal roots of *When Worlds Collide* are revealed just two minutes into its opening sequence, when a male voice-over narrative refers to "men of science." The familiar ideology becomes more apparent as the film shows male-only laboratories, female-free observatories and a UN meeting in which men from many nations discuss the end of the world. Joyce Hendron is often the only woman in exclusively male technical, political and professional environments. As the daughter of a professor and the film's love interest, she can trace her lineage back to the earliest science fiction films. Indeed, the other women in the movie too take on similarly traditional roles as cooks, secretaries and sexy stewardesses. In a curious early scene, a young woman, played by Kasey Rogers,[9] is crammed into a plane's cockpit with Randall, for no apparent reason other than to give him an opportunity to kiss her. Later, Randall indicates the shift of his attentions to Joyce Hendron by rebuffing a journalist's offer of money with the line, "No thanks. I'm working on a better offer."

All of this low-level sexism may seem petty in light of the film's radical presentation of Joyce Hendron as a humanitarian scientist and skilled mathematician. Perhaps it is, but it is also a reminder that tradition and stereotype are never very far from the surface. Indeed, 1950s science fiction cinema was built on conservative foundations that would serve as a constant challenge to the development of female roles.

Traditional Threats

The majority of science fiction movies of the 1950s fit into a category that can be described widely as "potential threat pictures." These span the entire decade and take the form of alien invasion films, creature features and monster movies, featuring what is sometimes known as the BEM—Bug-Eyed Monster. Titles for these films help to fuel that sense of threat; they include: *Zombies of the Stratosphere* (1952), *Invaders from Mars* (1953), *Killers from Space* (1954), *It! The Terror from Beyond Space* (1958), *Demons of the Swamp* (1959) and many, many others. The Japanese had their own particular style of monster movie, the "kaiju eiga," whose most famous character is Godzilla (*Gojira*, 1954). The science fiction credentials of these films rest on the concept of dormant creatures being disturbed by atomic explosions, an understandable preoccupation for postwar Japan. In North America and Western Europe, the primary focus was on the Soviet Union in what had now become the "Atomic Age." Wartime alliances had ended, leaving suspicions on all sides, which might be characterized simply as the Free West versus the Communist East, or the "Cold War." In real-world America, fear and suspicion found its most infamous outlet in Senator John McCarthy's House Un-American Activities Committee, which had set itself the task of rooting out communists on U.S. soil. McCarthy's most high-profile target was Hollywood, and so the proliferation of "threat pictures" is widely, but not exclusively, seen as response to this pervasive atmosphere of "reds under the beds" paranoia. It is perhaps best captured in the 1956 movie, *Invasion of the Body Snatchers*.[10]

Given science fiction cinema's record to date, it is perhaps unsurprising that women's roles in these "threat pictures" tend towards the familiar. Following a pattern laid down by earlier movies, not least the classic monster movie *King Kong* (1933), women in the 1950s are presented as victims, women-in-peril and damsels-in-distress in many films, including *It Conquered the World* (1956) and *The Monster That Challenged the World* (1957). These narratives are clearly intended to magnify the sense of danger for the male cinema-goer by threatening to take away his woman—not to mention the sense of fear generated in the female cinema-goer. This idea is replicated on promotional material and posters for the films of the period, many of which show semi-clad, attractive women being carried away by beasts, monsters, robots, colossal men and aliens. If they are not being carried off, they might be cowering beneath the threat, as Margaret Field is doing in the poster for the 1951 movie *The Man from Planet X*. Sometimes the threat is generated by the poster artist, despite no such peril existing in the picture. Examples of this tactic include the classic benign visitor film *The Day the Earth Stood Still* (1951), the film starring Robby, the decade's friendliest robot, *Forbidden Planet* (1956), and the title mentioned earlier, *It Came from Outer Space* (1953). Once again, it is Kathleen Hughes' bust that captures the attention here,[11] which inevitably leads to the question of sex.

In the 1979 edition of *The SF Encyclopedia*, Peter Nicholls widens the scope of the invasion films of the 1950s: "Just as white men traditionally fear that the black man is a sexual athlete too well endowed to compete against, so in sf the menace of the alien is often seen in sexual terms."[12]

As if to highlight this point, and so magnify the potential impact of the threat, there is a degree of female objectification in the films for this period. Once again, this is scopophilia and the "male gaze," rather than pornographic sex, and it can be seen in films such as 1954's *The Creature from the Black Lagoon* and its 1955 sequel *Revenge of the Creature*. They show off their use of 3-D technology by including underwater shots of female victims swimming. The sexual element is more prurient in other films, such as the 1952 West German remake of *Alraune* and the U.S. film of the same year, *Captive Women*, in which females are treated as breeding stock following a devastating atomic war. The savage woman appears again that year in *Untamed Women*, and again the following year in *The Mesa of Lost Women*, which charts attempts by a male scientist to

Exaggerated threats: scenarios that don't come to pass in advertisements for the *The Day the Earth Stood Still* (1951) and *Forbidden Planet* (1956).

create race of "savage women." This trend for fantasy also takes the form of a clutch of movies with lurid tiles such as *Bride of the Monster*, updated for the Space Age to *Bride of the Atom, She Devil* (1957), *The Astounding She-Monster* (1958), *The World, the Flesh and the Devil* (1959), *The 30-Foot Bride of Candy Rock* (1959).

Despite all of this sexual aggression and objectification of women, a contradiction seems to permeate science fiction cinema of the 1950s. Sex is often implicit, but rarely explicit. Even when the female is the potential aggressor, as in the 1954 British film *Devil Girl from Mars*, promises of sex turn to titillation, rather than anything graphic. The "Girl" of the title is the leather-clad Nyah, played by Patricia Laffan; she has travelled from Mars where a "battle between the sexes" has reduced the virility of the men, forcing her to Earth in order to find healthy human men to take back as breeding stock. *Devil Girl from Mars* is slow and dull, and, like the vast majority of science fiction films of the 1950s, fails utterly to deliver on its promises of sex.

Perhaps all of this pushing back against the sexualized creature is patriarchal cinema's way of pushing back against Peter Nicholls' alien "menace." The threat may still be there, but it is neutralized by human—that is, Western democratic—free will. This notion sits at the heart of the 1958 film with one of the most recognized titles of the decade, *I Married a Monster from Outer Space*. This may sound like a comedy, along the lines of *Earth Girls Are Easy* (1988); however, it is a serious attempt to address the issues of the "sexual alien menace" head on. The menace in *I Married a Monster from Outer Space* is another alien looking for a human woman to help repopulate a dying planet—this time the alien is male. He finds a potential mate, Marge Farell, played by Gloria Talbott, takes the physical form of her fiancé, Bill, and replaces him; however, this simulacrum does not have that "little extra something" needed to make him truly human. Farell, a savvy, red-blooded, patriotic, American woman, realizes that something is amiss, and the alien plot is foiled, but not before the alien has professed his love for her. Marge is not interested; she returns to her rightful husband, Bill.

I Married a Monster from Outer Space presents at least two allegories. In the first, Marge Farell represents American values, which not only rebuff Communist aggression, but they convert the aggressor[13] to a U.S. way of thinking. In the second, she represents an extension to the male Self; she is the "serviceable Other," described in Chapter I, created and used by the male to reinforce his position. When this human woman willingly returns to the human man, she takes her place again as a member of the "ordered-collective," as described by Edward Sampson and others. Femininity-in-peril is not used merely to present victorious masculinity through the damsel-in-distress formula; it also allows the male hero to claim possession of the female—regardless of whatever threat lies outside their ordered (Western patriarchal) society.

Central to the success of that ordered society in *I Married a Monster from Outer Space*, and many other 1950s science fiction films, is its authentic visual representation, achieved through its *mise en scène*—the combination of visual elements that make up the screen image.

AUTHENTIC VISIONS

In *The Marrying Kind: Working-Class Courtship and Marriage in 1950s Hollywood*, Judith Smith celebrates Hollywood's post-war move towards working-class realism as a reaction to what she calls its "ordinary presentation of homogenous classlessness... Filmed in black and white with mostly unknown actors on location where working-class people lived and worked, these productions claimed an aura of 'authenticity' beyond what moviegoers expected from mainstream Hollywood."[14]

If Smith likes the idea that cinema in general was beginning to show believable people in authentic settings, then she may well have applauded science fiction's shift away from the stylized sets of the 1930s and the studio lots of the 1940s towards what feels like more "ordinary" locations in the 1950s. Settings for the invasion films range from real cities in movies such as *The Flying Saucer* (1950) and *The Blob* (1958) through small, rural towns in *Invasion of the Body Snatchers* (1956) and *Space Master X-7* (1958) to the memorable desert locations that are backdrops to the events in many films, including *It Came from Outer Space*, *I Married a Monster from Outer Space* and *Them!* (1954). The desert was clearly successful enough to influence British producers to find similarly isolated locations in *The Stranger from Venus* (1954), *The Quatermass Xperiment* (1955), and others. As Vivian Sobchack points out in *Screening Space: The American Science Fiction Film*, deserts and their proxies had a dual role, as "cheap locations which were 'neutral' enough to admit the introduction of the extraordinary and fantastic into what was, after all, a real and familiar world...."[15]

Locations, then, were playing their part in the genre balancing act mentioned in Chapter II, whereby "abnormal" elements of a science fiction story are grounded by the "normal" elements, creating a believable whole. Characters are part of that balance, and in a jittery post-war world in which fear and suspicion played a large part, conservative values were projected onto those characters. The result for female representation, in addition to a degree widespread objectification, was a proliferation of domestic roles not seen since the silent period. At the top of the list, once again, was the mother.

The mother in the Earth-based science fiction films of the 1950s is the rock on which family, society and humanity are built. To Linda Grant, "working class women remain[ed] symbols of an idea of motherhood, nurture, suffering, labour, strength and earthiness."[16] As such, she represents Sobchack's "familiar world," especially in invasion films such as *Beast with a Million Eyes* (1956) and *Invaders from Mars* (1953).

Seventy or more years of movement away from what Judith Smith calls Hollywood's "popular discourse celebrating domesticity and marriage..."[17] have opened this traditional role to accusations of overt gender stereotyping. It could, however, be argued that there should be no issue with presenting women as mothers at all; if this reflects society then so be it. As Heather Barker has pointed out: "If we cannot even portray on screen the myriad of personalities and accurate gender ratios relating to our own world, then how can we even begin to explore strange new ones?"[18]

Barker is complaining primarily about those films with few, or no female characters, as well as those that fail to recognize anything beyond stereotype.

Many mothers in 1950s science fiction cinema conform to a very restrictive sense of who they should be. Some of this is based within tradition; however, as the West entered the Cold War, conservative images of domesticity, family and motherhood were central to a feeling of security. Mothers like Mary Maclean, played by Hillary Brooke, in *Invaders from Mars* are at the forefront of that feeling. Defined entirely within her roles as mother and wife, and deprived of any character development, Maclean is killed off shortly after fulfilling her primary function, which is to reinforce the relationship—mediate, that is—between her son, David, and his father. Mary McClean's death serves largely to court audience sympathy for David. In this, she reinforces the "special tie women have with children," described by feminist writer Shulamith Firestone as "no more than shared oppression."[19] This is a domestic oppression that women were fighting on all fronts in the 1950s, as Erica Sheen observes: "In the U.S. and in Great Britain reconstruction of the economy required the stimulus of new technology, particularly domestic technology with its broad market and self-creating demand."[20]

Science fiction cinema generated its own demand by magnifying social fears and then attempted to legitimize itself by resting on social stereotype. The idea that science fiction cinema reflects society at the time in which it is created is not new. Indeed, Bonnie Noonan takes this a little further in *Women Scientists in Fifties Science Fiction Films* with her contention that "ideology of the 1950s, particularly as it affected issues of gender, 'saturates,' to use Bakhtin's term, the B science fiction films of that era."[21] The ability of patriarchal forces to skew reality in order to magnify male desires has already become a recurring theme of this history. How then would science fiction cinema represent the growing number of post-war, real-world women who were no longer willing to conform to sexual and domestic stereotypes?

Professional Space

When the sciences and technologies created and developed during World War II were eventually put to peacetime use, they generated a huge number of new jobs in new, often science-based, professions. Old jobs in old professions were taken up again by male soldiers returning from active duty, and in America the *Servicemen's Readjustment Act*, known also as the "GI Bill of Rights" potentially provided a level of education to those men wanting to move forward into the new world. Even so, as Sheila Lewenhak points out in *Women and Work*,

> For about twenty-five years, from 1945 to 1970, the main belligerents in the Second World War and other advanced technological countries suffered from a labour shortage or had

"full employment" which alleviated the harsh competition that had characterized the previous hundred and more years.[22]

Lewenhak uses quotes around "full employment" above because she means "for men"; however, opportunities had already opened up for women through the war. In the United States in 1945, married women outnumbered single women in the workplace for the first time in modern history, and this trend would continue, helped by the general view of men "that it was a good idea for wives to earn and increase the family income...."[23] There were, however, restrictions to this, not least those revealed in the rest of that quotation: "provided that at the same they took almost total responsibility for home and family work." This attitude helped to fuel the domestic representation of women so common to the invasion films discussed in the previous section; however, expectations about women returning to what Germaine Greer calls work with an "ancillary aspect"[24] were at odds with the reality of postwar, female, career ambitions.

Genre Résumé

The earliest paid employment for women and girls in science fiction cinema is the domestic service seen in the silent films of Chapter I. She is the cook who accidentally spills the energy potion into the soup in *The Pill Maker's Mistake* (1906) or the pretty maid who makes the male inventor's wife jealous in *Hair Restorer* (1907). Service to men becomes service to country during the First World War, for example when the female post office worker thwarts the invasion of the "Nordeners" in the 1914 British film, *If England Were Invaded*. By and large, jobs for women on screen reflected their roles in society—until the arrival of the suffragists.

When science fiction began to wonder what the future would be like if society were run by women, it merely transposed "male" jobs, clothes and attitudes onto women. There was clearly an assumption that women in these futures would choose to continue where the men left off. As a result, she is the Mayoress of New York in the 1911 film *One Hundred Years After*, in which a man awakes in the year 2011 to find that all of the jobs have been taken by women. He joins a band of male suffragists and wins the vote for men. A similar concept underpins the 1914 film *In the Year 2014*, where the corporate and financial world is controlled by women, including Mrs. Jones and her daughter.

These and other female professionals form part of a response to male fears about female suffrage in films intended to show the potential shortcomings of female-run futures. As such, it is not clear how they fit, if at all, in the development of the genre's professional women. This remains the case for films not directly about female suffrage. In *Just Imagine*, the 1930 musical featured in Chapter II, the supposedly egalitarian society of 1980 New York employs a female census taker, played by Vera Lewis. The post is an official one, but, rather in the manner of the suffragist films, the function of this role is to provide a target for the ridicule of the male character MT-42. All of the decision-making officials in *Just Imagine* are male; and none of them is ridiculed. And so it goes: female professionals in early science fiction cinema either follow orders or are mocked for giving them.

The general attitude seems dated, but it is worth pausing to consider the number of corrupt, ineffectual or inept female CEOs, politicians or generals that survive into the 21st century, in movies, including: *Babylon A.D.* (2008), *Prometheus* (2012), *Elysium* (2013), *Divergent* (2014), *The Giver* (2014), *Jurassic World* (2015) and *Okja* (2017). Of course, men also run dysfunctional future societies, which are an essential part of science fiction's stock-in-trade, and the increase in the number of despotic female leaders may merely be a result of the increase in the number of women taking active roles in the genre's movies. This will be discussed further in Chapter VII. Suffice it to say here that in many ways these figures, along with the leaders in the failing future-societies above, are versions of the despotic leader already identified in the form of queens of Mars, Aelita, and Boo-Boo (*Just Imagine*, 1930). Science fiction cinema has habit of latching on to certain roles and remaining with them; repetition of success is, as noted before, a security against failure, which brings this résumé to the genre's longest-serving female professional outside the sex industry: the journalist.

While Lois Lane, in her various incarnations alongside Superman, is probably the most famous female journalist, the role can be traced back through the genre as least as far as the 1920 chapter serial, *The Screaming Shadow*. Neva Gerber plays the rich journalist, Mary Landers, who helps to break a network of unscrupulous professors who are using African monkey glands to develop their "youth elixir." It is not clear if Landers is employed or is working as a citizen journalist in the manner of the "gentlemen scientists" of the 18th and 19th centuries, and the film does include a "high priestess of the virgins of eternal youth,"[25] played by Frances Terry; however, the journalist role is a clear departure from the lovers, wives, sisters and daughters of male scientists of the period.

The high profiles of Hollywood columnists Hedda Hopper and Louella Parsons may have helped to maintain the journalist as the "acceptable face of female employment" in cinema. Whatever the reason, it was the primary professional work available to the female character in science fiction film between

1940 and 1949. She appears in *Ne le Criez Pas sur les Toits*, a French film made under Nazi occupation, and remade in Mexico in 1948 as *El Supersabio*, and she is in the 12-part cinema serial, *King of the Rocket Men* in 1949. She survives into the 1950s in *Bride of the Monster* (1956), as a science magazine editor in *The Deadly Mantis* (1957), as an expedition reporter in *The Land Unknown* (1957), as a photojournalist in *Beginning of the End* (1959), and as a news photographer in the 1956 British film *Timeslip*.[26]

Daily Planet reporter Lois Lane herself appears in a 15-part *Superman* chapter series in 1948, which was updated to reflect the atomic age a year later for the serial *Atom Man Versus Superman*. This suggests that even the comic book hero was being affected by post-war scientific age. It was a shift in emphasis that would have a lasting effect on science fiction cinema's female roles.

DOMESTIC SCIENCE

Anecdotally, it seems widely recognized that science fiction cinema of the 1950s saw a sudden surge in the number of female scientists; however, in *Women Scientists in Fifties Science Fiction Films*, Bonnie Noonan argues that "the emerging woman professional, particularly in the fields of science, is often ignored in critical analyses...."[27] Noonan fills this perceived gap with her 2005 book, whose very useful filmography identifies at least 45 female characters with science connections across "114 B science fiction films from 1950 to 1966."[28] Some of these connections are marginal, around sixteen of the characters are assistants to, or supports for, male scientists, and so follow a direct line back to cinema's silent period, and a few are journalists chasing science stories. Noonan's general point, however, remains sound: the science-connected female has a greater prominence after 1949 than before. With good reason, Noonan also questions a statement made by Patrick Lucanio regarding women in these films; he writes: "her professional status is merely a ruse to get her near the invader, and, once the invader meets her she becomes the archetypal 'damsel in distress.'"[29] This is not always supported by evidence gleaned from the films—by Noonan and others. Besides, in its fifty-plus year history, the genre's filmmakers had become adept at placing women in peril in the service of their narratives without seeing the need to employ them as scientists first. Something else was going on.

During World War II, men had seen women doing important work in factories, on farms, and even around the frontline, much of which was being reflected on film. As Antonia Lant points out in *Blackout: Reinventing Women for Wartime British Cinema*: "The zone of sexual difference was invaded and commandeered, in the name of establishing a more urgent difference—that of nationality."[30] While the threat to the U.S. homeland during the Second World War was less, many of these experiences were shared there. Lant does warn that it meant only that "the war of the sexes was put on hold"[31]; however, attitudes were shifting, not least because of Sheila Lewenhak's "labour shortage." The post-war period was one of huge scientific advances, including: radar, jets, rockets, medicine and computers. Science is in the DNA of science fiction, so its cinema could not ignore the changes. Nor could it ignore the role of women in post-war society, especially as America was soon on a new, "cold" war footing. Peter Biskind picks up this point in *Seeing Is Believing: How Hollywood Taught Us to Stop Worrying About the Fifties*, "Like war films, sci-fi often presented America in the grip of an emergency ... these emergencies dramatized the necessity of consensus, of pulling together."[32]

Of course, this does not mean screen emancipation for women as a separate but equal force. Often, they are expected to take on "masculine" values, in order to be "just one of the boys, part of the male group that restrained the monster from the id."[33] Occasionally they are given male names, such as biology graduate student Stephanie "Steve" Clayton, played by Mara Corday in the 1955 film *Tarantula*. Mostly, they are treated as women in a men's world—on screen and off. An obvious example of this is the arrival of Joan Weldon as entomologist Dr. Patricia "Pat" Medford in *Them!* (1954). It is her bare legs that are seen first, as she descends from the body of a military plane, snagging her skirt as she goes.

Casual sexist comments betray an attitude that runs through 1950s movies, and tends to reduce the perceived professionalism of their scientific females; however, there is also a subtler sexism at large. It can be seen in a scene from the 1951 film, *The Thing from Another World!* Among the scientists and soldiers who are sent to investigate a crashed flying saucer in Antarctica is a solitary woman, secretary Nikki Nicholson, played by Margaret Sheridan. Although this is one more woman than appears in the 1982 remake,[34] Nicholson's function is governed largely by her gender. Not only is she the film's nominal love interest, but when it becomes clear that the seemingly invulnerable "thing" rampaging around the research station is actually a vegetable, Nicholson's suggests that the way to destroy the creature might be to "cook it." Her plan succeeds (the creature is fried to death across electrical contacts); and so the men owe their redemption to the woman's knowledge domestic science.

These perceived limitations have a wider implication, one that continues to affect the genre in the 21st century. The female scientist in science fiction cinema tends to specialize in what genre critics Robert Scholes and Eric Rabkin describe as the "soft sciences"—what are now likely to be called "life sciences":

disciplines taking animals, plants or people as subjects.[35] She does not generally crunch numbers or split atoms using computers or physics—the "hard sciences"; instead she reflects the values of Mother Nature using zoology, biology, psychology, and the like. As a result, only 2 of the 14 qualified scientists identified by Noonan are from Scholes and Rabkin's "hard sciences"; they are nuclear physicist Dr. Ruth Adams, played by Faith Domergue in *This Island Earth* (1955) and Mara Corday's mathematician and systems analyst, Sally Caldwell, in *The Giant Claw* (1957).

These observations appear to support Judy Wajcman's contention, in *Feminism Confronts Technology*, that "the traditional conception of technology is heavily weighted against women,"[36] which she later links with computer science and "the obsession with control."[37] This theme underscores Biskind's suggestion that the strong, independent entomologist, Dr. Medford, who supports her scientist father in *Them!*, is not included to celebrate women, but rather to reflect "a paranoid fantasy of a world dominated by predatory females."[38] Times had changed, though, and a more pragmatic approach was required: "better give an inch than lose a mile, better let Pat Medford assert herself, or face a far more serious challenge to male power in the future."[39] Consequently, that future is filled with safe, "soft" science fiction females, up to and including Amy Adams' linguist, Dr. Louise Banks in *Arrival* (2016). James Cameron does make Dr. Lindsey Brigman, played by Mary Elizabeth Mastrantonio, a marine architect in *The Abyss* (1989),[40] but it is worth noting that her first appearance—as bare legs and heels stepping down from an aircraft—is a conscious homage to Dr. Medford's arrival in *Them!*

It is easy to overlay these developing roles with negative readings; however, in the preface to her book, Bonnie Noonan writes about the influence that these female characters had on her as a girl:

> My primary impulse, however, and the encouragement to which I responded, did not much reflect my interest in a scientific career, but my desire to have a career at all and to have that career taken seriously, as were the careers of the cinematic scientists to whom I looked for a vision of my future.[41]

Despite the suggestion above that female scientist roles have been restricted and restrictive, Noonan's anecdotal comments serve as a reminder that statistical research done sixty years after the events will not tell the whole story. For the young Bonnie, the female scientists of the fifties were inspirational—whether "soft" or "hard." It is her perception of these roles that makes them important to the development of the female in science fiction cinema. It is not clear, however, to what degree the genre's restrictions encouraged her decision to become a molecular biologist rather than a rocket scientist.

Male Space

The 1950s was the decade when science fiction would become science fact. Nazi rocket technology along with scientists captured at the end of the Second World War would give both the United States and the Soviet Union a hand-up in what would become the "Space Race." The USSR dominated the early years with two major firsts: the launch of an artificial satellite, *Sputnik*, in 1957, and pictures of the far side of the Moon, courtesy of *Luna 3*, in 1959, leaving the 1960s free for the pursuit of human space travel and eventually the Moon. Hollywood, however, would not wait that long—nor, apparently, would it hesitate to put a woman into space.

Rocketship X-M was released in 1950. It tells the story of a trip to the Moon that is accidentally diverted to Mars. Onboard the "RXM" are four men and a female research chemist, Dr. Lisa van Horn, played by Osa Massen. It is worth noting that the 1917 landmark film *Himmelskibet*, with its strong, female, Martian, mediator figure was made in Denmark. Casting a Dane in this role may also have been a reference to Gerda Maurus' performance in *Frau im Mond*, the 1929 German silent movie (both films are discussed at the end of Chapter I). Despite this pedigree, male characters in *Rocketship X-M* take many opportunities to reference the fact that Dr. Van Horn is "just a woman," or even "a girl"; however, these references are regularly dismissed, rebuffed and argued away.

One of the unsung female space traveler pioneers of the genre. Osa Massen as Dr. Lisa van Horn in *Rocketship X-M* (1950).

> Dr. Lisa Van Horn: I suppose you think that women should only cook and sew and bear children?
>
> Col. Floyd Graham: Isn't that enough? There is such a thing as going overboard in the other direction too, you know.

While there are some dubious lines of dialogue, on balance it seems that *Rocketship X-M* is ultimately challenging those who question the idea of a female astronaut. Indeed, Dr. Van Horn proves to be cool and competent throughout the trip, and, as the mission leader explains to the press, she is here on merit:

"The reason Miss Van Horn is making this trip is because of her pioneering research with monotonic hydrogen. That enabled her to develop the first rocket fuel powerful enough and concentrated enough to make this flight possible."

Rocketship X-M was not a commercial success, possibly because it has an unorthodox ending (like *Frau im Mond*). As a result, Dr. Lisa van Horn's impact on the audience, the genre and the industry will have been reduced, making this an important role in the history of female representation in science fiction cinema, but not necessarily influential to its development. It was a false start.

Released a few months after *Rocketship X-M*, the highest profile science fiction movie of 1950, *Destination Moon*, set the female development needle back to zero. Written with the help of science fiction writer, Robert A. Heinlein and overseen by Hermann Oberth, the former Nazi rocket scientist who had been the science consultant on *Frau im Mond*, *Destination Moon* had the distinction of being "relatively scientifically accurate for its time."[42] It also won an Academy Award for Lee Zavitz's special effects. Viewed today, it is a dull, ponderous, somber treatise on the practicalities of space travel. Like *Woman in the Moon*, it is hampered by drawn-out sequences documenting Oberth-inspired technical procedure; unlike *Woman in the Moon*, however, it contains no female astronauts. The role for women in this celebrated film is emphasized thirty seconds into a theatrical trailer, when a pair of caption cards appears. The first seems to promise female involvement, the second quickly takes it away:

> Never before has any woman…
> …sent her man on such an exploit!

It is possible that this is a mocking reference to *Rocketship X-M*, but it is also interesting to note that *Destination Moon*'s producer, George Pal, went on to include a prominent female scientist in his next movie, *When Worlds Collide*. In the meantime, it was *Destination Moon*, not *Rocketship X-M*, that would set the template for female astronauts in the genre. As, Marie Lathers points out in *Space Oddities: Women and Outer Space in Popular Film and Culture, 1960–2000*, "A few films have endeavored to imagine a competent female astronaut professional, but these have been rare."[43]

Cinema had seen human female space travelers before, but they had largely been fantasy space opera characters, such as Dale Arden in Universal Pictures' multi-chapter series, led by the male hero, Flash Gordon (1936/38/40). Leaving aside *Woman in the Moon*, the first *bona fide* female astronaut appears to arrive in 1941 with a film made in France under Nazi occupation. Inspired by Einstein's *Special Theory of Relativity*, *Croisières Sidérales* features a female space traveler who returns to Earth to find that the planet and her lover have aged 25 years in her absence; she then sends her lover off on the same mission. It is not clear if this film was ever released in English-speaking territories; it is unlikely that it was available there in 1941. Its influence on American filmmakers of the 1950s appears to be negligible, as only a handful of the space exploration pictures produced during the decade feature female space travelers. They include: *Flight to Mars* (1951), *World Without End* (1956), *It! The Terror from Beyond Space* (1958) and *From Earth to the Moon* (1958). The 1953 picture *Project Moonbase* features Donna Martell as Moon Flight Commander Colonel Briteis (bright eyes), which feels a little like giving with one hand and taking with the other.[44] It is tempting to use *When Worlds Collide* to help boost these numbers, but nobody in this film is a professional astronaut; events have forced them to become accidental space travelers. What is more, it is the men who pilot the ship that takes the forty or so passengers to Zyra. Despite a few isolated examples, evidence from the 1950s points to the idea that space travel, unlike science, was an overwhelmingly male pursuit. Tracing this line through to the 1990s, Sobchack observes that "astronauts are clearly those figures who centralize and visually represent the values and the virtues common to all the male protagonists of the genre in a single archetypal presence. They are cool, rational, competent, unimaginative, male, and sexless."[45]

Once again, it is a promise of sex that dominates, rather than actual sex. It underpins female representation in the space exploration movies of the 1950s. In Hollywood though, perhaps predictably, space is not where women go, but where women are found; and, again predictably, these discoveries tend to be objects of male desire. Following a thread that goes back at least as far as *Le Voyage dans la Lune* in 1902, male astronauts find fantasy women in exotic locations in *Cat Women of the Moon* (1953) and a 1958 version, *Missile to the Moon*. Hardy's witty description of this "inferior remake" includes the note that "the moon women (an assortment of beauty contest winners) wear mesh stockings and a continuous air of harassment."[46] The British entered this territory in 1956 with *Fire Maidens from Outer Space*, in which a single man visits the all-female society of Jupiter's 13th moon; however, the most well-known of these fantasy-women-in-exotic locations pictures is probably the 1958 film *Queen of Outer Space*, starring Zsa Zsa Gabor as Talleah, Queen of Venus. Bruce Lanier Wright observes that "Venus turns out to be inhabited by lightly clad showgirls,"[47] which of course is a theme common to all of these films. Sexual titillation underpins the 1957 UK film, *Escapement*, and it inspires many of the jokes for the 1953 comedy, *Abbott and Costello Go to Mars*, in which the popular pair crash lands on Venus (not Mars) where the despotic Queen Alura presides over an all-female population, played by former Miss Universe contestants.

Fantasy about what sexual temptations might be out there for male astronauts takes a slightly different tack for one of the decade's most recognized and celebrated films, *Forbidden Planet*. One of the very few genre movies of the period to be filmed in color CinemaScope, this was an expensive, experimental, "event" film for its studio, MGM. As result, its creators sought to minimize risk: the story was taken from Shakespeare, the special effects were created by Disney artists, and the only female character is the attractive, virginal Altaira, played by Anne Francis. The result is what M. Keith Booker calls "a virtual compendium of pulp science fiction themes...,"[48] replete with what Ace Pilkington recognizes as "sci-fi cliché."[49] Despite, or perhaps because of, this, John Brosnan calls it "possibly the best of all the space-travel pictures made during the 1950s...."[50]

Altaira is a young woman stranded on the planet Altair with her father, Professor Morbius. These two are Miranda and Prospero from Shakespeare's *The Tempest*, and like Miranda, Altaira has never met a man other than her father. She now meets men in the form of Commander Adams, leading what he describes as "eighteen competitively-selected super-perfect physical specimens, with an average age of twenty-four point six." The scene is set for the loss of Altaira's innocence. Once again, graphic sex is not on the agenda here, but rather it is male predatory objectification and titillation, which is highlighted in an exchange between Adams and Altaira, who is swimming:

> ALTAIRA: Come on in.
> ADAMS: I didn't bring my bathing suit.
> ALTAIRA: What's a bathing suit.

It is no accident that *Forbidden Planet*'s producers cast the petite Francis, "a successful model and cover-girl" and "The Little Queen of Soap Opera,"[51] for this role. Romping around her bucolic idyll in dresses so short that she must keep her forearm in her lap when she is seated, Altaira is an embodiment of the desirable virgin as described by Simone de Beauvoir in her classic 1949 feminist text, *The Second Sex*:

> Virgin lands have always fascinated explorers.... An object that men have already used has become an instrument; cut from its natural ties, it loses its most profound properties.... A virgin body has the freshness of secret springs, the morning sheen of an unopened flower, the orient lustre of a pearl on which the sun has never shone.[52]

In this film, exploration of the forbidden woman parallels exploration of the forbidden planet; Altaira loses her power when she gives herself to men.[53] When *The Virgin Film Guide* describes Francis as "failing entirely to transcend her ill-conceived, camp classic role,"[54] its critics somewhat miss the point: Francis was not supposed to transcend the role. Altaira represents a male fantasy fallback position that goes back through titillating Coppélia dolls to Méliès' *Corps de Ballet*, and forward through to the naïve Barbarella and the naked Ava

Making the best of a very traditional role. Anne Francis as the virginal Altaira Morbius in *Forbidden Planet* (1956).

in *Ex Machina* (2015). To paraphrase Lorraine Gamman and Margaret Marshment once again: Men do things; women are things. This is science fiction cinema.[55]

Narrative Place

While it is interesting to chart women's social and professional journey through the 1950s, there is a limit to what this reveals. Ultimately, the success of any character resides not in what she is (or is allowed to be), but in what she does (or is allowed to do). In *Invaders from Mars*, it is the female psychologist, Dr. Pat Blake, played by Helena Carter, who the young, motherless David McClean goes to for help to destroy the Martians; in *The Brain From the Planet Arous* (1957), Joyce Meadows as Sally Fallon keeps her wits about her when her boyfriend's mind is lost to the alien; and in *I Married a Monster from Outer Space*, it is the instinct of Marge Farell that saves the Earth from invasion.

The notion that the value of a character is best measured by her narrative function, rather than her social role or her professional position, was neatly illustrated back, once again, at the beginning of the decade.

GIANT LEAP FORWARD

Two enduring genre classics were released in 1951. In each, the arrival of an attractive, male outsider disrupts the life of an attractive, working female; he becomes the third element in an emotional triangle; and she is forced ultimately to make decisions about her future, his future and the future of humanity. The essential difference between these films is revealed by the detail. As noted above, in *When Worlds Collide* Joyce Hendron is a scientist and mathematician whose calculations confirm the destruction of the world; in *The Day the Earth Stood Still* Helen Benson is a secretary and mother whose actions prevent the destruction of the world. The second film was directed by Robert Wise, who would go on to make other genre favorites, *The Andromeda Strain* (1971) and *Star Trek: The Motion Picture* (1979). Arthur C. Clarke listed *The Day the Earth Stood Still* in his top ten science fiction films,[56] and its female star, Patricia Neal refers to it in her autobiography, *As I Am*, as "the best science fiction film ever made...."[57] This may not be an entirely objective critique, but Academy Award Winner Neal's continued regard for the film, almost 40 years, 30 features, 25 television episodes and many other awards later, does suggest a certain enduring quality to its female role. Indeed, the influence of Benson and Neal can be detected almost 50 years later in Kate Mulgrew's performance as Captain Janeway in *Star Trek: Voyager* (1996–2001). The television franchise's first female captain,[58] "the quintessential woman of the future,"[59] bears striking similarities to Helen Benson—in voice, appearance and demeanor.[60]

The Day the Earth Stood Still begins with the arrival of alien visitors bearing a message for humanity. Klaatu is a male humanoid, played by Michael Rennie, and Gort is an 8-foot tall robot; they land their flying saucer in the center of Washington, D.C. Klaatu is soon shot by a soldier and taken to a hospital, leaving Gort standing sentry in front of their flying saucer. At the hospital, Klaatu explains to a U.S. official that he can divulge the nature of his mission only to the assembled leaders of all governments of Earth. When this gathering proves impossible, Klaatu decides to take himself out into society to see what humans are really like. Enter Helen Benson.

Patricia Neal's character appears almost 24 minutes into *The Day the Earth Stood Still*, at the boarding house, where she lives with her 12-year-old son, Bobby. Klaatu, under the guise of "Mr. Carpenter" looking for a room, has arrived amid media hysteria surrounding the disappearance of the alien. Benson makes an immediate impact with her calm approach:

> BOBBY: I bet he's looking for the spaceman!
>
> HELEN BENSON: I think we've all been hearing too much about spacemen.

The next morning, at the breakfast table, Benson reveals a level of empathy that is lacking in the other characters. Sitting next to "Mr. Carpenter," she responds to more media hysteria:

> HELEN BENSON: This spaceman, or whatever he is: we automatically assume he is a menace. Maybe he isn't at all.
>
> MAN 2: Then what's he hiding for? Why doesn't he come out in the open?

MAN 1: Yeah, like that Heater fella [radio announcer] said: what's he up to?

HELEN BENSON: Maybe he's afraid.

WOMAN: He's afraid! Hm, hm!

HELEN BENSON: Well, after all, he was shot the minute he landed here. I was just wondering what I would do.

KLAATU: Hmm, perhaps before deciding on a course of action, you'd want to know more about the people here.

In their illustrated history of science fiction cinema, Douglas Menville and R. Reginald note that "it's only when he mixes with the average American citizens that one gets the feeling he's satisfied with what he sees."[61] Crucial to the current study is the fact that this satisfaction is ultimately provided by a woman, but not before Klaatu has attempted to communicate with Professor Barnhardt, the male scientist who serves as the other rational human voice in the film. The Professor promises to arrange for Klaatu to speak to a gathering of international scientists, who will then take his message back to their respective leaders. Klaatu is happy with this, but remains unwilling to share his message before this, even with Professor Barnhardt.

In order to ensure that the people of Earth take him seriously, Klaatu arranges for all powered devices across the planet to stop working at noon two days later. This standing still gives the movie its title; it is also the point at which Benson is given the information that Klaatu has denied everyone else. Trapped in an elevator with him, she alone is entrusted with the reason for his mission; even the cinema audience is denied this. Klaatu's request for Benson's discretion is increased later to a request for help when Klaatu realizes that he is in danger. Fearing that he may be killed by the military, he makes Benson memorize the words "Gort, Klaatu barada nikto"; this is what she must say to Gort to stop him destroying Earth in the event of Klaatu's death. Klaatu does die. Benson must now pluck up the courage to face the 8-foot tall sentry robot. She succeeds. Klaatu is resurrected by Gort and delivers his message, standing on his flying saucer. It is a warning to humanity, which has now acquired nuclear capabilities and rocket technology, that if their petty squabbles begin to threaten other planets, Earth really will be destroyed. With this, Klaatu and Gort leave.

It is difficult to over-emphasize the importance of Helen Benson's narrative function in *The Day the Earth Stood Still*, especially in the context of 1950s science fiction cinema—and the wider industry. Despite Germaine Greer noting that "the most overt kind of handmaidenship is practised by secretaries,"[62] and the restrictive 1950s ideal of what feminist writers have dubbed "the myth of motherhood,"[63] Benson's status as a secretary and a mother does not diminish her standing as a person; rather, it presents a degree of 1950s' "ordinariness"

Mother, secretary and savior of the planet. Patricia Neal as Helen Benson in
The Day the Earth Stood Still (1951).

to support her extraordinary action. Indeed, Edmund North's 1951 screenplay feels refreshingly honest in its suggestion that society, while it might expect women to be mothers and secretaries, can also demand even more of them when the chips are down.

North's narrative leap of faith is emphasized by the fact that his source material, Harry Bates' 1940 short story *Farewell to the Master*, contains no female characters at all. In fact, Klaatu is also incidental in this story, whose primary subjects are its narrator, Cliff Sutherland, and his focus, the robot Gnut. The title of the story is explained in Bates' haunting final words, "'You misunderstand,' the mighty robot had said. 'I am the master.'" Having shifted the emphasis of the story from robot-master to alien-messenger, screenwriter North upsets the balance of power by creating a new character to present humanity's rational but caring face. Helen Benson then subtly dilutes Klaatu's ability to treat the human race as a single entity bent on war. This woman becomes the film's human voice of reason. She is, of course, the mediator already familiar to science fiction cinema, not least through the silent films highlighted in Chapter I: *Himmelskibet* (1917), *Metropolis* (1927) and *Frau im Mond* (1929).

Science fiction writer Ray Bradbury recognizes the importance of the female voice in *The Day the Earth Stood Still* in his proposed sequel, *The Evening of the Second Day*.[64] In this incomplete 1981 screenplay outline, Klaatu's daughter, Klaata, arrives on Earth to assess humanity's progress and to reiterate her father's ultimatum. Klaata demonstrates her powers by "un-inventing" things. She begins fairly safely with needles, but moves on to a threat to un-invent oil, which would send humanity back to a pre-industrial age. The female Klaata's role is strengthened by the near absence of the powerful, male robot figure, Gort. Only his heart has survived, as a six inch "cube of pure glowing illumination," which pulses to mark the time left for humans to complete the tasks set by Klaatu and Klaata. By the time Bradbury wrote his screenplay, thirty years after the original film, the radical contribution of *The Day the Earth Stood Still* had been appreciated. This, however, was not always the case....

SMALL STEPS BACK

In her autobiography, Patricia Neal notes that the press at the time of *The Day the Earth Stood Still*'s release had more interest in her affair with Gary Cooper than in her film roles[65]; however this indifference towards Helen Benson has not been confined to the 1950s. John Baxter is satisfied to report Benson's contribution as a domestic role, stating that Klaatu enters into "a believable relationship with a young Washington widow ... and her son,"[66] rather than the fact that Benson saves the world from annihilation. Selective reviewing becomes inaccuracy in *The Virgin Film Guide*, which ignores Benson's role altogether, stating that "the wounded Rennie stops the robot from destroying the planet by uttering the now-classic phrase, 'Klaatu barada nikto.'"[67] He doesn't; she does. These and other comments reveal a patriarchal tendency to de-emphasize the contribution of female characters that would continue well beyond 1951. For example, Julian Petley's February 1985 *Monthly Film Bulletin* review of *The Terminator* (1984) fails even to mention Sarah Connor.

A 1954 British version of *The Day the Earth Stood Still* offers a unique opportunity for direct comparison, especially as *Stranger from Venus* also features Patricia Neal. Unlike *Devil Girl from Mars* from the same year, this film's title offers no adjective to advise the cinema-goer about the nature of the alien visitor, nor does this film place any women at the center of the action. Reprising her role as the understanding human on hand to gain the alien's trust, Neal, in *Stranger from Venus*, plays Susan North—perhaps a nod to the original's screenwriter. Despite being introduced to the audience during the pre-title sequence, Miss North has very little to do in this very low budget film. This, as Steve Chibnall observes, forces much of the action to be "claustrophobically confined to a small inn,"[68] which serves as the main backdrop for a dull, moralizing script, awkward performances and naïve plot. The landlord at the inn does have a daughter, Gretchen, played by Marigold Russell, who gets a few witty lines; however, Patricia Neal's character has been reduced to a childless, jobless love-interest, patronized by most of the men and wooed by the alien. Crucially, her essential function from the original film has been taken away, as Earth this time is saved entirely by the actions of men. Benson's essential function is also missing from the 2008 remake of *The Day the Earth Stood Still*, which reinvents her as a Princeton professor, but then gives her little to do in the narrative. She certainly does not get to save the Earth—more of which in Chapter VII's discussion of remakes.

As was the case with *When Worlds Collide*, even the original version of *The Day the Earth Stood Still* comes with a caveat. A cursory examination of the plot reveals the film's biblical connections: Klaatu arrives on Earth to save humanity from the wrath of heavenly forces, takes the name John Carpenter (JC), befriends children, calmly goes about his business in the face of provocation, is killed and resurrected, and finally ascends after delivering his sermon on the mount of his flying saucer. There are many other elements presenting deeper readings; suffice it to say that the film's religious allusions have been widely recognized.[69] This ties *The Day the Earth Stood Still* to what Mary Daly in *Beyond God the Father* describes as "the biblical and popular image of God as a great patriarch in heaven, rewarding and punishing according to his mysterious and seemingly arbitrary will."[70]

Adding to this theme is Mark Jancovich's argument that the film presents an authoritarian narrative in which "science is presented as the only potential saviour of humanity."[71] Science in the form of Professor Barnhardt is then joined by the exclusively-male military and Benson's overbearing boyfriend, Tom Stevens, in a cocktail of patriarchal symbols that feel very familiar. Heather Barker notes that the film makes "brave attempts to redress the balance"[72] by introducing the character of Klaatu, but, ultimately *The Day the Earth Stood Still* merely replaces familiar "human" patriarchies with a less familiar "alien" one—underpinned by religious allegory. If this reading is accepted, then Benson merely follows the example of the three Marys in John's Gospel.[73] She remains loyal to Klaatu throughout his stay on earth, representing Mary Magdalene through his days in the wilderness. Despite temptation, she has little chance of prevailing against his messianic status, for as Camille Paglia asserts, "Genesis is rigid and unjust.... It remade the world by male dynasty, cancelling the power of mothers."[74]

Helen Benson may not be the finished article, but her importance in the context of 1950s science fiction film is clear. She stands in stark contrast to other women of the genre, who—while visible and often active—remain narrative objects rather than subjects. Ultimately, it has been the placement of well-written, well-played, relatively radical female characters in successful films like *The Day the Earth Stood Still* and *When Worlds Collide*—and before them, *Frau im Mond*—that makes it easier for writers, directors and producers to take the next step in the representation of the female in science fiction cinema. Whether they take that step is another matter.

<hr />

The worlds that collided in 1950s science fiction cinema were not necessarily masculinity and femininity, but rather conservatism and modernity. Things were changing and this genre, a bastion of traditional representation, would have to change too if its cinema was still to hold a mirror up to nature and humanity. It cannot easily be said that the '50s saw sexism in the genre eliminated, or even significantly reduced for that matter; however, women definitely became more prominent in science fiction narratives. Themes introduced in the silent period, an aesthetic developed in the 1930s, and the pulp excitement injected in the 1950s would all eventually find homes in the spectacular genre juggernaut that emerged in the late 1970s. In the meantime, a period of uncertainty was looming on the horizon. A slow drift from black and white to color challenged science fiction cinema's identity, while social, scientific and sexual revolutions of the 1960s stalled its makers with conflicts of interest. The ship that was destined to become the biggest in the fleet seemed now to be rigged for silent running....

IV

INTERMISSION
Watershed Years, or, Destination Unknown and an *Annus Mirabilis*

Nineteen-sixty-eight has been identified by a number of commentators as a significant year in the history of science fiction cinema. And so it was. For five decades, movies released in that year have influenced the aims, ambience, aesthetics and ambition of the genre on screen. Fewer words have been devoted to the years running up to 1968, or indeed its effect on the years that followed—until *Star Wars* arrived in 1977. However, cinematic developments, scientific advances and social revolutions in the 1960s and 1970s created an interregnum period, with 1968 as its pivotal point—and female representation serving as a barometer for the changes it brought. New and diverse rights and roles for women off-screen led to uncertainty on-screen, where the monochrome professionals of the '50s met the Technicolor revolutionaries of the '60s. The result was a period whose destination seemed unknown: when science fiction cinema appeared unsure about what to do with its women.

―⚮―

Shifting Sixties

Although each decade's science fiction cinema may have a "feel" to it, there are no clean cut-off points between them. The genre that had grown hugely in popularity through the 1950s continued into the 1960s, now with extra confidence as it "finally emerged from the bottom half of the double bill,"[1] as Phil Hardy puts it. In *Alternate Americas*, M. Keith Booker argues that it was

Stanley Kubrick's *Dr. Strangelove, or: How I Learned to Stop Worrying and Love the Bomb* in 1964 that "essentially made the Cold War paranoia SF film obsolete."[2] Indeed, the "potential threat" films of the 1950s were slowly superseded by a growing number of diverse science fiction strands and sub-genres. Silly comedies sat alongside politically-motivated movies from Japan and West Germany, as well as visually arresting films from Italy and Mexico. A number of narratives grafted peripheral science fiction elements onto other genres to create hybrids, such as the British James Bond films. Even Alfred Hitchcock returned to the genre—albeit marginally—with *The Birds* in 1963.[3] This cornucopic decade was rounded off with big budget movies that brought more serious messages, prompting Hardy's chapter title for this decade of his encyclopedia: "Science Fiction Becomes Respectable."[4]

Respectability, such as it was, came at a price, not least an impact on female representation. The genre may have found a new zest, but its path through 1960s was unpredictable. When that happens, science fiction often calls on those elements that are never very far from the surface, and so some of the gains that women had made in the 1950s, such as the professionalization of female roles, were largely lost. The influential *Dr. Strangelove*, for example, features just one woman: Tracy Reed as secretary, Miss Scott, who spends her three-and-a-half minutes of screen time in a bikini. Many other factors also

Kubrick's Women #1: blink and you might miss them. Tracy Reed as secretary Miss Scott in *Dr. Strangelove or: How I Learned to Stop Worrying and Love the Bomb* (1964).

contributed to this period of upheaval. Society and science were developing apace, and cinema itself was changing. In America, the era of the all-powerful studios was coming to an end, and everywhere the move to color film began to influence the science fiction stories being told.

COLOR CINEMA

Elvis Presley's serious acting career ended when his films shifted from black and white to color. He did not appear in any science fiction movies, but there are parallels. His first post-army picture, the 1960 Technicolor musical-comedy *G.I. Blues*, was a clear departure from the dangerous, monochrome rock 'n' roll rebel pictures of the 1950s.[5] Color set Elvis on a light-comedy, industry treadmill that would produce a further 26 movies. His leading ladies suffered too. Ann-Margret's simple cipher, Rusty Martin, who first appears as a pair of sexy legs in *Viva Las Vegas* (1964), feels far removed from Carolyn Jones' complex *femme fatale*, Ronnie, who attempts to take control of her own destiny in the 1958 *noir*-esque *King Creole*. This effect can be seen reflected in science fiction cinema's female characters. Joyce Taylor's Saturday-serial style Princess Antilla, in the 1960 Metrocolor film *Atlantis, The Lost Continent*, is very different from Maria Montez's sultry black and white *Siren of Atlantis* in 1949—despite Hardy's description of the latter film as "a camp outing."[6] The time of production will have had an effect on these characters too, but the influence of the color format should not be discounted.

The transition period from black and white to color in mainstream science fiction cinema was far longer than the overnight switch from silent to sound. The first full color stock science fiction films[7] appeared in the early 1950s, with sporadic studio experiments, such as *When Worlds Collide* in 1951 and *War of the Worlds* and *Invaders from Mars* (both in 1953); monochrome's last gasps were taken twenty years later by smaller, independent outfits, with movies such as George A. Romero's influential *Night of the Living Dead* in 1968 and David Cronenberg's *Crimes of the Future* in 1970.[8] The tipping point was reached by the mid '60s, after which, more movies were made in the new color format.

It may not be scientific, but color really does make science fiction "feel" different. It made *Forbidden Planet* and *When Worlds Collide* seem like they were from the future back in 1951 and '56, in contrast, the 1961 black and white movie *The Day the Earth Caught Fire* feels like a relic of the past. However, the saturated hues of Technicolor and other processes have their own drawbacks: aliens do not seem quite so threatening in color. The bright red "Creature from the Id" created for *Forbidden Planet* does not have the same impact as even the man-in-a-rubber-suit seen in the black and white *Creature from the Black Lagoon*

(1954). This is perhaps why Ridley Scott would later keep his silver-grey creature lingering in the black shadows for most of *Alien* (1979). As another great director, Josef von Sternberg, put it, "A shaft of white light used properly can be far more effective than all the color in the world used indiscriminately." Color in the 1960s seemed to bring with it a certain, less serious, aesthetic.

Just as sound had turned science fiction towards the lighter musical comedies in the 1930s, color in the 1960s saw a rise in the number of frivolous films. Disney started early with the slap-stick, Jerry Lewis vehicle *The Absent-Minded Professor* in 1961, but many others, including in Italy, France Spain and Mexico, Japan and the UK experimented with color via lighter fare. The British pseudo–science fiction James Bond films lost their darker edge as they gathered more sexy women around the hero, and *Our Man Flint* gave this theme an American touch in 1965. The French and Italians brought a high-camp aesthetic to the genre, perhaps most notably with the 1967 film *Danger: Diabolik*, whose suave anti-hero is introduced with the tagline, "Out for all he can take, seduce, or get away with…" This sexual athlete was brought to the screen by producer Dino De Laurentiis, who would follow him a year later with a female counterpart, Barbarella. As the threats and seriousness of the 1950s' science fiction films waned, so too did the number of serious female characters—most notably, the science-related roles that had been developed after the Second World War. The genre was changing again, but not only because of color film; social attitudes were shifting too.

CHANGING SOCIETY

Much has been written about social revolutions in the West during the 1960s. The end of Britain's postwar period of austerity, the arrival of the contraceptive pill, a rise in the number of feminist texts, increases in migration, more liberal attitudes to sex, waning adherence to religious dogma, stirrings of sexual discrimination legislation, rising mass media and many other factors—charted in Reay Tannahill's *Sex in History*[9]—combined to create a more liberal society. Revolutions played out across the cultural landscape. Susan Douglas offers an example of this in her book, *Where the Girls Are: Growing Up Female with the Mass Media*, when she emphasizes the importance of all-girl pop groups to the development of choices and voices for young women of the early 1960s:

> Girl group songs were, by turns, boastful, rebellious, and self-abnegating, and through them girls could assume different personas, some of them strong and empowering and others masochistic and defeating.
>
> …

The songs were about escaping from yet acquiescing to the demands of male-dominated society, in which men called the shots but girls could still try to give them a run for their money.[10]

Linda Grant adds to the picture of this trend in her book, *Sexing the Millennium: A Political History of the Sexual Revolution*, when she highlights the importance of the "maverick, outrageous, insolent and stylish" *Nova* magazine, launched in 1965, for its work in "propelling women out of their traditional roles and forcing them to question every aspect of their lives and values."[11] Grant also sounds a note of caution, advising her reader to reconsider some of the histories told about this period of liberalization. Her doubts about the total success of this social adventure are encapsulated in a series of questions: "If there had been a sexual revolution, why did women still fear rape whenever they stepped outside the house? Where was the totally safe, totally effective birth control we had been promised? How could teenage girls who slept with their boyfriends stop being called sluts by their friends?"[12]

Many answers, of course, lie with the double standards that arise from a world still controlled by men. From a patriarchal perspective, the Sexual Revolution allowed men to have their cake and eat it too; it was an ideal encapsulated in the perceived, liberated readership in the 1960s of the women's magazine, *Cosmopolitan*: "The *Cosmo* Girl was guys' fantasy of the liberated woman, all legs and edible panties, with her own job and own studio apartment, adept at giving great head and getting great breakfast."[13]

Grant's description of *Cosmo* as "liberation with the politics sucked out" serves as a neat description of science fiction cinema's direction of movement as color film emerged from the monochrome shadows. Just the titles of the 1965 film *Dr. Goldfoot and the Bikini Machine*, its 1966 sequel, *Dr. Goldfoot and the Girl Bombs*, as well as the 1969 films *Curious Female* and *Some Girls Do*, give an indication of the genre's approach to these newfound sexual freedoms in the 1960s. It exploited them. The *Goldfoot* films rest on the genre's long history of sexy robots, as does the 1962 French film, *La Poupée*, and the 1964 film *Kiss Me Quick!*, with its comic references to Kubrick's *Dr. Strangelove*. When the sex act had been off the agenda in the 1950s, the vast majority of the robots were male; now that sex was back, science fiction cinema rekindled a tradition that goes back through *Metropolis* (1927) to the Coppélia-styled animated dolls of the earlier silent period.

In the late 1950s, science fiction cinema had responded to the arrival of rock 'n' roll, and attempted to appeal to its younger devotees, with a series of light, exploitation pieces, such as *Teenage Monster* (1957), *I Was a Teenage Frankenstein* (1958) and *Teenagers from Outer Space* (1959). This specific phenomenon did not last long, but its slight and silly spirit was revisited for the color films of the early sixties. Combined with a degree of casual nudity rarely seen in the genre before, these science fiction films typify a period of social change, when the genre naturally offered what Christine Cornea calls "a futuristic and playfully progressive framework within which to present the fashionable innovations of the day."[14] In the 1965 Spanish-Italian film, *La Decima Vittima*, Ursula Andress kills using a double-barreled brassiere-gun, and *Voyage to the Planet of Prehistoric Women* in 1968 seems to be a low-budget homage to a fantasy film released two years earlier: *One Million Years B.C.*, featuring the "sex symbol" of the day, Raquel Welch, and others, in fur bikinis.

Despite the darkness of a few films, such as the 1967 Argentinian *La Venganza del Sexo*, in which a depraved scientist uses captured women as sexual guinea pigs, the general aim of this "sexploitation" subgenre seems to be the kind of humor and titillation that would lead, once again, to *Barbarella*—perhaps the ultimate *Cosmo* Girl of male fantasy. It exploited a new, brazen approach to female sexuality that can be seen on the *Barbarella* posters that entice the potential cinema-goer with provocative phrases, such as, "Who takes sex to outer space?" "Who strips in space?"[15] and "The space age adventuress whose sex-ploits are among the most bizarre ever seen."[16] It is perhaps unsurprising that Jane Fonda, like Anne Francis, who had appeared in Technicolor in *Forbidden Planet*, preceded her acting career with some modeling, twice appearing on the cover of another of the period's iconic fashion magazines, *Vogue*.[17] Raquel Welch would journey to inner space as Cora Peterson in the 1966 color film, *Fantastic Voyage*, getting to outer space, however, was a different matter.

CONTROLLED SPACE

At the beginning of the 1960s, human space travel was still science fiction; by the end of the decade, it was science fact. On 16 June 1963, Soviet cosmonaut Valentina Tereshkova became the first woman in space, just two years after Yuri Gagarin's historic mission. Interest generated by the selection of a small group of female cosmonauts to the Soviet space program may have influenced the introduction of a female spaceship captain in the Soviet film *Planeta Bur* in 1962, and the initial selection of two female cosmonauts for the interplanetary mission in the 1963 Czech film, *Ikarie XB 1*. But, as Kim Newman points out in his 2013 *Sight & Sound* article, *Space, the Communist Frontier*, both of these women are pregnant; one is consequently cut from the mission and the other lies about her condition. Mónica Randall plays a female cosmonaut taken even less seriously in the 1965 Spanish-Italian comedy *Dos Cosmonautas a la Fuerza*. Beyond these examples, science fiction cinema was hardly moved by Tereshkova's achievement. It would be another twenty years before Sally Ride became NASA's first woman in space, so it is not surprising that the American industry continued its 1950s ambivalence towards the notion of female astronauts. *Voyage to the Prehistoric Planet* in 1965 re-used footage from *Planeta Bur* and introduced Faith Domergue as space station captain, Dr. Marsha Evans. Then a year later, Jerry Lewis returned in *Way ... Way Out*, which sets Connie Stevens' astronaut against Anita Ekberg's cosmonaut in competition for the film's sex-starved spacemen. This sexy, color comedy supports Piers Bizony's statement that "during the mid–1960s, Hollywood responded only sluggishly to the specific adventure of spaceflight unfolding so dramatically at Cape Kennedy."[18]

Western interest that did exist was directed largely at the real men of the NASA space programs, from the original "Mercury Seven" through Gemini to the astronauts of the Apollo missions. These all-male programs are reflected in the 1960 British comedy *Man in the Moon*, in which there is no hint that those going to the Moon, or indeed those with the power to send them there, would be women. Instead, the only female speaking role is taken by Shirley Anne Fields as Polly, an "exotic dancer" who provides support for her man and titillation for the film. This role can be seen again, updated in the form of Vivica A. Fox's Jasmine, in the movie *Independence Day*, thirty-six years later. These characters reflect Lynn Spigel's observation that real-life women "were barred from participating in the (aptly titled) manned space program."[19] Their roles— as so often in the cinema—were confined to being wives and girlfriends waiting at home, keeping house, and saying the right things for *Time Magazine* profiles on the family lives of the astronauts. In *Contest for the Heavens: The Road to the Challenger Disaster*, Claus Jensen highlights the supporting role of the wives when he reports what Neil Armstrong's wife, Jan, said when asked on the day of the Moon landing in July 1969 whether this was the greatest day of her life: "Living up to the very best tradition, as set long ago by John Glenn's Annie, she replied, 'No, that was the day when I married Neil.'"[20] Taking this attitude and other evidence into account in *Space Oddities: Women and Outer Space in Popular Film and Culture, 1960–2000*, Marie Lathers writes, "The history of women in space, reflected and often remolded in the representation of women in space in popular culture, may be read as the history of a deferral, of a problem deferred."[21]

That remolding has been part of a feedback loop in which fiction and reality seem to have conspired to keep women grounded. In the 1969 film, *Marooned*, the only female characters are three astronauts' wives, played by Lee Grant, Nancy Kovack and Mariette Hartley. When their screen husbands become trapped in orbit after the retro-rockets on their spacecraft fail, the women's patience, poise and stoicism mirrors that of the real astronauts' wives.

This film, with its close attention to realistic space-science, technology and jargon, has bought into the stereotype of what astronauts' wives should do and say. Virtually the same characters reappear in the 1995 movie *Apollo 13*, which recounts the events of a real space emergency just a few months after *Marooned* was released. Faced with the press corps after the launch of *Apollo 13*, Kathleen Quinlan's character, Marilyn Lovell, quotes the partners' mantra to a fellow astronaut's wife, played by Tracy Reiner: "Remember? You're proud, happy and thrilled"—which the younger wife duly repeats. *Apollo 13* is not strictly a science fiction film, but it borrows much from the genre, not least from *Marooned*, and it gives a lot back to the genre. It adds to what Edward James describes as the "bundle of perceptions"[22] that is used to help define what science fiction is in the Introduction.

The exchange between art, reality and reportage continues to sustain perceptions about what a woman can be and should be in science fiction cinema. It is another way to keep her as Lathers' "problem deferred." The wife, played by Joanna Moore, in *Countdown* may be an alcoholic, but she has apparently been driven to this by her husband, who works too hard—at being an astronaut. It could be argued that the problem was still being deferred in 1999, when director and writer Rand Ravich made the same assumptions about gender roles for *The Astronaut's Wife*.

Countdown was released in in the U.S. in 1968, the year when both Elvis Presley and science fiction cinema came in from the wilderness. The King had a television *Comeback Special* that would return him to the top of the charts; the genre enjoyed an auspicious year from which it would never look back.

Annus Mirabilis

In *The Encyclopedia of Science Fiction*, Peter Nicholls describes 1968 as "the single most important year in the history of sf cinema."[23] He supports his statement by listing some of the year's significant releases: *Charly*, for which Cliff Robertson became only the second actor to win an Academy Award for a performance in a science fiction film[24]; *Night of the Living Dead*, the low-budget, independent film which continues to influence zombie movies in the 21st century[25]; *Planet of the Apes*, the political satire that spawned a lucrative franchise; *Barbarella*, a sexy example of the Technicolor European pictures that had hit the genre; and Stanley Kubrick's space-age masterpiece, *2001: A Space Odyssey*. Nicholls continues with his praise for 1968: "Before then sf was not taken very seriously either artistically or commercially; since then it has remained, much of the time, one of the most popular film genres...."[26]

In the 1930s, female science fiction roles had stagnated, not least because the film industry was trying to respond to changes in technology. In the 1960s, film was trying to respond to changes in society, but those changes were coming very quickly—perhaps too quickly. Caught in the middle, filmmakers seem to be unsure again about what to do with their women: should they experiment with the new or retreat to the familiar? The result was a period of "diverse conservatism," a series of oxymorons that is encapsulated by three the films of that *annus mirabilis*, 1968.

"...BUT YOU'RE SO DAMNED UGLY"

Planet of the Apes is based on Pierre Boulle's 1963 French science fiction novel *La Planète des Singes*. The book recounts the human Ulysse Mérou's visit to the planet Soror, where apes are dominant. This "what if the roles of apes and humans were reversed?" concept played well in 1960s' commercial cinema, not least because it translated the "them" and "us" ethos that had fueled the 1950s' "potential threat pictures" into an allegory for a more pressing, contemporary issue: racial division. John Brosnan complains that "the allegorical and satirical elements are so obvious and heavy-handed they set my teeth on edge"[27]; however, as Jason Davis points out in *Planet of the Apes and Philosophy: Great Apes Think Alike*, this film and its four original sequels "invoked race and racial politics when other science-fiction movies left such issues off the screen."[28] Indeed, Adilifu Nama, in *Black Space*, calls *Planet of the Apes* "American SF cinema's most powerful allegorical response to the conundrum of American race relations at the end of the turbulent 1960s."[29]

The film was released at a pivotal time for the American Civil Rights Movement and just two months before the murder of Martin Luther King, Jr. Its significance could hardly be lost on the critics and audiences, but its power seems to extend beyond merely racial allegory. In his book *Science Fiction Film*, J.P. Telotte places *Planet of the Apes* under the wider sub-heading "environmental matters: threats to the environment and threats to the human species itself."[30] Nama also expands the field of influence, suggesting that that the source material "articulates multiple political and cultural subtexts beyond its intended message."[31] All of this potential may well have been the cue for left-wing, liberal screenwriters Rod Serling and Michael Wilson to widen the reach of the original story. Phil Hardy refers to their script as "literate" and "full of delicate comedy in which rational ape confronts irrational man."[32] It is significant to this survey that the most literate and rational of the apes comes in the form of the movie's most celebrated ape character: the female chimpanzee, Dr. Zira.

Although Zira is no token presence in the original *Monkey Planet*, she is held back by sexist social and professional restrictions. She is instrumental to much of the narrative; however, the power in Boulle's novel lies firmly with the male apes. Zira's husband, Cornelius, takes the plaudits for Zira's work, resulting in his promotion to "Director of the Science Institute," whereas Zira moves from being "Research Assistant" to "Director's Assistant." In the novel, she is never referred to as "Dr. Zira." It could be argued that Boulle is consciously working within the confines of 1960s' French society, or even that he is also criticizing gender inequalities through his allegory. But Zira is ultimately only required by Boulle to set up an uneasy *ménage à trois*, in which the sophisticated chimpanzee is measured against a savage human female. Franklin J. Schaffner's film is more sophisticated than this. For *Planet of the Apes*, Serling, Wilson and Schaffner elevate Zira from her proactive, but ultimately powerless, presence on the page to a central role as the film's conscience. Dr. Zira, the rational researcher, challenges authority in the form of militaristic gorillas and bombastic orangutans; she gently rebukes and cajoles Cornelius, in what is essentially a marriage of equals; and she serves as the film's focus of reason. The success of these changes is due, in no small part, to the performance of Kim Hunter, who had already won an Academy Award for her 1951 portrayal of Stella Kowalski, taming Marlon Brando's "ape-like" Stanley in *A Streetcar Named Desire*. A similar combination of intelligence, empathy and control in *Planet of the Apes* creates what Tom Milne, in his 1968 *Monthly Film Bulletin* review, calls a "soulful Zira."[33]

As well as being a stand-out female character of the 1960s, Dr. Zira is a significant figure in the history of female representation in science fiction cinema. The cynic might see reflected in this Lizzie Francke's comment in *Script Girls: Women Screenwriters in Hollywood* that "Hollywood soon caught up with feminism when it realized that there was an audience to be catered for,"[34] but this is the nature of commercial cinema. Audience demand is ultimately what supports the gamble with roles of this scope and quality. Besides, Zira is not completely free of the genre's well-worn female-character-risk-aversion techniques. As the central mediator between apes and humans, she reflects a traditional representation identified in Chapter I. And as an animal psychologist, Zira fits into the mold of "soft scientist" identified in Chapter III. Indeed, Zira benefits from her connection to a real-life female scientist: the superstar primatologist, Jane Goodall.[35] *Planet of the Apes'* producers capitalized on the Goodall phenomenon that followed her appearance on the cover of the December 1965 edition of *National Geographic* alongside a troop of African chimpanzees. Goodall was one of the so-called "Trimates," along with Dian Fossey, who studied gorillas in Rwanda until her murder in 1985, and Birutė Galdikas, who continues to work with orangutans in Borneo. The three great ape species championed by these women mirror those represented in *Monkey Planet* and *Planet of the Apes*. Of course, the success of Zira adds its own weight to expectations that women in science fiction cinema—and by extension, real-world science—are best suited to being mediating Mother Nature figures. This feedback loop is reflected in Londa Schiebinger's assertion that "primatology is widely celebrated as a feminist science"[36]—a notion supported in turn by Schiebinger's estimate that 80 percent of graduate students pursuing PhDs in primatology in 2001 were women.

While aspects of Zira's character may have been chosen and manipulated to conform to genre expectations, the ape could not easily be subject to sexual exploitation. About the only exchange is a little flirtation between Taylor and Zira:

> GEORGE TAYLOR: Doctor, I'd like to kiss you goodbye.
>
> DR. ZIRA: All right, but you're so damned ugly.

The sexual function in the narrative is given to the beautiful human savage, Nova. However, for this character, the movie rows back from the overt scopophilia that makes parts of *Monkey Planet* feel uncomfortable to the modern reader:

> It was a woman—a young girl rather, unless it was a goddess. She boldly asserted her femininity in the light of this monstrous sun, completely naked and without any ornament other than her hair which hung down to her shoulders.... Standing upright, leaning forwards, her breasts thrust out towards us..."[37]

And so it continues. Science fiction cinema's early exploitation of the young female was established in Chapter II, but clearly, there were limits to how far filmmakers in 1968 would be allowed—or would want—to go with this imagery for their family film. Their compromise was to cast former winner of the Miss Maryland beauty pageant, Linda Harrison, whose acting challenge is highlighted in production guidance in the studio's shooting script: "LINDA HARRISON hasn't a single line of dialogue ... and the role presents a challenge from which any young actress might understandably retreat. But this beauteous brownette welcomes it as another step in her career...."[38]

The Nova who reaches the screen in 1968 owes more to Raquel Welch's pelt-clad Loana, two years earlier in *One Million Years B.C.*, than to the prurient—arguably pedophilic—imagery created by Boulle; however, she still reflects Laura Mulvey's notions of a cinema that supports "the image of woman as (passive) raw material for the (active) gaze of man."[39] While it may be easy to dismiss Nova as yet another example of sexist representation of women, a distinction should be made between the sexy, if dull, character in the film and the blatant misogynistic treatment of Nova in Boulle's text. The leading men

Smart, sassy, soulful. Kim Hunter as Dr. Zira in *Planet of the Apes* (1968).

of both film and book are regularly placed in positions of power over Nova, but it is only Mérou, who takes advantage of this; Taylor, played by Charlton Heston, never indulges in the callous torments that, again, make the book an uncomfortable read in places. Instead, the movie rescues Nova from Boulle's casual misogyny.

Nova, like Zira, is ultimately a product of expectations generated by audience, industry and genre. Titillation is expected, but graphic sex is too much; and to avoid too much deviation from type, the filmic Nova does not develop intelligence and speech as she does towards the end of the book. Once the dangers of the book's base sexuality and Nova's only real potential for character development are removed, the screenwriters are left with very little to work with. The safest option in this instance appears to be: do nothing. Here, once again, is the "sexual inertia" phenomenon that runs though science fiction cinema....

"My name isn't Pretty Pretty, it's Barbarella"

Barbarella might be summarized as a curious mix of '60s psychedelia, naïve science fiction and a schoolboy fascination with the female form. Film critic Charles Champlin wittily dismisses it as a "camp visit to outré space,"[40] but Bonnie Noonan takes a more serious line in her study of *Gender in Science Fiction Films, 1964–1979*: "Jane Fonda's portrayal of a futuristic space heroine embodies so much of what was so right and so wrong about sexual liberation for women in the Sixties."[41] Whatever the misgivings, and there are many,[42] *Barbarella* is essential to this history for one simple reason: it is one of the most recognized examples of female representation in science fiction cinema. It cannot be ignored.

Barbarella began life in 1962, as Jean-Claude Forest's comic strip in the French publication, *V-Magazine*. In his online history of its development, Paul Gravett states that "Barbarella was the vanguard of a Sixties wave of liberated comics heroines in France and elsewhere."[43] His choice of words is interesting because, although the character Barbarella's relaxed attitude to sex has been linked to 1960s' female liberation and choice, it was really the comics that were liberated in what they could show; *V-Magazine* was, after all, and as Gravett points out, a "men's interest quarterly." It is this aspect of *Barbarella* that director Roger Vadim used as an opportunity to create a sex symbol of his new wife, Jane Fonda, just as he had done with his previous wives, Brigitte Bardot and Annette Stroyberg[44] As John Baxter points out, "Forest's sexually emancipated space woman becomes less independent and erotically acquisitive."[45] The established trappings of science fiction, coupled with the growing influence of a colorful, energetic European style of film, helped Vadim to present what William Hall, in a 1968 issue of *Photoplay Film Monthly*, sees as his aim to create perfect future woman:

> For if all goes according to plan the (female) shape of things to come will be packaged like this:
> SHE will be contoured as perfectly as 400 centuries of biological refinement (Vadim's words, not mine) can make her ... and that means around 36:22:36.
> SHE will be 5 ft 7 ins tall, and brainy—but not too brainy.
> SHE will be sweet-natured, sophisticated, sexy, and above all Eager to Please.[46]

Vadim seems to set his stall out from the beginning, with Barbarella's weightless strip-tease behind the opening titles. The sequence would appear to be setting the tone for the rest of the film, but Jane Fonda herself presents an alternative reading: "You know, Vadim only has me completely nude behind the opening titles. He said, 'Everybody will be waiting for that, so why don't we get it over with right away and get on with the picture?'"[47]

For those whose appetites are whetted by the opening sequence, the rest of the picture may well be a disappointment. Ironically, this was driven by commercial considerations, which forced the original X-rated movie to be "censored to garner a more profitable rating...."[48] The result, as with the presentation of

Nova in *Planet of the Apes*, is a compromise. Jane Fonda is squeezed into various fetishistic outfits and placed into various pseudo-pornographic poses for a voyeuristic camera that never quite delivers on the promise of that opening sequence. Despite its potential (and notoriety), *Barbarella* amounts arguably to little more than ninety minutes of trivial, Technicolor titillation. Central to the conflicts within the movie is Barbarella's individuality. Vadim may wish to present the male fantasy of a woman "Eager to please," as Hall puts it, but the original material will not always let him. Barbarella retains from the comic-strip the notion of a woman who is eager to please *herself*; in addition, she is wearing costumes designed by Paco Rabanne, who claims that he wanted through his garments "to turn women into modern warriors"[49] The confusion created by these conflicting aims neatly reflects a sixties' science fiction cinema unsure of what and who it is for. *Barbarella* is exploitative, but it is not always clear who is exploiting whom. As Hardy points out: "The film's most revealing failing is its lack of narrative drive, necessitated by Vadim's need to stop the action and present his scantily clad wife for the audience to ogle."[50]

Barbarella is a space traveler from a 41st century Earth which has eliminated physical sexual intercourse; instead, people take an "exultation transference pellet." Like Altaira in *Forbidden Planet*, Barbarella begins this film as a sexual innocent—a virgin. Her first experience comes as payment to the Catchman for rescuing her. When she discovers that he wants physical sex, her response, "Well, if you insist," echoes the bemused innocence of Altaira, when faced with men who want to kiss her. There is also an interesting connection with the 1930 film *Just Imagine*, which features in Chapter II. The Catchman's desire to do it "the old-fashioned way" reflects J-21's hankering for an "old-fashioned girl"; both films in turn reflect male responses to changing roles for women in society. This is not necessarily Paco Rabanne's claimed celebration of the "modern" warrior woman.

Barbarella then surprises its audience with a twist: she actually likes it the "old-fashioned way." And so from this point onwards, Barbarella's character takes on another male fantasy: she is the complicit innocent. Like Altaira, she is willing to participate, but she is not entirely sure about what she is participating in. This juxtaposition of *naïveté* and expertise creates an uneasy conflict that is identified, but underplayed, by film scholar Ian Christie in his statement that "most of the film's hilarity springs from the contrast between Miss Fonda's wide-eyed innocence and the astonishingly nasty situations she gets in."[51] Now addicted to sex, Barbarella offers it in trade, or as a reward, to a number of characters in her quest for the human fugitive, Duran Duran, in Sogo, the evil city of night. In one scene, disappointed that the rebel leader, Dildano, wants to have sex by the Earth's modern, "transference pill" method, she asks: "Couldn't we do it your way? I don't want to change your traditions."

The extent of Barbarella's sexual capacity becomes clear when she overloads Duran Duran's "excess machine," which is designed to expose its victim to fatal amounts of sexual pleasure. While Barbarella has now added "female sexual athlete" to her male-fantasy roles, Duran Duran exposes a patriarchal double standard in his verbal attack: "You've exhausted its power, it couldn't keep up with you. What kind of girl are you? Have you no shame?" But Barbarella has no shame; this is the point. She is Roger Vadim's fantasy woman: innocent, willing, and available to everyone—including her sexual alter-ego, The Great Tyrant of Sogo. Played with relish by Italian actress Anita Pallenberg, this evil queen relies on traditions that stretch back through science fiction cinema's history. She was also following a then recent trend for Technicolor updates, which included, *Queen of Outer Space* in 1958; a French/Italian version of Frank Aubrey's *A Queen of Atlantis* (1899) and Pierre Benoît's *Atlantida* (1920) in the form of *Aitinée l'Amante della citta sepolta* (1961); another French/Italian collaboration, *Maciste e la regina di Samar* (1965); and a British remake of Rider Haggard's 1887 novel *She*, starring former Swiss model, Ursula Andress.

Jane Fonda features in this example of the series of risqué posters produced for *Barbarella* (1968).

Pallenberg's character adds to all of this vanity plus a final male sexual fantasy—she is a vain, predatory lesbian, who attempts to ensnare Barbarella: "I am exquisite delight.... I shall share my delights with you." Despite Pallenberg's and Fonda's spirited performances, the dominant impression given by the film is of a director trying too hard. As Pauline Kael observes, "it's so obvious that he tries to shock only to please."[52]

A central irony to *Barbarella* is the fact that underneath all of its scopophilia and male fantasy is a good space pilot trying to do the right thing. In fact, Barbarella is one of the most proficient female astronauts seen in science fiction cinema to date. She has her own ship, she is described by the President of Earth as a "five-star, double-rated astro-navigatrix," she sticks to her mission, she has integrity, and she is serious, if naïve, about who she is. This sense of Self is expressed when she corrects the Great Tyrant of Sogo: "My name isn't 'Pretty Pretty,' it's Barbarella." This may be a nod to feminism and the primacy of the individual by the film's eight male screenwriters; however, it is far too late for that. This is a movie in which feminist attitudes are approached from a patriarchal perspective, turning a promising treatise into what John Simon in the *New York Times* calls "elucubrated, anemic pornography."[53] Ultimately, it offers a hard-wrought disappointment that echoes the "sexual inertia" present in *Planet of the Apes*. There may be more breasts in *Barbarella*, but science fiction cinema's confused attitude to sex remains. Barbarella's positioning as a sex object far outweighs any notion that the woman might be a good astronaut. In this respect, she represents merely a sub-clause in science fiction cinema's unwritten manifesto for the future of women in space.

"Did you have a pleasant flight, sir?"

In the June 1968 issue of the British publication *Monthly Film Bulletin*, *2001: A Space Odyssey* is described as "unquestionably the most ambitious and generally successful science-fiction film ever made."[54] With the benefit of two decades' perspective, Phil Hardy goes further, calling it "undoubtedly the most influential film of the sixties,"[55] which is supported more recently by M. Keith Booker's assertion that the film "resurrected science fiction at a time when the genre had largely faded from view." Bonnie Noonan brings the plaudits full circle with her description of *2001* as "the quintessential science fiction film of all time"[56]; and more recently still, it was clearly a significant influence on Christopher Nolan's award-winning 2014 movie, *Interstellar*. For fifty years, Stanley Kubrick's tour de force has been regarded by many as the greatest accomplishment in science fiction cinema. Indeed, Piers Bizony even projects his praise into the future in his must-have book, *2001: Filming the Future*: "It will take the passing of many more generations of human explorers before the questions raised by *2001* are answered, and the film becomes redundant at last."[57]

Bizony takes care in his text to refer to "human," "our," "civilization," "humanity" and so forth, avoiding gender-specific terms. This is well intentioned, but it also feels like an implicit acknowledgment of the elephant in this particular room: that is, the role of women. It is difficult to ignore the fact that this most celebrated and visionary of all science fiction movies has no place for female characters outside their traditional and established roles within the genre's cinema. It is perhaps useful at this stage to take another look at the generalized observations about female role development made during Chapter I's survey of the silent period:

a. She is absent
b. She is a narrative bystander or token presence
c. She supports the male characters
d. Her roles are restricted by tradition
e. Her reactions are governed by stereotype

Women are absent entirely from the second half of Kubrick's 139-minute film, as *Discovery One* continues its voyage through space to Jupiter. In fact, the final female appearance comes around the 60-minute point, when astronaut Frank Poole receives a birthday message via video from his parents. It is significant that Poole's mother, a token presence played by Ann Gills, is back on Earth, because, as Constance Penley observes in *NASA/Trek: Popular Science and Sex in America*, roles in space-bound science fiction are closely related to wider ideas and expectations about female representation:

> If we accept that "space" remains one of the major sites of utopian thinking and that "going into space" is still one of the most important ways we represent our relation to science, technology, and the future, we need to examine the stories we tell ourselves about space and about women in space.[58]

Kubrick's science fiction masterpiece—part art, part prediction, part philosophy—charts the past, present and future evolution of humanity, but it does virtually nothing to develop a role for women through that evolution. The five-strong crew of *Discovery One* is entirely male, as is the omnipresent HAL 9000 computer that controls the ship.

In their book, *Alien Woman: The Making of Lt. Ellen Ripley*, Ximena Gallardo and C. Jason Smith make an interesting point that *2001* "harmonizes quite nicely with the less urbane *Planet of the Apes*..., which explores the devolution of the human species and evolution of the apes...."[59] It is, however, that less urbane, or sophisticated, narrative that offers a place for women in space—

albeit through the short-lived Lt. Stewart, played by Dianne Stanley. This character does not appear in Boulle's original *La Planète des Singes*; it was invented by screenwriters Serling and Wilson, presumably to reflect their progressive liberal views. That is somewhat undermined by the fact that Stewart is killed off during the opening sequence, before the ship lands, before the narrative gets going, and before she has had a chance to say or do anything. In fact, it is not clear why she is included at all. Perhaps there is a suggestion here that space is not a safe place for women. Attempting to define Stewart's role, Gallardo and Smith draw attention to her description as the "New Eve,"[60] suggesting parallels with the role of Ellen Ripley in *Alien³* (1992); however, the supporting dialogue, which appears about an hour into *Planet of the Apes*, raises a few issues. "Did I tell you about Stewart? Now, there was a lovely girl. The most precious cargo we brought along. She was to be the new Eve—with our hot and eager help, of course."

The inclusion of a female astronaut may have been well-intentioned at a time when America had none, but Taylor's dialogue, and its retrospective justification for the inclusion of Stewart, labels her as "cargo" and positions her as NASA breed stock. It is not a huge leap from here to *Barbarella* and the notion that women would be in space for a reasons other than detached, scientific professionalism. Perhaps then *2001*, with its female absence, is more honest than those movies that include women in order merely to present them as sexual prizes—or "cargo." Kubrick's space is a sterile environment in which sex, emotion and gender appear to have no place at all. Even the reductive nature of the dialogue dehumanizes the characters, who seem to be caught in

Kubrick's Women #2: silently serving men on the *Aries-1B*. Edwina Carroll as a stewardess in *2001: A Space Odyssey* (1968).

a competition with computer and alien intelligences to be the most inert. Women are not treated particularly badly in *2001*, certainly by the standards of Kubrick's next genre project, *A Clockwork Orange* (1971); it is merely that they, like the women of the early silent period—and indeed Kubrick's previous genre project, *Dr. Strangelove*—are largely sidelined. Feminist academics Hélène Cixous and Catherine Clément have recognized this approach as symbolic of the "phallocentric"—male dominated—cultural and social constructs of religion, family, language, and art, in which "either woman is passive or she does not exist. What is left of her is unthinkable, unthought."[61]

Where women do appear in *2001*, their roles are "governed by stereotype," most famously, perhaps as the stewardesses played by Edwina Carroll, Penny Brahms and Heather Downham. These women are in space, but they are clearly here as "narrative bystanders" and "supports for the male characters." This is encapsulated in a line of dialogue delivered by the uncredited Chela Matthison, as the space station receptionist who greets Dr. Floyd: "Did you have a pleasant flight, Sir?"

Not all female representation in *2001* is rooted this deeply in gender stereotype, but when the film does move with the times, it treads carefully, working within traditions already established by the genre. Onboard a space station on his way to the Moon, Dr. Floyd meets three Russian scientists: Drs. Kalina and Shretniva,[62] played by the uncredited Irena and Krystyna Marr, and the wife of a friend of his, Elena, played by Margaret Tyzack. It is possible that these characters were included in recognition of the Soviet Cosmonaut, Valentina Tereshkova, who had become the first woman in space in 1963. Back in the 1950s, the genre's tentative steps towards the introduction of scientific women had been enough to inspire a young Bonnie Noonan to become a scientist[63]; a decade or so later, *2001* appears to represent a step back from this. Kubrick's scientists have no narrative function beyond small-talk. Most of the useful information and intrigue conveyed in their scene comes from the conversation between Dr. Floyd and a male scientist, Dr. Andrei Smyslov. The role of the women is largely to watch and listen as the men talk: their "token presence" restricts them even within what is already a restrictive new tradition for women in the genre.[64]

None of this will challenge *2001*'s position as what Bizony calls "the epitome of science fiction film-making"; however, his description of Kubrick's movie as "a dazzling manifesto for our future in space" and "a useful inspiration for many years to come,"[65] is open to challenge. But who will it inspire? The success of *2001*, coupled with its plausible prediction of space travel, added considerable weight to the idea that space was not a place for women—unless they were supporting men. *Barbarella* severely restricts the representation of women in space, but Jane Fonda's character does at least have a narrative role, a structural function and relationship with the spectator. Even in 1968, *2001: A Space Odyssey*'s representation of women had a closer connection with past philosophies than with current feminism; it certainly has no eye on a female future. It is, to paraphrase Bizony, "a dazzling manifesto for [a male] future in space"—and one that would exert a huge influence on the genre's future films and filmmakers.

Serious Seventies

In an online review for a book of fantasy essays, Geoff Willmetts offers his personal memories of women's roles in science fiction film films of the 1960s: "for a lot of SF films, the woman was the token character. Even when she was given the lead, as with 'Barbarella' (1968), the rest of the cast was still mostly male. Nothing to do with sexism but more the role in society at that time."[66] The obvious response to this is that, while *Dr. Strangelove*'s almost exclusively male cast says something about the military and political people who make decisions (and mistakes) in then-contemporary America, *2001: A Space Odyssey* has an opportunity to present an alternative future, but one that is does not take. This may have something to do with sexism. To be fair to Kubrick, he may be using *2001* to suggest that mistakes will continue to be made if men continue to make the decisions. At any rate it seems difficult to reconcile the very different approaches to women that are apparent in the prominent 1968 movies outlined above: *Planet of the Apes, Barbarella* and *2001*. Add to this mix a woman as a military expedition member in *The Bamboo Saucer*, benign female aliens in *The Monitors* and ten sexy assassins in *The Blood of Fu Manchu*, and it becomes harder to see women reflecting one particular "role in society." Indeed, this short list supports Annette Kuhn's note of caution, in *Hollywood and the New Women's Cinema*, about simplified readings: "Given the complexity of the institutional structures of the film industry, not to mention the coded operations of film texts, the relationship between social climates and the content of films is obviously not a simple one."[67]

Through the 1960s, science fiction cinema had taken a swing at everything, and was beginning to look like Hardy's genre of "all shapes and sizes."[68] This was evident in the diversity of female roles, which seem to be the result of filmmakers struggling to find a place for women that would remain true, not to their role in society, but to the genre's defining axiom: female representation reflects male expectation.

Following the commercial success of *Planet of the Apes*, the artistic success of *2001* and the critical success of *Charly*, the end of the decade was beginning to look rather different. Science fiction cinema, as Peter Nicholls pointed out (quoted above), would now be taken more seriously. This was an opportunity to take women more seriously too—and perhaps to let them make some of the decisions. What the genre would do with that opportunity remains to be seen; meanwhile, female voices off-screen were becoming louder.

Movement of Women

By the early 1970s, many female writers were following the 1963 lead taken by Betty Friedan with *The Feminine Mystique* by making significant contributions of their own to a discussion that Germaine Greer identifies in *The Female Eunuch* as "the second feminist wave."[69] Shulamith Firestone's *The Dialectic of Sex: The Case for Feminist Revolution* (1971), Kate Millett's *Sexual Politics* (1971), Juliet Mitchell's *Women's Estate* (1971) and others were forming what Marleen Barr later terms "statement of problem,"[70] which, put simply, registered the limitations of traditional female representation. Soon, feminist science fiction novels, such as Joanna Russ's *The Female Man* (1975) and Marge Piercy's *Woman on the Edge of Time* (1976), attempted to address this, and in so doing, helped to shift conversations towards the need to make "patriarchal structures which constrain women obvious and perceptible."[71] In *Faces of Feminism: A Study of Feminism as a Social Movement*, Olive Banks points out that, although social changes had been affecting American women throughout the 1960s, and the number of books on women had been increasing since 1959, political change (like changes in the movie industry) had consistently lagged behind social action.[72] But now the world political climate was beginning to change too, as women's rights movements experienced a huge boost of energy and support after the relatively slow start of the 1960s. Linda Grant notes that the 1970 Oxford Women's Conference led to the formation of many feminist organizations,[73] and Sheila Lewenhak points out that the United Nations designated 1975 as "International Women's Year" in order to "encourage member countries to introduce measures to help women to equality as citizens and workers."[74]

It may not have been essential, or indeed profitable, to actively support the women's movements; however, it was clearly dangerous to actively ignore their growing influence. There is evidence that the movie industry was making attempts—some cynical, some sincere—to reflect political, social and family issues raised by women's movements. In 1968 Katharine Hepburn won an historic third Academy Award for her portrayal of the powerful Eleanor of Aquitaine in *The Lion in Winter*; Glenda Jackson won in 1973 for her role in *A*

Touch of Class, a comedy about divorce; and Jane Fonda finally became an Oscar winner for her 1971 portrayal of a complex prostitute character in *Klute*. However, science fiction filmmakers, appear to have been unsure about whether to risk the larger budgets that came in the wake of *Planet of the Apes'* success. Fonda's nomination for her role in the 1979 genre film *The China Syndrome* may have helped later to loosen the reins, but even in this celebrated film, Fonda continues a genre tradition by playing a television news reporter. Underlying all developments appears to be the fear that female protagonists will threaten the commercial film industry axiom: cinema exists to magnify patriarchal stereotypes.

As if to emphasize these considerations, even Dr. Zira began to be side-lined in the inevitable sequels that followed the successful *Planet of the Apes*. Her prominence is gradually reduced during her journey through *Beneath the Planet of the Apes* (1969) and in *Escape from the Planet of the Apes* (1971), her female primatologist role is usurped by the human Dr. Stephanie Branton, played by Natalie Trundy. In this reversal story, three apes return to 1970s' Earth to discover a society controlled by humans. Denied of a meaningful role, Zira is reduced to feminist-parody and self-mockery throughout. In one notable scene, she is invited to speak at the Bay Area Women's Club, where she attempts to lend her voice to the feminist cause: "A marriage bed is made for two, but every damn morning it's the woman who has to make it. We have heads as well as hands: I call upon men to let us use them." The sentiment may be noble, but the notion that feminists were asking men to "let" women use their heads betrays a lazy approach to the issues. The largely comic nod to feminism in this *Apes* film undermines much of the headway made in the 1968 original. Zira's fate appears to have been set back in late 1968 with Pierre Boulle's screen-play for a proposed sequel to the first film. *Planet of the Men* dramatically reduces Zira's personal and professional role by placing more emphasis on the general conflict between apes and humans. The script remains unproduced, but it cast a long shadow: its new, female-free focus would eventually filter through to the screen in the last of the original series. Zira is killed off at the end of this third film, so there is no place at all for her (or indeed any other prominent female ape) in *Conquest of the Planet of the Apes* (1972) or *Battle for the Planet of the Apes* (1973).

A more subtle example of this attenuation of female success can be seen in *Charly*, the fourth of Peter Nicholls's important films of 1968. It is based in part on Daniel Keyes' 1959 Hugo Award winning, short story, *Flowers for Algernon*, a first-person account of Charlie Gordon's involvement in a scientific experiment which raises his IQ from 68 to over 200. His name is altered, but the protagonist remains male for the film version; however, Dr. Strauss, one of the scientists conducting the experiment, is changed from male to female. The other, Dr. Nemur, remains male. What screenwriter Stirling Silliphant then does is divide the academic responsibilities between these two scientists. The male Dr. Nemur attends to Charly's cognitive intelligence, while the female scientist, played by Lilia Skala, is responsible for Charly's emotional intelligence. This professional distinction is not present in the original text. Combining the functions of the teacher, landlady and work colleague, who are all sympathetic to Charlie's plight in the short story, Dr. Strauss' role is now to "mother" him. And so the (traditional) caring female position has now been formalized through a (feminist) professional role. It may seem a subtle distinction, but once again it points to science fiction's tendency, even in its most celebrated films, to seek safety in convention and stereotype.

General Retreat (Backlash)

By now, science fiction's retreat in the face of perceived external threats should come as no surprise. In the 1930s, it was sound, in the '40s it was war and in the '50s it was communism. Each time, female representation took a step towards forms of stereotype while the genre dealt with the existential danger. In the 1970s, the perceived threats included women themselves, which made the resulting retreat look a little more like a backlash.

For many critics and commentators, this apparent backlash was led by Stanley Kubrick's first movie following *2001*: his adaptation of Anthony Burgess' novel about youth in a future Britain, *A Clockwork Orange*. The film's tagline, "Being the adventures of a young man whose principal interests are rape, ultra-violence and Beethoven" gives a clue to its content and approach. The rape scenes in this film, one of which is accompanied by an ironic rendition of "Singin' in the Rain" by the anti-hero Alex, were always going to generate criticism—especially within communities and political movements that were trying to address social issues in a serious and sensitive way. In his 2016 conference paper on Kubrick's journey from *Dr. Strangelove* to *2001*, Simone Odino quotes archive material from the London-based Stanley Kubrick Archive to suggest that the director aimed to tackle "woman's place—and her displacement—in the modern world."[75] Evidence of this in those two films is thin, so it may be that Kubrick wanted *A Clockwork Orange* to address this subject head-on. Indeed, Kubrick's intentions may have been, like Burgess's, to expose the nature of violence towards women; however, the manner of his presentation met with vehement opposition. Pauline Kael argues that "Kubrick carefully estranges us from these victims so that we can enjoy the rapes and beatings"[76]; Danny Peary is also blunt about the director's perceived misogyny:

Kubrick's Women #3: the female "furniture" of The Korova Milk Bar in *A Clockwork Orange* (actors uncredited, 1971).

"(his treatment of women is insulting). Kubrick makes their abuse at Alex's hands more palatable by making them grotesque, mannered, snobbish figures."[77]

While arguments will continue forever about whether *A Clockwork Orange*'s rape scenes glorify, condemn or merely expose violence towards women, Vivian Sobchack draws attention to the arguably more subtle visual impact of the film, especially in the Korova Milk Bar sequences. During her discussion about the "wonder of alien visual surfaces," she argues that the bizarre, white-washed female figures that have been placed in the bar are eventually made familiar through repetition: "the strange postures of the sculptures become defined in terms of furniture and vending machinery and finally the Korova is accepted by the viewer...."[78] However, these figures are in subdominant sexual positions,[79] with their nipples and pubic hair highlighted with fluorescent paint; it is a blatant, arresting sexualization that, once again, raises questions about Kubrick's intentions. Odino's "displacement" of women in a modern world is certainly in evidence here.

In her work on Allen Jones, the American pop artist whose concepts initially inspired the Korova figures, Laura Mulvey discusses' the examination of fetishism through his "Women as Furniture" exhibition and his published works.[80] She observes that "the female genitals are always concealed, disguised or supplemented in ways which alter the significance of female sexuality" in a manner that is "infinitely more subtle in its understanding of fetishism than the kitsch design Kubrick finally used for the movie."[81] In addition to this, the female figures are impractical as tables, as intended; instead, they serve, for the most part, as foot-rests—literally supports—for men, clearly telegraphing the female function as passive, sexual object of male sadomasochistic desire. As with the rape scenes, it is not clear whether Kubrick is expecting his viewer to be shocked, to accept the repeated images in the way that Sobchack describes, or to enjoy what Molly Haskell, in *From Reverence to Rape*, describes as Kubrick's "violent abuse and brutalization" of women.[82] Whatever his intentions, the weight of critical feeling about *A Clockwork Orange*, as well as death threats against his family,[83] caused Kubrick to ban the film from British screens for the remainder of his life.

Kubrick's film is not alone in its ability to divide critics. The concept of the idealized woman is controversially explored in the 1974 Bryan Forbes picture, *The Stepford Wives*, in which the men of Stepford, a small Connecticut community, systematically replace their wives with more biddable, artificial replicas. Adapted by William Goldman from Ira Levin's 1972 novel, the film was designed as an allegory, a warning about the damaging influence of male-controlled media over the image of women. By presenting a cynical look at the female-robot-as-male-fantasy thread that runs through science fiction cinema, *The Stepford Wives* could be said to offer a rare, honest appraisal of the genre's own treatment of women. The film, however, was adversely criticized by feminists, many of whom saw the idealized, obedient mothers, hostesses, housewives and lovers of Stepford as an affront to their attempts to challenge the status quo. The film's defense was not helped by screenwriter Goldman's original vision of Stepford's "perfect" housewives as "*Playboy* models walking around the town in tight t-shirts and summer shorts...." By way of a defense, the screenwriter adds that "if you are so insanely desperate, so obsessed with women being nothing but sex objects that you are willing to spend the rest of your days humping a piece of plastic ... well, that plastic better goddam well be in the form of Bo Derek."[84]

Director Forbes is careful not to over-sexualize the women in *The Stepford Wives*, but the potential is there and it seems that the damage had been done. It is easy to see reflected in the film as a whole Germaine Greer's assertion that "there are stringent limits to the variations on the stereotype, for nothing must interfere with her function as sex object."[85] This is supported by Goldman's comments.

Sex was a preoccupation of the general, more-liberal cinema of the 1970s, leading to a few experiments in science fiction pornography. The American movie *Flesh Gordon* was a hard-core film, softened for general release in 1974, and the French *Spermula* was released in 1976; both titles offer a clue to their nature and content. Conventional pornography, however, proved far less popular in mainstream science fiction than the titillation of the "sexploitation" films. What did appear during this period was a sense of male anger. *Zeta One* (1969) is a clear product of a backlash against feminism, but more was to come via the "Trash" cinema that Tim Lucas in his 2015 *Sight & Sound* article describes as "a gleeful celebration of everything that might appeal to a mainstream audience."[86] In the science fiction realm, low-budget, non-mainstream filmmakers were taking this ethos and melding genre trappings with horror to present a brutal misogyny. A few of these themes will be returned to in Chapter VI, when another backlash rears its head. For now, it is worth noting that these "Trash" sub-genre efforts should not be mistaken for the relatively tame "sexploitation" offerings of the 1960s.

Dark commentary on women's newfound sexual freedoms did, however, filter through to the mainstream in various guises: even the award-winning *Charly* includes a rape scene. The angry-man approach is present in the casual misogyny of 1975's *A Boy and His Dog*; it is present in the casual voyeurism in *Logan's Run* in 1976; it is certainly present in the casual brutality of *Demon Seed* (1977), and in the casual "sexual harassment" in *The Man Who Fell to Earth*, as identified by Billie Wright Dziech and Linda Weiner in their essay, *The Lecherous Professor*. Despite Cornea's "progressive framework" of the 1960s, it seems that—sex or no sex—the genre was slowly but surely turning its focus back to a male point of view.

MOVEMENT OF MEN

Male anger, guilt, fear of feminism, attempts to avoid patriarchal stereotype, and commercial considerations all play a part in the noticeable side-lining of women for many of the high-profile science fiction movies of the early-to-mid 1970s. It is not difficult to see the shadow of *2001* in the token and silent females in some of the modest-to-high budget, technological, and often macho films that followed with regularity over the next few years.

Marooned won the 1969 Special Visual Effects Academy Award for its depictions of space, but there are no female astronauts on its *Ironman One* spacecraft; and in 1970, Susan Clark as Dr. Cleo Markham becomes a sexual pawn in a battle between man and computer in *Colossus: The Forbin Project*. The focus in 1971 of *The Omega Man*—the last man on Earth—is a clue to its priorities, although it does feature the rare inclusion of black woman, in the form of Rosalind Cash as Lisa. In 1972, *Silent Running*, directed by Douglas Trumbull, who had been the photographic effects supervisor on *2001*, has no female characters at all—although Cheryl Sparks is one of the performers inside the "male" Maintenance Drone 2, Huey. Also in 1972, Andrei Tarkovsky's *Solaris*, which has been referred to as the Soviet *2001* for is scope and vision, fails to reflect the Soviet Union's progressive attitude to real women in space. An adaptation of the 1961 novella by Stanslaw Lem, this movie is notable for many reasons, not least for this study is the fact that its concept echoes the treatment of women in the genre. An energy force on the planet Solaris turns the thoughts of Kris, the man in the space station overhead, into reality. The women created as a result are therefore male constructs, conforming to (often sexual) male fantasies. The notion is turned on its head when Kris loses control of his fantasy and it starts to control him—which may or may not be a portent of things to come in science fiction cinema. In the meantime, 1972, a good year for the genre, was not a good year for women: *Soylent Green* is another genre vehicle for Charlton Heston; and *Westworld* is a vehicle for Yul Brynner as the iconic, mute, macho, gun-slinging robot in a theme park whose female robots are almost entirely slaves, servants and sex workers, including Linda Grave Scott's "Parisian" prostitute, Arlette. *Rollerball* in 1975 is largely a James Caan vehicle and what Jonathan Rosenbaum called at the time an "embodiment of mindless masochism"[87]; and while the 1976 film *Logan's Run* is somewhat gentler, this is still, as the name suggests, a story about a man finding freedom—accompanied by Jenny Agutter, who is, on occasion, completely naked. Finally, for this indicative, although not exhaustive, list is 1977's *Capricorn One*, whose all-male astronaut crew, supported by astronauts' wives, makes it feel not unlike *Marooned*, from a decade earlier.

Most of the screenplays for these films were adapted from existing literature, so the producers had some idea of what they would be getting, including the number and type of female characters. *En masse*, they contribute to the distinct feel of the 1970s' science fiction movies: emotionally inert, sterile celebrations of space-age technology. The trend is partially explained by Susan Thomas's suggestion, in her essay *Between the Boys and Their Toys*, that "the function of androids, robots and computers is to act as a channel, or alter ego, through which the (male) audience can solve its emotional dilemmas."[88] Like so much of the genre's output, these films now feel rooted to their decade, as though they could not have been made in any other period. The cold, clinical, corporate approach that informs many of these films is the defining feature of George Lucas' first theatrical feature, *THX 1138*, a film that critiques consumer capitalism by suggesting that it will eventually reduce people and places to a bland homogeneity. In this more sophisticated version of the restrictive, egalitarian future society seen in *Just Imagine* back in 1930, men and women have bald heads and alpha-numeric strings for names, they are drugged into conformity, and are forbidden to have sex for pleasure. It is a man, THX, who finally breaks free, after being prompted (tempted) to stop taking his drugs by a woman, LUH, played by Maggie Omie. Towards the end of his revealing examination of this film, J.P. Telotte provides the following summary: "What *THX 1138* offers us, then, is a fantastic vision clearly focused on the very problematic relationship we have both to our own world and to those we might conjure up as an alternative."[89]

It is a lesson that might also guide a study of female representation in science fiction cinema. Namely, that criticism of what is being offered is one thing; knowing what to replace it with is quite another. As Judy Wajcman points out in *Feminism Confronts Technology*, even those feminists who were capturing attention with respect to gender inequalities in science in the 1970s did not always cast their nets wide enough. "Despite the advances that were made through the critique of science in the 1970s, gender-conscious accounts were rare ... the radical science movement focused almost exclusively on the capitalist nature of science ignoring the relationship of science to patriarchy."[90] Indeed, a corporate capitalist ethos had entered Hollywood itself with the sell-off of the old studios. This filtered through to science fiction films, and would really get up to speed as the genre entered the 1980s. Perhaps, then, it is this new capitalist focus that caused women to be sidelined by the genre through the 1970s, leaving men with their machines.

One notable exception to this appears early in the decade, in the form of Dr. Ruth Leavitt, played by Kate Reid, in Robert Wise's *The Andromeda Strain* (1971). While Bonnie Noonan lists this character alongside earlier female scientists, who "are content (or not) to operate as reliable, indispensable technicians,"[91] Dr. Leavitt does at least have an impact on the narrative—following Helen Benson in Wise's earlier film, *The Day the Earth Stood Still*. Dr. Leavitt discovers the means to neutralize the killer strain of space-bacterium that gives the movie its title. Despite this, the female scientist is diminished by other elements of the narrative—just as Dr. Strauss had been in *Charly*. The female Dr. Ruth Leavitt replaces the male Dr. Peter Leavitt from Michael Crichton's 1969 source novel; however, the character chosen to be female has a weakness. Leavitt's ability as a scientist is affected by illness and she has to be rescued at one point by her medical colleague. Kate is no longer a Nobel Prize winner, nor the Professor of pathology that Peter had been; nor is she the surgeon who saves the day. Dr. Kate Leavitt is a spinster with epilepsy. It is another example of the genre giving with one hand and taking with the other; and it is allied to what Lisa Tuttle describes in her discussion of female roles in science fiction literature as: "an object lesson to girl readers that career success equals feminine failure."[92]

In his seminal 1970 book, *Science Fiction in the Cinema,* John Baxter makes a distinction between the genre's literature as supporting "logic and order" and its films as supporting "illogic and chaos."[93] He then divides films into two categories: "the loss of individuality, and the threat of knowledge." Clearly, these are historian's generalizations; however, the "threat of knowledge" posed by women in the 1960s and '70s did lead to her "loss of individuality." Baxter's pessimistic view of science fiction cinema held true—at least, until the return of George Lucas.

———❧———

A palpable tension runs through the movies of the interregnum period that followed the genre's golden age explosion. Back in the 1950s, women's roles had been subject to a managed expansion: restrictions remained, but these were supported by a sense that women should be content with the concessions that had been made. By the mid–1960s, it was clear that women were not happy with their allotted square of turf; however, the monoliths of commerce, genre and tradition were difficult to budge. Industry guilt, confusion and fear led in turns to innovation, stagnation and retreat. A new approach was needed. Three events in 1977 together feel like a cultural changing of the guard: the death of cinema icon Charlie Chaplin severed a link with the birth of popular mass media; the death of rock 'n' roll icon Elvis Presley closed a chapter on its teenage years; and science fiction replaced these leviathans with a film that would re-shape the territory. As well as placing the genre at the center of the cultural landscape, it would also be pivotal in giving women a new direction—and a new hope.

V

GOLDEN ERA
Blockbusters and the Development
of Female Heroes

If 1968 changed science fiction movies, 1977 changed the movie industry. The genre had already shown that it could be thought-provoking, critically acclaimed and profitable. Soon it would prove itself to be a genre of mass entertainment (later *the* genre of mass entertainment). On the cusp of greatness too were women's roles, but there were still a few rites of passage to navigate. A-grade success for the B-movie genre made the late 1970s a confusing time: executives, inherently wary of the new, were tempted again to throw their money behind tried and tested formulae—those that required women once again to conform to stereotype, tradition and convention. But a new force was rising. Young filmmakers from new film schools revamped old rules with fresh ideas. Women would be expected to step up to the plate like never before. And they did. The scene was set for the roller-coaster that was to become the golden era for women in science fiction cinema.

———∞———

First Steps

Back in 1976, the huge commercial and financial success of *Jaws*—the biggest box-office hit to that date—established Steven Spielberg as a cinema director of note. *Jaws* is not science fiction, unless it can be argued that the shark's actions are triggered by an external scientific event (as with the monsters of the Japanese *Kaiju Eiga* of the 1950s). Spielberg's next feature was definitely science fiction, and it signaled a significant move for the genre—if not initially for the representation of women within it. A rewritten and expanded version of Paul Schrader's script for *Watch the Skies*, with elaborate special effects added,[1] the 1977 release, *Close Encounters of the Third Kind*, tells the story of a man who is haunted by visions which are eventually revealed to be premonitions of a visit to Earth by benign aliens. He has a wife, played by Teri Garr, who supports him until his behavior becomes too erratic; then she leaves with their children. Another mother, played by Milinda Dillon, becomes more active towards the end of the film, as she searches for her missing son, but that is the extent of prominent female involvement. This is a story about men looking for the truth. The large amount of time, effort and money invested into *Close Encounters* was an indication that Columbia Pictures was prepared to take science fiction seriously, or rather, that the producers were willing to trust a relatively young film-school graduate who seemed to have his finger on the pulse of the cinema-goer. Indeed, 20th Century–Fox was doing a similar thing with Spielberg's friend, George Lucas, whose huge commercial success with *American Graffiti* in 1973 had allowed him to make his own spectacular science fiction film—albeit with a little over half Spielberg's budget. *Star Wars*, like *Close Encounters*, continued the Seventies' strand of techno-centric, science fiction cinema, but from a very different direction. Spielberg's film mixes mundane domesticity with protracted tension to create a thought-provoking essay with a touch of 1950s aesthetic; Lucas mixes even earlier influences with futuristic sets to create a breathless romp around space. The only significant similarity between these science fiction cinema events of 1977 is the scarcity of women.

ACCIDENTAL FEMINIST

It is common knowledge that the original *Star Wars* trilogy is very male-centered; indeed, this is now the subject of parody. In *It's a Trap*, the 2010 *Family Guy* spoof of the third *Star Wars* film, *Return of the Jedi* (1983), Luke (Chris Griffin) reveals to Han (Peter Griffin) that Leia (Lois Griffin, voiced by Alex Borstein) is his sister. "Of course it's her," replies Han, "she's the only chick in the galaxy." Later, at the arrival of Mon Mothma (Angela, voiced by Carrie Fisher), Han quips, "Hey, check it out, it's another chick! The only other chick in the galaxy!" It is no secret that roles for woman in science fiction film in general, and *Star Wars* in particular, have been patchy. Despite this, no history of science fiction film can ignore *Star Wars* because, along with *Close Encounters* to a lesser degree, it represented a huge shift in the industry's attitude to the genre—and that would have an effect on female roles. These commercial and critical successes, which had built on the earlier impact of *Planet of the Apes* and *2001: A Space Odyssey* (both 1968) prepared the way for women to thrive. Without *Star Wars* and Leia, there might not have been *Alien* and Ripley, and then perhaps no *Terminator* and Sarah Connor. Besides, while Leia is clearly not the gritty warrior that Ripley and Connor would become, neither is she a weak damsel-in-distress. Lucas seems to have attempted to walk a middle way.

Almost a decade after *2001* and the real-life moon landings, Lucas was relying on his audience's familiarity with space travel to establish his *mise en scène*: "'I suppose it's space fantasy,' Lucas said at the time. 'But we don't explain anything. We take the hardware for granted....'"[2] He takes his themes and characters for granted too—and that includes the women. Unable to secure the rights to remake the "space fantasy" *Flash Gordon* as a feature film, Lucas took many elements from the Saturday morning chapter serials and mixed them with other genre allusions. Indeed, when Lucasfilm and 20th Century–Fox later sued the producers of the series *Battlestar Galactica* (1978–9) for plagiarism, their case collapsed because, as science fiction writer, historian and expert witness Brian Aldiss points out in *Trillion Year Spree*, these films exploit the same genre traditions: "The lawyers' first formal question to me was this: 'What was your initial response to *Star Wars*?' I replied, 'I experienced the delights of recognition.' They thought about it. Then they smiled."[3] (The series was canceled after 21 episodes before the suit could progress; the case was dropped.)

It could be argued that *Star Wars* began a trend for borrowing, alluding and re-cycling that has sustained science fiction cinema for the last forty years; the recent escalation of this trend will be discussed in Chapter VII. Meanwhile, *Star Wars* did cast its net wider than most for what Lucas called at the time a "modern mythology to give kids a sense of values, to give them a strong mythological fantasy life."[4] As a result, its homages include pulp science fiction, traditional fairytale, world mythology and mysticism, as well as the work of Japanese filmmaker, Akira Kurosawa. His 1958 film *The Hidden Fortress* gave Lucas, amongst other things, the squabbling plebeians, R2-D2 and C-3PO, and the sassy princess, Leia.[5]

Princess Leia Organa, played by Carrie Fisher, combines all of these earlier influences and more, but she was also created at a time when female voices were being raised—if not always heard. It was this era and environment that created the "Women of Punk" who appeared on the 2017 episode of the BBC Radio 4 program, *The Reunion*. These punk pioneer contributors subscribed to the notion that, back in the mid–1970s, "Women could dress how they liked, behave how they wanted and develop their own sound without being manipulated by the mostly male gatekeepers of the record industry. Young women who didn't fit the traditional mold of femininity found a new tribe in punk."[6] In the radio broadcast, singer Toyah Willcox points out that some punk women were expressing their right to rebel by exposing their breasts. Princess Leia does not go quite this far, but her breasts did prove to be an issue. Nineteen-year-old Carrie Fisher was famously taped down under her diaphanous, Fay Wray style gown—a result of Lucas' pronouncement that "there are no bras in space." It is doubtful that Lucas was showing affinity with the punks in rebellion a few miles from the Elstree Studios where much of *Star Wars* was filmed. Instead, despite Fisher's complaints that "They have these ads that make it look like I go around the galaxy seducing robots"[7]—and despite Leia's beauty first attracting Luke to her hologram message—Lucas' aim was to ensure the kind of sexless space environment on film that Vivian Sobchack explores in her essay, "The Virginity of Astronauts." This is not to say that the human characters portrayed in *Star Wars* are androgynous; they do have recognizable gender, but sex itself, as in the 1950s, is off the agenda. If Leia's representation leans towards "boy in a dress," this may well be due to what Dale Pollock identifies in his 1983 biography, *Skywalking: The Life and Times of George Lucas*, as the director's admitted lack of understanding about women in general, resulting from little prior contact with them: "Lucas admits that he's always had problems developing women in his movies—he can make them strong and independent but seems to have no idea of what they're thinking or feeling."[8]

Ironically, it may be this lack of insight that led to Leia's distain for both the traditions of female representation in the genre and the imperial forces of institutionalized patriarchy. She may display the hallmarks of damsel-in-distress, literally a princess, trapped in a tower: a sexless icon of an age of medieval Romanticism[9]; however, she subverts this nominal role. She shows no fear to anyone, as is seen in her, almost comic, audacious and frank exchange with the villain, Grand Moff Tarkin:

> PRINCESS LEIA: Governor Tarkin. I should have expected to find you holding Vader's leash. I recognized your foul stench when I was brought on board.
> GRAND MOFF TARKIN: Charming to the last. You don't know how hard I found it signing the order to terminate your life!
> PRINCESS LEIA: I'm surprised you had the courage to take the responsibility yourself!

Leia's vitriol and sarcasm is shared with the male heroes too, in lines like: "This is some rescue!," "Will someone get this walking carpet out of my way!" and "Listen. I don't know who you are, or where you came from, but from now on, you do as I tell you. Okay?" It is not clear how much dialogue doctor Gloria Huyck (along with her husband, Willard)[10] brought to this portrayal, but in many ways, it was Lucas' shortcomings as a writer of women that ultimately created what amounts to an accidental feminist in Princess Leia.

Star Wars was released in the U.S. in May 1977, followed by other territories through '77 and into '78. This gave little time for the larger studios to respond in kind for the 1978 season. That response would have to wait until

"**I recognized your foul stench when I was brought on board.**" Carrie Fisher as Princess Leia confronts Peter Cushing's Grand Moff Tarkin, in *Star Wars: Episode IV—A New Hope* (1977).

1979. In the meantime, Universal did manage to get a theatrical release for what is essentially a television movie, *Battlestar Galactica*, and MGM released a remake of *Invasion of the Body Snatchers*, both of which benefited from the success of *Star Wars*. The rest of 1978 was left largely to smaller, nimbler production companies who were able to exploit the new science fiction climate with films like, *The Bees, Deathsport, Attack of the Killer Tomatoes!* and other "exploitation quickies"; their names give an indication of their content, and it is not difficult to guess at the roles they offer women. During this relative lull between the massive impact of *Star Wars* and the wider industry's big-budget responses, one film was released that is, perhaps surprisingly, significant in the study of women in science fiction cinema.

FALSE DAWN

Coma, the 1978 movie adapted and directed by Michael Crichton, from the 1977 novel by Robin Cook, is a medical murder mystery set in Boston Memorial Hospital, where patients have been lapsing into unexplained coma, during routine surgery, at an alarming rate. The reason for this is revealed by Dr. Wheeler, who investigates the phenomenon at great personal risk, confronting external powers and the internal hospital hierarchy. Of central importance is the fact that this narrative takes a female perspective. Dr. Susan Wheeler, played by Geneviève Bujold, is a woman. This is her story.

Female professionals had already proven that they could hold their own in the 1950s with capable characters such as Dr. Lisa van Horn in *Rocketship X-M*, and Helen Benson had shown that a mother and secretary could step up to the plate in *The Day the Earth Stood Still*; however, these women play important roles in stories about men. As with the genre's earliest female characters, they support male action. Barbarella had been given her own story, but she is, of course, a figure of heterosexual male desire. Dr. Wheeler is different. Contrary to Elizabeth Cowie's complaint, in *A Discussion of Coma*, that "as a character she is 'strong,' but as an actant within the narrative she is 'weak,'"[11] Dr. Wheeler is in fact the essential element within both plot and narrative. As Pauline Kael observes: "With her slightly moldy Peter Pan pertness, she's irreducibly curious—that's her sexy-witch essence.... Dr. Wheeler's suspiciousness—the sneaky expressions she gets when she doesn't go along with what her superiors are telling her—is all we've got to hang on in this sterile environment."[12]

In her introduction to part three of *Women in Film*, Charlotte Brunsdon cautiously welcomes films like *Coma*, which "bear the traces of feminist struggles"[13]; however, she goes on to suggest that the main criticism of films such as these is, ironically, that the female characters are not sufficiently representative or ordinary. Nonetheless, it is clear from the dialogue in *Coma* that Crichton is aware of the significance of this female role, so much so that the sexual politics does feel rather forced at times. A key early argument between Dr. Wheeler and her partner, Dr. Bellows, played by Michael Douglas, is triggered by his crass assumption that she is going to cook dinner, despite the fact that they have both just returned from long shifts at the hospital. This gives Crichton the opportunity to have Dr. Bellows voice an anti-feminist accusation: "You don't want a lover, you want a goddam wife!" It also introduces the concept of male opposition that Dr. Wheeler will meet in various guises throughout the film. While the male Dr. Bellows is happy to conform blindly and blithely to the rules of a system in which he is accepted, the female Dr. Wheeler is not; she finds herself pushed around, pressured and patronized by the patriarchal medical hierarchy. In their book *Alien Woman: The Making of Lt. Ripley*, Ximena Gallardo and C. Jason Smith identify Dr. Wheeler as one of the women of 1970s' science fiction cinema who "either relied on a man or was finally crushed by the evil forces plotting against her."[14] It is true that Dr. Wheeler needs Dr. Bellows to save her at the end of the film, but she is not the victim here. Through dogged, solo determination, it is the woman who brings down a prominent part of the patriarchal system. Rather than be punished for it, like the strong females in earlier genre films, she eventually educates and converts her man to her cause.

It has been argued that *Coma* is not science fiction at all because it merely extrapolates from current medical practice. Cowie judges the film largely on its merits as a detective narrative, Kael calls it a "formula exploitation thriller"[15] and Christine Geraghty in *Three Women's Films* calls it a "fantasy/narrative."[16] It is all of these and more. The notion of patients being held in computer-controlled stasis until their organs can be harvested conforms to Peter Nicholls' requirement of an "explicable novum": a new element supported by known science. What is more, the Jefferson Institute, where the bodies are held, suspended on wires, is clearly presented as a science fictional environment. It might be helpful also to see *Coma* in the light of a Jennifer Rohn's recent genre formulation, "LabLit" (Laboratory Literature),[17] which, as Olga Pilkington points out in her introduction to the first anthology of essays on the subject, focuses on stories of real scientists doing real science in real environments. LabLit is a circle on a Venn diagram that intersects with science fiction and other related genres and sub-genres at various points. To deny *Coma* its place on this diagram would be to deny *Frankenstein* its place also. Besides, many film critics and commentators include *Coma* in their (pre–LabLit) studies of science fiction.[18]

In their study, Gallardo and Smith use *Coma* alongside *The Stepford Wives* (1975) and *Demon Seed* (1977) in order to help place *Alien* (1979) in context. This is reasonable, as there is clearly a contrast in styles and approach, but perhaps the difference between Dr. Susan Wheeler and Lt. Ellen Ripley is not so great. Each character is gritty and determined, each experiences prejudice, and each is the subject of voyeurism as their film reaches a point of dramatic jeopardy. One comes when the camera takes a position below the skirted Wheeler as she climbs a ladder during a tense sequence. The other appears as Ripley's

Caught between Leia and Ripley. Geneviève Bujold as Dr. Susan Wheeler in *Coma* (1978).

famous "strip" sequence, in which the low-set camera watches her undress to her briefs as she prepares to get into her spacesuit and confront the alien. It is hard to know if Ridley Scott watched *Coma* before making *Alien*, and even harder to prove that Wheeler was a direct inspiration for Ripley; however, it would not be surprising—not least because of the visual similarity between Geneviève Bujold and Sigourney Weaver in a number of *Coma's* scenes.

Direct influence or not, *Coma* pre-figures *Alien* in many ways, however, it did not foment immediate revolution or start an instant trend. As so often with key films such as *Frau im Mond* (1929), *The Day the Earth Stood Still* (1951), *Planet of the Apes* (1968) and it represents a false dawn. Michael Crichton clearly picked up on novelist Robin Cook's feminist message, but he still chose to include a naked shower scene for Bujold; however, it was not this familiar, patriarchal scopophilia that held the film back. Instead the message was lost in the maelstrom that became the science fiction film industry's attempts to capitalize on the global commercial success of *Star Wars*.

COMMERCIAL CONSIDERATIONS

Independent feminist filmmaker Lizzie Borden's 1983 *cri de coeur*, *Born in Flames*, is a rallying call from an imagined near-future, where women are fighting for a utopia in which everyone has an equal voice, regardless of race, class, creed, color, sexuality, gender and so forth. When it becomes clear that this socialist revolution will fail because it cannot create enough jobs, the revolutionaries call for the "women's army" to take over the methods of production and wealth generation, with the cry: "we will not stop fighting until we get proportional representation in government." At the end of the film, these Marxist feminists blow up the twin towers of the World Trade Center in New York City. Today, these buildings are indelibly linked with the events of 11 September 2001; in 1983, the phallic towers represented to Borden's feminist freedom fighters a combined threat to society: patriarchy and capitalism.

Up to now, this history has focused largely on patriarchy in general and male control of the often scopophilic image in particular. *Born in Flames* is a reminder that patriarchy comes in many guises and feminism has many responses. Borden's Marxist feminists would know that chipping away at on-screen female representation does not address the deeper issue of off-screen power. Since the breakup of the old American studios following anti-monopolies legislation in the 1950s, corporations had slowly been taking over Hollywood—and those corporations were run largely by men. As Linda Gordon states in *The Struggle for Reproductive Freedom: Three Stages of Feminism*, "liberation is going to require a struggle against capitalism and male supremacy as two connected, but not identical, forms of domination."[19]

David McClintick exposes very close ties between the American film industry and financial institutions in his 1983 tale of corporate corruption *Indecent Exposure*, with the telling tagline: "A true story of Hollywood and Wall

Street"; however, the ultimate arbiter is almost always the box office. Wealthy individuals, such as the businessman Howard Hughes, have been able to produce loss-making films that satisfy their personal preoccupations, but in the main, an individual film must make a stand-alone profit to satisfy CEOs and shareholders. Films that make a big profit, inevitably inspire imitators—and within months of its release, *Star Wars* had become the highest grossing film in history. Commercial considerations had forced a step-back in the development of female roles before—for example, at the arrival of sound on film—but *Star Wars* was on an altogether different scale. It was not clear yet how such a strong merging of traditional roles and box office success would affect the representation of women in science fiction cinema. For the big-budget films that inevitably began to emerge in 1979, from studio-cum-corporations hoping to replicate the box-office success of *Star Wars*, it was difficult to ignore women altogether. The genre had developed to a point where female characters were expected to be involved in some way—not just as part of the furniture, as in *A Clockwork Orange*, but as professionals and named individuals. Ironically, the profile of Princess Leia had contributed to the latter. Women could not easily be ignored, but they could be sidelined—again. For the industry, *Star Wars* really was a "have your cake and eat it moment"; producers could return to the safety of tradition, stereotype and convention—and make money doing it.

The movie version of *Superman* indicated a direction of travel in December 1978, with its no-nonsense journalist, Lois Lane, played by Margot Kidder, encapsulating both familiar and feisty, not unlike Princess Leia. Helped, no doubt, by the considerable charm of Christopher Reeve and the well-publicized, fleeting appearance of Marlon Brando, the film made its $55million budget back before the end of the year. Paramount also stayed on familiar territory when it dusted off its television property, *Star Trek*, for *The Motion Picture*. This first feature for a franchise that has now stretched to 13 films across three incarnations is able to offer little more than the familiar Nichelle Nichols' as Lt. Uhura and former Miss India model, Persis Khambatta, as the sexualized Deltan, Ilia. *Buck Rogers in the 25th Century* presents further strong-but-familiar roles in the form of Princess Ardala and Colonel Wilma Deering, played by Pamela Hensley and Erin Gray respectively; and while Walt Disney Studios tried to bring a new story to the screen with *The Black Hole*, its single female character, Dr. Kate McCrae, played by Yvette Mimieux, is secondary to the male characters—and ultimately becomes a damsel-in-distress. The result, according to Brosnan, "is interesting, but otherwise the movie fails on every level."[20] The most successful independent film of the year was George Miller's Australian hit *Mad Max*; however, this is a throwback to the masculinized worlds of 1970s' American films, such as *Rollerball* and *Death Race 2000* (both

1975). For a short period, female roles seem to have returned to characteristics identified in the silent films of Chapter I: traditional, token or absent.

Despite what reviewer Tim Pulleine in 1979 called its "commercial astuteness,"[21] one British/American film that appeared to buck this trend was Ridley Scott's *Alien*, featuring Sigourney Weaver as Ellen Ripley. Her place in the pantheon of female science fiction cinema characters is assured, but it is also assumed that it was *Alien* that put her there. Indeed, Scott's film has already been mentioned in this chapter in a manner that takes for granted that the reader already knows of its existence and significance. For those who don't, *Alien* takes, to continue Pulleine's review, "*Star Wars* hardware, the approximate storyline of *Jaws*" and "some regurgitated business from *The Exorcist*" for its loose remake of the 1951 film *The Thing from Another World!* To further underscore its debt to the past, the film also has links with both the 1958 film, *It! The Terror from Beyond Space*,[22] and A.E. van Vogt's 1939 science fiction story, *Discord in Scarlet*.[23] The commercial spaceship *Nostromo*, returning to Earth after a mining mission, is diverted to a planet transmitting what appears to be a distress call. The crew is woken from cryosleep and sent to investigate. On the planet, they find an abandoned spaceship and a clutch of eggs containing alien creatures, one of which is brought back to the *Nostromo*. Once onboard, the alien develops into a killing machine that then slaughters the crew, leaving just one person alive: a woman, Ellen Ripley.

It is hard to gauge accurately now the affect that Ripley had on audiences at the time. Her role is not particularly large, this is not exclusively her story, she saves only herself and the ship's cat, and it is really just events that transpire to make her the accidental hero of the piece. Tim Pulleine continues:

> ...Sigourney Weaver's pragmatic heroine—played off not only against Veronica Cartwright's hand-wringing stereotype [Lambert] but also against Tom Skerritt's cynical resignation [as Dallas]—is recognisably a Hawksian woman removed from a Hawksian context of interdependence. But such intimations remain on the periphery of the movie.[24]

Although Pulleine recognizes Ripley's connection with the strong, no-nonsense women who appeared in many of the films of director Howard Hawks (not least, Rosalind Russell's news reporter role in *His Girl Friday* [1940]), it is her place on the "periphery" that is significant. *Alien* is an ensemble piece and, crucially, women are as active—if not as numerous—in the ensemble as men. They are not here to make up the numbers, nor merely to support male derring-do. Both women and men are presented as flawed, brave, pathetic and heroic. Any of the crew of the *Nostromo* could have been the last person standing; it happens to be Ripley. She does not succeed because she is necessarily faster, smarter or stronger, or even because she is a woman. She just happens to be a woman who happens to survive—an evocation of the "last girl standing" trope made popular by horror films of the period, such as *Halloween*. It is uncertain whether Ripley, as one of the crew of a deep-space mining vessel, meets Charlotte Brunsdon's requirement of the "ordinary" that was deemed missing from *Coma*, but within the context of *Alien*, she is not particularly extraordinary. Like Helen Benson before her, Ripley does extraordinary things when called to do so. This is key to the strength of both characters. Of course, Ripley does not really just "happen" to survive; that decision is made by Ridley Scott and screenwriter Dan O'Bannon. This decision is key to the strength of their contribution to the representation of women in science fiction cinema.

Much has been said and written about Ripley and the 1979 film that introduced her. And while Pulleine's statement that *"Alien* signifies nothing very much—except, of course, at the box office,"[25] is inaccurate, so too, perhaps, is the retrospective significance heaped on Ripley's shoulders in the years following the film's sequels. Gallardo and Smith seem to acknowledge this when they focus on the development of the character across all four *Alien* films that had been made when they wrote their book, *Alien Woman: The Making of Lt. Ripley*. The first *Alien* was merely an important starting point for a character who becomes arguably more interesting and significant once she is given her own story.

Hero(ine)'s Journey

Years before he became a filmmaker, George Lucas had an experience that would directly affect *Star Wars*, science fiction cinema, and, ultimately, women's roles within it. A near-fatal car crash in 1962 forced on Lucas a period of rest and recovery, during which he read voraciously. Among the many philosophical and sociological works that he studied was Joseph Campbell's 1949 book, *The Hero with a Thousand Faces*, in which the author shows that myths derive from universal fears, needs, wants and dreams; they usher in rites of passage, attempt to make sense of death, and offer guides to life. In this influential work, Campbell argues that these shared elements mean that myths from around the world, through time and across cultures can be boiled down to a series of common features: a "monomyth," or a classic pattern for the hero's journey. This pattern is followed by Luke Skywalker. Later, Christopher Vogler would align Campbell's work with the standard 3-act, 120-minute screenplay structure in *The Writer's Journey: Mythic Structure for Storytellers and Screenwriters*, whose widespread influence has helped to homogenize the genre.[26]

Across the original three *Star Wars* films, Luke completes the three stages of the traditional hero's journey to enlightenment: "Separation" (*A New Hope*),

"Initiation" (*The Empire Strikes Back*), and "Return" (*Return of the Jedi*). Campbell dissects each stage further. The first "Separation" stage follows five phases, which in turn govern the destiny of Luke through the first film:

I.   The Call to Adventure
II. Refusal of the Call
III. Supernatural Aid
IV. The Crossing of the First Threshold
V.   The Belly of the Whale

To begin his separation from his life as a farm boy, Luke is called to adventure by the arrival of R2-D2 with a hologram message from Leia. Fearing his uncle, Luke refuses the call and agrees to have the droid's memory erased. Luke's supernatural aid arrives in the form of Ben Kenobi, who encourages him to answer the call to adventure. Luke refuses again, but then fate intervenes to kill his uncle and aunt (Beru, played by Shelagh Fraser, the film's only other human female). With nothing left for him on his home planet, Luke crosses the first threshold by leaving Tatooine for the first time. It is a journey that will force him to enter the belly of the whale in the form of the Death Star. Ben's role in Luke's final glory is predicted in Campbell's words: "it may be that he here discovers for the first time that there is a benign power everywhere supporting him and his superhuman passage."[27] There are various ways to align Luke with Campbell's hero myth. Indeed, phases from later stages are evoked, as Luke follows "the road of trials" in his "return" to the Death Star. John Shelton Lawrence has pointed out that there are limitations to the depth of this link between *Star Wars* and the monomyth[28]; indeed, Ben Kenobi (and later Yoda) arguably owes more to Carlos Castaneda's *Tales of Power*.[29] There is little doubt, however, that Campbell's influence did at least set Luke on his journey, which set up a chain reaction.

In the preface to her book, *Women Scientists in Fifties Science Fiction Films*, Bonnie Noonan recalls that "as a girl, I felt I would never be able to be the male hero who was automatically entitled to participate in the adventure."[30] Two decades after Noonan's disappointment, *Alien* invited Ripley to participate, but it was Campbell's hero's journey that would influence her next step—and usher in a new generation of *bona fide* female science fiction heroes.

PENDULUM PROTAGONISTS

In psychoanalytical terms, a cinema-goer's willingness to enjoy and accept what is on the screen is a function of her imagination (the unconscious, unfettered id) and her sense of reality (the socially structured super-ego). Imagination is pleasurable; this is what brings audiences to the cinema, but too much, according to Christian Metz (who was introduced in Chapter II) has the potential to alienate people. This "cinematic paradox" demands a balance: enough imagination to be exciting, but grounded in enough reality to be believable. Perhaps more than any other genre, science fiction relies on this id/super-ego transaction.

In story terms, the cinema-goer wants to see imaginative plot and character development, which might include a journey from something ordinary, or believable, to something extra-ordinary. For the 1951 audiences of *The Day the Earth Stood Still*, the arrival of a flying saucer in contemporary Washington, D.C., followed by Helen Benson's journey from mother and secretary to mediator and savior, did just this. It may seem surprising that Dr. Susan Wheeler in *Coma* had not been sufficiently "ordinary" for the critics cited by Charlotte Brunsdon, but this perhaps indicates the distance that women still had to travel in the socially structured (super-ego) mind of the 1978 audience. Surely then, Sarah Connor, as introduced in James Cameron's *The Terminator*, would be safe bet. She is, as M. Keith Booker points out in his essay on this 1984 movie in *Alternate Americas*, "a completely ordinary young woman"[31]; she is a waitress—and not a particularly good one at that. This overt ordinariness contributes to the success of Sarah Connor's character. It gives room for development once Cameron and fellow writer, Gale Anne Hurd, apply elements of Campbell's hero's journey.

Before her call to adventure. Linda Hamilton as Sarah Connor in *The Terminator* (1981).

To begin her separation from her life as a waitress, Sarah Connor, played by Linda Hamilton, is called to adventure by the arrival of a cyborg from the future, played by Arnold Schwarzenegger. This "terminator" is working its way through the Sarah Connors listed in the telephone directory, killing them in turn; it soon reaches Hamilton's Connor. She is rescued just in time by a stranger, Kyle Reece, who explains to the terrified waitress that he is a warrior from the future and that she is destined to become the mother of the savior of humanity. Reece is soon arrested by police and interrogated. Seemingly safe at the same police station, Connor watches a video of the interrogation; at this point, like Luke Skywalker, she refuses the call to adventure, and accepts the professional diagnosis of Reece as "a loon." But when Schwarzenegger's cyborg decimates the police station, Connor and Reece—her supernatural aid— escape again, and she accepts her calling. Connor crosses a threshold when she helps Reece to make pipe bombs in preparation for combat with the terminator. When Reece is killed, Connor alone must enter the "belly of the whale," which comes in the form of an automated factory. Here she eventually destroys the cyborg.

Sarah Connor's trajectory through *The Terminator* can be summarized simply using Joseph Campbell's own description of what he names "the nuclear unit of the monomyth": "A hero ventures forth from the world of common day into a region of supernatural wonder: fabulous forces are there encountered and a decisive victory is won: the hero comes back from this mysterious adventure with the power to bestow boons on his fellow man."[32]

Campbell's monomyth is not the only narrative element borrowed for *The Terminator*. Like *Alien* and *Star Wars*, Cameron's film takes much from low-budget and pulp science fiction traditions, or, as Booker says, "we have rarely seen so many *clichés* collected in one place."[33] Indeed, *The Terminator's* producers were sued for plagiarism by cult fantasy author Harlan Ellison,[34] whose screenplays for the television series *The Outer Limits, Soldier* and *Demon with a Glass Hand*, had featured warriors traveling back through time and changing their future. When a film has been written about as much as *The Terminator*, it is often instructive to skip back to original reviews to gauge the impact on contemporary critics. In Julian Petley's February 1985 *Monthly Film Bulletin* appraisal, it is Arnold Schwarzenegger as the time-traveling warrior, along with the film's female producer, Gale Anne Hurd, who receive most of the attention; Linda Hamilton and Sarah Connor are not mentioned at all. Writing in 2006, it is difficult for M. Keith Booker to avoid mentioning Sarah Connor, but it is interesting to note that his essay largely echoes Petley's focus on the impact of Schwarzenegger and the notion of "man vs. machine."[35]

Connor's importance is drawn out in Rebecca Keegan's celebration of

Cameron's life and work, *The Futurist*, but the director's quoted words initially seem confusing: "In writing I like to be fresh, and at the time of *The Terminator*, that kind of female character hadn't really been done."[36] "Fresh" may not be the most appropriate way to describe the traditional elements of Connor's character, nor indeed the traces of Dorothy's journey through Cameron's favorite, indeed "perfect," film, *The Wizard of Oz* (1939)[37]; however, there is one simple, key element that sets Connor apart from most female science fiction characters that had gone before. Although the space dedicated to Connor is limited, Booker's essay does provide a very important clue about what helps to make this female character "fresh":

> Meanwhile, the central female character, Hamilton's Sarah Connor, is certainly attractive, but her evolution in the course of the film from seemingly helpless girl to strong, capable woman … makes her far more than a conventional object of masculine desire. In particular, she provides a potential alternative object of *feminine* identification in the film.[38]

Central to Sarah Connor's revolutionary status in science fiction cinema is simple: her character develops. Ripley and Wheeler survive to the end of *Alien* and *Coma* but their characters, albeit objects of identification for female viewers, remain essentially the same: strong, opinionated and resourceful. In *The Terminator*, Cameron takes this a step further, by presenting Connor as a developing hero of her own journey through an action picture. This crucial factor is picked up by many later commentators, including the authors of *Empire* magazine's *The Ten Definitive Science Fiction Films of All Time*, who note that "her transformation over the course of the film is miraculous,"[39] and Martin Scorsese, who, in his 1993 introduction to the first British television broadcast of the uncut version of *The Terminator*, remarks on the transformation from "waitress to goddess."[40] To eliminate any doubt, Connor's transformation from waitress to warrior is cemented by the line of dialogue she is given just before finally crushing the cyborg: "you're terminated, fucker."

Revolutionary though this character development undoubtedly is, it still has its limitations. Once Connor has transformed from what Jackie Stacey describes as "classic feminine behaviour, forgetful, clumsy, unpunctual, and indecisive"[41] to what Heather Barker calls the "prototype Warrior,"[42] there is no turning back. In this instance, the call to adventure represents a narrative cusp point through which the pendulum of female representation has swung. The result is a simple characterization that reflects what Germaine Greer argues is a patriarchal preference for binary opposition. Greer focuses on the apparent need to identify non-linear gender differences as male or female[43]; however, this same desire to divide, categorize and polarize is used by Hélène Cixous and Catherine Clément to expose what they call "dual, hierarchical oppositions" in language in general, and in female descriptions in particular:

Where is she?
  Activity/Passivity
  Sun/Moon
  Culture/Nature
  Day/Night[44]

To Cixous and Clément, these binary oppositions contribute to the sub-jugation of women because they replace one aspect of the male-defined female with another. It is this "patriarchal pendulum" that limits Sarah Connor's devel-opment in *The Terminator*, as she can be either/or, but not both. In short: she is not a complex character. Once again, as with *Star Wars* and *Alien*, it is com-mercial acceptability that ultimately dictates female character limitations. Per-haps, then, the financial success of all three films would loosen some of the shackles for their respective sequels.

CRUCIBLE CHARACTERS

One of the criticisms leveled at *Star Wars* soon after its release in 1977 was its absence of non-white human characters. This complaint is magnified by the suggestion, documented by Adilifu Nama in *Black Space*, that "the aliens of the film signify black people"[45]—not least, the evil Darth Vader. Related issues have continued to follow *Star Wars*, as Anne Cranny-Francis demon-strates in her 1990 chapter, *Feminist Futures: A Generic Study*: "the characters Luke Skywalker, Han Solo and Princess Leia enact a patriarchal, bourgeois (liberal humanist), white supremacist narrative in a setting uncannily similar to today's USA."[46] The race issue was addressed in the 1980 *Star Wars* sequel, *The Empire Strikes Back*, although it is fair to say the inclusion of Billy Dee Williams as the "duplicitous"[47] Lando Calrissian did not satisfy everyone.

The first draft of *The Empire Strikes Back* was written by a woman, expe-rienced screen and science fiction writer Leigh Brackett; however, any hopes that existed for better on-screen roles for women were not met at that stage in the film's development. The only specified female speaking role in this early version, apart from Leia, is a nurse.[48] Brackett died of cancer shortly after deliv-ering her script to George Lucas, so it is impossible to know what further changes she would have made. The eventual, produced screenplay was written largely by Lawrence Kasdan from Lucas' notes.[49] The men removed the nurse, leaving Princess Leia as the only female character of note; however, they did realize that this high-profile returning role would need to develop in some way for the sequel.

Now wearing androgynous jump suits, rather than familiar feminine robes, Leia takes on the mantle of rebel leader. Her pep talk on Hoth, to X-wing fighter pilots, who are about to go to battle with the Empire, evokes the spirit of Queen Elizabeth I in her famous, self-written speech at Tilbury Docks, to her sailors as they prepare to face the Spanish invasion of England in 1588: "I am come..., in the midst and heat of the battle, to live or die amongst you all.... I know I have the body of a weak and feeble woman: but I have the heart and stomach of a king...."[50]

This particular character development seems to have had an impact on screenwriters Chris Weitz and Tony Gilroy, who give Jyn Erso a similar speech in *Rogue One*. It is an indication of how far female characters have come in the *Star Wars* galaxy that Felicity Jones's character is central to that 2016 film; whereas, back in the '80s, Carrie Fisher's gratitude for any sort of character development becomes clear in Robert Greenberger's interview with her for *Starlog* magazine on the set of the 1983 second sequel, *Return of the Jedi*: "'It is interesting that they give the female so much power,' says Fisher, and drops her voice, which takes on an ominous tone as she adds: '*And I get even more, now!*'"[51] All of this feels like an obvious consequence of the commercial success of *Alien*.[52] *Star Wars* had already combined traditional values with a more stubborn female stance, but now the latter was being lifted a little, leading to what *Starlog*'s cover describes as, "The Lovely & Lethal Princess Leia." However, this still feels like George Lucas' calculated attempt to meet the needs of a changing genre without taking too many commercial risks. For these, it is necessary to look to other sequels—and to James Cameron.

Ridley Scott's *Alien* had presented Ripley as the last of an ensemble crew, and Cameron's *The Terminator* had told Connor's story as her pendulum swung through her own cusp point on her journey from waitress to warrior. Characters in sequels, however, cannot easily have a pendulum swing; they cannot go back through the point of no return, so they have to do something else. Cameron was asked to write and direct the *Alien* sequel, *Aliens*, released in 1986. Following the success of *The Terminator*, he was in a good position to push Ripley much further than Leia would ever go. He also took the opportunity to create a far more complex character than he and Gale Anne Hurd had initially created with Connor. To do this, Ripley in *Aliens* would have to evolve; she would have to become multi-faceted.

Despite this seemingly modest aim, the notion of a female role developing into a fully-rounded character was not (and is still not) common to science fiction cinema. Heather Barker's useful argument, used in Chapter III to support a wide variety of female characters—whether they be mothers or astronauts—might be re-deployed here to support variation within an individual female character—allowing her to be a mother *and* an astronaut: "If we cannot even portray on screen the myriad of personalities and accurate gender ratios relating to our own world, then how can we even begin to explore strange new ones?"[53]

Attempts at multifaceted female roles had arguably been seen before, as far back as *Metropolis* (1927) and *Frau im Mond* (1929). Zira came close in *Planet of the Apes* and two sequels, before being pushed to the periphery and eventually killed off. In each of these of these cases, and others, the female characters are supports in male stories. Sarah Connor had been given her own story in *The Terminator*, but her character arc had been simple. John Pym's contemporary *Monthly Film Bulletin* review for *Aliens* describes it as "efficient," "busier," "less quirky" and "essentially unchanged" from *Alien*,[54] but what that misses is the fact that the sequel presents front-and-center the notion of a complex female character with her own story. The nature of that complexity is also important. Despite being debilitated by bad dreams, Ripley turns out to be the most mentally stable of the humans in this film; most of the others are soldiers, but she turns out to be the most resourceful and resilient; and she can switch from personal disdain for the company man, Burke, to compassionate empathy for the young girl, Newt, played by Carrie Henn, as the moment requires. The binary swing of the pendulum has been replaced with a complex, sometimes chaotic, crucible of characteristics, which Ripley dips into as she struggles to make meaning of her life.[55] The result is described by director, Tim Smit on IMDb.com as "survival of the fittest, corporate greed, feminism, and motherhood, all wrapped in a beautiful sci-fi shell"[56]; he continues, "Ripley went from

Surrogate daughter and intelligent fighter. Carrie Henn as Rebecca "Newt" Jorden and Sigourney Weaver as Lt. Ellen Ripley in *Aliens* (1986).

being a victim in *Alien* to a strong female leader providing us movie fans with an icon who is often imitated but hardly ever surpassed in film history. Game over, man. *Game over!*" Ripley's status as "victim" in *Alien* is debatable, but the point about imitation is well made. Smit has, however, chosen to avoid this in his own genre film, *Kill Switch*, which is advertised on the back of this IMDb editorial. Instead, he focuses on a man who saves his family from disaster. Game over, indeed.

The *Aliens* scene that has perhaps gained most attention, and some imitators, is Ripley's climactic fight with the alien queen using an industrial load-lifter. Protecting her surrogate child, Newt, whom she has returned to rescue, Ripley snarls the now iconic, line "Get away from her, you bitch!" In doing so, Ripley replaces the stock, trite battle of the sexes with a new hero's battle for survival. This, and the film around it, is a statement: if the fight is just, this woman will take on all comers. It is this essence that Cameron takes as his guide for his next science fiction sequel character development: Sarah Connor in *Terminator 2: Judgment Day* (1991)

Girls Will Be Boys

In many ways, Sarah Connor is a less rounded character than Ellen Ripley; but, ironically, it is James Cameron's mission to strengthen the female role that flattens her off. Between *Aliens* and *Terminator 2*, Cameron wrote and directed the 1989 feature *The Abyss*, which features Mary Elizabeth Mastrantonio as Dr. Lindsey Brigman, a brilliant but bitter marine architect, described by a male colleague as "Queen bitch of the universe"; it is a reputation that she revels in at times: "It's not easy being a cast-iron bitch. It takes discipline and years of training." Mastrantonio's character is revealed to be rather more nuanced than this as the film progresses, but it is Brigman's angry, almost comic, "man-hating feminist" sensibility that Cameron melds with Ripley's toughness to re-create Sarah Connor for *Terminator 2*.

Although Connor begins her sequel locked in a mental institution, she is essentially a full-fledged fighter from the start. The pendulum that swung to reveal the tough woman emerging from her hero's journey at the end *The Terminator* appears to be stuck here now, unable to move. This self-imposed restriction surely contributes to film critic, Amy Taubin's description of Connor as "a dumber, male-identified version of Ripley."[57]

Cameron's efforts to test the boundaries of the masculinized female produced a character with seemingly no reverse gear. Ripley's success had relied on a process described by Christine Cornea as "gender blending,"[58] rather than a wholesale move towards the masculine—not least through her maternal role.

After answering the call to adventure. Linda Hamilton as Sarah Connor in *Terminator 2: Judgment Day* (1991).

In *Terminator 2*, there is an attempt at a gender balance through the transposing of Sarah's spiritual role as a mother-of-the-future into the more corporeal mother-of-John figure; however, further evidence from the Special Edition suggests that Cameron was not fully committed to this deepening of his female lead for the theatrical release. The 1997, *Terminator 2* Special Edition restores scenes in which Kyle Reece, Connor's "supernatural guide" and lover in *The Terminator,* appears to her in a fantasy sequence. He lifts her spirits, encourages her to fight on and appeals to her role as a mother. Through her tears, Connor tells Reece that she loves him, eventually chasing him along a corridor in her satin nightdress. This short sequence softens, and so deepens, Sarah Connor's character; it reminds the audience of the sex scene in the original *Terminator* film and it projects Connor's femininity forward through the rest of the Special Edition. Removing the sequence leaves Connor as an angry, masculinized cipher. According to Rebecca Keegan, Cameron now views this as a mistake, as "its removal from the theatrical release meant Sarah Connor was all warrior."[59] Indeed, it reflects the younger Cameron's drive towards a self-contained, female, all-action hero, which works against what Booker sees as Connor's intended character development: "Hamilton's evolved Sarah is not really the kind of feminist icon that might seem threatening to some male egos."[60]

Cultural critic Lynne Magowan is not so sure. For her, Connor's character is "ultimately unhinged and hysterical."[61] The character loses all credibility for Magowan in the sequence in which Connor bursts into the home of Skynet scientist, Dr. Miles Dyson, threatening to kill him and his family. She is eventually talked down by her teenage son, John, but not before it is clear that she has lost perspective and control. For Magowan, Connor does not drive the narrative in *Terminator 2*; instead, she is swept along by a story in which she becomes an efficient killing machine solely to reinforce her role as a protective mother. Moral power and emotional focus now shifts to John, where it remains for the rest of the film, as Tony Rayns observes in his *Sight & Sound* review: "The price she has to pay for her independence, inevitably, is exclusion from the tremulous male bonding between her son and the T-800; it's hard to project her role beyond the final fade out."[62] Rayns' 1991 comment is prescient: Sarah Connor is a distant memory in the 2003 sequel, *Terminator 3: Rise of the Machines*, leaving Schwarzenegger's T-800 and the now-orphaned John alone to fend off a new, female, cyborg in the form of Kristanna Loken.[63]

Just as the success of *Star Wars* had helped to secure Leia's role in the sequels, the success of the *Alien* and *Terminator* movies would inspire many stock female science fiction imitators through the 1980s and '90s. However, films such as 1994's *A.P.E.X.*, described by Hardy as a *Terminator* "rip-off,"[64] miss the point. As does the 1995 film *Galaxis*, whose star, Brigitte Nielsen, had appeared ten years earlier mirroring Arnold Schwarzenegger in the fantasy film *Red Sonja*. Rather than replicate the human complexities and subtleties of Ripley's (proto)post-modern feminist, they emphasize the pseudo-lesbian, militarized and militant radical feminist of popular stereotype. Their model seems to be drawn equally from another *Aliens* character: the overtly masculinized Private Vasquez, played by a very taut and muscular Jenette Goldstein. Indeed, Cameron's screenplay even seems to predict audience and industry responses to this character in an exchange of dialogue between the male soldier, Hudson, and female Vasquez while she is warming up with behind-the-neck pull-ups:

> PRIVATE HUDSON: Hey Vasquez. Have you ever been mistaken for a man?
> PRIVATE VASQUEZ: No. Have you?

Hudson turns out to be a whiner and somewhat of a coward, which contributes further to *Aliens'* reversal of patriarchal expectations.

Christine Cornea writes in detail about the presentation of masculinity and femininity in her 2007 book, *Science Fiction Cinema: Between Fantasy and Reality*. She builds on a field of discussion that emerged earlier, as commentators responded to the notion that these masculinized women might feed the idea that all feminists wanted to emasculate men. Linda Mizejewski is rather more balanced in her approach when she discusses the parallel de-masculinization of men in films like *Total Recall* (1990). Her argument leans, as do others, towards a loss of gendered identity across the board.[65] Christine Cornea sums up one of the central issues in this wide-ranging debate: "the mere borrowing, by a female character, of what have been previously understood as masculine traits does not necessarily lead to a representation of equality between the sexes."[66]

To appropriate Laura Mulvey here, it might seem that creators of female characters in the 1980s and '90s were "torn between the deep blue sea of passive femininity and the devil of regressive masculinity."[67] Ultimately, it is hard to gauge whether these sweaty, muscular, gun-toting, kick-boxing heroines represent a feminist revenge response, or a just new projection of heterosexual male fantasy. In truth, however, despite the column inches dedicated to them over many discussions—including this one—these memorable women should perhaps be placed in perspective. That is, they might be more accurately described as prominent examples of a "general uplift" in female roles across science fiction cinema through the 1980s and early '90s.

A Thousand Faces

When women appeared as beautiful, cruel despots, destined to be destroyed by men with ray guns, it was easy to see what was going on. Science fiction was presenting "what if" scenarios, exploring the consequences, and then reverting to the preferred status quo: patriarchy. Developments in female representation through the 1980s and '90s generated far more complexity, making it increasingly difficult to make value judgments. Ripley's "strip" towards the end of *Alien* is described by Gallardo and Smith as "highly voyeuristic, highly sexual, and obviously written for an actress...."[68] This could also be used to describe Barbarella's strip at the beginning of her film. The presentation of Ripley, however, is balanced by many other factors; she is a more complex character than Barbarella. Roger Vadim's intentions are clear, Ridley Scott's are ambiguous, and so the debate about Ripley continues.

Then there is the notion of subjectivity: to suggest that a particular form of representation is right and another wrong is to deny the viewer his preference, her point of identification, or their imagination. The secretary might save the world, the politician might destroy it; the sexy astronaut might be the sole voice of reason and the waitress may become the mother of the savior of humanity. All have their *fortes*, each has her flaws. Perhaps the most important feature of female representation during the two decades that followed *Star Wars* is the apparent lifting of restrictions. For a while, the industry allowed its writers and directors the scope to explore what women could be, and audiences by-and-large accepted it. The result is a mélange of fascinating roles—some good, some bad, some ugly—that combine to populate the Golden Era of female representation in science fiction cinema.

This demonstration of diversity can be seen in the six *Star Trek* movies produced in the years following *Star Wars*—that is, those films featuring the original crew, including Lt. Uhura, played by Nichelle Nichols. The ride is not always smooth, but the direction of travel seems clear: during this period Captain Kirk leads his *Enterprise* crew from "where no man has gone before" to "where no man—no *one*—has gone before."[69]

WHERE NO WOMAN HAS GONE BEFORE?

Star Trek is a science fiction institution. What is now referred to as a "franchise" began life as a 1966 television show, whose success relied heavily on pulp genre themes and a strong relationship between its three leading male characters: Capt. Kirk, Mr. Spock and Dr. McCoy. Fifty years later, the same basic elements drive the recent film series—the third theatrical incarnation. *Star Trek*'s continued reliance on deep-rooted external and internal patriarchal and genre conventions has always made it difficult for women to break into. The narrative forces that compelled Ripley and Connor to develop in their sequels would only work here if returning female characters, such as Lt. Uhura, were give their own *Star Trek* stories. To date, this has not happened. Rather than develop established female characters, what the first movie series would attempt to do is present some new ones.

Although Paramount Pictures was emboldened enough by the success of *Star Wars* to reincarnate *Star Trek* as *The Motion Picture* in 1979, its producers clearly felt that references to the more serious *2001: A Space Odyssey* would give their film more *gravitas* than other action-adventure style movies being produced at the time. The result was rather slow and ponderous, and not generally well received by critics.[70] Despite being directed by Robert Wise, whose earlier genre works, *The Day the Earth Stood Still* (1951) and *The Andromeda Strain* (1970), had introduced significant female roles, *The Motion Picture* relies on static, patriarchal representations of female characters.

The most prominent of these is Lt. Ilia, a Deltan, played by former "Miss India," Persis Khambatta. Ilia is a figure of interest for the crew as soon as she arrives on the *Enterprise*; the reason for this is revealed in her first line of dialogue to Kirk: "My oath of celibacy is on record, Captain. May I resume my duties." So, within seconds, the professional nature of the female character is offset—undermined, even—by sexual intrigue, in what is another example of the give-with-one-hand-and-take-with-the-other mentality that has followed female representation through science fiction cinema history. It suggests that by 1979 Paramount felt obliged to include a professional woman, but not confident enough to let professionalism define her. Indeed, Nurse Chapel, played by Shannon Quinlan in the television series, had become Dr. Chapel, played by Majel Barrett for *The Motion Picture*; however, this promotion, and the fact that she was married to *Star Trek* creator Gene Roddenberry, does not appear to have qualified her to add anything important to the narrative. Ilia does become central to the plot of *The Motion Picture* when the computer-based entity, V'ger, abducts and replaces her with a perfect facsimile, replicating all of "her brain-patterns and memories." What the "mind of pure logic" does not replicate, however, is Lt. Ilia's Starfleet uniform; instead, V'ger sends her back in a very short, thigh-revealing, white jacket outfit, complete with high-heeled silver shoes. It is a logic-defying narrative distortion that reinforces the notion that Ilia has been included as a love/sex interest for the film. It is not the best of starts for the *Star Trek* motion picture series.

In 1977, Nichelle Nichols had been asked by NASA to help recruit more women and minority representatives to its astronaut program. Backed by her company, Women in Motion Inc., Nichols used the considerable influence afforded by her *Star Trek* profile to boost female applications to the program from fewer than 100 to 1,649; minority-group applications also rose: from 35 to 1,000.[71] This was clearly an achievement for Nichols in what feels like a progressive move by NASA; however, in his forensic examination, *Contest for the Heavens: The Road to the Challenger Disaster*, Claus Jensen offers an alternative perspective on this widening of NASA astronaut recruitment policies: "In a crew of seven or eight not everyone needed to be a superman or be made of the finest stuff. Older and younger astronauts joined the ranks, as did women."[72] Jensen goes on to suggest that the space agency was less than enthusiastic about this increasing diversity, seeing women (and other under-represented groups) in space during this period merely as a necessary evil, and a publicity exercise to secure government funding. It is tempting to imagine the same pressures being felt by commercial filmmakers at the time—at least, those anxious to be seen as inclusive.

If this anxiety did indeed exist, Walt Disney's response to it came in *The Black Hole*, released in the same year as *Star Trek: The Motion Picture*, 1979. Yvette Mimieux's role as the professional scientist and astronaut Dr. Kate McCrae is undermined by her reduction to damsel-in-distress for the film's formulaic climax; nevertheless, it represents a giant step forward from her part as the mute slave-girl and victim, Weena, in the 1960 classic, *The Time Machine*. If any acting career can be used to demonstrate the shift in female representation in science fiction over time, it is Mimieux's. Dr. McCrae mostly plays second fiddle to her male colleagues, but she also pre-dates Dr. Sally Ride's historic flight as America's first real-life female in space by four years. A rather more gritty space-based role is taken by Frances Sternhagen in the 1981 Sean Connery vehicle, *Outland*, a version of the classic 1952 Western, *High Noon*. Sternhagen plays the irascible Dr. Marian Lazarus, the medical officer on a mining colony. This is not her story, but in a rare departure for the genre, it is Dr. Lazarus who stands alone with the hero for the dramatic climax of the film.

Back on the USS *Enterprise*, things were changing too. Although the second *Star Trek* feature shrewdly looks back to the original television series for story inspiration,[73] 1982's *The Wrath of Khan* would need to look to the future for its female roles. As a result, Kirstie Alley joins the crew as the efficient, intelligent Vulcan, Saavik, and Bibi Besch appears as geneticist, Dr. Carol Marcus. To further emphasize the break with the past, Dr. Marcus is Kirk's former wife—and it transpires that it was she who left him. Of course, Dr. Marcus' role as a "soft" scientist, the classic female science role discussed in Chapter III, does root this role in some level of tradition; however, given Jane Killick's description of the traditional *Star Trek* female as "captain's crumpet,"[74] it is clear that some distance has been traveled already from the television series. Indeed, in her 1992 *Starburst* article, "Star Trek Sex: The Female Frontier," Killick identifies two particular examples of "misogyny" in the original episodes. In the first, a beautiful, female android dies "moments after she breaks her programming to become an independent human being"; in the second, when Kirk swaps bodies with an ambitious, beautiful, female alien, "the episode treats women's ambition as something malevolent."[75]

Whether these examples constitute overt misogyny or casual oversight is hard to say, but Killick's general point about lax approaches to the integrity of female roles is reasonable. A similar attitude is taken towards Saavik in *The Wrath of Khan*. At the beginning of the movie, she fails the *Kobayashi Maru* test, in which trainee captains are given a no-win scenario that always results in the destruction of their starship. The test, which takes place in a simulator, is designed to challenge the student captain and to build character. It can be argued initially that, despite her humiliation, Saavik's treatment has been no different from that of other Starfleet trainees: they were all tested and they all failed. All except James T. Kirk, that is. When this fact is discovered, the level playing field that the female Saavik had been on is tilted in favor of the male. It may seem subtle, but it is another example of the chipping away at female success and the glorification of male success that has always destabilized equality in science fiction cinema. For an indication that this has continued into the 21st century, look no further than the 2009 franchise reboot feature, *Star Trek*. A lengthy sequence in this film revisits, and expands on, Kirk's victory in the no-win *Kobayashi Maru*. A year after *The Wrath of Khan*, in 1983, strides that had been made to level Princess Leia's playing field faltered when she was given a gold bikini to wear in *Return of the Jedi*. This retreat prompted Heather Barker to write: "She was a sarcastic and spunky idea which unfortunately got hopelessly lost as the trilogy unfolded."[76]

In 1984, Helen Mirren reversed this trend a little with her practical, savvy and well-rounded Russian spaceship captain, Tanya Kirbuk, in *2010*, the sequel to *2001: A Space Odyssey*. In the same year, *Starman's* re-visit to the plot of *The Day the Earth Stood Still* places Karen Allen in a more traditional role as grieving wife Jenny Hayden; but, as in the 1951 template, it is the woman who stands by the male alien when all around them is danger and chaos. These are watchwords for the new female characters in the next *Star Trek* feature: *The Search for Spock*, released in 1984. When the "soft" scientist, Dr. Carol Marcus, had created the "Genesis Probe" in *The Wrath of Khan*, the writers might have been accused of womanizing the weapon; in what might be called its "coming of age" movie, the franchise would now begin to weaponize its women—in the form of Klingons. This seems to be a popular decision, as female Klingons, the warriors of the galaxy, reappear to take more prominent roles in the fifth and sixth *Star Trek* movies: *The Final Frontier* (1989) and *The Undiscovered Country* (1991).

Before that, the series returns to more traditional fare with the 1986 film: *Star Trek IV: The Voyage Home*, in which the *Enterprise* crew time-travels to Earth of 1986, in order to find a whale to bring back to save their future Earth. Significant to this plot is Catherine Hicks as cetacean biologist, Dr. Gillian Taylor—a whale specialist. Leaving aside this "soft" scientist role, Dr. Taylor serves as a guide for the, now socially inept, crew from the future, as they navigate this new world of the past. In her essay, "Between the Boys and Their Toys," Susan Thomas demonstrates how the film *Short Circuit*, released in the same year as *The Voyage Home*, presents Ally Sheedy as Stephanie Speck, an intermediary between a futuristic robot and a socially inept male scientist. The sexual and scopophilic tensions prove more problematic than in the *Star Trek* film, but it is interesting to note that both films lean on the female-as-mediator role that stretches back through the genre to silent films discussed in Chapter I. Even the female Klingon, Azetbur, played by Rosana DeSoto in *The Undiscovered Country*, eventually becomes a mediator, in a bid to broker peace between the Federation and the Klingon Empire, stating, "War is obsolete, General, as we are in danger of becoming."

In fact, it is the female Vulcan who becomes obsolete in this film. Now in the form of Lt. Valeris, played by Kim Cattrall, she carries much of the intelligence and *gravitas* of Spock and the female Saavik in earlier films; however, there is a development: Lt. Valeris betrays her fellow *Enterprise* crew members.

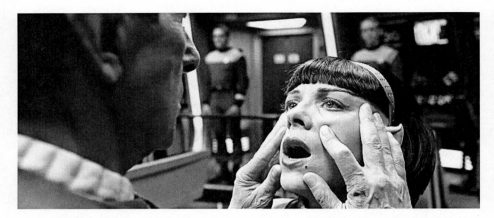

Leonard Nimoy as Mr. Spock interrogates Kim Cattrall as Vulcan Lt. Valeris in
Star Trek VI: The Undiscovered Country **(1991).**

This act does not necessarily reflect misogyny on the part of the film's writers, after all, both female and male characters have right to go rogue; however, it does lead to an extraordinary scene in which Spock forces Valeris to reveal her thoughts in a Vulcan mind-meld. Criminal or not, Lt. Valeris' obvious distress makes it difficult to watch this scene without regarding Spock's act as a violation of the female—perhaps even as a form of rape.

    Star Trek movies do not tell women's stories. As Killick points out: "What everyone wanted to see when they went to the cinema was Kirk, Spock and McCoy reprising their familiar roles. The female characters could only be peripheral, and were not allowed to assume power."[77] This ethos is abundantly clear in the film barely mentioned above: *Star Trek V: The Final Frontier.* Hampered by an unoriginal premise, immature dialogue, and an improbable screenplay, this fails even to hit its basic marks.[78] Largely a display of male bonding and impotent machismo, the film not only halts the cycle's development of female characters, but even reduces their significance to a level unprecedented in any *Star Trek* incarnation. Lt. Uhura is, of course, present as a member of the USS *Enterprise* crew, but her central scene, in which she performs a semi-naked dance to divert the attentions of male guards, serves only to expose this character to ridicule. Nichols' dance is used by Christopher Tookey, perhaps rather unkindly, to exemplify the advancing ages of the principal male actors of the series: "Lieutenant Uhura's dance of the seven veils might pass muster in a glamorous granny competition, but is embarrassing in any other context."[79]

    Despite some developments in female roles through the original film series, it is clear that what *Star Trek* does best is shoe-horn women into patriarchal frameworks. Nichelle Nichols observed this from the beginning, noting that director, Robert Wise, "brought to *Star Trek: The Motion Picture* a new, all-encompassing vision of how our 'universe' would look and sound, and for the cast that meant unisex." Nichols was not happy with this; she continues:

> I really disliked the bland unisex approach, not simply because it was unattractive, but that it just wasn't Uhura. Bob Wise had made it clear that he did not want to see fingernail polish, jewelry, or any other personal extraneous adornment. When I showed up on the set with Uhura's long silver nails, jade earrings, and high heeled boots, he was not pleased, but I argued that it was right for Uhura. When they finally submitted to the court of last resort—Gene [Roddenberry]—he agreed. "Absolutely," he said. "This is not the military, and that is Uhura expressing her individuality. Besides she's a special woman."[80]

The steady, modest integration of diverse female roles—Uhura, Saavik, Azetbur, Valeris—into a domain as patriarchal as *Star Trek* can be taken as a good indication that things were changing across the genre as a whole. Indeed, *Star Trek*'s conservative stance is close to where the heart of the genre lies. As a result, its female roles are more representative of the period than the celebrated, masculinized examples discussed earlier in this chapter. Would science fiction cinema's natural gravity be enough to pull the female characters back into line, or would her new-found energy enable her to escape once and for all?

——— ∞∞∞ ———

Women's roles came a long way in the two decades that followed 1977: there is little doubt that this was a golden era, characterized by increased diversity, visibility, quantity and quality across female characters. In truth, however, much of that success rests on the profile of very few characters, and these have become icons, not just for women in the genre, but for the genre itself. Ripley led the way with guns, guts and attitude because her success in this most male of realms blurred the distinctions between masculine and feminine. The question, then, is where does female representation go from there? Will it develop? Can it develop? In many ways, this period laid the foundations for female representation in 21st century science fiction cinema; however, the line between the two points is not as straight, and the legacy not as direct, as might first seem. The genre's post–1970s women did not enjoy an inexorable rise to glory; instead, their progress was diverted by a series role reversals and pastiche performances that would temporarily turn the foundation stone into a gravestone. Ironically, the era that had opened with an alien's death would close with an alien resurrection....

VI

Dangerous Times
Identity Crises and
a Millennial Mélange

Give a woman a gun and she'll be poster-girl for the genre; teach her to respect the gun and she'll become a *bona fide* hero. By the mid–1990s, it began to feel as though the struggle for female representation in science fiction cinema had been won. Women were accepted—and expected—in roles previously reserved for men. They could now be whatever they wanted to be. The battle was over. However, careful attention to movies of the period reveals a subtle shift: fewer prominent female characters were driving the narrative. Echoing the experience of their professional colleagues of the 1950s, women were once again becoming conspicuous elements in films about *men*. Something had gone wrong. In the cut-throat world of blockbuster cinema, a successful formula is all too often mistaken as the formula for success. Imitation replaces innovation, and so science fiction cinema soon seemed more interested in poster-girls than protagonists. But worse was to come, as feminist icons found themselves in a new struggle with a familiar patriarchal beast: the backlash.

―∞―

Familiar Undercurrents

Choose any film in any genre at any time and all sorts of representations will be found. Whether these are good, bad or indifferent will be affected by subjectivity and focus. This book is not about disability, so it can have little to say about whether Dominique Pinon's Vriess in *Alien: Resurrection* (1997) or Peter Sellers' Doctor Strangelove are reasonable portrayals of characters who are also wheelchair users. The same applies to race, religion, sexuality, class and so forth. Focusing on the representation of a particular category brings dangers, not least the sense that the author is "looking for trouble"; that is, trying to find damning evidence of discrimination against the subject group. It should, however, be clear by now that women have indeed been discriminated against in science fiction cinema. Their representation is affected by male power and its adherence to narrative traditions in the pursuit of commercial gain: men, myths and mammon. It is not difficult to find "trouble" because it is always there, bubbling under the surface.

Chapter V of this history gives the impression of a generally linear progression in the development of female roles in science fiction film, as women advanced from doing some meaningful things in the narrative to having their own stories told and then sometimes to driving the narrative and making decisions. Of course, the reality is a little more nuanced than this. The slow, grudging integration of woman into the *Star Trek* film franchise, accompanied by a few blips and reversals, is an indication that not everyone was as keen as James Cameron to give women a rifle and a *raison d'être*. Reflecting the wild, watershed years of the 1960s, many producers, faced with the developing trends in the 1980s and '90s, just did not know what to do with their women. As a result, a combination of inertia, resentment, fear and opposition led many filmmakers to kick back against the changes—or at least to ignore them. To add depth to this survey, therefore, it is important to return briefly to the 1980s to chart the undercurrents that would eventually lead to the end of the "Golden Era."

Old Habits Die Hard

Back in 1977, visual effects had contributed greatly to the success of *Star Wars* and *Close Encounters of the Third Kind*; between them, they took all of the visual and technical prizes at the 1978 Academy Awards ceremony. Lucasfilm, with its subsidiary ILM, headed a transformation in cinema effects, that eventually led to the revolution in digital graphics and projection that is still being felt today.[1] Other production companies in the 1980s renewed their conviction that the genre is the natural home for the kind of high-profile effects that draw the attention of awards panels. Walt Disney had tested the space-spectacle route with modest commercial success in their 1979 film *The Black Hole*, but in 1982, the studio leaned on its legacy as an animation specialist to make a graphically enhanced, live-action classic.

Steven Lisberger's *TRON* looks like no other science fiction movie—certainly nothing released before the CGI era. It tells the story of Flynn, a male computer hacker played by Jeff Bridges, who becomes trapped inside a computer, teams up with the male title-character and his male friend, and fights the malevolent male forces of the Master Computer Program and his hench-man. Many of these ideas would re-emerge twenty years later in the 2003 *The Matrix* sequels, *Reloaded* and *Revolutions*. Scientifically, *TRON* is naïve, even silly, but despite Phil Hardy's description of it as "in effect a video version of *Fantastic Voyage* (1966),"² it does try to present something original. *TRON* is a unique, landmark science fiction film; its treatment of women, however, feels rather familiar.

Susan Thomas points out that Lora, played by Cindy Morgan, is initially indispensable to Flynn as a mediator between the human world and the machine world, but "once the balance of power is restored Lora is rediscovered as a threat."³ That may be a little strong, but she certainly has no further role in the film. At the end of *TRON*, Lora's computer alter-ego Yori (who, inciden-tally, now has a 21st century *Twitter* account describing her as "A smart, pretty program"⁴), becomes the film's love interest for a few minutes, before Flynn returns to the safety of his own machines. In so doing, he aptly reflects a genre and an industry that regularly returns to traditional plots and characters in the face of new, expensive technologies. It happened with the introduction of sound, color and widescreen, and it happened at every new special-effects cycle—including the widespread introduction of computer graphics. *TRON*'s new vision is used to tell an old tale of male derring-do with female support. To see an example of how expensive effects continued to affect the represen-tation of women, look no further than the heterosexual-male-fantasy figures of Gem and her fellow "sirens," played by Olivia Wilde, Serinda Swain, Yaya DeCosta and Elizabeth Mathis, in the 2010 sequel *TRON: Legacy*.

Picking up on the trend developed in the 1970s, tales about men and their machines continued into the 1980s in films like *Firefox*, a 1982 vehicle (literally) for Clint Eastwood as a USAF pilot. *WarGames* (1983) features another male computer hacker—and another technically illiterate female mediator and voice-of-reason, in the form of Ally Sheedy's Jennifer. A boy who is good at computer games is drafted into an alien fighting corps in the 1984 movie, *The Last Starfighter*, and in 1985, the boy actually becomes the machine in *D.A.R.Y.L.* In the highest grossing movie of that year, Michael J. Fox as Marty McFly travels back in time in a DeLorean car for *Back to the Future*. The plot leaves his girl-friend, another Jennifer, played by Claudia Wells, asleep on the porch in 1985, while Marty chases after his own mother in 1955. It is a token-support role for Wells, but the scenario does give Lea Thompson, as Marty's young future mother, Lorraine, one of the wittiest lines in all science fiction cinema. Tired of Marty's moralizing and ignorant of who he really is, she admonishes her future son: "Marty, you're beginning to sound just like my mother."

Only science fiction cinema could set up and deliver this pay-off line. It certainly has a rich store of mothers from which to draw the cultural memory. Lorraine may not be the mother of the future savior of humanity, but, like Sarah Connor, she is essential to the existence of the male protagonist, who becomes more central as the film series develops.

In 1986, *Short Circuit*, as mentioned before by Susan Thomas, sees a woman mediate between men and their machines, and in the revisit to the 1958 genre classic *The Fly* in the same year, Geena Davis gets caught up, along with some prostitutes, as her man attempts to tame nature through technology. The 1987 movie *InnerSpace* is a re-tread—more so than *TRON*—of the classic *Fantastic Voyage*, but this time the incredible journey is an exclusively male affair. In the same year, **batteries not included* does make an attempt to pair women and machines, but Jessica Tandy is somewhat wasted in this Spielberg-produced attempt to reproduce the cute-alien dynamic of his *E.T. the Extra-Terrestrial*, which had been the highest grossing film of 1982. Incidentally, *E.T.* essentially takes the story of *The Day the Earth Stood Still*, leaves the alien as male, but gives Helen Benson's role to a boy. As he had done in *Close Encounters*, Spielberg (now in cooperation with screenwriter Melissa Mathison) makes *E.T.*'s primary female role a pseudo–1950s suburban American mother, played by Dee Wallace. The sidelined female is, of course, not new to science fiction cinema; she has been seen throughout this study: from her absence in the silent period, though her domesticity in the 1950s to her token presence in the 1970s. These representations undoubtedly reduce the impact of women in the genre; however, they surely do less harm than the reduction to a mechanized, sexual commodity that she experiences in what is one of the most misogynistic mainstream science fiction films of the 1980s.

Cherry 2000 was released in 1987. It features Melanie Griffith as the human, E. Johnson, and Pamela Gidley as Cherry, a life-partner robot whose primary talent is indicated in the film with the line, "When you get one of these fired up, it's like slamming an octopus." Sex permeates science fiction movies of the mid–1980s, from the relatively tame *Weird Science* (1985), through the exploitative nudity of the *Mad Max*-inspired *Desert Warrior* (1985), to the even more overt Polish film, *Seksmisja* (*The Sex Mission*, 1984). Sex robots are not new to the genre either; however, *Cherry 2000* is notable for its attempts to imbue its gynoid with a personality—and then blithely disregarding it. Indeed, the ability to distil a female "spirit" drives the plot of this extension to the genre's "men and their machines" strand.

When his Cherry 2000 model breaks, Sam takes her personality chip, places it (her) in his pocket and goes in search of an identical physical replacement for his beloved robot. The movie charts Sam's dangerous quest through a wasteland—where women are victims of brutalization and rape by vigilante

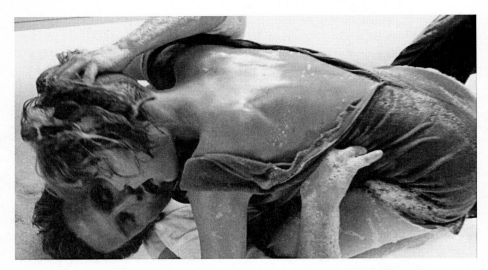

"It's like slamming an octopus." Pamela Gidley as the Cherry 2000 gynoid, on top of David Andrews as Sam, in *Cherry 2000* (1987).

men—and onto his relationship with E. Johnson, who features, holding a large gun, on the posters for this movie. Johnson helps Sam to find a replacement body for Cherry, into which he installs the personality chip. His "perfect woman" is back in his possession. By now, however, affection between Johnson and Sam has convinced him that he would rather be with the human woman. This might be considered a positive move in his emotional development, were it were not for the manner in which Sam leaves Cherry. He asks her to fetch him a cola, which she of course does unquestioningly, then Sam and Johnson fly away, leaving Cherry alone at the vending machine in the wilderness. It is a moment of genuine pathos, of pity felt by the viewer—if not the filmmaker.

There is an attempt to vindicate Sam's callous rejection of Cherry by showing her left in ignorant bliss—she is, after all, merely a robot—but this ending really only reinforces the misused and misplaced patriarchal power that underpins *Cherry 2000*. In so doing, it also serves as a proxy for the science fiction film industry. One notable, previous, misogynistic low-point had been the 1975 film *A Boy and His Dog*. But even though its final scene suggests that the girlfriend, played by Susanne Benson, has been eaten by the male protagonists, that film somehow feels less callous because it does not linger on the final moments of its discarded female. In *Cherry 2000*, it seems that the male protagonist is allowed to assume an existence without a conscience because the female is assumed not to be conscious of her existence.

Knowledge Is Power

The eventual fate of Cherry is far removed from that of Ava, the gynoid played by Alicia Vikander, who takes control of her own existence at the end of in the 2015 British film, *Ex Machina*. While Alex Garland's award-winning film does present its synthetic female possessions naked at various points, its primary focus is the 21st century science fiction cinema's preoccupation: artificial intelligence. This has been explored recently through prominent female characters in *Her* (2013) and *Lucy* (2014), as well as the television series *Humans* (2015) and *Westworld* (2016), all of which will be returned to in Chapter VII. Back in the 1980s, when home computers were beginning to appear on the domestic market, the brain of the female computer was more likely to be dismissed than engaged in phenomenological and existentialist debate.

There is a curious scene involving a female-voiced chess computer close to the beginning of John Carpenter's 1982 remake of the 1951 genre classic *The Thing from Another World!* Kurt Russell, as MacReady in *The Thing*, is playing a game against the computer, voiced by Adrienne Barbeau. She announces, "Check-mate"; unhappy at this, MacReady pours whisky into the memory-card slot of the machine and mutters, "Cheating bitch!" The computer sparks, smokes and dies. From a narrative-logic perspective, this makes no sense: MacReady and his colleagues are, after all, snowed into an Antarctic research station with precious few forms of entertainment. From a female representation perspective, MacReady's action is viewed by teacher and feminist Lynne Magowan as "a clear example of symbolic annihilation of the woman."[5] Whether this is the intended message is unclear; however, Bill Lancaster's screenplay for *The Thing* contains no further female characters. The 1951 original, *The Thing from Another World!*, unsurprisingly has no computers, but it does contain the scene described in Chapter III, in which Nikki Nicholson, played by Margaret Sheridan, saves the Antarctic base with her knowledge of domestic science. Gendered science is discussed in those earlier chapters in relation to "soft" and "hard" disciplines, but this example widens the discussion to encompass the general notion of gendered knowledge.

Cognitive science—which studies the perception, understanding and acquisition of knowledge—envisages society as a potentially predictable, ordered mechanism. By asking if all problems can be solved intellectually, rather than emotionally, cognitive science feeds on, and in turn feeds, the idea of a purely scientific world.[6] This, of course sits at the heart of many of science fiction's "what-if" concepts, although not necessarily the human responses in its stories. In his book *Celebrating the Other: A Dialogic Account of Human Nature*, first encountered above in Chapter I's discussion of the Self and the Other,

Edward Sampson interrogates the idea of cognition: "What is the source of this order, meaning, and intelligent behaviour? The cognitivist's answer: the individual's mind—often the individual's brain."[7]

Sampson goes on to argue that, by placing emphasis on the individual as the potential site of all knowledge, cognitive science goes further than all other Self-celebratory theories in reducing the value of the Other. It follows then that the man doing things on the cinema screen—the male Self—would potentially be strengthened by the idea that knowledge too is perceived as male. This is more or less what Elizabeth Cowie suggests in her discussion of the 1976 film *Coma* when she states that Dr. Susan Wheeler "is given a pre-eminently masculine trait, the desire for knowledge...."[8] Sampson goes further, arguing that the creation of pure knowledge, unfettered by emotion, and at the expense of all forms of Other, serves to reinforce an already dominant ideology. If this is true, then cognition—part of the bedrock of science fiction—supports a white, heterosexual, male vision of the universe, and so by extension normalizes the white, heterosexual, male gaze.[9]

An example of this can be seen in developments through versions of H.G. Wells' 1898 novel *War of the Worlds*. In the original book, the alien invasion of Earth is halted by God, using infectious organisms to which the visitors have no immunity. In Byron Haskin's 1953 movie, male scientists are on the way to developing their own bacterial weapon, but nature beats them to it. In the 1996 virtual remake, *Independence Day*, human male knowledge triumphs over the aliens, despite the logic flaw highlighted in the witty question posed in Caroline Westbrook's *Empire* magazine article, "Incoherence Day?," "And how ... is [Jeff] Goldblum *able* to download said virus from a normal, ordinary, earthly computer to one that has probably never caught a whiff of Windows 95...?[10] Steven Spielberg's 2005 version of *War of the Worlds* brings the sequence full-circle by returning victory to "the tiniest creatures that God in his wisdom put upon this earth."[11]

As Judy Wajcman demonstrates many times in *Feminism Confronts Technology*, social structures have regularly gendered knowledge—especially scientific and technical knowledge—as male.[12] Despite counter-examples, such as Joyce Hendron's mastery (itself a masculinized term) of the "Differential Analyzer" in *When Worlds Collide* (1951), science fiction cinema regularly places knowledge in the minds of male characters, who then share it with female characters, who in turn serve as proxies for lay members of the audience. This happens in *WarGames*, when David explains to Jennifer how computers, modems and so forth, work. Explaining digital technology to 1980s' teenagers is one thing, but when Yvette Mimieux's Dr. Kate McCrae is used as a substitute for ignorant viewers in *The Black Hole*, it begins to look like her function is

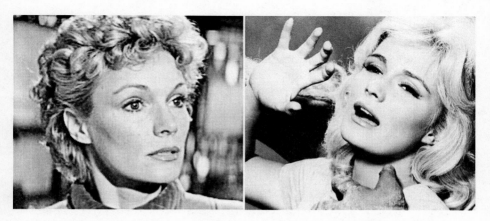

So far and yet so near. Yvette Mimieux as Dr. Kate McCrae in *The Black Hole* (1979), and as Weena in *The Time Machine* (1960).

merely as a foil for the male Dr. Durant's delivery of the necessary exposition: "The most destructive force in the Universe, Harry: nothing can escape from it, not even light." Dr. McCrae responds with a statement which clearly outlines her information as given: "I had a professor who predicted that, eventually, black holes would devour the entire universe." The value of McCrae's contribution is then further reduced, as her male colleague confirms the validity of her statement with another of his own: "Why not? When you can see giant suns sucked in and disappear without a trace." Exposition aside, the message given in these early exchanges in *The Black Hole* is that the male scientist's knowledge is his own, but the female scientist's knowledge is second-hand.

First-hand female knowledge in science fiction cinema comes most readily in the form of computers, but, once again, 1980s filmmakers often used this as an opportunity to perpetuate gender stereotypes through the anthropomorphization—the overlaying of human behaviors—of the female artificial intelligence. When V'ger, the "mind of pure logic" starts to appear irrational in *Star Trek: The Motion Picture*, even the logical Spock gives it a gender: "V'ger is as child, Captain. We should treat her as such."

The "computer metaphor" has been a favored tool for cognitive scientists attempting to isolate the organizing structures and principles within the human mind. As Sampson suggests, it enables them to "look at the computer and find an information-processing device that will serve as a perfect model of the human mind."[13] Anthropomorphization and then gendering of computers has a direct effect on their characters. A generalized rule can be drawn from the difference between HAL in *2001: A Space Odyssey* and Nell, the mother computer in the 1980 movie, *Battle Beyond the Stars*: male computers think; female computers feel.[14]

Indeed, a similar conclusion can be drawn from a comparison between HAL and his female counterpart, SAL, voiced by Candice Bergen, in the *2001* sequel *2010*, released in 1984. The new film takes trouble to explain HAL's murderous actions in *2001* as a logical result of his programming; whereas SAL's logical and cognitive capabilities are de-emphasized. Like V'ger, she is treated—and acts—like a child. Before being disconnected, as part of a test, SAL asks her male creator, Dr. Chandra, "Will I dream?" Chandra replies, "Of course you will. All intelligent beings dream." SAL is not seen again. Later, the viewer is reminded of SAL's question, when the same is asked by the reinstated HAL. This time Dr. Chandra considers his answer, before replying, "I don't know." It is a more honest answer, betraying a perceived bond between men and their computing machines.[15]

In her survey of science fiction cinema, *Between Fantasy and Reality*, Christine Cornea extends the notion of gendered cognition to include what she calls the "mind/body dichotomy"[16] in the 1995 film *Johnny Mnemonic*. She notes that Jane, played by Dina Meyer, receives modifications that enhance her body, whereas the male hero's alterations expand his mind: he is presented as "logical and unemotional." Back in 1982, that mind/body dichotomy is central to the existential philosophy that underpins one of the most celebrated science fiction movies of all time.

"I'M NOT *IN* THE BUSINESS—I *AM* THE BUSINESS"

Although it was slow initially to make an impact at the box office in 1982, *Blade Runner*'s reputation and following has grown considerably since. By 1996, Paul M. Sammon was claiming on the cover of his book, *Future Noir: The Making of Blade Runner*, that Scott's film was the "most influential SF film ever made." That is hard to quantify; however, it is undoubtedly true that *Blade Runner* remains a unique, landmark science fiction film; its treatment of women, however, feels rather familiar. And that previous sentence may be familiar too; it was applied above to *TRON*, released in the same year. Scott's soaring technical vision and high-concept science fiction, like Lisberger's, takes very few risks with plot and character, choosing instead to source them from tried-and-tested filmic and genre traditions.

Blade Runner is set in a murky, dystopian LA of 2019, where it seems always to be raining. It essentially tells the stories of two male characters. Rick Deckard is a down-at-heel detective whose job it is to hunt down and kill illegal androids—or "replicants." Roy Batty is a replicant who has arrived on Earth to seek his male maker. Batty hopes that Dr. Tyrell will be able to extend his in-built, 4-year life-span. He cannot. In the film's long, climactic chase and confrontation sequence, Batty, having killed Tyrell, saves his own would-be killer, Deckard, before delivering a final, dying monologue, in which he talks about his memories being lost in time "like tears in rain." Touched by this display of "humanity," Deckard is moved to re-evaluate his own existence, an act that is given significance in the 1992 Director's Cut, which hints at the notion that Deckard is himself a replicant.

One assessment of the treatment of the female characters in *Blade Runner* appears in Marleen Barr's 1991 essay, "Metahuman 'Kipple' Or, Do Male Movie Makers Dream of Electric Women?"

> The male replicants are menacing and strong while the females are provocative to the point of exaggeration. It is reasonable to expect a bleached blonde Pris-as-pleasure object to appear dressed in a short skirt revealing her garters. But, is it really necessary for Zhora to die while running through the city in panties, metallic bra, boots, and transparent raincoat?[17]

Even Paul Sammon appears to have misgivings about the treatment of women: "Most tellingly, both of Deckard's 'retirements' are women—and he shoots one in the back."[18] Zhora, played by Joanna Cassidy, is actually shot multiple times and lacerated by glass as she stumbles to her death in slow-motion. The "retirement" of Darryl Hannah's Pris is also presented in disturbing, graphic detail—unlike that of any of the male characters. The nature of the female deaths may have added to Barr's complaint that Zhora, despite being a combat replicant, is re-framed as a pleasure-model replicant, joining Pris as an object of desire. They join the serviceable Others discussed in Chapter I, which, as Barr points out, "can be understood as one group's power to define and control another group."[19] Ultimately, Zhora and Pris are of little more narrative significance than the robot sex-workers that Ridley Scott inserts into the background to give "science fiction texture" to his 2017 *Alien* re-tread, *Alien: Covenant.*

The title of Barr's essay refers to *Blade Runner*'s source novel. Philip K. Dick's 1969 short story, "Do Androids Dream of Electric Sheep?" In this text, Deckard's object of desire is an expensive bio-engineered sheep, which he keeps as both a pet and a status symbol. In *Blade Runner*, Deckard's possessive attentions switch to Dr. Tyrell's personal assistant, Rachael, played by Sean Young, who is revealed as a replicant early in the film. This transfer of male possessive attention supports Barr's central argument that *Blade Runner* has "speciesism as its subject and sexism as its unconscious component."

Indeed, Deckard's treatment of Rachael, especially during the scene in which he forces her to kiss him, has attracted much critical attention, including from Cornea: "The aggression with which he approaches Rachel seems totally uncalled for and rather shocking in context of their relationship up to this point."[20]

Perceived sexism may also be connected to Rachael's alignment with one of cinema's stock female object-of-desire characters: the *femme fatale*. This figure is most readily found in the classic *films noirs*—typically 1940s' American movies with a sense of foreboding and menace, often employing smoke and shadow to add to the mood. The "fatal woman" is a beautiful, seductive lure for the male hero, who is motivated by her charms to do something that he might otherwise not do. Rachael's role as *femme fatale* has been suggested by many commentators, often building on *Blade Runner*'s general connection with *film noir*; however, she does not fit the mold entirely. Rachael looks the part and she certainly contributes to Deckard's out-of-character decisions, but she is not necessarily plotting his downfall or using her femininity to get her way in the manner that is expected of the classic *femme fatale*. She is fatal in so far that she kills the replicant Leon to save Deckard, but it is never quite clear what Rachael's intentions are towards the hero. This can, of course, be interpreted as a strength of the character. Director Scott makes much of the silences in *Blade Runner*; in her own silences, Rachael may be scheming, or she may be pondering her existence, but her self-interrogation never seems to extend much beyond tearful cognizance of her own impotence. As a result, Rachael appears as an unwitting innocent—a child lost in a world of adults.

In her essay, "Ramble City: Postmodernism and *Blade Runner*," Giuliana Bruno suggests that, despite possessing artificial memories, Rachael attaches more value to the tangible photograph of her mother: "that photograph represents the trace of an origin and thus a personal identity, the proof of having existed and therefore of having the right to exist."[21] Like the cinema spectator, Rachael chooses to suppress the fact that the image might be an artificial construct. For this reason, the viewer might be less likely to condemn Rachael's seeming resistance to existential enquiry. Cornea reads an additional layer of meaning into the photograph: "The film also implies that what they are really seeking is the lost mother; a mother that will provide them with a secure historical lineage and a sense of subject-hood."[22] This suggestion is supported by the fact that Leon kills his interrogator at the mention of his mother. Once again, the mother is being use by science fiction as a touchstone for humanity.

Whatever the reading, and whatever the effect it has on perceptions of Rachael, it remains the case that most of the cognitive reasoning in *Blade Runner* is done by the male characters. Indeed, Roy Batty's ontological and existentialist enquiries arguably position him as the most "human" of the film's characters. His encounter with his "father," Tyrell, shares many of the Freudian Oedipal

Future *femme fatale.* **Sean Young as the replicant Rachael in** *Blade Runner* (1982).

entanglements that deepen Luke Skywalker's confrontations with his estranged father, first in *The Empire Strikes Back* (1980) and later *Return of the Jedi* (1983). This is, of course, another trope of science fiction, but one with far more significance than Rachael's drift through the lives of powerful men. As she points out to Deckard in what is a candidate for the most apt line of dialogue spoken by any woman in science fiction cinema: "I'm not *in* the business—I *am* the business."

It is perfect description for the journey that Sigourney Weaver and Ellen Ripley would take as their roles began to develop through the "Golden Era" of female representation.

Alien Resurrection

In her 1992 *Sight & Sound* article, "Invading Bodies: *Aliens*[3] and the Trilogy," Amy Taubin describes the dramatic sequence at the end of *Alien*[3] (1992), in which Ripley sacrifices herself by falling backwards into a lake of molten metal, just as an alien creature bursts from her chest: "She wraps her arms around it, pressing its hissing mouth to her breast—to prevent its escape, but also to nurture it. A most complicated gesture, and quite unlike any other I've ever seen in movies."[23] Barbara Creed sees further significance in this as an image of virgin birth:

> Ripley's death is represented as if it were a holy sacrifice. The close-up shot of Ripley's face, with shaven head and expression of blissful resignation, bears a striking resemblance to the face of Falconetti in Carl Dreyer's *The Passion of Joan of Arc*, as she, too, is consumed

by the flames. The medieval surroundings of *Alien*[3] thereby assume a new significance; Ripley's death is represented as a supreme sacrifice akin to that of an ancient androgynous god or religious saint.[24]

In his alternative description of this as "an absurd 'transcendent' finale,"[25] Kim Newman puts his finger on a wider significance for Ripley, one that is born of co-producer and star Sigourney Weaver's power to influence the character and the narrative for this second *Alien* sequel. Rather than merely transcending events to become the sole survivor *within* the narrative, she now *is* the narrative. To emphasize the power of the female in this new dynamic, much is made in *Alien*[3] of the fact that Ripley is the only woman on a prison colony inhabited entirely by men. She is accused, abused and almost raped, but, once again, she succeeds in the end—and on her own terms.

In many ways, Ripley loses impact in this film because she (or is it Weaver?) has become too powerful. The men of the prison refuse to kill Ripley, even when they discover that she is carrying the alien creature's baby; for that reason, the alien will not kill her either. Protected by both man and beast, Ripley is invested with the invulnerability of the Virgin Mary, much in the manner described by Creed above. Everything else is now subordinate to the female human's new relationship with the female alien. Indeed, the embrace in the climactic scene of the film looks remarkably like a tacit admission that Ripley has become the monster.

MONSTROUS FEMALE

The title of this section is inspired by Barbara Creed's 1994 book, *The Monstrous Feminine: Film Feminism, Psychoanalysis*, an examination of the horror film that also has something to bring to discussions about science fiction film— especially when female aliens are concerned. Creed's work draws on the notion of abjection (whereby an object or image is rejected as unpleasant) as presented in Julia Kristeva's 1982 essay, "Powers of Horror." Creed states that women in horror films are often linked to nature, rather than culture, through reference to reproductive functions: "in this way woman is again linked to the abject through her body."[26] Creed argues that, with its images of menstruation, archaic mother, *femme castratrice*, repugnant birth and so forth, the horror film often distils the female into an abject-essence that de-emphasizes her human characteristics, and so denies viewer identification. In an earlier essay, "Gynesis, Postmodernism and the Science Fiction Horror Film," Creed states that "one of the most interesting developments in the hybrid genre has been a concentration on imagery connected with the female reproductive cycle."[27] The *Alien* series presents the clearest development of these ideas within the combined horror/sf genre; however, science fiction cinema alone has not traditionally presented primal female monsters in the way that Creed describes for horror— otherwise, they would, arguably, become horror (as *Alien* is often described). What the genre has instead is a long tradition of alien females with emphasized human characteristics that invite identification.

Alignment with nature came early in science fiction cinema, with the various mythological—and, crucially here, beautiful—Mother Nature figures of the silent period, introduced in Chapter I. However, figures such as the Queen of the Polar Regions and the Fairy Queen of the Oceans tended to be beneficent; their popularity quickly waned. Their place was quickly taken by despotic—and, again, beautiful—queens and early *femme fatale* figures in films such as *Aelita: Queen of Mars* (1924) and *Die Herrin von Atlantis* (1932). These powerful females are doomed by their own ambition, but they are still not abject and "dirty" in the manner described by Creed. These are clean and attractive "monstrous females," who have been constructed as "Hegelian Others" to be destroyed. They are patriarchal warnings about the dangers presented by the female, so identification with real women is essential.

Traditional science fiction women remain on the culture side of the "culture/nature" dynamic that is essential to Creed's notion of the "male/female" distinction in horror film. The female is generally part of the cultural "Us" against the anti-cultural "Them." This can be seen in the domestic women who support the fight against the invaders in films around World Wars One and Two and the Cold War of the 1950s. Even when the genre's females become evil or destructive, they tend not to be visceral and abject. For example, Nancy Archer, the title character played by Allison Hayes, in the 1958 film *Attack of the 50 Foot Woman* is presented as a feminine, and even a sexy, point of identification—although her exaggerated height in the movie's posters leaves no doubt that she is a threat.

These genre distinctions have the potential to change when science fiction absorbs more horror elements, as it did in the 1996 *Star Trek: The Next Generation* movie, *First Contact*. Even here, however, Alice Krige's Borg Queen is framed as attractive and alluring—like the *femme fatale*. Perhaps more science fiction than horror, this "vamping Borg Queen," as Leslie Felperin calls her, is a sexualized grotesque. Sex itself, while promised—or threatened—is not delivered in *First Contact*. As Vivian Sobchack points out in "The Virginity of Astronauts," the genre tends to de-emphasize these female biological functions, and this is the case with the Borg Queen. She remains a sanitized view of what the genre might become. Felperin continues: "If *Star Trek* is a kind of ongoing American epic, it would seem to be entering a baroque, self questioning phase here."[28]

Despite being a relatively safe incarnation of the monstrous female, the Borg Queen does represent a threat to male dominance through a characteristic that is central to Creed's examination of the monstrous feminine in the horror genre. She appears to be able to procreate without relying on men. Her "children" are cyborgs created from the assimilated husks of many species, races and genders. Like the monster in *Alien*, she is not fussy about the nature of the host. In this, she represents what Creed calls the archaic, parthenogenetic mother—a direct attack on patriarchy:

> If we posit a more archaic dimension to the mother—the mother as originating womb—we can at least begin to talk about the maternal figure as *outside* the patriarchal family constellation. In this context, the mother-goddess narratives can be read as primal-scene narratives in which the mother is the sole parent. She is also the subject, not the object, of narrativity.[29]

Creed uses these ideas to examine *Alien*; she is especially interested in its various representations of sex and birth—including face huggers and bursting chests. The creature in *Alien* makes its visceral mark in the clean environment of the spaceship, but as the film series develops, the environments and the representation of the female take on more elements of what Creed recognizes as horror.

In her 2015 round-up of then-recent slasher movies and torture porn for her *Black Static* magazine column, Lynda E. Rucker's identifies a horror genre dichotomy: "As tiresome, lazy and misogynistic as the rape-torture-murder-of-women trifecta in film after film can be, women's bodies are also in many ways an ideal site upon which to enact horror because they are uniquely vul-

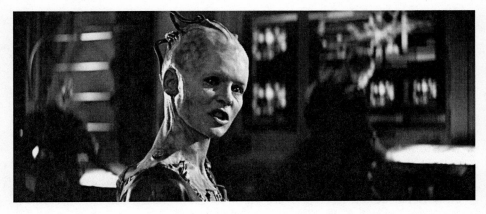

Monstrous horror meets alluring science fiction in the Borg Queen, played by Alice Krige in *Star Trek: First Contact* (1996).

nerable in ways that male bodies are not."[30] Rucker goes on to discuss pregnancy and childbirth as consequences of that vulnerability.

Whether the drawing of horror's abject elements into the female characters of *First Contact* and *Alien³* represents a backlash against strong women of the "Golden Era" is hard to say. The concept reappears in *Splice* (2009), but the line connecting these two points is tenuous. Science fiction's well-established modes of female presentation tend to co-opt other approaches. As discussed throughout this history, its model is too strong to be set aside. Besides, the *Alien* series gradually turns the female "vulnerability" taken from horror into a strength. In the first film, the creature is born through John Hurt's chest, making motherhood an equal-opportunities event. This is extended in *Aliens*, and by the end of *Alien³* Ripley has taken ownership of the alien birth. The stage is set for the fourth film, in which she will merge genetically with the female monster—and extinguish the male threat altogether.

"FATHER'S DEAD, ASSHOLE"

The third *Alien* sequel, *Alien: Resurrection*, was released in 1997. Its French director, Jean-Pierre Jeunet, had scored a critical hit with the surreal dark comedy *Delicatessen* in 1991 (co-directed with Marc Caro) and would go on to make the quirky, multi-award-winning *Amélie* in 2001. Bringing an Americana and pop culture perspective to this fourth *Alien* project was screenwriter Joss Whedon, who had created *Buffy the Vampire Slayer* for the original 1992 film and had co-written the 1995 Pixar film *Toy Story*. He is now known for his multi-layered, inter-textual referencing in projects like *Serenity* (2005), *Dollhouse* (TV, 2009–10) and *Avengers Assemble* (2012). The question, then, was what would these two maverick, postmodernist filmmakers take from their earlier work and the previous *Alien* films to put into this new female-led project? The answer seems to have been: "everything."

Ripley in this third sequel has been cloned from DNA collected during the events of the previous film; she is a resurrected hybrid: part human and part alien. The creature that was bursting out her at the end of *Alien³* is removed by caesarean section at the beginning of *Alien: Resurrection* by scientists who want to weaponize it, leaving Ripley with no real further plot function. To Whedon's narrative, however, she presents a rich psychological breeding ground; she is a link between the parthenogenetic alien mother of the horror genre and the surrogate human mother of the science fiction genre. This union creates a female character with a fierce independence, supported by enhanced physical and cognitive capabilities, coupled with innate animalistic mother instincts. As a result, Ripley is now the most formidable essence in the film;

her hold on the narrative is absolutely secure—which is both a blessing and a curse.

Ripley's relationship with the alien becomes most overt—and disturbing—towards the end of *Alien: Resurrection*, when she is drawn into the lair of the new alien queen, who is also her surrogate daughter. Thanks to Ripley's DNA, the hybrid queen has evolved a new reproductive system, bypassing the need for eggs and face-huggers. Developing Barbara Creed's horror-film concept of the "monstrous womb," which "belongs to woman or a female creature who is usually about to give birth to an alien being or brood of terrifying creatures,"[31] *Alien: Resurrection* not only recreates the archaic mother, but makes that mother partly human. This parthenogenetic mother, with her female/female reproductive system, may come from a horror tradition, but it plays on patriarchal science fiction's long-held fears about societies that do not require men to keep them going.

The new creature that the alien queen duly creates is a grotesque chimera with expressive human eyes, and a murderous alien appetite. After fighting with her grandmother instincts, Ripley finally rejects her genetic progeny by throwing some of her own acid blood at a spaceship window to burn a tiny hole; the creature is sucked through this into the vacuum of space. Michael Eaton picks up on the uncomfortable, real-world allusions created by this gruesome, visceral scene, which "—with its end-product of minced-up tissue fragments, blood and bone—cannot help but recall a Right-to-Life campaign."[32] Ripley has been forced to make a choice between human and alien, which is to say between life and death—or even between science fiction and horror. As Eaton continues, "abortion is seen here as deliverance not for Ripley but for the whole human race."

This finale is all very psychologically powerful, with the potential to elevate Ripley's character to a level not attained before. However, the moment has already been weakened somewhat by memories of an earlier encounter, in which Ripley kills an older alien. She is challenged by Call, played by Winona Ryder:

> CALL: I can't believe you did that.
> RIPLEY: Did what?
> CALL: It's like killing your own kind.
> RIPLEY: It was in my way.

Ripley's offhand response—one of many throughout the film—hardens her in much the same way that Sarah Connor was hardened for *Terminator 2: Judgment Day* in 1991. With fewer nuances and a shallower character crucible to dip into, Weaver's role, rather than deepening psychologically, soon begins to hemorrhage viewer sympathy. This is transferred to Call, who eventually usurps Ripley as the film's most effective point of emotional contact. Part way through the film, Call is revealed to be a gynoid—a female robot—designed to serve humans with unquestioning loyalty; as such, she is crucial to *Alien: Resurrection's* next feminist message: that of injustice repaid.

Repayment comes in a sequence in which Call takes control of the spaceship computer, which, for Whedon and Jeunet's film is, perhaps predictably, called "Father," rather than "Mother." The change of gender enables the filmmakers to set up an ironic twist. Call locks an escape door against the malevolent male scientist, Wren, who then cries out to the computer, "Father? FATHER!" The sequence inverts Ripley's own exasperated cry of "MOTHER!" to the computer towards the end of the original *Alien* film in 1979; it also reflects Christ's cry to his own father as he suffered on the cross. The female outsider's response to the male establishment figure comes when Call addresses Wren through the ship's feedback speakers: "Father's dead, asshole."

It is another potentially powerful and empowering moment. However, once again, it is weakened by the screenplay's sustained mockery of the same feminist sensibilities that had given succor to Weaver and Ripley eighteen years earlier. For example, when Call is unable to communicate remotely with the spaceship, her excuse is witty and played for laughs: "I burned my modem, we all did." This thinly veiled reference to the myth of the bra-burning radical feminist[33]—along with many similar lines of dialogue—signals a pendulum-swing back to the open-season on outspoken women that had characterized the suffragist films of the silent period, as discussed in Chapter I.

And so it goes. *Alien: Resurrection* is loaded with witty, ironic and comic lines, but they do not come naturally, as they had done in the light comedy *Back to the Future*; instead, they clash with other themes, making it difficult to discern what the screenwriter is trying to do or say. This fourth film is so overloaded that the serious gets lost in the frivolous, and vice versa. The challenge to patriarchy through the parthenogenetic mother or the potential lesbian relationship between Ripley and Call work on one level, but these deepening relationships with the alien and the alienated are regularly diluted by the antics of the other characters, who are largely ciphers and comic turns. *Alien: Resurrection* works on many levels, but not all together.

The starkest example of this is a sequence, described by Eaton as "the omphalic centre of the picture...."[34] The critic's choice of the word "omphalic"—relating to the navel and umbilical—is apt in many ways. This is the sequence in which Ripley discovers past incarnations of herself in genetic development; it is also a scene of considerable navel gazing for a franchise that has become enamored of itself and its central character. Ripley enters a biology lab and sees:

Unlikely allies: the alien and the alienated. Sigourney Weaver as the resurrected Ellen Ripley and Winona Ryder as the gynoid Call in *Alien: Resurrection* (1997).

> Nothing less than a Freak Museum, or more precisely, a variant of what the old carny barkers of the US fairground would have called a "Punk Show": a display of deformed human foetuses floating in liquid in glass jars. Except that in this instance the exhibits are mutant products of a hybridisation between human and alien life forms. This is a veritable "Ripley's Believe It or Not" Odditorium.[35]

Ripley also encounters a living, mutant, malformed version of her human self, who begs to be killed. Ripley duly does the deed in what is a genuinely powerful, emotional moment of release, revenge and catharsis—an action supported by the viewer and by Call. All of that is undermined, once again, by a humorous punchline—this time from Johner, the film's central image of mindless machismo. Looking into the burning lab, he says: "What's the big deal man? Fuckin' waste of ammo. Must be a chick thing."

Alien: Resurrection offers tantalizing windows onto a number of feminist treatises. Shulamith Firestone's aim of freeing women from biological maternity[36] is mingled with Judy Wajcman's argument that reproductive technology in male hands is "intrinsically an instrument of domination."[37] Continuing Vivian Sobchack's notion of 1980s' science fiction's "inverted millenarianism"[38] (in that it does not necessarily celebrate the future), the film dismantles the glorious, clean, male-controlled, futuristic artificial reproduction and nurturing presented in films like *Just Imagine* (1930) and *Logan's Run* (1976) and returns it to the defiled realm of Victor Frankenstein's errant ambition and blatant disregard for humanity. The "Frankenstein Syndrome" is inverted in parallel with Luce Irigaray's call to replace the notion of "phallic woman" with "non-phallic woman" or just "woman."[39] "Such a version of feminism," according to Lynda Glennon, "is neither equal rights nor androgyny, but matriarchy,"[40] which leads to Marilyn Frye and a question posed by the notion of male exclusion: "Do you have to be a lesbian to be a feminist?"[41] *Alien: Resurrection* is all of these things—and none. For they are drowned by a droll satire that might best be summed up as Ripley's own *Divine Comedy*—or maybe it is *Paradise Lost*.

Ultimately, perhaps, it is naïve to imagine that a collaboration between Whedon and Jeunet would be other than an exercise in shallow postmodernism.[42] After all, by 1997, the *Alien* franchise had become so familiar that their film could do little but riff on its own themes and reflect on the embarrassment of riches which now seemed to lie before the genre's enfranchised women.

A New Watershed

The *Star Trek* movie series had already featured female Klingons, but the introduction of—albeit moderated—horror elements in the form of *First Contact*'s Borg Queen was still quite a departure for the franchise. Its combination of old and new is, to Leslie Felperin, "so satisfying because it keeps throwing such sly curve balls even as it offers tried and tested pleasures."[43] The film's inclusion of Alfre Woodard's black, woman rocket-scientist, Lily Sloane, might also feel like a curve-ball for a genre that is, as Adilifu Nama claims in *Black Space*, is notable for its "overt omission of black representation and racial issues...."[44] Sloane is not mentioned in Nama's book, perhaps because *First Contact* does not make a racial issue of her appearance; instead, she is neatly integrated into a series that is trying to find an identity for its next generation. As Felperin notes: "The first series' cold-war warriors with ray guns have given way to the *Next Generation*'s technocratic peacekeepers.... Captain Kirk and crew seldom had any self-doubts that they were in the right, Picard et al. on the other hand are racked with doubts."[45]

It is this sense of doubt, and the change of approach, that identifies *First Contact* as a possible proxy for female representation in the genre in the final years of the 1990s. By 1996, it felt as though women had done, or at least could do, just about all of the jobs in science fiction movies, leaving a sense of "what next?" Looking at the releases for the next few years, it seems that filmmakers of the period, like their predecessors in the 1960s, did not really know what to do next with their women, but this time, they were spoiled for choice. In the watershed year of 1997, prominent female characters came in all forms—including the marginally surreal.

"The just-plain-crazed emotional climax when a being genetically engineered as a perfect warrior is horror-struck by the whole idea of war is a daft final irony."[46] That quote could almost be from a review for *Alien: Resurrection*; instead, it is Kim Newman's description of Leeloo, the very different kind of alien who features in *The Fifth Element*—another chaotic, creative confection, directed by another Frenchman: Luc Besson. Unlike Ripley, Leeloo, played by Milla Jovovich, is a sexy, sexual-innocent with the power to destroy Earth. The film is colorful, frenetic and often silly, with many retreats into traditional female representation, including provocative costumes designed by Jean-Paul Gaultier, echoing Paco Rabanne's role on *Barbarella* in 1968. But somehow *The Fifth Element* succeeds with its on-screen comic book approach in way that *Barbarella* does not; it also succeeds with its humor in a way that *Alien: Resurrection* does not.

The year 1997 continues with aliens being hunted by a very serious Dr. Eleanor Arroway, played by Jodie Foster, in *Contact*. Arroway is a radio astronomer on the SETI (Search for Extra-Terrestrial Intelligence) project, a role reputedly based on the American astronomer Dr. Jill Cornell Tarter in Carl Sagan's original source novel. It is interesting to see a film that inverts science fiction cinema's usual father-and-son pattern by presenting a tale of father (and father-figures) and daughter. This is not to be confused with the father/daughter pairings in Christopher Nolan's 2014 film *Interstellar*. These are instead rooted more firmly in the tradition of women standing in the shadows of their scientist fathers, one that can be traced back to the silent period and films such as *The Comet's Comeback* (1916) and *The Carter Case* (1919). Instead, *Contact* presents Dr. Ellie Arroway's personal enquiry in face of patriarchal interference. In so doing, it has closer links with the 1978 film *Coma*, not least through the important comments that it makes about the obstacles that men still place in the way of women who are trying to succeed in professional scientific environments. Philip Strick draws attention to the importance of casting in these challenging roles when he notes that Arroway and *Contact*'s narrative as a whole are "well suited to Jodie Foster's intense and haunted performance."[47] It is no coincidence that this quality is central to Geneviève Bujold's performance as Dr. Wheeler in *Coma*.

Contact joins a number of 1997 movies that include meaningful roles for women, often with equal or greater status with men. This collection of films starts to reveal a sense of the growing diversity of the female experience in the genre: *Starship Troopers*, *Cube*, *Gattaca* and *Event Horizon*. These may not all contain great female roles, but they do offer potential, as well as a sense that the genre was beginning to mature in one important respect: women could be good, evil, winners, losers, intelligent or ignorant—just like men. The impact and diversity 1997's releases seem to bode well for the future; however, given that *Alien: Resurrection* appeared to be sounding a retreat for Ripley, there was a danger that these films, rather than indicating a secure, settled home for female roles, instead represented a last gasp for their "Golden Era."

Fin De Siècle

A number of commentators have noted how many aspects of the film industry run in cycles: studios come and go, themes re-emerge, styles appear, disappear and reappear, even old technologies and formats can find themselves in favor once again. The multi-award winning 2011, black and white, almost-silent movie *The Artist* may not have made dialogue redundant, but it did stimulate nostalgic interest that, arguably, helped to create a cinema audience for the likes of the 2016 musical, *La La Land*. In her 2011 book, *American Film Cycles*, Amanda Ann Klein adds popular trends, social preoccupations and political undercurrents to a discussion that includes cycles within film genres.

At some point, discussions about film genres will include the four-part life-cycle proposed by film scholar Thomas Schatz.[48] Building on the work of Christian Metz, introduced in Chapter II, Schatz argues that genres cycle through the following phases:

1. Innovation/experimentation
2. Classical/established
3. Parody/pastiche
4. Deconstruction/refinement

The development of science fiction cinema can be matched against this cycle in a number of ways. For example: by taking the silent period as marking the genre's innovative beginnings; identifying levels of establishment from the arrival of the talkies to the classics of the 1950s; moving on to the chaotic color period and the establishment of pastiche and parody in the late 1970s; and then finishing with the closely managed refinement that has occurred with the application of computer graphics. Variation can be added to this model, by noting that epicycles are created when each technological revolution has referred the genre temporarily back to the innovation stage.

The Schatz Cycle also offers a useful framework for thinking about female representation in science fiction film; however, it is harder to match this back to the beginnings of the genre. After all, it is difficult to argue effectively that the absence of women or even their token presences were "innovations." Having said that, the start of the cycle might be set to any of various points of first contact discussed in earlier chapters: her first active on-screen appearance, the first female scientist, the first woman astronaut, the first non-male protagonist, and so forth. Taking *Star Wars* as a starting point, an application of the Schatz Cycle might suggest *Alien* and *The Terminator* as innovators, the *Star Trek* film series as a barometer for the establishment of classic trends; *Tank Girl* (1995) and *Barb Wire* (1996) as indications that parody and pastiche was in the air; and *Alien: Resurrection* as evidence that the female roles were beginning to be deconstructed. This encompasses the "Golden Era" for female representation in science fiction film.

However, no theory is ever that neat. It can also be shown that at every stage of every cycle—however it is framed—each of these elements is vying for attention. This means that there will still be innovation at the point that the genre is being deconstructed—and so it has been with female roles. As the genre approached the end of the century, and the "Golden Era" began to wind down, all phases of the Schatz Cycle could be identified together, arguably bringing a richness to the female characters of the genre.

It is worth now taking a brief look at the mixed-bag of approaches to female representation—some old, some new—that colonized science fiction cinema as it as it approached the new millennium.

INNOVATION

While female fortunes may have entered uncharted onscreen territory around 1997, off screen, women were continuing on an upward trajectory. Historically, it was in the screenplay that most female contributions could be found; Julia Crawford Ivers' 1916 film *The Intrigue* is identified in Chapter I as the earliest traceable example of a science fiction film written by a woman. Women continued to contribute regularly as science fiction screenwriters, working on pre–1990s projects as diverse as *Metropolis* (1927), *Flash Gordon* (1936), *The Invisible Woman* (1940), *The Blob* (1958), *Daikaiju Gamera* (1966), *The Omega Man* (1971), *E.T. the Extra-Terrestrial* (1982) and *Howard the Duck* (1986).

As the density of screenwriters began to trail off in the mid–1980s, the baton was picked up by female producers. Again, Julia Crawford Ivers is a very early example of this role, although director Alice Guy-Blaché is likely to have produced her own 1900 short, *Chapellerie et charcuterie mécanique*, before the industry distinguished between writers, producers and directors. Clara Kimball Young's production company made *Without a Soul* in 1916 and Marion Davies produced *The Young Diana*, starring herself, in 1922; women science fiction producers then seem to be absent until Helen Ainsworth produced *The 27th Day* in 1957. With the exception of a few films in the 1960s and '70s, including

Close Encounters of the Third Kind, co-produced by Julia Phillips, it was not until the 1980s that female producers started to appear in larger numbers. Many more films were produced by women during the "Golden Era" than ever before. That could be simply because there were more opportunities in the industry, or it could be that on-screen and off-screen events are connected. It is possible that a new generation of female filmmakers had been inspired by what was happening to female characters. Women (and men) were applying an experience and understanding of female ability on-screen and applying it to potential aptitude off-screen.

Tangible evidence for this is hard to muster, although many of the reasons for the rise of the female producer are discussed by Mollie Gregory in her 2002 book, *Women Who Run the Show.* "Securing the Perimeter" in the 1980s led to a "Breakthrough"[49] in the '90s, which in turn led to the many female producers who work in the science fiction film industry today. The situation is developing with time, which can be seen in the number of women listed in the Filmography section of this text. Some of today's producers had kick-started their careers at the beginning of the "Golden Era" and are now instrumental in shaping the 21st century genre, most notably Gale Anne Hurd and Kathleen Kennedy. Indeed, since taking over from George Lucas as President of Lucasfilm, Kennedy has been called "the most powerful woman in Hollywood."[50] Innovations in industry practices in the mid–1990s did not, however, make the genre immune to the lures of the past.

CLASSIC

The postmodernist approach that had affected *Alien: Resurrection* can be found throughout this mixed-bag, *fin de siècle*—end-of-the-century—period, as the genre began to look back to its classics for inspiration. This included a modest number (by today's standard) of remakes, including a joint U.S.–UK feature length version of the long-running BBC television show, *Doctor Who*— clearly an attempt to capture the spirit of this quintessentially British television show for a wider audience. Something was lost in translation. This was also the case for the 1995 film version of the British genre comic strip *Judge Dredd* and for Tim Burton's witty but financially unsuccessful *Mars Attacks!*, his homage to the 1962 trading card series. Other attempts to capture existing magic met with varying success. The 1997 live-action version of *The Men in Black* comic book was a hit, whereas the movie version of the American hit television series *The X-Files* only just turned a profit. These were early soundings for what would become the post-millennium era of the remake, more of which in Chapter VII. These films betray an explicit hankering for the past that was present, but implicit, in some of the big studio movies through the period: *Stargate* (1994), *Waterworld, Outbreak* (both 1995), *Deep Impact*, directed by Mimi Leder, and *Armageddon* (both 1998). All of these nostalgia films deliver to the viewer—at some level—a concept, style, story, aesthetic or just a general feeling, of the classics of the genre. It is a sentimental look back that impacts many of their female characters too. This is no less true for the biggest box office hit of 1996, *Independence Day*.

The roots of Roland Emmerich's movie go back to the U.S. invasion films of the 1950s, and to H.G. Wells' 1898 novel *War of the Worlds*. The four central male characters collectively save the world through feats of derring-do, while their women—three wives and a daughter—take up compromise positions between the strong, independent figure that cinema audiences had come to expect and the subordinate role demanded by this exercise in nostalgia. It is a modern compromise that has carried through to the films of the 21st century; its roots can be seen in an exchange between Jasmine Dubrow, played by Vivica A. Fox and Mary McDonnell's First Lady, Marilyn Whitmore:

FIRST LADY, MARILYN WHITMORE: So, what do you do for a living?

JASMINE DUBROW: I'm a dancer.

FIRST LADY, MARILYN WHITMORE: Ahh. Ballet?

JASMINE DUBROW: No. Exotic.

FIRST LADY, MARILYN WHITMORE: Oh, I'm sorry.

JASMINE DUBROW: Don't be. I'm not. It's good money. Besides, my baby's worth it.

Independence Day recalls and replicates a world in which women were restricted in what they could do and be. It also recalls a scene in the 1960 British comedy *Man in the Moon*, in which Shirley Anne Fields, as Polly, innocently describes her job as a stripper, while she is taking her clothes off: "It's funny to think people pay me money to do this. And there's nothing to it really."

Polly's dialogue is meant as titillation in a way that Jasmine's is not, but both films project a notion of "woman in control" that is not really supported by the rest of the narrative. In *Independence Day*, Margaret Colin, as Presidential Press Secretary Constance Spano, does reveal a degree of control in her back-story, as she left her man to pursue her career. She is, however, eventually returned to the fold in way that supports Constance Penley's observations about classical cinema:

> It is by now well known that the narrative logic of classical film is powered by the desire to establish, by the end of the film, the nature of masculinity, the nature of femininity, and the way in which those two can be complementary rather than antagonistic.... Ironically, it is science fiction film—our hoariest and seemingly most sexless genre—that alone remains capable of supplying the configurations of sexual difference required by the classical cinema.[51]

What is more, as many of these nostalgia films show, the distance between conventional classic and perilous pastiche can be a short one.

PARODY

Back in the silent period, science fiction had been used to parody women's ambition in films such as *A la Conquête du Pôle*, which ridicules campaigns for female suffrage. Female roles specific to the genre itself would need to become established before they became targets, because parody, pastiche, satire and spoof take advantage of a level of familiarity. This had been achieved by the time that *Sins of the Fleshapoids* was experimenting with B-movie notions of gender stereotypes through its parody of robot societies in 1965. As might be guessed from the title, science fiction themes are also targeted in the 1972 Australian comedy *Shirley Thompson Versus the Aliens*. These are just two examples of witty self-reference in the genre.

The combination of familiar genre elements in *Star Wars* created a product that has become central to the pastiche creations of its own sequels and prequels, as well as its many imitators. Among the early parodies that drew liberally from *Star Wars* was the 1980 film *Battle Beyond the Stars*, a loose re-make of *The Magnificent Seven* (1960) and *The Seven Samurai* (1954). Already, then, a multi-layered parody, John Sayles's screenplay adds numerous female science fiction stereotypes, including the innocent virgin, vamp, rape victim, fecund virgin, Amazonian warrior, lesbian and damsel-in-distress. The central spaceship is clearly female, with a hull that features breasts with nipples, and a "mothering" computer called Nell, played by Lynn Carlin, who creates a womb-like home for her human inhabitants. This is arguably a more nuanced approach than was employed in *Barbarella*, which is taking advantage of stereotypes to sell sex, rather than comedy. The 1980 approach might also be seen as an attack on women in a post–Ripley genre; that is: women, now had a champion of their own, and so were "fair game" for the attack. This certainly seems to be the case with the 1985 *Mad Max* sequel, *Beyond Thunderdome*, which features Tina Turner as the outrageous, leather-clad, warrior-woman parody, Aunty Entity. The film is not intended to be a parody as such, but it is an effective pastiche of the type of post-apocalyptic narrative made popular by the original *Mad Max* in 1979.

The rather more gentle 1988 comedy *Earth Girls Are Easy* attempts to draw its audience into a world of inoffensive fun that melds the recognizable genre type of the fatuous female love interest with sassy sexuality of the empowered woman, in the style of the 1985 non-genre Madonna movie, *Desperately Seeking Susan*. This ethos seems to have been magnified for the post–*Terminator 2* film *Tank Girl*, which, in 1995, attempted to capitalize on the audience acceptance that science fiction women could now be whatever they wanted to be. For whatever reason, that mission failed at the box office[52]; and that may well have contributed—along with the 1996 *Casablanca* parody, *Barb Wire* (1996) and the marginal genre project *Catwoman* in 2004—to the chronic lack of women at the head of fantasy and comic book–based features for the next 20 years. The science fiction pastiche was rescued in 1997 by *The Fifth Element* and *Starship Troopers*, which may well have paved the way for Sigourney Weaver's well-balanced lampooning of Uhura in the successful 1999 *Star Trek* parody, *Galaxy Quest* (1999).

DECONSTRUCTION

Sigourney Weaver had already proven that she could offer a comic turn in the highest-grossing U.S. film of 1984, *Ghostbusters*, so her role in *Galaxy Quest* was not a total surprise. It is also closer than might first appear to *Alien: Resurrection*, whose post-modernist inter- and intra-textual referencing brings that film close to pastiche, and a parody of its own *Alien* lineage. Both films require a process of deconstruction in order to understand what is being commented on, which brings parody close to this final phase in the Schatz Cycle. Rather than making comedy from their discoveries, some filmmakers attempt to reconstruct the genre in a way that subverts its recognized forms and conventions.

This "knowing" approach was taken when Hollywood came to make a movie version of the classic 1960s' television series *Lost in Space*. The 1998 film retains the original's female/male pairings: parents, Maureen and John Robinson; children, Penny and Will; and the older Judy Robinson with fighter pilot, Don West. The update gives each female a modern, post–Ripley, nononsense attitude towards her correspondent male. She is the boss. This is graphically indicated in scene in which the men have been arguing about who got them into their current mess, and which of them is in charge. Dr. Maureen Robinson, played by Mimi Rogers, withers them with a reprimand, followed by a line laden with irony: "Now, if you've finished hosing down the deck with testosterone, I suggest you come with me. I may have found a way to get us off this planet."

It is a promising exchange, but ultimately, the plot of *Lost in Space* fails to deliver on the potential offered by its dynamic female characters: Lacey Chabert's punk Penny is surely inspired by Leeloo and Tank Girl, and Heather Graham's Dr. Judy Robinson is a 1950s' female scientist with 1990s attitude. The overall narrative, however, has not been updated. In the final act of the

Three strong females lost in a male melodrama. From left: Heather Graham, Mimi Rogers and Lacey Chabert as Dr. Maureen, Dr. Judy and Penny Robinson in *Lost in Space* (1998).

film, Mother Maureen and her two daughters remain in the relative safety of the spaceship home, while all of the male characters brave the dangerous environment outside in search of a means to escape the planet. The men then interact with versions of themselves, by virtue of a time-bubble created by boy-genius Will. The Freudian angst of the finale leaves the viewer in no doubt that this is another film about men and their fathers. The female Robinsons benefit initially from the industry's intention to nurture strong female characters that ran through the 1990s; however, there seemed now to be nowhere left to go with these and other characters. Many became, as Christine Cornea points out, "slimmed down" features of "cyber-thrillers"[53] like *Johnny Mnemonic* (1995).

According to Schatz, deconstruction of a genre often leads to innovation. The last year of the 20th century featured two science fiction cinema hits that offered glimpses of a technical future. *The Matrix* literally deconstructs its world bit-by-bit and re-presents it frame-by-frame in time-freezing 3-D. *Star Wars: Episode I—The Phantom Menace* paved the way for the digital projection of computer effects that dominates the cinema today. It should by now, however, come as no surprise that these revolutionary science fiction films delve into the past for their lead female characters. Despite her initial promise, Carrie-Ann Moss's leather-clad fighter, Trinity, ultimately evokes the three Marys of the *New Testament*, as she follows the new male messiah, Neo. Natalie Portman's Amidala is a Queen; what is more, she will become—as the 21st century reveals—the mother of the woman who arguably triggered the start of the "Golden Era," Princess Leia.

—❦—

The period 1977 to 1999 offered a mixed bag for female representation. On the one hand, it promised—and delivered—so much; on the other, it showed that, however complete the revolution may appear, convention and stereotype always seem to retain a degree of influence. Science fiction cinema's ostensible mission has been to seek out the new. Strong female characters driving the narrative had been this for a while, but once her shine came off, it was time to move on to the next new thing. However, the impact of these captivating female characters had been such that they were now part of the toolbox; they had been added to the conventions and stereotypes that science fiction filmmakers lean on in times of stress and change. The scene was now set for the biggest change to face the genre in a long, long time: the digital revolutions in production and projection. Attempts to capture the essence of old successes with the new formats would lead to a fresh danger. Women, and men, were set to become rubber stamp characters in a series of franchise films—to become studio weapons in the 21st century clone wars....

VII

21ST CENTURY
Computers, Corporations
and Consumers

When science fiction cinema of the 1980s turned its attention to the power of corporations, it criticized the corrosiveness of capitalism, the commodification of humanity and the threat to identity—and it gave birth to some of the genre's most celebrated female heroes. In the first two decades of the 21st century, computer generated imagery has given filmmakers unprecedented levels of creative power. At the same time, the commercial threat has permeated cinema: forces that are rarely seen on-screen are rarely without off-screen influence. These are the conglomerates that own the corporations that own the companies that own the creative concerns that used to control the movies. The art and industry of cinema is now, more than ever, a streamlined investment opportunity. Backlot and headline have been replaced by backend and bottom-line. Armies of executive producers and accountants wield vetoes over concepts, stories and characters borrowed for the screen. Women may be here in numbers now, but where have all the Ripleys gone? More importantly: will they be back, now that the dentists are running the candy store?

———∞———

Solid State of the Art

It was noted earlier that a change of decade does not necessarily flag a change in the style of science fiction cinema; with the notable exception of the arrival of sound-on-film in the late 1920s, watersheds are rarely that neat. However, the human capacity and desire to turn over a new leaf will have been magnified by the arrival, for most people in the West, of a new century and a new millennium.[1] It would not be surprising, then, to see a change in the kind of science fiction movies being produced.

The big science fiction cinema story of 1999 had been *Star Wars: Episode I—The Phantom Menace*, the long-awaited prequel to the original *Star Wars* trilogy. Much as the first "talkies" had done at the end of the 1920s, this film bridges the gap between decades. It looks backwards into the past for story inspiration, but it also has a clear eye on the future, specifically on George Lucas' dream of a fully digital cinema. That is: one in which computer technology is used in the creation, the manipulation, and—crucially—the projection of the image. Lucas had already made strides towards an all-digital *Star Wars* with his augmentation of the original trilogy to create the 1997 Special Edition releases; however, this was not universally well-received by fans and critics, many of whom felt that these much-loved films should have been left well alone.[2]

Lucas' tinkering was perhaps inevitable. The special effects boom that followed the original release of *Star Wars*, and morphed throughout the 1980s into the Computer Graphics Imagery (CGI) revolution of the 1990s led commentators to complain that special effects and grand images were hijacking the stories. The result, according to Brooks Landon, was a "self-referential celebration of the technologies of cinema itself."[3] The "image vs. idea" debate is not new to this genre or this survey. A number of commentators have decried the story that underpins the 1927 technical *tour de force*, *Metropolis*, and in his discussion about the expansion in the genre in the 1950s in his 1970 history, *Science Fiction in the Cinema*, John Baxter is rather dismissive of the genre's cinema compared with its literature: "the two fields of sf and cinema do not mesh; sf films usually succeed as cinema in proportion to the degree in which they fail as sf."[4]

Lucas was determined to make the digital technologies succeed for his *Star Wars Special Edition* stories and then his *Star Wars* prequel series, in which *The Phantom Menace* was followed by *Episode II: Attack of the Clones* in 2002 and *Episode III: Revenge of the Sith* in 2005. In this, Lucas was following a long tradition that gives rise to Garrett Stewart's pithy response to the generally held view that futuristic movies reflect today's society; instead, says Stewart, "Movies about the future tend to be about the future of movies."[5] *Star Wars* is, of course, not set in the future, but rather "a long time ago…"; however, as was noted in respect of sound and color in Chapter II and Chapter IV, this is precisely where the genre often retreats to when it wants to move forward with a revolutionary technology. Lucas' prequels betray a tradition covered throughout this survey in which stories, characters—especially female characters—have remained at the mercy of industry trends.

If the films of the first decade-and-a-half of the new millennium have been characterized by anything, it is the increased ability of CGI to render the impossible possible, and by the growing power afforded the custodians of what Terry Ramsaye in 1926 called "the Prayer Wheel of the Wish"[6]—cinema itself. Those doing the wishing are crucial. There is no space here to discuss further the history or merits of CGI; instead, of far more importance is the effect of its widespread adoption on female representation as science fiction cinema turned into the new millennium.

GENDER UN-BLENDING

The real world breathed a collective sigh of relief when the threatened "Millennium bug" failed to cause catastrophic damage to computers whose dates were set to tick from "99" to "00" on 1st January 2000. The battle for the digital realm posited by *The Matrix* in 1999 was confined to the cinema; Earth continued to turn on her axis and Trinity continued to support Neo through the 2003 sequels, *The Matrix Reloaded* and *The Matrix Revolutions*. If Trinity is an accurate measure, it would seem that female characters had some way to go before regaining the ground lost towards the end of the 1990s. Indeed, further ground would be lost in a real-life event that was far more important than the turn of a new millennium: the terrorist attacks on the U.S. on 11 September 2001.

Back in 1983, the feminist freedom fighters in Lizzie Borden's *Born in Flames* had attacked the priapic twin towers of the World Trade Center in New York City in order to damage patriarchy and capitalism. Glen Donnar's work on contemporary American cinema suggests that this was remarkably prescient, as real-world events had a similar effect: "the attacks on 9/11, which figuratively wounded normative masculinity, resulted in a re-assertion of traditional modes of masculinity by conservative commentators and news media. This arguably led to a similar, though inverse re-positioning of females."[7]

"Normative masculinity" had been challenged by science fiction in the 1980s, a period notable for what Christine Cornea describes as an "overwhelming concern with masculine identity and subjectivity."[8] Citing movies like *The Terminator* (1984) and *RoboCop* (1987), Cornea links this development to the U.S. presidential transition from Jimmy Carter to the neo-conservative Ronald Reagan. She then extends it to include the "heavily muscled female hero" and the "gender blending" personified by Sarah Connor and Ellen Ripley. As noted in Chapter VI above, these overtly masculinized figures (male and female) faded away somewhat towards the end of the 20th century. Pegging this demise to the presidency of Bill Clinton may be a step too far, but combining Donnar and Cornea does at least point to a suggestion that the genre's response to social, political and commercial uncertainties in the early 21st century was to continue on its path back to the familiar territory of male and female stereotypes—a process of "gender un-blending."

A new "concern with masculine identity and subjectivity" is apparent in some of the high-profile films that join *The Matrix* during this millennial transition period. In 2000, *Hollow Man* charted the psychological traumas of a man who has acquired the ability to make himself invisible; from the same year, *Battlefield Earth* is John Travolta's personal attempt to realize the works of the founder of the Church of Scientology, L. Ron Hubbard; the title of *The 6th Day* (2000) refers to human Creation Day in Genesis and features Arnold Schwarzenegger as Adam, a man whose existence is threatened by clones; *A.I. Artificial Intelligence*—a 2001 film which coincidentally shows the destruction of NYC's twin towers—follows a robot boy on his journey to discover that he is not unique; Tom Cruise's character discovers that his free will is threatened in *Minority Report* in 2002; and Jean-Luc Picard's individuality is threatened in the same year by a clone of himself in *Star Trek: Nemesis*. It seems that the genre's preoccupation with fathers and sons had been replaced, for now, with an even more narcissistic focus on versions of the male Self. This is perhaps why Carrie-Ann Moss's Trinity bears a striking resemblance to Keanu Reeves' Neo.

As Chapter V indicates, the classic *Star Trek* movies are not particularly

Gender blending. Carrie-Ann Moss as Trinity and Keanu Reeves as Neo in poster detail from *The Matrix Revolutions* (2003).

good at telling women's stories, and the final installments in *The Next Generation* series are no different. In 1998, *Star Trek: Insurrection* had featured Donna Murphy as Anij, a romantic interest for Captain Picard; in *Nemesis*, that role goes to Marina Sirtis as Counsellor Deanna Troi, now the wife of Captain Riker. The focus on attractive women in token roles is not unique to *Star Trek*, nor to science fiction for that matter; however, its place in the genre at this stage is highlighted by a feature in the *Yearbook 2000* edition of the science fiction entertainment magazine, *Starburst*. Under the title "SF Babes," Ian Atkins' presents what he calls the "Starburst Miss World 2000 competition" in which "Each girl is put through her paces in a variety of contests,"[9] with considerable weight placed on sexy clothing and instances of nudity. In reverse order, the finalists (from both cinema and television) are: Amanda Tapping (53), Traci Lords (60), Lexa Doig (65), Elisabeth Shue (67), Shannon Kenny (71), Gillian Anderson (72), Jayne Heitmeyer (75), Jennifer Sky (76), Jessica Alba (79), Thandie Newton (82), Rebecca Romijn (Stamos) (87), Sigourney Weaver (88). Xenia Seeberg (89), Angelina Jolie (90), Leela (the *Futurama* character voiced by Katey Segal) (91), Jeri Ryan (92), Rhona Mitra (93), Claudia Black (95), Carrie-Anne Moss (96) and Jennifer Lopez (97).

Atkins is not being entirely serious with this *Starburst* feature. Indeed, he labels it as "post-feminist irony," arguing that "if *Voyager*, *First Wave* and *Andromeda* [TV shows] are this shameless, why can't we join in the fun?" Amongst this "fun" are lines that give a good sense of where female science fiction role had reached by the year 2000. Of particular note is part of the entry for Elisabeth Shue:

> Elisabeth plays Linda McKay, the scientist in *Hollow Man* who starts off as a hesitant brainiac and then turns into a flamethrower-wielding Rambo when Kevin Bacon's see-though character takes first blood. In the Science Fiction world we call it "doing a Ripley." However, unlike Sigourney Weaver, it's unlikely Elisabeth is going to be called back for three sequels.[10]

This may be unfair criticism of Shue's performance, but it is also an accurate assessment of the way that female characters in 21st century science fiction cinema are regularly reduced to a Ripley reference. Atkins' "post-feminist" feature more accurately reveals a "post-modernist" environment, in which female characters are expected to add sexy-and-sassy to smart-and-strong.

This approach arguably holds together for the 2004 movie *I, Robot*, in which Isaac Asimov's original roboticist Dr. Susan Calvin is brought to screen-life by Bridget Moynahan; however, the all-things-to-all-people model is less successful in the 2005 movie *Æon Flux*. With a firm focus on the eponymous, super-efficient assassin played by Charlize Theron, director Karyn Kusama clearly intends to send a powerful, feminist message; however, she seems to have expended too much effort making sure that all of the boxes have an "A" grade in them. The net result for the Flux character is unfeasible toughness, impossible agility, unbelievable luck, and impractical costumes that are clearly designed with scopophilic intention. In short, she is not credible. According to Kim Newman in his critical *Sight & Sound* review, Kusama, "following up her 2000 debut *Girlfight*, segues from indie grit to mid-level studio anonymity like so many others before her."[11] Newman may have had Rachel Talalay in mind here, whose 1995 film *Tank Girl* also struggled to draw a female movie character from non-live-action roots. *Æon Flux* has the added disadvantage of being augmented by CGI, which can, as George Lucas showed with his *Star Wars Special Editions* and prequels, place rather too many temptations before the director. To be fair to Kusama, it may also have been difficult trying to stay true the spirit of the original character and story while meeting the expectations of nine producers from six production companies. This has become one of the perils of filmmaking in the 21st century.

Ironically, female characters in this uncertain post-millennial period seem to fare better in roles that do not expect them to carry the whole narrative. For example, the dramatic resolutions to the three main story threads towards the end of *The Matrix Revolutions* rely heavily on female intervention. Zee and Charra (Nona Gaye and Rachel Blackman) eliminate a giant machine adversary, Jada Pinkett Smith's Niobe expertly pilots a rescue ship, and Trinity pilots the ship that carries Neo on his way to becoming a sun-god. This may look like female occupation of the spaces left by men, and perhaps it is, but it might also indicate a genre that had become more comfortable with its women. In this new period of "concern with masculine identity and subjectivity" it would have been tempting just to hit the reset button, sending female roles back completely to the absence and tokenism of earlier years; however, women had come too far for that. The result was a temporary compromise that resulted in female characters doing interesting things in sub-plots and backgrounds.

The 21st century may have started with an expectation that women would continue to thrive in science fiction cinema, but the output of this early period suggests that they had not yet developed far from the mixed bag of diverse, sometimes interesting, often frustrating, roles that characterize female representation at the end of the 1990s.

TRICKLE DOWN

Back in 1998, the remake of *Lost in Space* had offered a glimpse of what a post–Ripley science fiction female might look like: outwardly competent, professional women caught in male-driven plots. The gates had previously been levered open for female-led narratives by Scott, Cameron and others, but of the characters that flooded through them, relatively few made the impact of Ripley or Connor. More were like Maureen, Judy and Penny Robinson, but their numbers were sufficient to generate enough momentum for a clear sea-change, one that would be felt into the early part of the 21st century. Despite films such as *Hulk* in 2003 still presenting the genre as a playground for male, Freudian angst, sustained attitudes towards women in the genre meant that they had become established. Now, as so often before, filmmakers were presented with a question about what to do with women who could not be ignored.

Added confusion may have been created by the sustained Japanese interest for animated films—anime—featuring significant female characters. Projects such as *Ghost in the Shell* in 1995, with its cyborg policewoman, Major Motoko Kusanagi, voiced by Atsuko Tanaka, helped to consolidate interest in anime within a wider, Western audience. A female character is central to both the 1999 movie *A.Li.Ce*, which features a girl who travels through space and time, and to *Spirited Away*, which won the Academy Award for "Best Animated Feature" of 2001. The latter film is not necessarily science fiction, but it is a high-profile example of the Japanese female-led fantasy narrative that would continue through *Ghost in the Shell 2: Innocence*, *Howl's Moving Castle*, *Appleseed* (all 2004), and *The Girl Who Leapt Through Time* (2006).

Titan A.E. in 2000 had shown that the serious animated science fiction story could be replicated in the U.S., and *Final Fantasy: The Spirits Within* in 2001 showed that it could also feature a prominent female character. It may have been this realization, along with the widening of interest in female anime characters that persuaded Paramount Pictures and others to spend $62million turning the 1991 animated television series *Æon Flux* into the augmented live-action movie of 2005.[12] As noted above, that approach failed, but it would eventually find massive success with James Cameron's *Avatar* in 2009. In the meantime, elements of the "Golden Era" of female representation continued to trickle down to other post-millennium characters. The profile of Trinity, generated largely by the posters and her first five minutes in *The Matrix*, helped to ensure that women on screen would continue to be "doing a Ripley," but this was not the only influence on female roles in this curious, transitional period.

Tim Burton's much-anticipated 2001 re-imagining of *Planet of the Apes* returns to the concept of a central female ape character that had been missing since Dr. Zira was killed off in *Escape from the Planet of the Apes* in 1971. For Burton, Helena Bonham Carter plays the chimpanzee Ari. She is not the scientist that Dr. Zira had been, but she does attempt to mediate between the apes and the humans, taking a moral and emotional position that ultimately backfires. Andrew O'Hehir is not overly complimentary about the movie, but he does suggest that it could have been rescued if Ari's relatively complex character had been given more of the narrative: "is there anyone or anything in the whole movie we care about besides Ari, the class traitor who has been branded as a human and a slave and then abandoned by the man she loves?"[13]

The writers, producers and director of *Planet of the Apes* are reluctant, however, to rest this expensive project on the shoulders of a female, non-human protagonist, and so Ari fails to meet her potential. This return to genre type is mirrored in former model Estella Warren's Nova-esque character, renamed Deanna for this movie.[14] Annoyance at her lack of development beyond Pierre Boulle's novel—or indeed female roles of the 1950s—is palpable in O'Hehir's complaint that "even though the planet's humans are reduced to primitivism and slavery, they still have access to lipstick, eyebrow pencil and other crucial styling aids."[15]

A similar complaint might be leveled at the arrival of Kristanna Loken as T-X, the new cyborg assassin in 2003's *Terminator 3: Rise of the Machines*, especially as she appears naked in her first scene. However, no more of Loken is seen here than was seen of Robert Patrick as the T-1000 in 1991's *Terminator 2: Judgment Day*, or indeed of Arnold Schwarzenegger himself as the T-800 in the original *Terminator* film in 1984. There is a logic to Loken's nudity that is not always apparent in other films of the genre. There is also a sense that she has been included to make up for the absence of Sarah Connor—a tacit admission, perhaps, that a *Terminator* film is incomplete without a strong, central female character. It is interesting to note that in *Terminator 3* the naked T-X is met with concern from the female driver, played by Carolyn Hennesy, who first encounters her: "Oh my God! Are you OK? Do you want me to call 911?" This is in contrast to the derision and abuse that Schwarzenegger's naked T-800 receives from the male punks whom he first encounters in *The Terminator*.

The nuanced 21st century approach to the presentation of the female body would mature further in films of the next decade, including *Ex Machina* and *Under the Skin*; however, it is certainly not echoed in the 2007 film *Transformers*. This is clearly intended to be a "boys and their toys" movie, so a degree of scopophilia is not unexpected; however, director Michael Bay's overt and routine objectification of Megan Fox as Mikaela Banes highlights just how difficult it is to identify trends or themes in a period when the representation of the female is so diverse. Even movies whose titles appear to offer female stories present problems for the analyst: films such as *The Girl from Monday* (2005), *Children of Men* (2006), *Zombie Strippers* (2008),[16] *Cyborg She* (2008), and *The Time Traveler's Wife* (2009) give an indication that the "feminist project"— whatever that may be—has led to a confusion of mixed messages in this post-millennium free-for-all.

Perhaps, then, *Transformers* should actually be seen as part of this decade's muted celebration of what women can be. She is a futuristic jet pilot in *Stealth* (2005), a super-smart, super-fighter in *Serenity*, at least three kinds of mother in *Babylon A.D.* (2008), plus the scientist and the creature in *Splice* (2009). Megan Fox is an updated version of Kathleen Hughes, mentioned in Chapter III, who had swung her well-upholstered breasts at the camera in 1953 for no other reason than to show that *It Came from Outer Space* was filmed in 3-D. But *Transformers* represents more than this; it is a CGI-fueled reflection of the wishes that the genre has always tried to fulfill. In 2007, that signaled a future in which science fiction cinema's reliance on CGI would have a marked effect on the development of its female characters.

MILLENNIAL HEROINES

It may be too early for this history to suggest a definitive *annus mirabilis* for the 21st century, but the science fiction movies released in 2009 already support its nomination as a watershed year. With *Moon*, Duncan Jones showed just how effective small, independent genre cinema could be, while *District 9* showed that CGI could be used in the service of intelligent stories. *The Road* presented gritty reality and *WALL·E* offered charming animation (and another female character named Eve). *Terminator Salvation* hammered a nail into the coffin of one franchise, while life was breathed into another: J.J. Abrams' rebooted *Star Trek*. Although Zoe (or Zoë) Saldana[17] plays Uhura with grit and energy, the male writers fail to take the role much beyond what Jane Killick in her 1992 *Starburst* article "Star Trek Sex: The Female Frontier," calls Nichelle Nicholls' "galactic telephonist in a mini skirt."[18] It is a limitation that is in turn neatly lampooned by Sigourney Weaver's character, Gwen DeMarco, in the 1999 *Star Trek* spoof, *Galaxy Quest*. In contrast, Saldana's second science fiction film appearance of 2009 was destined to have a greater impact on female roles within the genre.

At the time of writing this, James Cameron's *Avatar* is the highest grossing movie of all time, with worldwide box-office receipts of almost $2.8 billion.[19] Three sequels are slated for release between 2020 and 2024, and indications are that Saldana, as the alien Neytiri, and Sigourney Weaver, as the human Dr. Grace Augustine, have been retained for these projects. As always, care must be taken with unconfirmed film news, as details can change, but their rumored involvement at this stage does at least underscore the importance of these female presences to the original film.

This focus is not surprising, as Cameron's movies have almost always featured prominent female characters. It is variations of female representation

Making use of those big anime eyes. Zoe Saldana as Neytiri of the Na'vi in *Avatar* **(2009).**

that occupy most of the points of empathy in *Avatar*, beginning with the planet Pandora itself, the setting for most of the movie. Pandora's spirit, Eywa, is identified throughout as female, seeming to combine the Force from *Star Wars* with the Greek myth of Gaea. This, of course, draws on the genre's earliest female characters, the Mother Nature figures discussed in Chapter I, but in Cameron's "event film," they are writ large, as reviewer Andrew Osmond observes, "In *Avatar*'s most vivid moments, the characters seem uplifted from stereotypes to archetypes ... the exotic Na'vi tiger-woman, leaping into a fire-lit glade and loosing an arrow in mid-air."[20]

Eywa is worshipped by the Na'vi, Pandora's indigenous people, of whom Neytiri is one. She is a free-spirited daughter of the forest, not unlike Marya in the 1917 Danish epic, *Himmelskibet*, with which *Avatar* shares a surprising number of visual and thematic elements. Marya's father is the high priest; Neytiri's mother, Mo'at, played by CCH Pounder, is the spiritual leader of her people. She fulfills the function of the ancient Greek high priestess Pythia, Keeper of the Delphic Oracle, translating the will of Eywa to the Na'vi, contributing to what Chris Hewitt, in his *Empire* magazine review, calls a "love letter to humanity and spirituality."[21]

Although Weaver's Dr. Augustine does not present quite the same personification of the natural spirits as the Na'vi characters, she is nevertheless a xenobiologist, and so takes her place among the "soft" female scientists who permeate the genre. As an irascible iconoclast, however, she is recognizable as a "Cameron woman," and of course as Sigourney Weaver she also lends more than a hint of Ellen Ripley to the film. *Aliens* is brought even closer by the gun-toting, Hispanic helicopter pilot, Trudy Chacón, played by Michelle Rodriguez—a clear nod to the no-nonsense Private Vasquez, played by Jenette Goldstein in Cameron's 1986 movie. Cameron is careful in *Avatar*, however, not to jeopardize a lower age classification, so, R-rated lines like Vasquez's "Fuck you, man" are tempered here to become Chacón's "Freakin' daisy-cutters." Even so, the character does feel rather like an out-of-place antique of the genre, which seems ironic, given that she is surrounded by archaic Mother Nature figures. This is perhaps an indication that audiences had become wary of the leather-clad, kick-ass athlete type that was, in-truth, already looking tired when Trinity took on the role in *The Matrix* in 1999.

Avatar's female characters are far from cutting-edge or nuanced. They are tools for Cameron in what Osmond calls "the sublime pulp territory that he's now definitely conquered."[22] Saldana's Neytiri is modeled on an Amazonian warrior woman, with a visceral femininity and dangerous sexuality, plus she saves the male hero Sully's life on at least two occasions; however, she must be and do all of this from the sidelines. In the main, Neytiri is reduced to rolling her big, anime eyes at Sully's mistakes and to facilitating his actions. Like Marya in *Himmelskibet*, she is a mediator for her man. And yet, she is also a mediator for the genre. By being an iconic figure—as so many of Cameron's female characters become—and in such a hugely profitable movie, she shows, if nothing else, that a female character can thrive in the commercial environment of the science fiction cinema industry. Like the original *Star Wars*, *Avatar* is a double-edged sword. It relies on stereotype for its success, but it is that success which creates a platform for female characters in science fiction cinema going forward.

Neytiri's effect was not instant; many big-budget movies—such as *Inception*, *Iron Man 2*, *TRON: Legacy* (all 2010); *Captain America: The First Avenger* and *Rise of the Planet of the Apes* (both 2011)—continued to focus on male protagonists. However, in 2012, Ridley Scott picked up his *Alien* baton again to conduct Noomi Rapace as the smart and robust Dr. Elizabeth Shaw, taking the lead in the much-anticipated prequel, *Prometheus*. It is fair to say that Scott's third science fiction film was not as successful as *Alien* and *Blade Runner*, as critic Michael Brooke writes, "No one could accuse *Prometheus* of a lacking ambition or ideas, but the latter are too often presented as citations instead of component parts of a fully thought-through thesis."[23]

Despite Dr. Shaw's limited influence on the narrative, it is fair to say also that Rapace's presence and impressive performance in *Prometheus* must have added to growing expectations that women would once again routinely take the lead in science fiction films. This is clearly true of *The Hunger Games* from the same year, which taps into the teenage-girl market that had sustained the *Twilight* saga over five films, and presents it with a female hero in the form of 16-year-old Katniss Everdeen, played by Jennifer Lawrence. This model was so successful that it generated three *Hunger Games* movie sequels (2013, 2014 and 2015, which in turn gradually increase the number of prominent female characters). The model was used for a number of imitation projects, including *Divergent* in 2014.

It is interesting to note that both of these successful female-led projects originated as novels written by women: Suzanne Collins and Veronica Roth respectively. It throws up a question about who is best placed to create sympathetic female characters for the screen. Leslie Felperin had alluded to this in 1995, in her *Sight & Sound* review of *Tank Girl*: "the computer generated predictability of the script (written by a man, wouldn't you know) numbs the film."[24]

And that leads to vexed and current questions about whether Hollywood is able create new science fiction stories for the screen at all.

Déjà Vu

It has become a common cry that the cost of CGI, the fear of risk, a lack of imagination, and even laziness, have forced science fiction cinema to retreat into the past for inspiration. It is tempting for commentators to suggest that this "retreat signals a creative bankruptcy, emphasized by the growing number of 21st century science fiction and fantasy film sequels, prequels, and remakes."[25] By contrast, Nick Pinkerton condemns the repetitive, "steady influx of think-pieces decrying Hollywood recycling…" as an ironic "failure in the journalist profession…" In his March 2016 *Sight and Sound* article, "Rise of the Reboots," he points out that Hollywood has always recycled material, from Charlie Chaplin's Little Tramp character, through studio-era stars playing the same type in successive films, to direct and indirect versions of the same intellectual property—and to remakes.

Science fiction cinema is no different. The very early period was awash with multiple versions of the same concept and the first epic pictures were, like *Le Voyage dans la Lune*, adaptations of existing literature. Silent films were remade for the sound era, if not immediately, as with 1929's *The Mysterious Island*—itself a sequel to Jules Verne's *Twenty Thousand Leagues Under the Sea*—then later, as with Fox Pictures' remake of its 1924 film *The Last Man on Earth* as *It's Great to Be Alive* in 1933. Successful chapter serials were regularly revisited with sequel series, black and white classics have been remade in color, and English-language versions have been created from non–English originals. *Blade Runner* is available in at least four official versions, following the lead of *Close Encounters of the Third Kind*, which in 1980, according to James Bell, "initiated the trend for reissuing successful films with previously unseen footage."[26] In his article "Remake/Remodel: Director's Cuts & Alternative Versions," Bell identifies six additional science fiction films that have been "re-versioned": *Metropolis* (1927), *Gojira* (1954), *Videodrome* (1983), *Dune* (1984), *Repo Man* (1984) and *Brazil* (1985). All of this was before the current crop of re-makes, re-boots, re-treads and re-imaginings.

It is, however, this current penchant for recycling that seems to be exercising the critics, commentators and academics who write about today's science fiction cinema. Indeed, Pinkerton acknowledges later in his article that the situation has changed: "While Hollywood's quixotic desire to standardise success never changes, the manner in which it attempts to do so does...."[27]

Original writing has not disappeared from science fiction cinema, but it does seem to have been pushed down the agendas of producer teams hoping to guarantee a return on their investments by meeting what film theorist and historian David Bordwell calls "the popular demand for the same again but different."[28] How long audiences will continue paying to watch what is increasingly "the same again and barely different" remains to be seen. In the meantime, it has been affecting female roles.

ABSENCE: THE REMAKE

Female roles themselves have long been subject to the recycling process. The literary characters of Alraune and the Mistress of Atlantis have appeared many times. *Bride of Frankenstein* (1935) was created as a sequel to *Frankenstein* (1931) and earlier, in 1914, *The Exploits of Elaine* were successful enough to generate two further 1915 chapter serials: *The New Exploits of Elaine* and *The Romance of Elaine*. All of this was long before Ellen Ripley and Sarah Connor inspired their own sequels and a host of imitators. And of course, the recycling of female types has provided material for much of this book. The animated doll of Georges Méliès' 2-minute skit in 1900, *Coppélia: la poupée animée*, is reflected in *Metropolis*, *Blade Runner* and *Ex Machina*, showing that it is not only the bad movies that recycle ideas. Sometimes, however, recycled ideas can make bad movies.

A remake of Robert Wise's 1951 film *The Day the Earth Stood Still* was released in 2008 with Jennifer Connelly as the classic female character, Helen Benson—originally played by Patricia Neal. The movie had already been remade in 1954, as the low-budget British version, *Stranger from Venus*. Looser versions arguably appeared as *E.T. the Extra-Terrestrial* in 1982 and *Starman* in 1984, and a tighter case could be made for the 2016 movie *Arrival*. Indeed, although *The Day the Earth Stood Still* was based on Harry Bates's short story *Farewell to the Master*, the male alien Klaatu's crucial interaction with the human woman can be traced back through to films of a much earlier period, such as *When the Man in the Moon Seeks a Wife* (1908) and *A Message from Mars* (1913). Helen Benson's essential function is, however, missing from the $80million[29] remake of *The Day the Earth Stood Still*.

David Scarpa's new screenplay appears to start with good intentions, by promoting Helen Benson from secretary to successful career scientist; however, in doing so he immediately follows the genre's well-established trend for "soft scientists": Princeton professor Helen Benson is an astrobiologist. Despite this adherence to tradition, the new film seems embarrassed by the 1951 Benson's role as a mother, and so in 2008 she becomes the lone guardian to Jacob, whose black father died in the Gulf War. The film attempts to dilute Benson's maternal role by consciously shifting her away from the birth-mother stereotype, but then presents her as selflessly caring for Jacob, despite his animosity towards her. Whatever its narrative justification, this 21st century relationship feels forced because there is not enough recognizable reality to underpin it. The 1951 relationship between Bobby and his mother, who had become a widow in World War II, is familiar and immediately accepted; in 2008, too much needs to be explained about the current situation, the past and Benson's motives, which, ironically, draws attention to her role as proxy-mother. As veteran U.S. critic Roger Ebert notes, there is "more detail than we require, I think; just 'her son' would have been fine...."[30] In short, the film is trying too hard to do the "right thing." In effect, Benson's 2008 scientist role drags her towards the "acceptability" of the Mother Nature figure, while her mother role attempts to drag her away from the "restrictive" 1950s' ideal.

These social and professional roles, however, become far less relevant next to the fact that the woman in this 2008 reinvention has lost her crucial narrative function. In this ecologically updated story, the aliens have decided *en masse* not to waste time delivering a message to humanity, but rather to save Earth by purging it of humans altogether. With his original mission to deliver his ultimatum removed, Klaatu, played here by Keanu Reeves, has no real central function either. He has no reason to demonstrate the awesome power at his disposal, and so, as Kim Newman points out, "the Earth stands still as an afterthought."[31] As a result, Klaatu runs around aimlessly, while Professor Benson runs around aimlessly after him. She has been stripped of the essential narrative function that had once made her a powerful force—despite being a secretary and a mother. This is the science fiction axiom offered in Chapter I, updated now for the CGI age to: "Men do very little; women watch them."[32]

Dramas have always been re-packaged for a contemporary audience; this is what keeps Shakespeare fresh 400 years after the plays were written. Despite losing its female character, John Carpenter's 1982 remake of *The Thing* has more visceral impact than the 1951 original, as does David Cronenberg's 1986 version of the 1958 classic, *The Fly*. Both of these directors, and their screen-writers, understand the essential elements that drew audiences to the original versions. It is clear that the imposing robot, Gort, was the element of familiar appeal that attracted the producers of the CGI-heavy remake of *The Day the Earth Stood Still*, rather than the original film's unusually prominent female role. And therein lies an ironic consequence of the development of female representation in this genre. What was unusual, indeed ground-breaking, in 1951 was commonplace by 2008. And so, Helen Benson's role is reduced because she no longer brings anything special to the narrative. If this theory holds true, it presents the potential for other prominent female roles to be sidelined, or even stripped out of, new versions of films that were once the building blocks of female character development in science fiction cinema.

Ten years after Tim Burton had re-imagined *Planet of the Apes*, the series was re-booted again for the current franchise, beginning with *Rise of the Planet of the Apes* in 2011. This film takes many of its references from Pierre Boulle's source novel *La Planète des Singes*, but that influence does not extend to Zira— nor indeed to any meaningful female presence. Frieda Pinto plays Caroline Aranha, a chimpanzee specialist (a "soft" scientist) at San Francisco Zoo. The role is clearly a nod to Zira, but there the comparisons end. Despite her field of expertise, Aranha appears to show no curiosity about the nature and origin of her scientist-boyfriend's clearly exceptional male chimpanzee, Caesar. The female professional is sidelined even further in the 2014 sequel, *Dawn of the Planet of the Apes*, in which the nurse Ellie, played by Keri Russell, does little more than defend the apes in a few lines of dialogue, and use antibiotics to cure Caesar's wife. This movie is largely one of male concerns: between fathers, sons, male humans and male apes. The single named-ape female is Caesar's partner Cornelia, who is referred to only as "Mother." The inquisitive female, embodied in Dr. Zira (and later in Ari) has been silenced. The second sequel, *War for the Planet of the Apes*, released in 2017, does include 12-year-old Amiah Miller as Nova, a mute mediator between humans and apes, but it is a long way back to Zira from here.

It is interesting to note that the ape character that carries the most empathy, sympathy and gravitas in these films is the male orangutan Maurice— played by a woman, Karin Konoval. It seems odd, given the liberties already taken with the source material, that the filmmakers did not merely make this character female. There is no reason why it cannot be, except that, again, female role development is not the focus of these CGI-heavy remakes; instead, it is the remarkable motion-capture performances, led by Andy Serkis as Caesar. This technology has become so impressive and important by the third film that it seems to have taken all of the energy and imagination out of the writing. The dialogue skips between witty intra-textual references to earlier *Apes* material, while the story makes inter-textual references to another Boulle-inspired movie, *The Bridge on the River Kwai* (1957), as well as to Francis Ford Coppola's 1979 movie, *Apocalypse Now*—which was in turn inspired by Joseph Conrad's 1899 novel, *Heart of Darkness*. Despite all of this willingness to re-imagine, plus the power of modern movie technologies, there appears to be no space on the planet of the apes for a new female character.

GENDER: THE RE-IMAGINING

Ignoring for a moment its power to mitigate risk, the remake does offer filmmakers opportunities to revisit old themes and concepts from new perspectives. Notwithstanding Garrett Stewart's pithy comment above, science fiction cinema is often held as a mirror for modern mores; so, the remake is also a useful tool for comparison. Even more valuable to this study are the recent examples of films that make changes to their original gender roles.

It was noted earlier that the 1974 adaptation of Ira Levin's 1972 book *The Stepford Wives* generated debate about whether that film exposes or indeed perpetuates female stereotypes in the media. Frank Oz's 2004 remake attempts to dodge this particular debate by making it clear from the start that its chosen media target—the television industry—is shallow, fatuous, and exploitative of both men and women. The most obvious initial problem from the female perspective is the fact that the television industry depicted here is run by women. Nicole Kidman plays Joanna Eberhart, the heartless, megalomaniacal executive who is fired and forced to move to Stepford. An attempt is then made to dodge cries of "misogyny" by making the film a comedy. Bette Midler, as Bobbie Markowitz, works very hard to that end, but the messages become muddled when the film also tries to make serious statements. The most obvious example of this is the introduction of a homosexual couple, Roger and Jerry, who are implausibly welcomed "just like any other couple" by Christopher Walken's sinister patriarch, Mike Wellington, and his conservative coterie at the Stepford Men's Association. This welcome extends to Roger being "cyborgized" in the way that the other wives of the community have been. However, while all of the female wives have had their professional ambition removed by the homogenization process, this male "wife" has additional ambition inserted; he is then presented as the community's candidate for Senate. And so, the "perfect woman" here is a gay man.

In her 2004 *Sight & Sound* review, Liese Spenser places some of this chaos of mixed messages into contemporary American context:

> In a world in which Hilary Clinton bakes cookies for the news crews and über-housewife Martha Stewart implodes in a scandal of insider trading, there's no doubt that there's still mileage in this kind of material. But the remake eschews any simple message, lambasting Kidman's career bitch and Glenn Close's demented downsizer alike.[33]

In that final point, Spencer highlights what is perhaps the most incongruous aspect of this remake. It turns out that Mike Wellington, who has been controlling the female cyborgs of Stepford, is himself a robot, who is being controlled by his wife, Glenn Close's "demented" Claire Wellington. Ultimately then, this remake of *The Stepford Wives*—which seems so keen to avoid debate—begins and ends by blaming women for everything.

While the project is ultimately flawed, *The Stepford Wives* should perhaps be praised for its attempt to say something new. Otherwise, there may be a danger that a "damned if you do, damned if you don't" mentality will curtail attempts to revisit material from new perspectives. In Chapter VI, this survey suggested that Winona Ryder's Call—the first female synthetic in the *Alien* series—is trying too hard to be different. It could also make the argument that Kristanna Loken's T-X—the first female cyborg in the *Terminator* series—is not different enough to make her distinctive from the men. It could certainly make this case for the 2016 remake of the 1984 hit, *Ghostbusters*.

The "what if" concepts that sit at the heart of science fiction make the genre an ideal space for discussions not just about sexuality, but the notions of gender fluidity that are becoming more commonplace in the real world. In an online article, Guy Kelly refers to seventy-one current gender identification terms; he expands on the following selection: "agender, aporagender, bigender, butch, cisgender, demigender, demme, genderfluid, gender neutral, gender queer, intergender, nonbinary, polygender and transgender/trans."[34] The fact that these designations are not common currency in science fiction cinema— and probably never will be—leaves *The Stepford Wives'* gay re-formulation looking both cutting-edge and hopelessly inadequate.

At first glance, the 2014 Spierig brothers' film *Predestination* appears to be promising. As Anton Bitel notes, the inclusion of an hermaphrodite character suggests a film "concerned with issues of gender destiny...."[35] Indeed, the movie develops some of the criticism of casual sexism that Robert A. Heinlein scatters through his source material, the 1959 short story, *All You Zombies*. One sequence in the movie suggests that the only way women can reach space is by training as "companions" for male astronauts on long missions. It is a neat reflection of Lt. Stewart's role in *Planet of the Apes* (1968), as discussed in Chapter IV, and it is also a neat way of criticizing the early men-only policy of NASA; however, this film has a men-only policy of its own. The time-travel conceit at the core of *Predestination* requires characters to have knowledge, and to act on that knowledge in order to keep the time-cycle running. All of the knowledge and action resides with the male characters; all of the decisions are made by the men. Once the woman, Jane, has been used to create the baby needed to fuel the time-cycle, she is removed from the plot. She literally becomes a man, John. It is only then—as a man—that he gains knowledge and any potential power over his life or the film's narrative. This is a time travel film, so Jane inevitably returns, but always at the point where she is denied knowledge, leaving her, and the viewer, to sit and watch the men do things. It may be that the writer/directors have self-consciously created this Jane/John dynamic to highlight the genre's default position; perhaps this is one of the 'issues of gender destiny' highlighted by critic Bitel. Regardless, the lesson of *Predestination* seems clear: if you want to know things or do things in science fiction film, become a man.

Since making *The Matrix* series, the Wachowski brothers, Larry and Andy, have re-identified as women: the Wachowskis, Lana and Lilly. As trans-women with influence in the film industry, they potentially bring a unique perspective to science fiction film. It is hard to tell yet if this will eventually come through their work. Their 2014 film *Jupiter Ascending* adds to the genre another woman tossed around a male-driven narrative, with little power to affect her own destiny. Despite the prominence on posters and in trailers of the eponymous Jupiter Jones, played by Mila Kunis, the movie offers very little for its female lead. Indeed, it is not surprising that a film described by Adam Nayman as "perfumed and pricey sci-fi pulp"[36] should once again define its lead female character in terms of science fiction's most pervasive female role: she is a mother, remodeled from the DNA of a dead matriarch.

Perhaps this is the Wachowskis' own voice, or perhaps they need time to take stock and develop it further. In the meantime, the best place to find female points of view on screen in the second decade of the 21st century is television and the internet. Director Jennifer Phang, co-writer Jacqueline Kim and a host of creative women show that the small screen can be a place for strong women in their 2015 online movie *Advantageous*; and the British television show of the same year, *Humans*, examines the notion of the perfect woman through Gemma Chan's "synth," Mia. In 2017, it was announced that the BBC's *Doctor Who*, a series which has run intermittently in Britain since 1963 with twelve men in the leading role,[37] would be gaining its first female Doctor (the lucky 13th), in the form of Jodie Whittaker.

Traditionally, transfers from the small screen to the large screen have been more commonplace, but a recent resurgence in television has addressed this imbalance. For female roles, the switch has been beneficial, as multiple episodes give far more opportunity for potential character development than a single feature can. This maxim is borne out in two film versions of *The X-Files* movies in 1998 and 2008, neither of which allow Gillian Anderson as Dana Scully the scope that makes her character so compelling in the original television series. Perhaps this is why producers turned to television for their powerful remakes of *Westworld* (2016) and *The Handmaid's Tale* (2017)—the big winner at the 2017 Emmy Awards.

These shows are not, however, without their critics, who quickly pointed to their scenes of nudity, sex and rape as potential perpetuations of violent, anti-female cultural stereotypes.[38] Thandie Newton, who plays the brothel Madame Maeve Millay in *Westworld*, is not so sure. Presented as an intelligent, articulate activist for women's rights in Jane Mulkerrins' *You* magazine article, "It's MY BODY, MY CHOICE, MY TERMS," Newton—who, incidentally, named her daughter Ripley after the "feminine, but empowered" icon—argues that *Westworld* presents an important message. "When I read the first script, there was so much that I was horrified by, but the point of it is to shock us into the awareness that this is what we do to each other...."[39]

Newton may be right, but that will not silence debates about whether female nudity on screen represents post-modernist, post-feminist female empowerment or exploitation of a well-worn stereotype.

STEREOTYPE: THE REBOOT

Crucial to the central role that women play in *Westworld* is the fact that they are the first characters to become self-aware—a concept central to the 2015 British film *Ex Machina*. This is the story of a man's obsession with his sophisticated robot creation, Ava, played by Alicia Vikander. *Ex Machina* has been widely praised for its elegant and intelligent exploration of artificial intelligence, and not just in the movie press. In a *New Scientist* magazine article, cognitive and computational professor Anil Seth praises the film for "its engagement with current theories about the meaning of consciousness," adding that "everything about this movie is good."[40] Dan Smith disagrees: in his letter to *Sight & Sound*, published in the April 2015 issue, he argues that "*Ex Machina* is a voyeuristic movie (if there are any other kinds). Its initial justification for its objectifying gaze upon a woman trapped in a glass booth and on trial for her life ... is that she is after all just a robot. But there is a good deal of lingering on dressing and undressing."[41]

This "just a robot" stance had been the implicit justification for the callous treatment of Pamela Gidley's character at the end of *Cherry 2000* in 1987. *Ex Machina* writer/director Alex Garland's justification for the perpetuation of the sexualized robot trope is that, in order for his film to highlight society's objectification of young women, he must give the audience what it expects. This view was offered in an interview on BBC Radio 4's *Film Programme*, in which the presenter/interviewer Francine Stock had already noted in her introduction that there is "little surprise, perhaps, that this robot should be made in the form of a beautiful, young woman."[42] Garland may well be evoking memories of other mad scientists and their fantasy-female creations—Rotwang's robot Maria, Frankenstein's bride, and Tyrell's replicants, for example—however, he uses the same justification that has attended debates about perceived misogyny in *A Clockwork Orange* and the original *Stepford Wives*. Garland may well have misgivings about society's wider treatment of women, but he must surely also realize that its repetition over time in high-profile movies, such as his, has helped to keep these stereotypes alive.

Perhaps *Ex Machina* gets away with this because it is an accomplished, intelligent film with real science at its core. The female robot does not perform a sexy dance in the way that Caity Lotz's character—another Ava—does in another British film, *The Machine*, in 2013. Instead Ava's nudity in *Ex Machina* might be read as an indication of vulnerability, like Ripley's "strip" towards the end of *Alien* (1979). It could be argued that part of Ava's education and exploration is the examination of her own body. It could be argued that Garland is enticing his audience in the way that the low-budget 2014 Canadian movie *Debug* does, by ensuring that every female character appears in her bra and/or briefs at some point in the story. *Debug* is not in the same league as *Ex Machina*, but comparison does lead to wider questions about when stereotype is acceptable or necessary. For example, what is the audience to make of the final sequence of *The Hunger Games: Mockingjay—Part 2*, which shows Katniss Everdeen returned to her bucolic idyll as a wife and mother, despite fighting her way, alongside an unusually high number of female fighters, to victory through four films? Perhaps this is her chosen prize, but it is rather different from the ascension to heaven that greets the male heroes of *Dune* and *The Matrix* series. Where the male savior becomes a god, the female savior becomes a mother.

Mothers are not the issue here. It is not surprising that a role so central to the concept and reality of creation should have sustained through more than 100 years of science fiction cinema. The real issue is how essential that function is to the "what if" conceits that underpin the genre. Opinions on this matter will differ. In the 2010 European film *Womb* (also known as *Clone*), the male hero grows up to have an accidental sexual relationship with his mother; in the 2017 movie *The Space Between Us*, she is merely a vessel to transport the male protagonist; in the celebrated 2013 film *Gravity*, motherhood provides the emotional touchstone and the central character flaw.

For a British newspaper interview about *Gravity*, director Alfonso Cuarón stated that "the studio told me very early that nobody wanted to see a film set in space that stars a woman.... But you know, it's something I didn't even question...."[43] Cuarón's stance is laudable, and supported by evidence; however, the Dr. Ryan Stone who emerges in *Gravity* suggests that she did not have his full confidence. To make Sandra Bullock's character more palatable, she is given a few familiar female characteristics, including a link with biology and medical sciences, large gaps in her knowledge, reliance on the man (alive and dead) and emotional instability. She is also a mother. Indeed, it is Dr. Stone's own perception of her failure as a mother—her daughter was killed in an accident—that saddles her with psychological demons that surely would have been discovered during the NASA selection process.

It is tempting to suggest that Cuarón held out for a female lead character because he and his fellow writer, son Jonás, required a chaotic, car-wreck of a character to drive the emotional element of an otherwise sterile, technology-heavy narrative. The woman here may have more presence than in previous special-effects showcase movies—such as *Destination Moon*, *2001: A Space Odyssey* and even *Star Wars*—but that presence is required by the narrative as a point of weakness. Whatever the merits of its 3-D spectacle, and Bullock's impressive performance, the overall effect of *Gravity* is to take a potentially strong, modern female character and then systematically undermine her.

The 2016 movie *Arrival* was made for less than half the budget of *Gravity*. Its central character is also female: Dr. Louise Banks, played by Amy Adams.

No kick-boxers here. Amy Adams as linguist Dr. Louise Banks in *Arrival* (2016).

She is also a bereaved mother who is psychologically damaged by the death of her daughter. And, as she points out, she is not a scientist: "You want science? Talk to your father." Instead, it is Dr. Banks' knowledge as a linguist that drives this story. This female-linguist role had also been seen before in Amelia Hall's all too brief appearance as Professor Mabel Chapel in *Iceman* (1984). In *Arrival*, however, Dr. Banks' discipline and expertise guide the viewer through the sometimes convoluted narrative, and she eventually saves the world. As a mediator between "Us and Them," she has a recognizable connection with female characters going back through *Avatar* (2009), *The Abyss* (1989) *Short Circuit* (1986), *Starman* (1984), *Planet of the Apes* (1968), *The Day the Earth Stood Still* (1951), *Metropolis* (1927), and even the 1927 French curiosity, *Sur un air Charleston*, in which a woman communicates with an alien visitor through dance. However, *Arrival* manages to use, subvert and transcend the female stereotypes in a way that other films do not. Dr. Banks is attractive without being objectified, smart without being obnoxious, and flawed without being undermined. It is a crucible of characteristics that make her one of the most rounded and satisfying characters of the 21st century so far.

A New New Hope for the Future...?

The ability to bend female stereotypes to a better purpose in films like *Arrival* might suggest that science fiction cinema is maturing. Indeed, if a bastion of machismo like *Mad Max* can enable women to claim its territory and reclaim the stereotypes in a movie like *Fury Road* (2015), then perhaps the genre has already reached maturity. Director George Miller's third sequel to the 1979 genre classic uses its female characters to cover as many representation bases as possible: skin color, hair color, age, disability, sexuality, body modification, nudity and more. It also deftly handles issues of sexual violence without voyeurism and presents the amputee, warrior, woman Imperator Furiosa, played by Charlize Theron, as a rounded character. Indeed, she becomes a potential successor to Max himself, which is a matter of concern to Aaron Clarey, who has declared foul play in a number of interviews and blog posts, arguing that Furiosa as "an impossible female character" who has been included "in an effort to kowtow to feminism."[44] This may be true; after all it seems a long, long way from the damsel-in-distress of *The Perils of Pauline* (1914). However, Clarey's fury, which includes the argument that "feminism has infiltrated and co-opted Hollywood," masks the continuing plight of most female characters in the genre. For many years, genre expert Kim Newman has used the pages of *Sight & Sound* magazine to draw attention to this, and he seems set to continue: his May 2014 review for *Escape from Planet Earth* mentions a "noxious subtext with a villainess"[45] and in April 2016, he writes of the semi-spoof *Deadpool*: "Vanessa's line from the trailer about not being a damsel in distress has been dropped for the film—presumably because the makers realised that she'd become precisely that."[46] Newman's September 2017 review for *Spider-Man: Homecoming*—the penultimate genre release before this survey was completed—does offer something more, with its observation that "Peter is stuck not on a cheerleader but the captain of the academic decathlon team."[47] Welcome though they may be, these tweaks are surely no match for the onslaught of media messages and publicity surrounding today's science fiction films.

LOOK-AT-MY-ASS SF

Science fiction cinema has long embellished its posters to sell its movies. The female threat posed in the *Attack of the 50 Foot Woman* is exaggerated by the image of a scantily clad woman who appears to be at least 200 feet tall. Prurient peril is added to *Forbidden Planet* in the classic 1956 poster that shows an unconscious, buxom Altaira being carried by Robbie the Robot, something that never happens in the movie. Some suggestions of sex do at least run through *Forbidden Planet*, which is not true of *The Day the Earth Stood Still*, whose 1951 poster shows a sexualized Helen Benson in a state of peril, again, never seen in the movie. Bruce Lanier Wright's comment that the posters for this film are "somewhat more conventional than the film itself" highlights the common thread of "adult" images that run through these advertising materials, and others collected in his book *Yesterday's Tomorrows*. Many more can be found in posters for films that pre-date the U.S. Production Code Administration, whose introduction, as discussed in Chapter II, had a marked effect on the style and content of science fiction films around the world. The poster for the 1928 version of *Alraune* is particularly noteworthy for its risqué image of a stylized Brigitte Helm.

Provocative posters never disappeared completely, but a number of online commentators, including Andrew Bridgman at www.dorkly.com have noticed a 21st century trend for images that clearly reflect the "scopophilia" and "male gaze," also discussed in Chapter II. The posters in this trend typically show a woman with her body facing away from the camera, but looking back over her shoulder into the lens. The camera angle is low, which draws attention to her, usually well-defined, buttocks.

Examples of this "look-at-my-ass SF" image can be seen in posters for *Daredevil* (2003), *G.I. Joe: The Rise of Cobra* (2009), *TRON: Legacy* (2010), *Avengers Assemble* (2012), *The Dark Knight Rises* (2012), *Divergent* (2014),

21st century "Look-at-My-Ass SF" posters. For *Daredevil* (2003), *G.I. Joe: The Rise of Cobra* (2009), *TRON: Legacy* (2010), *Avengers Assemble* (2012), *The Dark Knight Rises* (2012), *Jupiter Ascending* (2015), *Divergent* (2014), *Ex Machina* (2015) and *Deadpool* (2016).

Jupiter Ascending (2015) and many others, including *Ex Machina*. The trend is so well established that is lampooned in a *Deadpool* poster in which the male hero adopts the same pose, next to the tagline, "Bad Ass. Smart Ass. Great Ass."

Deadpool's use of this stance draws attention to a key difference between the traditional "male gaze" and what might be termed an "invited male gaze." While these women are still objectified, they appear to have a choice; this is "look-at-*my*-ass SF" rather than "Look-at-*her*-ass SF." This distinction sets up a cynical suggestion that designers may be using the suggestion of female agency and complicity to assuage male guilt and head off criticism. On the other hand, it may also be a reflection of the increasing roles that women and girls play in the consumption of science fiction products. It is an extension of Vivian Sobchack's 1988 observation that "the American SF film, no matter how abstract individual images may be, finally grounds itself in comprehensibility, in its necessary commerciality."[48]

Bridgman's website Dorkly.com is a fan site, offering, like many others, "a fun take on fandom."[49] This fun increasingly extends to fans dressing up and playing in the costumes of their favorite, often science fiction, character—cosplay. A staff member at *Dorkly* hints at the extent of its scope, effectively turning Sobchack's observation into a prediction: "It's kind of amazing to see how the hobby of cosplaying has evolved from 'goofy excuse to wear spandex' to a 'multi-million dollar artform with its own celebrities and industries.'"[50]

A cursory glance through the Dorkly website and elsewhere on the internet suggests, anecdotally, that at least 50 percent of the fans within this creative zone of the genre are female. Constance Penley draws attention to a similar trend in her 1997 exploration of science fiction fan "slash" culture, *NASA/Trek.* Here she notes the number of women fans who write gay fantasy fiction about their screen favorites: stories involving Captain Kirk and Mr. Spock (Kirk/Spock, Kirk-slash-Spock) were popular at the time.

When cosplay became the subject, in 1996, for an episode of the hit television show *Friends*, it was presented as a vehicle for male desire. In "The One with the Princess Leia Fantasy," directed by Gail Mancuso, Ross suggests to Rachel that if she were to dress as Princess Leia in her gold bikini costume from *Return of the Jedi*, it might spice up their sex life. Rachel complies with this request, although the outcome is not entirely what Ross was hoping for. Twenty or so years later, the gold bikini is still a very popular cosplay costume, but it appears alongside far more overt and sexualized outfits that, crucially, appear to be chosen by the women wearing them. It might be easy to suggest that this "choice" is—like that implied in the "look-at-my-ass" posters—an illusion, driven by assumptions made about an imagined male consumer for this cosplay; however, it is becoming increasingly dangerous to make these blanket, "male gaze," assumptions. The video for the American pop star Ariana Grande's 2014 song "Break Free" opens with a *Star Wars* inspired introductory crawl that includes the words: "It is just one step ahead of present day reality and two steps ahead of present day sexiness." The video itself is a chaotic mix of post–Spice Girls science fiction kitsch, with inter-textual film references and a clear message of "Girl Power." Dressed in a science-fiction–esque corset, Ariana Grande is the hero of her own genre narrative in which she kills alien creatures with her blaster rifle and destroys a robot using rockets that emerge from her bustier. The action is interwoven with an homage to Jane Fonda's striptease from the title sequence of *Barbarella*—although without the full nudity. This may be just as well, as Ariana Grande's core fan-base is pre-teen and young-teen girls, as suggested by her "Choice Music: Female Artist" win at 2014 Teen Choice Awards. Given this constituency, it is difficult to know the intended message being sent by "Break Free." Science fiction and fantasy feature strongly in the movie categories at these awards, which include a prize for the "Choice Hottie: Female" (also won by Grande). All of this, along with the "look-at-my-ass SF" poster used for the teen-targeted movie *Divergent*, points to a confusing, modern liminal space where young people are seemingly taught that female power is equated with robust sexual imagery.

These particular incarnations of that strand have some way to go before they become like the pornographic cosplay that has now colonized sections of the internet; however, they do make a contribution to an on-going "empowerment vs. sexualization" discussion.[51] The impression that women have more power and so are willing accomplices in their subjugation and objectification presents a dichotomy that is neatly encapsulated in the genre career of Scarlett Johansson.

SCARLETT FEVER

Scarlett Johansson began her genre career with a 2005 Michael Bay film that has the feel of 1970s' science fiction. In *The Island* she plays Jordan Two Delta, one of the "products" of a human farm that clones rich clients to enable replacement body parts to be harvested as required. *THX 1138* (1970), *Coma* (1978) and *Logan's Run* (1976) are all evoked here, but it is the latter that informs Johansson's role, especially in the second half of the movie, when she spends most of her time running after her running man. The CGI-augmented action that shifts the aesthetic in the second part of *The Island* is there throughout the ongoing series of Marvel movies in which Johansson plays Natasha Romanoff, also known as Black Widow. The character name may evoke the spider who eats the male after mating, but it is really Johansson's character that is the victim in a series of ostensibly ensemble stories that are really tales of male angst, fathers and sons, and "boys with their toys."

When Black Widow first appears in the 2010 Marvel film *Iron Man 2*, the low-set camera focuses initially on her back-side, which it follows as she walks across the room. It is a moving example of the "look-at-my-ass SF" that features on so many posters. Even more overt focus is placed on the female-ness of this character in *Avengers Assemble* (2012), when the male villain refers to her as a "mewling quim." This sexually abusive, and frankly bizarre, archaic language is not repeated in the series, but it sets the tone for the sexualization and gradual side-lining of Black Widow through *Captain America: Winter Soldier* (2014) and *Avengers: Age of Ultron* (2015), until she becomes a token presence in *Captain America: Civil War* (2016).

It is in non–Marvel films where Johansson's more interesting roles can be found. In *Under the Skin* (2013), she plays an alien visiting Earth, trapped in a human body. I.Q. Hunter considers it a remake of the 1954 film *Devil Girl from Mars*, but one "which is rather less fun than the unassuming original,"[52] but *Under the Skin* does add more to the debate about "necessary" nudity highlighted above by *Ex Machina* (2015). *Her* (2013) updates the genre's approach to computers and cognition, discussed in Chapter VI, with its presentation of a despotic female entity; and *Lucy* (2014) updates *Charly* (1968) and *Johnny Mnemonic* (1995), exploring notions of knowledge gained and lost from a female perspective. Finally, for now, the female body, AI and lethal force are brought together in stylized form for the 2017 CGI-augmented, live version of the 1995 anime classic, *Ghost in the Shell*, in which Johansson plays the iconic Major Kusanagi.

All of these movies rest on stereotype at some stage, but when the intention is honestly to tell a female story with style, the stereotypes start to feel like the legitimate contents of a toolbox. This may be what eventually rescues *Ex Machina* from censure. What is more, it seems that when women are the focus of a modern science fiction narrative—or work alone within it—their roles are more diverse and interesting. This is perhaps not surprising; however, it does present a reversal of the ensemble setup that proved so successful for Ripley in *Alien*. Women working in co-ed teams in the 21st century are instead regularly tied to two modern stereotypes, both of which have their roots in the 1980s: the despotic leader and the "fighting babe."

Capitalism and the military-industrial complex became preoccupations of science fiction films in the 1980s. The *Alien* series is a key example of this. Since then, greedy organizations have remained through *Resident Evil* (2002) *Avatar*, *District 9* and more; and ruthless corporate entities are now routinely represented by autocratic female figureheads. For example: *Babylon A.D.*

(2008), *Prometheus* (2012), *Elysium* (2013), *Divergent*, *The Giver*, *Transcendence*, *Escape from Planet Earth* (all 2014), *Jurassic World*, *Hunger Games: Mockingjay—Part 2* (both 2015) and *Okja* (2017)—although this final example does knowingly lean towards parody for its "corporate bitch."

The second modern stereotype, "fighting babe," clearly carries the DNA of Leia, Ripley and Sarah Connor, but she has morphed through Trinity, River Tam (*Serenity*, 2005) and Neytiri to become a super-charged, attractive, mixed-martial-artist. She may still carry a gun, but it is less likely to be an oversized blaster rifle, as favored by Private Vasquez in *Aliens* (1986), and she is often objectified by the camera and other (male) characters. She is part of a trend that might be better described as "look-at-my-ass-kickboxing SF." Charlize Theron is not impressed, as she told John Hiscock in a British *Telegraph* interview: "I'm not a fan of scrawny little girls pretending to kick butt."[53] Trudy Chacón in *Avatar* may represent more a return to the big guns of the 1980s and '90s, but the IMDb.com profile of Michelle Rodriguez, who plays her, gives an indication of the basic appeal of this type: "Known for tough-chick roles, Michelle Rodriguez is proof that there is a cross between beauty and brawn."[54]

Of course, not all female characters in the genre display the brutality and robustness that characterize the callous leader and the accomplished fighter; however, there seems to be a general expectation that the female character will be smart and sassy with a no-nonsense attitude—even if she still has no control over the narrative. Such is the success of this modern powerful/powerless female hybrid that she has found her way into children's animated features, such as: *Capture the Flag* (2015) and *Smurfs: Lost Village* (2017)—which features Rodriguez as the voice of the "tough-as-nails warrior," Smurfstorm.[55]

The ethos is captured by the female-clothing retailer, GWBB (Girls Will Be Boys), whose website, incidentally, features quite a few images of women from behind. Its "About Us" page sets out the company mission statement:

> GWBB represents a lifestyle for those that understand, reflect and embrace the definition of the modern Tomboy.
>
> …
>
> 4. Navigates effortlessly in a man's world but is also feminine and sexy when she desires.
>
> …
>
> Strong, independent, accepted, active, stylish, physically fit, vibrant, free spirit, trendsetter.[56]

The full GWBB statement of intent might also serve as a manifesto for female characters in the biggest science fiction properties of the 21st century.

Battle of the Franchises

Speaking on BBC Radio in 2017, around the time of the release of *Alien: Covenant,* Ridley Scott claimed that he was planning to make the *Alien* franchise "bigger than *Star Wars.*"[57] This apparent focus on money and legacy, rather than stories and art, reflects Sobchack's comment above about the "necessary commerciality" of the American science fiction film. It also recalls Christian Metz's work on the nature of cinema itself, *The Imaginary Signifier,* in which he argues that cinema is "peculiar to a historical epoch (that of capitalism) and a state of society, so called industrial civilisation."[58] To Metz, the rise of the modern franchise as a technology-reliant money-making machine would be an inevitability. CGI has streamlined the generation of the product to the point where the franchises have become their own genres, drawing on all four stages of the Schatz Cycle, discussed in Chapter VI: innovation/experimentation; classical/established; parody/pastiche; deconstruction/refinement. Twenty years after *Alien: Resurrection* paved the way with baroque postmodernism, they have become pastiches and deconstructions of themselves.

"Re-boot" suggests a new start, and after the parochial, television feel of the ninth and tenth *Star Trek* movies, *Insurrection* and *Nemesis,* J.J. Abrams' *Star Trek* re-boot did feel new. The franchise's female fans, increasing in number via cosplay, fan fiction and the spin-off television shows, might have expected some experimentation with the female characters too, but with so many self-references and in-jokes to deliver, Abrams' movie was perhaps always destined to settle back into well-worn stereotypes—feeding David Bordwell's "popular demand for the same again but different." Kirk's mother appears briefly, in the form of Jennifer Morrison, and the death of Spock's mother, played by Winona Ryder, has a psychological effect on her half–Vulcan son. While Zoe Saldana's Lieutenant Uhura conforms to a number of "modern stereotypes," her primary role is in psychological support of Spock. She is his girlfriend.

In 2012, Ridley Scott provided a reminder through the *Alien* prequel *Prometheus* that women could be strong-willed and effective without being kickboxers; however, the narrative, with its broad references to the classic *Alien* themes, fails to do justice to the potential of Noomi Rapace's Dr. Elizabeth Shaw. A classic of the *Star Trek* franchise provided the model for the 2013 movie *Star Trek Into Darkness,* which is based on the 1982 movie *Star Trek II: The Wrath of Khan,* which was in turn inspired by the original television series episode "Space Seed." Dr. Carol Marcus is back, now younger and played by Alice Eve. She is smart and sexy, and appears briefly in her underwear in a shot reminiscent of the closing sequences of *Alien;* however, this is not her story.

Despite initial appearances, *Star Wars: The Force Awakens* (2015) is not really Rey's story either. Daisy Ridley plays this character in a retread of the journey followed by Luke Skywalker in the original *Star Wars* movie. It seems that Nick Pinkerton may be right: "the eternal hero with a thousand faces may be limited to fewer and fewer bankable names."[59]

This lack of originality presents a quandary for those looking at, and for, female development in the genre. When 1980s science fiction cinema discovered that the hero's journey—long the preserve of men—could be taken by women, it began to tell female stories. *The Force Awakens* is not one of those, but it is a self-conscious attempt to inject a female perspective into one of science fiction cinema's biggest properties. When Rey shouts at Finn, as he tries to drag her out of trouble, "will you stop holding my hand!," the inference is the unspoken "I am not your usual science fiction film heroine!" She is right. She may not be the finished article, but she is getting close. By summer 2016, even the *Star Trek* franchise had begun to the see the potential of a prominent female hero, and so *Star Trek Beyond* introduces Jaylah, a bald, beautiful alien played by Sofia Boutella. Her tough role is balanced by a Lydia Wilson's bad alien, Kalara, and Anita Brown's good alien, Tyvanna, in what is the most female-focused cast of all *Star Trek* movies to date.

Despite Tim Hayes' complaint that "the results show the straightjacket of franchise engineering,"[60] *Rogue One*, the *Star Wars* story released at Christmas 2016, does take one step further than both *Star Trek Beyond* and *Star Wars: The Force Awakens* in the journey towards a bona fide female narrative. This is Jyn Erso's story; however, it is still familiar, Felicity Jones plays the orphaned

Are we looking at the future here? Felicity Jones as Jyn Erso in *Rogue One* (2016).

child who initially refuses the call to fight the Empire, then saves the day after a reconciliation with her father. Katherine Waterston's character, Janet Daniels, in *Alien: Covenant* (2017) is even more familiar. For this second *Alien* prequel, Ridley Scott returns not only to the ensemble cast that carried Ellen Ripley to initial success in 1979, but to the entire plot of the original movie. In truth, it all feels a little familiar.

This new wave of female characters in franchise films could be a commercial recognition of the power of the female consumer as reflected in the cosplay community. There could be a deeper, psychological reason, linked to the "id/super-ego transaction" discussed in Chapter II. Throughout the genre's history, unfamiliar concepts have been balanced against familiar, or "normal," elements to create interesting but acceptable narratives. Social position was once that normalizing factor; now, perhaps, these stories have become so familiar that they will support anyone in the lead role. Or it could be that women have become so familiar in the genre that they no longer seem out of place. Perhaps they are now a "normalizing factor."

Sonequa Martin-Green certainly seems at home in her role as Michael Burnham, the narrative focus—albeit curiously named—of the latest *Star Trek* small-screen incarnation, *Discovery*. However, as noted above, a television series often offers more freedom for female character development and experimentation than a feature film is able to. And that is the subject of a whole new book.

———⊗⊗⊗———

Despite the seeming sophistication of its vision and its dominance in the marketplace, 21st century science fiction cinema is subject to the same forces that have always affected female roles. The advance of technologies, social influences and financial pressures have, once again, forced filmmakers to see former triumphs as a route to future success. For the female roles of the new millennium this meant an attempt to rekindle the magic of Ripley and Connor, but without the muscles. The kick-boxing babes who emerged may not permit a return to the domesticity of a bygone age, but nor do they generate the impact of that near-gone era. There are glimmers of hope, but these may fade if the same selection, distillation and repetition process continues to homogenize the movies themselves. It is uncertain how long science fiction cinema will continue to eat ever more expensive versions its own tail; at the moment, the women (and men) of this genre seem to be trapped in one big sausage machine—which, ironically, is where this survey of female representation in science fiction cinema began.

CONCLUSION
Invisible Woman

When you came in here, didn't you have
a plan for getting out?—*Princess Leia*

This has been a history. It has attempted to lay some facts out and make some connections between them. If one requirement of the Conclusion is to take these observations and summarize the role of the female in science fiction cinema over time, I would return to the silent period and paraphrase the words offered in Chapter I: "women support men doing things." Despite many developments in the interim, this maxim still underpins much of the genre. If another requirement of the Conclusion is to make predictions, I would need to be a little more circumspect. After all, I have been wrong before:

> As feminism continues to develop its multiple debates, inevitable further fragmentation increases the amount of ever more complicated socio-political argument. As science fiction film continues to develop its love affair with the visual image, inevitable simplification of its message decreases its tolerance for socio-political argument. In consequence, then, this renewed divergence suggests that the opportunity to utilise science fiction film as a platform for feminist debate has been missed.[1]

Nineteen years after those words were written, it appears that change may actually be in the air. In order to chart that potential change here, it is worth returning to Marleen Barr's 1987 text *Alien to Femininity: Speculative Fiction and Feminist Theory*, which was introduced earlier to illustrate how second-wave feminist movements in the 1960s and '70s were challenging traditional representations of women. Barr identifies three phases of developing feminist thought, along with their literary equivalents:

213

1. "Statement of Problem"
2. "Radical Feminist Solutions"
3. "Moderate Womanist Solutions"[2]

Science fiction cinema has traditionally trailed behind this particular curve, but it may now—just—have reached the cusp of phase 3. With apologies to Barr, a skewed version of her outline now forms a framework for discussion on the current state of female representation in the genre.

STATEMENT OF PROBLEM(S)

The 1976 movie *Logan's Run*, with its simple escape and discovery story, would not be made in the same way today. That is a fairly obvious statement; remakes are always more complex in plot and vision than the original. And yet, these modern complexities often fail to reach as far as the female characters. Scarlett Johansson's role, chasing Ewan McGregor around in the 2005 film *The Island*, is barely more sophisticated than Jenny Agutter's supporting role, chasing Michael York around in *Logan's Run*. This initial "problem" will not be solved while the genre continues to draw its female characters from the same well.

This stems from the central "problem," which has been highlighted so often in this text that it has become the underlying theme: it is the cinema industry's coupling of capitalism and patriarchy. Put more bluntly: it is male control of the money-making well. This problem is magnified by science fiction's enhanced ability to make manifest the male imagination. However, counterexamples do exist, and analysis of these present a potential model for change, which begins with this: It must be *her* story.

This is obvious too. It is also too simplistic. If the hero of her own story spends most of the movie naked, or is sexually abused, or is a secretary, or even a biologist, the role will be open to complaints of sexism, misogyny, gender stereotyping, laziness and more. This is a tough square to circle, because the alternatives are also problematic. The no-nonsense, leather-clad, kick-boxing fighter has herself become a female stereotype in the genre, and so is now open to similar complaints—especially when much of the focus is on her backside. Any screen presence might be deemed better than mere absence; however, absence might be preferable to overt objectification and misogyny. If women tread paths previously taken by men, their voices may be diminished; however, if they tread distinct paths of their own, they run the risk of being boxed in and denied access to the rich tapestry of storytelling traditions.

Perhaps balance is required. If men spent more time naked, sidelined, abused and ignored, the ignominy of objectification and rejection might be shared. But that feels like a race to the bottom in a mission to make characters the worst they can be, rather than the best. There are already too many science fiction films peopled by ciphers and cardboard cut-outs. More are not required. It is surely preferable to have good—even great—female characters, but attempting to identify what that means is tricky. It recalls the ongoing mission to define science fiction itself, discussed in the Introduction.

In her attempt to weave fantastic fictional elements into a liberal definition that also acknowledges science fiction's relationship with other genres, Vivian Sobchack offers this somewhat unwieldy summary:

> The SF film is a film genre which emphasizes actual, extrapolative, or speculative science and the empirical method, interacting in a social context with the lesser emphasized, but still present, transcendentalism of magic and religion, in an attempt to reconcile man with the unknown.[3]

Unwieldy it may be, but what Sobchack's definition provides is a frame of reference. It is an all-encompassing list of what science fiction film *can* be; it is not a description of what every science fiction film is. Perhaps, then, a more productive way to address the notion of great female roles is to identify what she can be, but not require her to be everything. For if a counsel of perfection is maintained, it should be made clear right now that there has never been— and will never be—a great female science fiction character.

Is it of consequence then that female scientists in the genre's films traditionally focus on the "soft," life sciences? Should it matter that the most common female role is the mother? Should the appearance of "feminine" traits in female characters be criticized as sexist, or should they be applauded as a vanguard against the genre's descent into bland, unisex homogeneity? Nichelle Nichols was very clear on that matter when she insisted that Lt. Uhura be allowed to wear make-up and jewelry in the 1979 feature *Star Trek: The Motion Picture* and returned to wearing skirts, rather than pant suits, in 1984 for *The Search for Spock*.[4] Does it matter that this translates into Zoe Saldana's Uhura being the only member of the senior bridge crew not wearing pants in the 2009 re-boot, *Star Trek*? Or does it matter more that she is the only lead character who does not get to save a colleague? After all, as Neytiri in *Avatar*, Zoe Saldana wears virtually nothing, but this does not stop her helping to save her planet—and her man.

It is easy to forget context and perspective, which is a reminder of Bonnie Noonan's comments, quoted in Chapter III, as she explains the effect on her young self of seeing active women in professional science settings in the films of the 1950s: "the encouragement to which I responded, did not much reflect my interest in a scientific career, but my desire to have a career at all and to have that career taken seriously...."[5] Noonan has avoided the temptation to set up retrospective weighing scales with "progressive representation" in one pan and "regressive elements" in the other; instead her book, *Women Scientists* in *Fifties Science Fiction Movies*, provides context and perspective, and values the overall impression created by these characters. In this spirit of openness, I decided to go out on a limb and list my top ten female science fiction film characters. I attached no prior criteria to this exercise, instead allowing the "overall impression" principle gleaned from Noonan to guide my selection:

Friede Velten	Gerda Maurus in *Frau im Mond*, 1929.
Lisa van Horn	Osa Massen in *Rocketship X-M*, 1950.
Helen Benson	Patricia Neal in *The Day the Earth Stood Still*, 1951.
Altaira Morbius	Anne Francis in *Forbidden Planet*, 1956.
Zira	Kim Hunter in *Planet of the Apes*, 1968.
Leia Organa	Carrie Fisher in *Star Wars*, 1977.
Susan Wheeler	Geneviève Bujold in *Coma*, 1978.
Sarah Connor	Linda Hamilton in *The Terminator*, 1984.
Eleanor Arroway	Jodie Foster in *Contact*, 1997.
Louise Banks	Amy Adams in *Arrival*, 2016.

On further analysis, these seem to be characters who stand out from the crowd in their particular era and so may have had an influence on what followed (although, it is too early to say that for Louise Banks). These subconscious

Handing the baton to the next generation. Lt. Uhura, as played by Nichelle Nichols in *Star Trek III: The Search for Spock* (1984), and Zoe Saldana in *Star Trek Beyond* (2016).

criteria are hardly surprising from someone who is coming to the end of writing a book on the subject. Indeed, thinking about that, an honorable mention should go to Uhura, but she is primarily a television character who loses significance in the *Star Trek* feature films. *Fury Road*'s Imperator Furiosa is the best of the recent crop of fighting females, who, along with Ripley would make list #2.

In reality, of course, this is a list of favorite characters in films that I would be happy to watch again tomorrow, which returns this discussion to the central problem. My favorites will not influence what comes next, but somebody's will. And that somebody for the vast majority of science fiction cinema history has been a man.

Radical Feminist Solutions (On Screen)

Taking a line of best fit, one that smooths out oscillations in female fortunes across a century or so of science fiction cinema, might yield a development journey that looks something like this:

She is nothing

She is something

She does something

She responds to the narrative

She develops within the narrative

She is the focus of the narrative

She drives the narrative

She is the narrative

The high-profile female action characters who now occupy prominent positions in some of the genre's biggest franchises would appear to occupy the final four stages of this journey. They represent the genre's most radical shift away from the days when she was absent or a mere token presence. It is interesting, then, to see how, or indeed if, this development has affected wider perceptions of female roles. To help with this, a call for characters was put out to a few of the critics, commentators and academics whose work has been cited in this text. They were invited to provide a "list (up to 10) of the 'best' female characters in science fiction cinema." No criteria were specified. Their personal selections provide fascinating insights, so they have been included below.[6]

Bonnie Noonan

It is interesting to see that Noonan remains serious about the importance of careers, but with greater emphasis now on the scientific nature of those careers. This may reflect her training as a molecular biologist. Her own criteria are as follows: "a. Highly credentialed in science and/or space travel; b. Crucial member of a scientific investigation/space expedition; c. Able to stand up against opposition to her importance; d. Authoritative when necessary; e. Prevails due to intellect rather than physical force."

Dr. Lisa van Horn	Osa Massen in *Rocketship X-M*, 1950.
Dr. Patricia Medford	Joan Weldon in *Them!*, 1954.
Dr. Lesley Joyce	Faith Domergue in *It Came from Beneath the Sea*, 1955.
Dr. Cleo Markham	Susan Clark in *Colossus: The Forbin Project*, 1970.
Dr. Ruth Leavitt	Kate Reid in *The Andromeda Strain*, 1971.
Officer Ripley	Sigourney Weaver in *Alien*, 1979.
Dr. Diane Brady	Lindsay Crouse in *Iceman*, 1984.
Agent Dana Scully	Gillian Anderson in *The X-Files* [TV], 1993–2002.
Dr. Ryan Stone	Sandra Bullock in *Gravity*, 2013.
Dr. Louise Banks	Amy Adams in *Arrival*, 2016.

J.P. Telotte

Unsurprisingly for someone who has published so many valuable insights into the genre, Telotte provided notes for each of his selections. Sadly, there is not enough space to include them all here, but in general they emphasize the importance of duality and independence within characters. Telotte's general criteria for selection are also very enlightening: "I've simply pulled figures who resonate for me and who seem to reflect something(s) important about what I term the science fiction imagination, *i.e.*, a part of our larger cultural imagination that allows us to address/make sense out of the problems and possibilities that emerge from a world where science and technology hold sway." In "no particular order," his list is:

Maria	Brigitte Helm in *Metropolis*, 1927.
Ripley	Sigourney Weaver in the *Alien* series, 1979/86/92/97.
Nikki	Margaret Sheridan in *The Thing from Another World*, 1951.
River Tam	Summer Glau in *Serenity*, 2005.
Sarah Connor	Linda Hamilton in *The Terminator 1&2*, 1984/91.
Rachael	Sean Young in *Blade Runner*, 1982.

Major Kusanagi   Atsuko Tanaka in *Ghost in the Shell*, 1995.
Princess Leia   Carrie Fisher in *Star Wars IV–VI*, 1977/80/83.

Marie Lathers

This list was also accompanied by interesting personal criteria notes: "The best female characters in science fiction cinema are bold and independent, active and intelligent. They are not mere followers, but leaders. They often outwit their male counterparts, and are often responsible for saving humankind and planet Earth. They are not reduced to their sexual and reproductive function, but make use of all of their skills. They may be evil, especially if they are aliens, but they stand out for their independence and intelligence."

1. Ripley   Sigourney Weaver esp. in *Alien*, 1979.
2. Ellie Arroway   Jodie Foster in *Contact*, 1997.
3. Aelita, Queen of Mars   Yuliya Solntseva in *Aelita, Queen of Mars*, 1924.
4. Friede Velten   Gerda Maurus in *Frau im Mond*, 1929.
5. Lisa van Horn   Osa Massen in *Rocketship X-M*, 1950.
6. Nyah   Patricia Laffan in *Devil Girl from Mars*, 1954.
7. Zira   Kim Hunter in *Planet of the Apes*, 1968.
8. Uhura   Nichelle Nichols and Zoe Saldana in *Star Trek* [film/TV].
9. Dana Scully   Gillian Anderson in *The X-Files* [TV/film].
10. Rachael   Sean Young in *Blade Runner*, 1982.

Lynne Magowan

As a teacher, Magowan is fascinated to observe the connection that her students have with science fiction film characters: "I find it difficult to watch Scarlett Johansson as Black Widow. But kick-boxing babes in lead roles have made it easier than it used to be to engage female students with the genre." She also provided a rationale for each, including "males gaze at your peril!" for Zhora. Her edited countdown is:

10. Furiosa   Charlize Theron in *Mad Max: Fury Road*, 2015.
9. Vampire Girl   Maila Nurmi in *Plan 9 from Outer Space*, 1959.
8. Lt. Nyota Uhura   Nichelle Nichols in *Star Trek* film and TV series.
7. Ellen Ripley   Sigourney Weaver in the *Alien* series, 1979/86/92/97.

6. Dr. Ellie Arroway   Jodie Foster in *Contact*, 1997.

5. Zhora   Joanna Cassidy in *Blade Runner*, 1982.

4. Lady Jessica   Francesca Annis in *Dune*, 1984.

3. Barbarella   Jane Fonda in *Barbarella*, 1968.

2. Princess Leia   Carrie Fisher in *Star Wars IV–VI*, 1977/80/83.

1. Sarah Connor   Linda Hamilton in *The Terminator 1&2*, 1984/ 91.

Ace and Olga Pilkington

It is interesting to see the drift towards television with the Pilkingtons' list; they are not the only commentators tempted by these roles; as Ace observes, "there's a lot more characterization in a ten-year series than a two-hour film." Their criteria for selection, edited here, remain fascinating: "We looked for characters who were intelligent, attractive, and capable. If they were also professional, assertive, and highly educated that was even better. When they have problems (or other people do), they deal with them effectively. Most of them make big differences in the societies where they find themselves, often against great opposition." In preference order, they are:

1. Prof. Lesley Joyce   Faith Domergue in *It Came from Beneath the Sea*, 1955.

2. Altaira Morbius   Anne Francis in *Forbidden Planet*, 1956.

3. Lieutenant Uhura   Nichelle Nichols and Zoe Saldana in *Star Trek* [film/TV].

4. Amb./Pres. Delenn   Mira Furlan in *Babylon 5* [TV], 1994–8.

5. Capt. Kathryn Janeway   Kate Mulgrew in *Star Trek: Voyager* [TV], 1995–2001.

6. Seven of Nine   Jeri Ryan in *Star Trek: Voyager* [TV], 1995–2001.

7. Dr. Ellie Arroway   Jodie Foster in *Contact*, 1997.

8. Col./Dr. Samantha Carter   Amanda Tapping in *Stargate SG-1* [TV], 1997–2007.

9. Dr. Susan Calvin   Bridget Moynahan in *I, Robot*, 2004.

10. Molly Woods   Halle Berry in *Extant* [TV], 2014–5.

Matthew Wilhelm Kapell

A drift even further away from cinema here, but that in itself is an interesting comment on the wider genre, especially as Kapell provides specific insight into his Heinlein selection: "my first novel that I can remember with a female protagonist, and it is the 'model' of how I envision strong women in older, written SF." His eclectic list, in "no particular order," is:

Lt. Ellen Ripley	Sigourney Weaver in *Alien*, 1979.
Mina Harker	Various in *Dracula* and most associated films.
Sarah Connor	Linda Hamilton in *The Terminator*, 1984.
Honor Harrington	novel character, David Weber novels.
Dana Scully	Gillian Anderson in *The X-Files* [TV], 1993–2002.
Laura Roslin	Mary McDonnell in *Battlestar Galactica* [TV], 2004–9.
Dana	novel character, *Kindred*, Octavia Butler, 1979.
Ellie Arroway	Jodie Foster in *Contact*, 1997/Carl Sagan novel, '85.
Anzha	novel character, *In Conquest Born*, C.S. Friedman, 1986.
Friday	novel character, *Friday*, Robert A. Heinlein, 1982.

I was once rebuked for not including the 2005 film *Æon Flux* in a piece about women in science fiction cinema. I had not seen it at that time, but once I had, I still did not want to include it. Charlize Theron's "perfect assassin," to paraphrase one of the movie's taglines, seems to be a synthetic response to a male notion of radical feminism—despite the film's female director. With very little plot or character development, plus questionable dialogue and costumes designed to draw the male gaze, *Æon Flux*, rests almost entirely on a promise that *Total Film* makes in its review of Theron's 2017 film, *Atomic Blonde*: "Kick-ass action. Charlize Theron is totally badass."

It is interesting to see how few of the characters in the commentators' lists above conform to this modern female stereotype. Instead, their measured responses reformulate and re-present "radical" as "revolutionary," rather than "man-hating feminist"; these are characters who are enough ahead of their time, and their peers, to appear nonchalantly radical. There are many complex characters, here, sharing J.P. Telotte's description of Major Kusanagi as "a truly liminal figure, always detached, always in charge, yet also unsure of who/what she really is." This often manifests itself in a vulnerability in these listed characters that, perhaps surprisingly, connects the final two characters offered up for this exercise.

Christine Cornea

Rather than provide a list, Cornea draws attention to "two recent representations within the genre, which I think make for an interesting comparative coupling." These are:

Imperator Furiosa   (Charlize Theron in *Mad Max: Fury Road*, 2015)
Louise Banks   (Amy Adams in *Arrival*, 2016)

Cornea points out that Banks' "heroic status is not based upon her physical fighting prowess." This is a self-evident characterization that runs counter to what appears to be a general trend, but, as Cornea goes on to point out, *Arrival's* complex and thoughtful narrative "seems to open up the prospect of a female perspective in mainstream sf film." It is interesting to note that it is this type of female character—one whose perspective is shared with the audience—that dominates the lists included above. More interesting still are Cornea's comments about the other half of this comparative coupling:

> Imperator Furiosa, as an example that is certainly worthy of attention, is really driven by the excited responses to this character from my students. When the film was first released, female students in particular were noticeably thrilled with the fact that this female character takes center stage and, in some respects, replaces the male hero, Max, in terms of offering a hope for the future.

An argument could be made that Furiosa shares with many of the nonaction nominees above a sense of psychological vulnerability that is not always apparent in action characters. The result is a more rounded character and, once again, a shared female perspective.

More significant to this conclusion is the similarity between Christine Cornea's experience and Lynne Magowan's observation that female action characters have helped her female students to engage with the genre in a way that they did not before. This also links back to Bonnie Noonan's personal recollection, whereby women in 1950s films gave her younger self hope of a career of some kind—any kind. This is one reason why the Introduction to this text mentions the avoidance throughout of qualitative terms like "progressive" and "regressive"; they cannot hope to take all perspectives into account.

Various attempts over the years to offer radical feminist solutions to the stated problem essentially created a science fiction cinema that presents male expectations of female expectations. This was always going to produce unsatisfactory results, because, as Gloria Foster's Oracle says in *The Matrix Reloaded*: "What do all men with power want? More power." Those student responses to Imperator Furiosa and Dr. Banks suggest that what is required is a different way of thinking.

MODERATE WOMANIST SOLUTIONS (OFF SCREEN)

When astronomers believed that the universe was geocentric, they needed to invent epicycles to explain why planets sometimes appeared to move backwards in their orbits around the Earth. Once they realized that Earth is in a heliocentric system, the heavens ran a lot more smoothly—at least for the scientists. The authorities remained skeptical. For a century or so, the workings of science fiction cinema have been androcentric. Women have revolved around men, sometimes appearing to falter, until the imposition of an epicycle got them going again. The overall direction may have been forwards, but the journey has not been a smooth one. While there seems to have been a general shift away from this model on-screen, some cinema authorities appear to remain skeptical. Perhaps it is time for an off-screen revolution: a gynocentric science fiction universe. Its form, however, may need to take account of Germain Greer's warning to women from *The Female Eunuch*: "If women understand by emancipation the adoption of the masculine role then we are lost indeed."[7]

The hopes and aims of many may be to find a whole other way of doing things, but finding the ideal model to deliver this may well be tricky. In his editorial for the November 2014 issue of *Sight & Sound*, Nick James offers the obvious way forward: "Film theory teaches us that the male gaze is so deep-rooted in cinema as to be structural. The obvious answer to such a problem is to bring more women into filmmaking and commentary."[8]

James may be correct in the long term, but the success of this strategy so far has been patchy. In recent decades an increasing number of female writers, directors and producers, have come to science fiction cinema, but this has not necessarily translated into the presentation of female points of view on screen— at least not in high profile projects. Movies such as Lynn Hershman-Leeson's *Conceiving Ada* (1997), Gabriela Tagliavini's *The Woman Every Man Wants* (2001) and Madeleine Olnek's *Codependent Lesbian Space Alien Seeks Same* (2011) all offer female perspectives, courtesy of women writer-directors; however, these are not films with wide distributions and large studio budgets and backing. For that, go to the recent *Planet of the Apes* franchise, which, despite the input of Amanda Silver as writer and producer, has no prominent female ape character and barely a notable female human either.

Of course, this is not necessarily Silver's fault, nor the fault of any of the women who work on high-profile science fiction projects that continue to mine traditional female representation. They are working within the confines of a patriarchal industry, just as Ella O'Neill was when she wrote her parts of the 1936 space opera *Flash Gordon*, or Karyn Kusama was when she directed the ill-fated *Æon Flux* in 2005. It is the same industry that stripped the female protagonist out of the title of Luc Besson's official adaptation of the French comic strip, *Valérian and Laureline*, before presenting it as the 2017 event movie, *Valerian and the City of a Thousand Planets*. Sergeant Laureline has not disappeared entirely; she remains, played by model Cara Delevingne, wielding her blaster, wiggling her bottom and essentially running around after the movie's male hero.

Laureline fits into a tradition of female sidelining, which is beginning to look old in the face of changes happening elsewhere in the high-profile movie market. As of the end of August 2017, the most financially successful films of the year so far were female led: *Beauty and the Beast* and *Wonder Woman*. Indeed, the latter has become "the highest-grossing non-sequel action flick of all time."[9] *Star Wars: The Last Jedi* inevitably joined their ranks shortly after its December release. In the 21st century, eight science fiction films have received nominations for Best Picture at the Academy Awards: *Avatar* and *District 9* in 2009, *Inception* in 2010, *Gravity* and *Her* in 2013, *Mad Max: Fury Road* and *The Martian* in 2015, and *Arrival* in 2016. Only three were nominated during the previous 74 years.[10] Of the eight 21st-century nominees, five feature women in prominent or lead roles. None of the 20th-century nominees do.

Studio heads, producers, marketing managers and accountants will understand that this data suggests that the audience—the market—is shifting. They will understand the commercial need to shift the gaze along with it; however, that requires a paradigm shift in industry thinking. It is why characters such as Laureline, along with Black Widow in *Captain America: Civil War* (2016) and Gamora, played by Zoe Saldana in *Guardians of the Galaxy Vol. 2* (2017), continue to arrive; they seem to betray a reluctance to let go of the traditions that have sustained the genre for over one hundred years. Or perhaps a careful compromise is being played out here. Charlotte Brunsdon has seen this before. In her 1987 examination of feminism on screen, *Films for Women*, she refers to movies which "attempt to capitalise on a discernible new audience," adding that,

> while some women have given a cautious welcome to these films, arguing that they do indicate shifts in definitions and representations of femininity, others have been particularly angered, feeling that political ideals have been exploited to provide fashionable—and profitable—entertainment.[11]

It is tempting to wonder if recent developments in science fiction cinema would meet with the same response. Regardless, Brunsdon's lesson is clear: take nothing for granted. Indeed, she points out that many early feminist films "took a feminist politics for granted, and built from there, rather than polemicising to establish that politics."[12]

It may seem that cinema is a long way from using science fiction actually to promote feminism, but according to Aaron Clarey, who received much attention for his calls for boycott of *Mad Max: Fury Road*, that process has already started. After watching the trailer, Clarey, predicted irately that "*Fury Road* was not going to be a movie made for men. It was going to be a feminist piece of propaganda posing as a guy flick."[13] Clarey is part of the "Men's Rights Movement" that Casey Jaye explores in her 2016 documentary, *The Red Pill*.[14] It presents the central argument of the movement as this: In the rush now to promulgate the female perspective, men are being denied their own perspective. After one hundred years of male-dominated science fiction film, this may be a hard pill to swallow, but even the documentary's feminist director Jaye, initially skeptical of the Men's Rights Movement, reaches the conclusion that an anti-man stance does not help anyone.

The dangers of polarized opposition can be seen in the furor that surrounded the movie *Passengers* after its release in 2016. Jennifer Lawrence plays Aurora Lane, a passenger in cryosleep on an ark ship, which is traveling through space to colonize a distant planet. Chris Pratt plays Jim Preston, another sleeping passenger, except that he is accidentally woken 90 years too early. After some time alone on the ship, Preston gives in to temptation and wakes Lane from her cryosleep, in order to have a companion. He then tells her that her waking was also an accident. The two are now alone on the ship for 90 years. They fall in love, have sex, and then the trouble begins. Detractors have referred to this as a rape narrative; Tomris Laffly does not go this far, but he does call the film "an outdated and offensive fairy tale in disguise,"[15] pointing out that, although the screenplay does explore the morality of Preston's actions, largely through the anger of Lane, it also "brazenly milks the viewer's sympathy for Jim," and "manufactures the perfect excuse for Aurora to team up with Jim again and forgive him."

Passengers does have its issues, although perhaps not as many as are suggested by comments across the internet. Laffly's description of the film as "insulting to women" is not unreasonable; however, this film is no more insulting than the majority of the genre's output for a hundred years. For some of its duration, *Passengers* actually makes a better job than most of interrogating and questioning the actions of the male protagonist, but ultimately this is still primarily a movie about male action. Jennifer Lawrence's character conforms to an observation made in Chapter I about movies made one hundred years ago; it is one that has been applied above to *Logan's Run* and *The Island*: "men run around; women run around after them." It is this age-old, fundamental issue that remains when the hoopla surrounding *Passengers* is stripped away.

There are no easy answers to these issues. However, notwithstanding the dangerous power of social media to escalate and magnify grievances unchecked, these debates may well turn out to be healthy for the genre. They highlight century-old issues that would not have been aired a century ago. And so, studios are becoming aware of the "offense" being caused by some of these representations. It is necessary now to head these critiques off at the pass, which is perhaps why Kathleen Kennedy, President of Lucasfilm, has convened a story steering group whose task it is to guide the *Star Wars* feature narratives over the next few years.[16] Most of the group's members are female, including its Chair, Kiri Hart, which may account for the push towards the promotion of female perspectives in the franchise; although Disney, which now owns *Star Wars*, does have a long tradition of placing leading female characters in prominent roles in its movies. Whatever the proportion of influence, the combination appears to provide a "womanist solution" that is set to be the model for a successful science fiction franchise for some time to come.

The journey to this point has not been a smooth one; the journey forward will doubtless not be entirely smooth either. Whether the current situation will lead to revolution is not clear; however, it does feel as though the genre has reached a tipping point. Female science fiction film characters are closer to glory than at any time in their history. Whatever the model, it will surely require more of the industry to recognize that women are now not just *in* the business, they *are* (at least half of) the business.

Epilogue

In order for a physical book to be produced, the author must stop at some point and allow the publication process to take over. However quick that process is, it is inevitable that a history to the present day will be dated the day it goes into print. This is especially true of a study of a film genre as current and dynamic as science fiction. All of this will be understood by the reader, so no further words should be necessary here. However, as the manuscript's post-submission period saw the release of at least two significant science fiction movies, this epilogue has been written to bridge the gap between delivery and printing, taking this historical survey to the end of 2017—with a quick muse about possible futures.

One of those significant late 2017 releases was *Blade Runner 2049*, the long-awaited sequel to the influential 1982 genre classic, *Blade Runner*. Critical responses to the new movie have generally been good, with reviewers praising it for remaining true to the atmosphere of the original while developing the story with a degree of intelligence. Female roles have developed too. Their impact, however, resides not in a newfound power to influence the narrative, but in their professional roles within this imagined world—most notably Robin Wright's tough police officer, Lt. Joshi, and the no-nonsense replicant, Luv, played by Sylvia Hoeks. Despite these female characters, *Blade Runner 2049* remains a story about male angst and the search for Self. It also retains the thread of female-as-commodity which ran through *Blade Runner*. Ana de Arnas plays Joi, a disposable virtual-woman designed to please her man in multiple environments; in a particularly gruesome scene, a newly "birthed," naked female replicant is dispatched with a blade once it is clear that she is not pregnant (and is therefore useless); and Sean Young's character Rachael appears just as she was in the 1982 movie, only to be shot through the head when she is no longer required in this one. While *Blade Runner 2049*'s much-praised re-creation of the original movie's *mise en scène* owes much to the art direction and cinematography, the importance of the tone re-generated by these discarded women should not be discounted.

Although *Star Wars: The Last Jedi* does not share *Blade Runner 2049*'s flirtation with misogyny, it does dilute the Rey-led narrative, promised at the end of *The Force Awakens* (2015), in favor of a psychological exploration of Luke's journey as a Jedi master after the events of the original trilogy. Rey is left to continue her re-tread of Luke's earlier journey, by mirroring elements of his paths through *The Empire Strikes Back* (1980) and *Return of the Jedi* (1983). As if to balance this side-lining of Rey, *The Last Jedi* introduces a number of plot threads involving influential women. General Leia and Vice-Admiral Holdo, played by Carrie Fisher and Laura Dern respectively, take turns to be in charge of the rebel forces, while Rose Tico, played by Vietnamese-American Kelly Marie Tran, takes control of Finn in a quest to disable the First Order's tracking device. Often, these powerful women expose the rash, gung-ho nature of male actions, and often women can be seen in control rooms, starship bridges and fighter cockpits. The result appears to be a competition with *Rogue One* (2016) to be "the movie with the most equal gender balance."

It is interesting to note that both *Blade Runner 2049* and *The Last Jedi* make efforts to address the historic gender imbalance in science fiction cinema. They also toy with other audience preconceptions generated by years of entrenched tradition. Most notably for this survey is the notion of the hero's noble lineage: the genre's well-trodden preoccupation with male heroes in search of their fathers runs through this book. This is both inverted and subverted in each of these new films. Ryan Gosling's character, K, is looking variously for a father-figure and a mother-figure, only to be disappointed by the news that he is not the messianic progeny of replicant Rachael. He is nothing. Rey is a woman looking for a father figure, only to be deflated by Kylo Ren's news that her parents were "filthy junk traders" who sold her for drinking money. She is nothing. These set-ups and revelations are clearly designed to play with the expectations of audiences used to fairytale endings. On the surface, they deliver surprises akin to the arrival of Schwarzenegger's good T-800 cyborg that fueled the *Terminator* franchise in *T2: Judgment Day* (1991); however, they also signal a move toward a self-assured, postmodern knowingness that arguably undid the *Alien* franchise in *Resurrection* (1997). It is, of course, possible that the final film of the third *Star Wars* trilogy (slated for release in 2019) will reveal that Kylo Ren was lying, and that Rey is in fact the result of a union between Captain Phasma and some long-lost Kenobi.

Guessing the future can be a dangerous game. That said, it is tempting finally to take a brief look at releases scheduled for 2018, in order to muse about their potential for female representation. The science fiction and superhero juggernaut seems set to roll on, with remakes, sequels and franchise spin-offs such as: *The Predator, Jurassic World: Fallen Kingdom, Maze Runner: The Death Cure, Pacific Rim: Uprising, Avengers: Infinity War, The New Mutants, Ant-Man and the Wasp, Solo: A Star Wars Story* and doubtless more. A cynic might predict that any increased female involvement there will take the form of malevolent CEOs, kick-boxing babes and a sidekick or two—perhaps even a female Wookiee. There are, however, some potentially interesting lead female roles among the re-treads. *X-Men: Dark Phoenix* may be able capitalize on the success of *Wonder Woman* (2017), if Sophie Turner is given a chance to shine in this title role. And with Yukito Kishiro's classic manga *Alita: Battle Angel*, producer James Cameron will once again place Japanese female characters at the center of the action—this time in the form of Rosa Salazar in a movie co-written by Laeta Kalogridis. Even the "boys and their toys" series, *Transformers*, seems set to experiment, with *Bumblebee*, written by Christina Hodson, presenting Hailee Steinfeld in what appears to be the protagonist role. *Mortal Engines* also has female writers in Fran Walsh and Philippa Boyens, alongside Peter Jackson, but the cast list as it currently stands looks less promising.

Perhaps the most promising movie scheduled for a 2018 release is *Annihilation*, Alex Garland's directorial follow-up to his critically acclaimed *Ex Machina* (2014). Garland's screenplay is adapted from Jeff VanderMeer's novel, which follows four women (a biologist, a surveyor, a psychologist and an anthropologist) as they journey into the mysterious Area X. Given that most of these roles conform to science fiction cinema's tradition of the "soft" female scientist, it will be interesting to see if Garland attempts to use this to challenge audience preconceptions, as he claims to have done in *Ex Machina*.

Whatever happens, female roles seem set to develop further, as women continue to take center stage on various media platforms. S.J. Clarkson has recently been named as the director of the next *Star Trek* movie, and the first woman in that role. On Christmas Day 2017, the long-running British television series *Doctor Who* unveiled Jodie Whittaker as its first female Doctor, after fifty-four years and 12 male incarnations. Also in 2017, the *PlayStation* fantasy game series, *Uncharted*, released *The Lost Legacy*, a stand-alone story with female protagonists for the first time in ten years and eight chapters, previously led by Nathan Drake. It is doubtful whether Chloe Frazer and Nadine Ross will become as iconic as Lara Croft from the *Tomb Raider* series, but their portrayals are somewhat closer to women that the game player might expect to meet on the street. This "normalization" of the female action character can be seen in the *Star Wars* themed product commercials screened in theaters along with the UK release of *The Last Jedi*. Most of these feature girls and young women as protagonists—wearing virtual-reality goggles, wielding light sabers, using the force, and so forth. These adverts in turn represent a real-world focus that has been brought into sharp focus recently by Hollywood celebrities using Twitter hashtags such as #metoo, #timesup and #glassceiling to draw attention to the treatment of women in the movie industry—on-screen and off. The year 2018 and beyond is shaping up to be a very interesting period in many ways.

And there we really must stop. By the time this book goes to print, this epilogue will be out-of-date too; however, musings about interesting female roles will continue to be added to webpages at www.deanconrad.com. Perhaps in another twenty years these will be drawn together in an updated version of this printed volume.

APPENDIX
Female Representation
in Science Fiction Cinema—
A Selection

The movies in this section have been selected to give a sense of how female roles in science fiction cinema have developed over 120 years. It is not an exhaustive list, these are not necessarily the greatest films of the genre, nor do they all contain "great" female characters. Instead, the aim has been to cover a range of roles, concepts, themes, stereotypes and so on. Rather than aim for the "first" of each type (robot, scientist, astronaut and so forth), the list leans towards some of the more notable examples. There is more overt personal opinion here than in the main text, which should point towards titles that are recommended as good films to watch, rather than just those deemed necessary for study. Finally, listing by decade can be somewhat artificial, as cinema styles rarely divide that neatly; however, it feels right to include at least one film from each decade, in order to give a better sense over time of the development of female representation in science fiction cinema.

The 1890s

Photographic images that move had been around for a few years before 1895, but the new ability to project them onto a screen expanded the audience and so increased potential revenue. An industry was born. In its earliest days, cinema was a novelty promoted by entrepreneurs to make money out of curious thrill-seekers. With a few tweaks, this might also serve as a description of the science fiction film industry. Indeed, it has been argued that, to early audiences, all films were science fiction.

La Charcuterie mécanique
(Lumière Brothers, France, 1895, b/w, silent)

The Mechanical Delicatessen is considered by many to be the first science fiction film. It is a 1-minute piece in which a live pig is pushed into one end of a large wooden box, then, thanks to the magic of cinema, it emerges at the other end as sausages, chops, hams and so forth. These "trick" films formed the basis of the early genre, and the sausage machine concept appeared a few more times under different guises. There are no women in *Charcuterie mécanique*. In fact, the absence of women from most of the early pictures says a lot about the nature of the genre and the industry. A comparison with 2017 release *Okja* gives good indication of the considerable distance travelled by women— and pigs.

The 1900s

Filmmakers quickly realized that the ability to manipulate time and space makes film the perfect medium for fantasy stories. Cinema's first complete decade saw French, British and American independent filmmakers expand science fiction's offering with crazy inventions, silly science and speculative fiction. The genre's female characters conformed in the main to their traditional narrative roles as pretty lovers, nagging wives and Mother Nature figures.

Chapellerie et charcuterie mécanique
(Alice Guy-Blaché, USA, 1900, b/w, silent)

This may well be the first science fiction film directed by a woman, which alone makes it interesting for this study. The idea is not particularly original, as it joins a number of films during this period that developed the concept presented in *La Charcuterie mécanique* (above). There are no women in this 4-minute adaptation either; however, cats are turned into hats! Guy-Blaché was a pioneer of early cinema, with hundreds of short film credits across many genres to her name, so it is inevitable that her work would encompass this one. Her 1906 marginal genre film *Les Résultats du Féminisme* muses on the consequences to society were feminism and the work of the suffragists to be left unchecked. It was a popular subject before World War I began to alter perceptions about women in society.

Le Voyage dans la Lune
(Georges Méliès, France, 1902, b/w, silent)

The face of the Moon with a space capsule stuck in his eye is one of the iconic images of all silent cinema. This is the original science fiction cinema epic. Stage magician Georges Méliès reveled in the new medium of film, as it enabled him to do tricks that he could only dream of before: making people vanish instantaneously was a favorite. The women in this space story take roles that were to follow them through the history of the genre. On Earth, they are the attractive assistants to scientists who would come into their own in the 1950s in films like *The Thing from Another World!* (1951). On the Moon, they are Selenites, beautiful alien ancestors of the likes of Leeloo (*The Fifth Element,* 1997) and Neytiri (*Avatar,* 2009). They are led by an alien queen—another staple of female representation in the genre (see: *Aelita, Queen of Mars,* 1924 and *Star Trek: First Contact,* 1996, in this list).

An Animated Doll
(Unknown, USA, 1908, b/w, silent)

The robot is one of science fiction cinema's most enduring themes, with examples coming from every decade—although they do become scarce in the 1940s and '50s. The earliest female robots are actually animated dolls, inspired by Délibes' 1870 ballet, *Coppélia;* for example, in the 1900 Georges Méliès short, *Coppélia: la poupée animée.* That film, like so many, is long lost. In *An Animated Doll,* a boy steals an automaton for his sister, who plays with it until the owner retrieves it. The girl cries. There is no suggestion here of the sexual element that would often characterize the robot in later movies (*Metropolis,* 1927, *Westworld,* 1973, *Blade Runner,* 1982, *Ex Machina,* 2015), but active boys and passive girls is a theme that will permeate the genre.

The 1910s

War and its consequences dominated Europe for much of this decade, decimating its film industries and giving America the foothold that it would never lose. Domesticity was still the norm, but not the limit, of female representation in the genre. When women were not propaganda pawns for the war effort, they were targets for anti-suffrage attack, but if there is one thing that is worse than being talked about, it is not being talked about. Women were now on the science fiction map—just.

A la Conquête du Pôle
(Georges Méliès, France, 1912, b/w, silent)

This film is in this list for three central reasons. Firstly, its formulaic plot—involving men on an epic journey somewhere—places beautiful young women in their usual assistant-to-men roles. These are repeated throughout Méliès' work. Secondly, it joins other genre films of the day by ridiculing female political movements. The fate of the suffragist leader is particularly brutal, as she is impaled on a church spire. Finally, the climactic sequence appears to involve a woman rescuing men trapped at the North Pole—a revolutionary turn for the genre. It is not entirely clear that this is a woman, but it is not clear that it is a man either. This ambiguity may well come from the master magician Méliès attempting to have his cake and eat it.

Wake Up!
(Laurence Cowan, UK, 1914, b/w, silent)

As war arrived in Europe, many filmmakers positioned themselves for propaganda—and women quickly became part of the message. A number of films feature brave, active women in order to present a united front for the enemy. These include *England's Menace* and *If England Were Invaded* (both 1914); others, such as *An Englishman's Home* (1914), place women in peril. *Wake Up!* does both: Lord Pax's daughter retrieves plans crucial to the defeat of the enemy, while girls are murdered in their beds to show the brutality of that enemy. Female characters are, of course, being exploited here, but now that the mold was broken, it would become harder to return them to being passive observers.

Himmelskibet
(Holger Madson, Denmark, 1917, b/w, silent)

Another early epic of the genre—and an early example of the female mediator character, who will return in many science fiction films, including: *Metropolis* (1926), *Planet of the Apes* (1968) and *Arrival* (2016). Lilly Jacobson plays Marya, daughter of the High Priest of Mars, who falls in love with a visiting human. She intervenes to save the men when they disrupt the peaceful Martian idyll. Many elements of the basic story are shared by *Aelita: Queen of Mars* (1924), but perhaps more notable is the endurance of some of the characters, themes and visual styles: some can be found again in *Avatar* (2009).

The 1920s

The American studios may have shaped the industry during this decade, but a fair amount of on-screen style came from a resurgent Germany and the newly formed Soviet Union. This was the last decade of the "silents" and by the end of it, cinematographers, writers and directors had honed their arts on surprisingly sophisticated science fiction projects. The vast majority of the stories are still about men, but this post–World War I environment provides active female roles, albeit often as rich heiresses, villainess and "fallen" women.

Aelita: Queen of Mars
(Jakov Protozanov, USSR, 1924, b/w, silent)

The plot for this is apparently based on a story by Tolstoy, but is bears many similarities with *Himmelskibet* (1917). A man travels to Mars, where he falls in love with the Martian Queen, Aelita, played with dramatic gusto by Yuliya Solntseva. What sets this film apart is its impressive Constructivist/Deco sets and costumes. Protozanov's film indicates the avant-garde, artistic ambitions of the pre–Stalinist Soviet Union, the nation which would later become the first to send a woman into space (Valentina Tereshkova, 1963). Aelita's strongest genre legacy is the beautiful, petulant, fashion-conscious queens who followed. Notable amongst these are Zsa Zsa Gabor's outrageous Talleah in *Queen of Outer Space* (1958) and Anita Pallenberg's deliciously evil Great Tyrant in *Barbarella* (1968).

Metropolis
(Fritz Lang, Germany, 1927, b/w, silent)

It is a testament to the vision of Fritz Lang and his design team that, ninety years on, the robot Maria is still one of the most iconic images of science fiction cinema. The stunning robot design, brilliant cinematography and revolutionary special effects make *Metropolis* a must-see classic. It is also an early example of the style-over-substance thread which remains in the genre today. Thea von Harbou's story, in which the underground worker drones rebel against their surface-dwelling masters, borrows themes from, amongst other things, the Russian revolution and Karel Čapek's 1920 robot play *R.U.R.* Brigitte Helm's Maria is notable for her dual function: as a human, she is a mediator (heart) between the workers (hands) and the masters (head); as the robot, she incites rebellion and dances semi-naked in a night club.

Frau im Mond
(Fritz Lang, Germany, 1929, b/w, silent)

This is another genre classic—and a landmark female role—from director Fritz Lang and his screenwriter wife, Thea von Harbou. The German studio UFA produced many visually stunning and technically brilliant films during this period, and again, the cinematography here is impressive. Gerda Maurus plays Friede Velten, an independent-minded woman who is well able to hold her own with four men and a boy on their trip to the Moon. German women had won the vote 11 years earlier, and much has been made of Velten's "male" clothing, with even a suggestion that her "phallic" tie projects feminist sympathies. Her fate in the film is echoed in the final shot of Dr. Brand's in *Interstellar* (2014), but Lang's film would have had far more lasting impact if it had not come at the end of the silent period—making it virtually obsolete as soon as it was released.

The 1930s

The arrival of sound changed the film industry almost overnight. The early 1930s saw much experimentation across Europe, but by the second half of the decade, science fiction cinema was dominated by American product. A diet of Saturday morning serials, techno-thrillers and gothic horror lead to a consolidation within the genre that in turn fed stagnation in the development of female roles. Little of note would happen now until after the Second World War.

Just Imagine
(David Butler, USA, 1930, b/w)

The arrival of sound-on-film in the late 1920s led to many screen experiments across the cinema industry of the early '30s. This was science fiction's most expensive contribution—a futuristic musical comedy. This might sound cozy, but *Just Imagine* is a good example of the genre's habit of grounding its stories about the future in tradition, convention and stereotype. In this imagined future 1980 society, men and women are seemingly equal, but the law treats them very differently. The smiling, singing and dancing disguise an underlying misogyny that aims to keep women in their place. The impressive future-city populated by attractive female pawns will return in *Blade Runner* (1982); the disguised misogyny will be seen again in the firm-breasted, badass, kick-boxing babes who wield very little real power in so many movies of the 21st century.

Bride of Frankenstein
(James Whale, USA, 1935, b/w)

Since *Frankenstein*, science fiction has been attracted to the notion of man creating man—taking the roles of God and woman. This is identified in Chapter II as "The Frankenstein Syndrome." However, the male holy grail for this genre has been to turn the tables on nature completely, enabling man to create woman. This sequel to James Whale's 1931 classic, *Frankenstein*, does just that. In reality, the film is a rather dull re-tread of the original until the final 15 minutes, when Elsa Lanchester emerges as the bride of the title—and creates one of the enduring female icons of science fiction and horror cinema. Iconic imagery aside, Whale's new film would have been more interesting if it had taken the line of the 1985 film *The Bride* by exploring what happens next.

Flash Gordon
(Frederick Stephani, USA, 1936 [13 chapters], b/w)

In its heyday, the Saturday morning serial drew many people (largely children) to their local cinema for a weekly dose of derring-do. Buster Crabbe as Flash Gordon was a favorite, starring in 40 episodes across three *Flash Gordon* space opera series (plus 12 episodes as Buck Rogers). These serials were well-regarded then and are still fun to watch today. The key female roles—the virginal Dale Arden, played by Jean Rogers, and the dangerous Princess Aura, played by Priscilla Lawson—give an indication of what happens to science fiction when it does not know where to go next: it returns to convention, tradition and stereotype. Ironically, the science fiction chapter series had begun in 1914 with *The Exploits of Elaine*—although, even here, Pearl White as Elaine Dodge does spend much of her time as the damsel-in-distress.

The 1940s

The Second World War dominated the first half of this decade and all but wiped out non–U.S. science fiction production until the British made a limited postwar return. Chapter serials increased, as did the number of U.S. patriotic characters and proxies for conservative masculinity. The result was a continuation of the stagnation that had set in during the second half of the 1930s—and a very fallow period for female roles.

Superman
(Spencer Gordon Bennet and Thomas Carr,
USA, 1948 [15 chapters], b/w)

Superman is one of those patriotic proxies mentioned in the decade summary above, along with Captain Marvel (1941) and Captain America (1944).
Of central importance to this survey is the character of Lois Lane. As a heroine
to be rescued, she retains links with a traditional past, but as a journalist, she
helps to pave the way for the professional women who proliferated through
the 1950s and beyond. The female reporter had already been seen in the 1920
chapter serial *The Screaming Shadow* and non-genre films such as *His Girl Friday*
(1940), so Lois Lane is not a complete leap into the void. She does however,
represent an important post–World War II development, as women built on
the gains made after World War I.

The Perfect Woman
(Bernhard Knowles, UK, 1949, b/w)

This curious British comedy borrows from the well-established theme of
the sexualized female robot. When a genre starts to laugh at itself, it is a sure
sign that the tropes are entrenched, and films like *Earth Girls Are Easy* (1988)
and *Galaxy Quest* (1999) show that parody and pastiche are good places to see
genre stereotypes at play; however, *The Perfect Woman* feels more like exploitation. Borrowing further from *The Tales of Hoffmann* and drawing-room farce, it
sets up a string of mix-ups involving a robot doppelgänger for the scientist's pretty
niece—who then spends much of her time in her underwear. Incidentally, this
film features Stanley Holloway, who starred in *My Fair Lady* (1964)—a version
of George Bernard Shaw's 1913 play *Pygmalion*, which was in turn inspired by
the ancient myth in which a man discovers how to create his perfect woman.

The 1950s

If two world wars had contributed to America's domination of the film
industry, the Cold War would shape its domination of science fiction though
alien "Them versus Us" narratives. While the men who created the genre generally considered women as part of "Us," female characters thrived as science
professionals and mothers, but once this golden age turned its attention to
space travel, women became "Them" again, and were generally confined to
Earth or presented as sexy space maidens.

Rocketship X-M
(Kurt Neumann, USA, 1950, b/w)

Dale Arden had already been into space alongside Flash Gordon, but this film may well feature the first bona fide professional female astronaut in American science fiction cinema. In a clear nod to Gerda Maurus' performance in *Frau im Mond*, the Danish Osa Massen is excellent as the cool, calm, collected chemist, Dr. Lisa van Horn, on a mission to the moon with four men. She is here on merit, as the person who developed the fuel that makes the rocket go, but this being 1950, a fair amount of the dialogue refers to her gender. It is not always clear if the filmmakers are sneering at the idea of a woman in space, or are sneering at people who sneer at the idea of a woman in space. Regardless of that, it is Massen who wins in the end, despite the unorthodox climax— another element of this film that owes something to *Frau im Mond*.

The Day the Earth Stood Still
(Robert Wise, USA, 1951, b/w)

Robert Wise—editor on *Citizen Kane* (1941), and the director who would bring *The Sound of Music* (1965) and *West Side Story* (1961) to the screen— presents here a genre rarity: a woman who saves the world. In the most radical female role since *Frau im Mond* (1929), Patricia Neal—who would later win an Oscar for her performance in *Hud* (1963)—plays Helen Benson, the mother and secretary who mediates between humans and the alien visitor, Klaatu. From an apparent female stereotype, Benson emerges to become the film's voice of reason—like Maria in *Metropolis* (1927), Zira in *Planet of the Apes* (1968) and Louise Banks in *Arrival* (2016). The 2008 remake of *The Day the Earth Stood Still* does no justice at all to this landmark of female representation in science fiction cinema.

Them!
(Gordon Douglas, USA, 1954, b/w)

This is one of the best of the crop of classic U.S. films from the golden age of science fiction cinema. Most critics put the alien invasion films down to anti-communist paranoia, although there are anti-liberal, "authoritarian" readings of films like *The Day the Earth Stood Still* (1951). Through the 1950s some female assistants-to-male-scientists had started to build on their war work to become scientists themselves; however, they still meet certain "expectations" for female representation. Many of them specialize in what have been described as the "soft sciences": disciplines taking animals, plants or people as subjects. In *Them!*, Dr. Pat Medford, played by Joan Weldon, is an entomologist, who works as second fiddle to her scientist father and becomes the film's love interest. The first glimpse of her is of as a pair sexy legs climbing out of the plane—a very 1950s approach, that was used again by James Cameron in *The Abyss* (1989).

Forbidden Planet
(Fred M. Wilcox, USA, 1956)

It is easy to forget just how good Anne Francis is in this science fiction re-working of Shakespeare's *The Tempest*. Playing the sexy-innocent Altaira (Miranda), with her tiny dresses and dubious lines must have seemed a thankless task; however, Francis brings something special to the role—understanding, perhaps, that faux naïveté is the essence of the characterization. MGM threw everything at *Forbidden Planet*: a big budget, sumptuous color, Cinema-Scope and Walt Disney special effects. Little wonder then that they avoided risk by resting on a characterization that hadn't changed much in 350 years. News of a remake for the 21st century has been attached to Joel Silver, producer of *The Matrix* (1999). If Altaira becomes a kick-boxing babe, something of the character may well be lost.

The 1960s

As it slowly took hold, color film brought a different aesthetic to cinema in the 1960s. Added to this, The Beatles, the pill, second-wave feminism and other cultural and political upheavals made this a decade of huge uncertainty. Science fiction was also unsure of itself—and certainly not clear about what to do with its women. The result was an artistic kaleidoscope that focused in on one year that seemed to bring the genre's creative contradictions together in a series of diverse projects: 1968.

Barbarella
(Roger Vadim, France/Italy, 1968)

There is little doubt that Jane Fonda as Barbarella is one of the most recognizable female figures in science fiction cinema. There are arguments that she takes control of sex and her sexuality, and so becomes a feminist icon, but others maintain that this film represents a kitsch exploitation of the director's wife at the time. From Fonda's opening zero-gravity striptease, through Paco Rabanne's lingerie-inspired costumes, to the BDSM city of Sogo and the orgasm machine, this film clearly projects heterosexual male-fantasy. It is also notable for the less-than-subtle lesbian intentions of Anita Pallenberg's Great Tyrant of Sogo. Based on Jean-Claud Forest's comic strip, Vadim's film has Barbarella stumble from one "erotic" scenario to the next, with an innocence not unlike Altaira's. Like *Forbidden Planet*, this film has also been a target for a remake for many years. It is going to be tough to top this original.

2001: A Space Odyssey
(Stanley Kubrick, UK/USA, 1968)

Science fiction cinema's most consistently celebrated movie, routinely recognized as a masterpiece of the genre, has scant place for women. This is a fiction about men going into space just before real men landed on the Moon. It is in this list as a reminder that the development of female roles in the genre has never been linear: steps forward have often been followed by steps back, as filmmakers struggle to make sense of external forces. Kubrick's *2001: A Space Odyssey* may be his measured response to the social upheavals of the 1960s, including feminism, but does it represent a prediction or a hope? The film is less violent, but perhaps, in its way, just as misogynistic as the director's next science fiction project, *A Clockwork Orange* (1971).

Planet of the Apes
(Franklin J. Schaffner, USA, 1968)

Like *Barbarella*, this is based on French science fiction literature—this time Pierre Boulle's 1963 novel, *La Planète des singes* (translated as "Monkey Planet"). It is interesting to see the evolution of the central female characters. The young, naked girl, Nova, reappears as the adult Linda Harrison's pelt-clad savage, in an echo of Raquel Welch's character in *One Million Years BC* (1966); chimpanzee Dr. Zira, played by Kim Hunter, the film's voice of reason, continues a tradition passed down through *Himmelskibet* (1917), *The Day the Earth Stood Still* (1951) and *Metropolis* (1927); and Dianne Stanley's Lt. Stewart is invented for the film, only to be quietly killed off during the title sequence. The first two characters survive in spirit into Tim Burton's 2001 "re-imagining," but their spirit is dead in the "rebooted" series (2011, 2014)—until Nova returns as a girl again (fully clothed) in *War for the Planet of the Apes* (2017).

The 1970s

Science fiction cinema seemed to come out of the 1960s with a focus on "men and machines," a "boys and their toys" mentality that may have been influenced by the NASA Moon landing in 1969. Taking their place alongside men in men's stories, women feel rather like pawns and playthings. In many ways, female representation in this decade echoes the absence and token presence that characterized the cinema of the early silent period.

The Andromeda Strain
(Robert Wise, USA, 1971)

Bucking the decade trends, Robert Wise's first science fiction film since his 1951 classic *The Day the Earth Stood Still* offers another significant female character—and one that is male in Michael Crichton's source novel. Kate Reid plays the re-gendered, professional, no-nonsense scientist, Dr. Ruth Leavitt, who has some of the driest, wittiest lines in the movie. Despite retaining epilepsy for her film incarnation, Leavitt confidently navigates what is essentially a man's world—complete with sexism, stereotypes, and female nudity. When an unknown virus from the Andromeda Galaxy threatens life on Earth, it is Dr. Leavitt who discovers the crystalline structure which will eventually be its undoing. And so Wise, again, presents a woman who saves the world. Female characters in his next genre offering, *Star Trek: The Motion Picture* (1979), have less impact.

Solaris
(Andrei Tarkovsky, USSR, 1971)

A psychological masterpiece from the haunting novella by Stanslaw Lem, this film takes for its subject the implicit nature of the science fiction film itself: a vehicle for male fantasy. Orbiting the planet Solaris in a space station, Kris is visited by an apparition of his dead wife. The planet has the power to materialize human thought; therefore, the women in this film are by definition male-constructs, and so they conform to (often sexual) male fantasies. This is not revealing in itself, but the notion is turned on its head when Kris loses control of his fantasy, and it starts to control him. A treatise on desire and isolation, this has been dubbed the "Soviet 2001." Tarkovsky certainly shared Kubrick's famed perfectionism—and the run of the studio. Steven Soderbergh's restrained 2002 remake of *Solaris* had a very tough act to follow, but it is also worth a visit.

The Stepford Wives
(Bryan Forbes, USA, 1975)

Is this misogyny or a feminist warning from the future? If science fiction is a crucible for male fantasies, it might be easy to see this film as anti-feminist—especially coming at a time when "women's lib" was high in the public mind.

However, replacing the wives in a town with dull, robotic simulacra seems an odd way to create a male utopia. Male fears about feminism have instead tended to generate films that warn about the perils of female dominance in society. For example, *Les Résultats du féminisme* (1906), *One Hundred Years After* (1911) and *Percy Pimpernickel, Soubrette* (1914) are all paranoid responses to the women's suffrage movements of the early 20th century. On balance, this film version of Ira Levin's original "what if" novel, *The Stepford Wives*, is an interesting genre study; the 2004 re-imagining is not.

Star Wars
(George Lucas, USA, 1977)

Lucas famously bound bits and pieces from film, literature and culture with the writings of Campbell, Jung and Castaneda to make his space opera. The execution is first-rate and its influence on the genre at large is unquestionable. Some do question the importance of Carrie Fisher's Princess Leia, arguing that she is basically a fairytale princess in a tower waiting to be rescued by her knights in shining (white) armor. The traditional reference cannot be denied; Lucas originally wanted to re-make *Flash Gordon* (1936), however, Leia is so much more than Dale Arden. She is a gutsy, feisty fighter, who can easily hold her own with and against the men. The success of *Star Wars* gave prominence to a central female role, and that paved the way for Ripley and the rest. *Star Wars* is only just catching up again with Jyn and Rey, but for the most interesting of George Lucas's female characters, step outside the franchise and back to *THX 1138* (1971).

Coma
(Michael Crichton, USA, 1978)

Forgetting the science fiction for a moment, this is a fine study of female struggle in a patriarchal environment—one that had been seen in *The Andromeda Strain* (1971) and would be revisited in *Contact* (1997). Geneviève Bujold portrays surgeon Dr. Susan Wheeler, who is patronized and pushed aside, but she keeps springing back. Her diligence and detective work lead her to the discovery that the comas in her hospital are being induced, so that the victims can be stored and their organs harvested when required. The central concept— if not the determined central female character—were borrowed for the 2005 film *The Island*. Sitting quietly between *Star Wars* (1977) and *Alien* (1979), *Coma* is often overlooked; however, Dr. Wheeler provides the missing link between Princess Leia and Lieutenant Ripley.

Alien
(Ridley Scott, UK, 1979)

Anecdotally, this is #1 in the females-in-science-fiction-film canon, because Sigourney Weaver as Ellen Ripley is said to have inspired the tough, lithe, gun-toting women who followed in many films, including: *The Terminator* (1984) and *The Matrix* (1999). Filtered through millennial changes, she may also be responsible for the attractive mixed martial artists in the current crop of comic-book inspired movies. As "last woman standing" from an ensemble cast, Ripley draws on a tradition that was already a staple of the horror genre; it was far less common in science fiction. A great deal has been written about what is meant by the "strip" sequence at the film's climax. Does it betray the implicit sexism of a male director, or is Ridley Scott merely showing that Ripley is a vulnerable human being?

The 1980s

This was a new golden period for science fiction cinema. *Star Wars* had lent credibility and clout to the genre, and special effects unleashed its creativity. The resulting blockbusters generated sequels that would develop into the franchises whose influence now dominates the industry. Many female characters were strengthened by this heady, corporate-capitalist environment. They would emerge to see some of their influence last into the 21st century.

Blade Runner
(Ridley Scott, USA, 1982)

The inspiration for this genre classic come from philosophical science fiction writer Philip K. Dick and his 1969 short story "Do Androids Dream of Electric Sheep?" The existentialist inquiry that underpins the concept is conducted largely by the two central male characters, leaving the women to represent strippers, sex workers and *femmes fatale*. As replicants (robots), they are literally male-created, fantasy figures, whose roots reach back beyond *Metropolis* (1927), and they are subject to fair degree of sexist violence. In short, these are not the greatest female roles in the genre, but thanks to Ridley Scott's *noir*-esque vision, they are some of the most memorable. Indeed, Sean Young as Rachel has one of the most apposite lines spoken by any female character in science fiction cinema: "I'm not *in* the business.... I *am* the business." Whether this insight rescues Scott from cries of misogyny is hard to say. The Director's

Cut, released in 1992, places women and men on a more equal footing, by making victims of both.

Return of the Jedi
(Richard Marquand, USA, 1983)

This film is included in this list as an example of how the genre has routinely given with one hand and taken back with the other when it comes to female representation. Princess Leia developed through *The Empire Strikes Back* (1980) to become a more rounded character. At the beginning of *Return of the Jedi*, she goes undercover as a bounty hunter to rescue Han Solo from the gangster Jabba the Hutt. She is then captured and forced to wear the famous metal bikini as Jabba's slave. Of course, this was not the first time that a female science fiction character had been presented as a sexual object, but to do this to such a high-profile character was to normalize that representation for a generation of young people. Arguably, the sexualized Western cosplay phenomenon, and the likes of Quorra and Gem in *TRON: Legacy* (2010), can be traced back to this film.

Born in Flames
(Lizzie Borden, USA, 1983)

Written, directed and produced on a tiny budget by Borden, *Born in Flames* is a gonzo-documentary-style filmed manifesto. It is an example of the use of the genre to send a political message. Borden's Marxist, socialist-liberal, feminist statement is potentially all the more powerful because it came at a time when science fiction cinema was developing into a corporate machine. *Born in Flames* presents a near future in which a socialist government has promised a voice for all minority groups; however, utopia turns to dystopia when it becomes clear that this ballot-box revolution cannot create enough jobs. Borden's central message is diluted somewhat by repetition, over-statement and hectoring, but the final image of an explosion at the top of the twin towers of New York City's World Trade Center is both powerful and prescient. Are these symbols of patriarchal-capitalist oppression?

The Terminator
(James Cameron, UK/USA, 1984)

It is easy to recall Sarah Connor as the tough, gun-toting, guerrilla-fighter of *Terminator 2: Judgment Day*, but her beginnings were far more humble—

and arguably more interesting. Linda Hamilton portrays the clumsy waitress and intended victim of Arnold Schwarzenegger's iconic T-800 cyborg assassin in *The Terminator*. Connor's radical development through this first film is not merely an attempt to create an interesting character arc; it is an insurance policy. In order to ensure that 1984 audiences accept the finale's feisty fighter, her character is "balanced" with the more familiar "feminine" traits and characteristics. This balancing act is played out throughout the genre. Sometimes the alter-egos are contained in one character, as in *Metropolis* (1927) and *Solaris* (1971); sometimes they are shared, as in *Just Imagine* (1930) and *Blade Runner* (1982). The star of this film may be Schwarzenegger, but, as with *Alien* (1979), the foundation has been laid for that female-focused sequel.

Aliens
(James Cameron, USA/UK, 1986)

Generally regarded as the best movie of the *Alien* series, *Aliens* does not have to concern itself with Ripley's backstory, or to explain her nature. She is accepted as a no-nonsense, organized and resilient woman. Building on his work with *The Terminator*, James Cameron develops Ripley's female-fighter role, but is careful again to emphasize her feminine side. She becomes a surrogate mother here to the orphan, "Newt," played by Carrie Henn in her only movie acting role to date. During Ripley's climactic power-loader battle with the alien queen—a sequence taken from Cameron's earlier short film, *Xenogenesis*—she snarls the now-famous line, "Get away from her, you bitch!" This is balanced by a softening of her prejudices against "synthetics," after Bishop saves Newt. Responding to Ripley's own heroism, Bishop says, "not bad for a human." It is an important moment for the genre: here is a female science fiction character beginning to be defined by her actions and her humanity, rather than her gender.

The 1990s

There was no reason to think that the formulas that had made a success of science fiction cinema through the 1980s should not get the genre through the '90s. This proved to be the case until innovation was replaced by imitation and the formulas lost their power towards the end of the decade. Change was in the air for female characters too, as Ripley and Connor clones lost their appeal. The result was a period of variety for science fiction cinema as the new millennium approached.

Terminator 2: Judgment Day
(James Cameron, USA/France, 1991)

Creating a sequel can be a blessing and a curse. The element of surprise is lost, but there is more opportunity to develop the characters. *Terminator 2* returns some of the surprise element by making Schwarzenegger the good cyborg. Sarah Connor is no longer the hapless victim-cum-accidental hero; she is now a trained fighter with the knowledge needed to save her son John, the future savior of humanity. Unfortunately, this also makes her somewhat one-dimensional, and she becomes redundant once John has bonded with the cyborg. Attempts by the next two *Terminator* films, *Rise of the Machines* (2003) and *Salvation* (2009) to shift the narrative emphasis onto John Connor are reversed to a degree in *Genisys* (2015), in which Emilia Clarke appears as an alternative Sarah Connor from a different timeline. It is clearly aimed at fans of *Terminator 2* and *The Sarah Connor Chronicles* television series, but no one can quite match Linda Hamilton's performance.

Tank Girl
(Rachel Talalay, USA, 1995)

The tough female character had become commonplace in the genre by the mid–1990s, so the fun, witty, sexy, and just a little bit "edgy" British comic-strip that inspired this film must have felt ideal for the times. Unfortunately, *Tank Girl* falls well short of its potential—and even the promise of its own title sequence. This is probably because it tries a little too hard to be funny and quirky, from its opening voice-over through its over-the-top performances, to the silly action climax. The inter-cut comic-strip sequences are effective, but they also remind us of *Tank Girl*'s roots, and that live-action comic-strip is hard to pull off. This watered-down, humorless comedy is disappointing fare from a female director. Twenty years after *Tank Girl*, her post-apocalyptic, desert-dwelling female fighter spirit was raised again in George Miller's far more successful *Mad Max: Fury Road* (2015).

Star Trek: First Contact
(Jonathan Frakes, USA, 1996)

While Alice Krige's Borg Queen role may be rooted in a tradition which goes back to the alien leaders in the likes of *Le Voyage dans la lune*, *First Contact* does show that in 1996 it could still be done really well. Part of the strength of this character (apart from Krige's well-judged, deliciously evil performance) is the fact that she has a motive. The Borg Queen is given something to do and some (fairly) intelligent lines to speak; both of which are unusual traits for these female despot characters. As rocket engineer, Lily Sloane, Alfre Woodard is a black, female "hard" scientist—perhaps unique to the genre, until *Black Panther* (2018). *First Contact* may feel like just a bigger version of a *Next Generation* television episode, but it does a little more for female representation than most in the genre, including many other *Star Trek* movies.

The Sticky Fingers of Time
(Hilary Brougher, Spain, 1997, b/w & color)

With a growing gay following, this has been billed as a "lesbian science fiction film"—but not by its female writer/director, who has approached the subject as a serious genre effort. The dubious title may not have helped her cause here, but titles aside, this is an entertaining, if slightly confusing, film. Made on a low budget, although not quite the shoestring of *Born in Flames*, this film attempts many of the same things as Lizzie Borden's 1983 film, but in a gentler way. Brougher shows that science fiction can be a place for women to flex their creative muscles, both off-screen and on. Female characters can shape the narrative and, yes, they can have relationships with each other. This message is undermined slightly by the suggestion of a male "puppet-master" character, but this of course may be part of Brougher's plan.

The Fifth Element
(Luc Besson, France, 1997)

This film succeeds where *Barbarella* (1968) and *Tank Girl* (1995) did not. It takes comic-strip elements (though not an actual comic strip here) and melds them with witty dialogue and brilliant visuals to create a genuinely entertaining science fiction film. Contributing to this success are some effective supporting performances and the quirky brilliance of Milla Jovovich as Leeloo. It is true that this female role relies greatly on traditional representation, but somehow this movie gets away with it. The sense of fun even rescues its corny "the fifth element is love" climax in a way that the "love conquers everything" message at the end of Besson's *Valerian and the City of a Thousand Planets* (2017) does not.

Contact
(Robert Zemeckis, USA, 1997)

Zemeckis' previous big science fiction film offering, *Back to the Future* (1985), offered some fairly thankless female roles. *Contact* goes some way towards making up for it. The female scientist at the center of Carl Sagan's original novel was reputedly based on the American astronomer Dr. Jill Cornell Tarter, director of the SETI (Search for Extra-Terrestrial Intelligence) Institute. Jodie Foster here plays Dr. Eleanor Arroway, a radio astronomer driven by her desire to communicate with her dead father, a notable departure for a genre whose stories have so often focused on fathers and sons. The story gets a little silly once aliens are introduced, but, like *Coma* (1978), it presents a good study of the political, scientific and personal obstacles that can beset a woman in a patriarchal world. 1997 was a good year for women driving science fiction narratives; this is one of the best examples.

Alien Resurrection
(Jean-Pierre Jeunet, USA, 1997)

Ripley is back here to mark the point at which the *Alien* franchise became fully self-aware: smart enough to wink back at itself; strong enough to turn the genre on its head. The mothership computer has become "father"; the male androids have turned into Winona Ryder's sympathetic gynoid, Call; and Ripley has become the alien's mother. Full circle. It is only a matter of time before the creatures are loose onboard and then it becomes a game of "spot the victim": the black, the white, the woman, the man, the gay, the disabled, the alien. But not Ripley. She now IS the narrative; everything else is peripheral. Her gender is not questioned, but it is hardly recognized either, and so a feminist dream has become an androgynous nightmare. When Call takes over the ship's computer and announces, "Father's dead, asshole," she is only partly right.

The Matrix
(The Wachowski Brothers, USA, 1999)

The first five minutes of this film belong to Carrie-Anne Moss, as the super-tough, leather-clad fighter, Trinity. She is the link between the "masculinized," gun-toting women who evolved though the 1980s and early '90s and the more "feminized," largely unarmed, fighters who can be found throughout the genre in the second decade of the 21st century. For the remaining two hours of *The Matrix* Trinity reverts to stereotype, supporting her man and helping to verify one of the genre's defining axioms: "men do things; women chase round after them." The clue may be in her name, which evokes the trinity of Marys who follow their own Messiah through *The Bible*. As with *Star Wars* (1977), the success of *The Matrix* extended the life of its female character, and so some of Trinity remains in *The Force Awakens* (2015) and *Rogue One* (2016).

The 2000s

The end of the 1990s had offered a mixed bag for women, as the genre once again entered a period of indecision. The turn of the new millennium, coupled with the exponential rise of CGI, added uncertainty, pushing the genre back towards the "safety" of men-and-machines. Female roles had come too far to be reduced entirely to convention and stereotype, but Ripley and Connor were fading memories. The result is a period of trickle-down and transitional development for female roles.

Terminator 3: Rise of the Machines
(Jonathan Mostow, USA, 2003)

It is tempting to decry the naked Kristanna Loken near the beginning of this film as gratuitous; however, male nudity in the other *Terminator* films is logical requirement of time travel—and so it is here. Loken is the new, advanced T-X cyborg. Her arrival in the window of a clothes shop—amid the female mannequins—signals some of the franchise wit and self-awareness that had been seen in *Alien: Resurrection* (1997). The female T-X is faster and stronger than Schwarzenegger's clunky old male T-800 version, but perhaps more interesting is the fact that the story has moved completely away from Sarah Connor and onto John Connor—who acquires a female sidekick in the form of Clare Danes. A female terminator feels like a step forward, but the film indicates a genre retreat towards the traditions of female representation which opened the first *Terminator* film.

Æon Flux
(Karyn Kusama, USA, 2005)

This is not a great film. It does, however, allow a good comparison between an early CGI-enhanced, super-athletic female fighter, of the type that proliferated after the turn of the millennium, and the self-assured action heroine who emerges in *Mad Max: Fury Road* (2015). They both feature Charlize Theron in the lead role. Like *Tank Girl* (1995), *Æon Flux* tries much too hard to match the atmosphere and impact of its source material. Very little is grounded in reality, and so characters, motives, actions become unbelievable—as do the action sequences themselves. Theron's recent route through the genre is an interesting one: a beleaguered wife in *The Astronaut's Wife* (1999), the failed Flux and the sidelined wife in *The Road* (2009) morph through an autocratic company executive in *Prometheus* (2012) to her celebrated role in *Fury Road*. It's almost a template for female roles through the 21st century so far.

The Time Traveler's Wife
(Robert Schwentke, USA, 2009)

A caption card in the theatrical trailer for *Destination Moon* (1950) entices the viewer with the line: "Never before has any woman…"; the promise of female derring-do hangs for a moment, until it is dashed by the following card: "sent her man on such an exploit!." Sixty years later, *The Time Traveler's Wife* appears to be doing the same thing, except that Rachel McAdams' Clare does not even do any sending. Her man just goes. There are some interesting moments when Clare's greater knowledge makes it appear that she is the time traveler, but beyond this, the film generally takes the male line—ignoring the shared perspectives of Audrey Niffenegger's well-received source novel. *The Time Traveler's Wife* offers no explanation for its fantastical element, and so, like that other love story through time, *Groundhog Day* (1993), it may not be science fiction at all.

Star Trek
(J.J. Abrams, USA/Germany, 2009)

Lt. Uhura, played originally by Nichelle Nichols in the *Star Trek* television series, is too important a character not to be represented in this list; however, her appearances in the classic film series adds very little to her television role. Indeed, *The Final Frontier* (1989) includes a scene in which Uhura dances and sings as a sexy, silhouetted siren, confirming that this was a franchise that told men's stories. The re-boot promised more. It is a well-made, enjoyable movie, and Zoe Saldana is effective as Lt. (Nyota) Uhura as far as the role goes, but this really is a missed opportunity. Once again, this film is about the men; all of them—even Sulu—get to be heroes in this movie. Uhura gets to be Spock's girlfriend. It would have been a mistake to turn Uhura into a kick-boxing super woman, but a little extra something to do in the narrative might have done more justice to this iconic character.

Avatar
(James Cameron, USA/UK, 2009)

To date, this is the highest-grossing movie of all time—in any genre. Billions have been taken at the box office for a story that could have been sketched on the back of a napkin. As a result, the characters, both male and female, are lost in a maelstrom of convention, stereotype and tradition. Zoe Saldana plays Neytiri of the Na'vi, a proxy for Mother Nature; Sigourney Weaver plays Dr.

Grace Augustine, an irascible biologist; and Michelle Rodriguez plays a clone of the masculinized Private Vasquez from Cameron's 1986 movie *Aliens*. What is important about *Avatar*, however, is not its originality, but its success. Just as *Star Wars* had done in 1977, this commercial genre juggernaut featured a prominent female character at a time when women were beginning to drift into the background again. Zoe Saldana's career benefited, as did the female protagonists who began to emerge again in films such as *The Hunger Games* (2012), *Prometheus* (2013) and *Gravity* (2013).

The 2010s

Franchises were firmly in control as the genre entered the second decade of the 21st century. For women, this was a double-edged sword. Existing characters and formulae can be a straightjacket for writers and directors, forcing them to return to the past for representation. The huge amounts of money made by these properties does, however, give a sense of a bullet-proof medium, allowing producers to experiment more with narrative elements—and that includes female characters.

Prometheus
(Ridley Scott, USA/UK, 2012)

This film was not particularly well received by critics and fans, but Ridley Scott was at least trying something new at a time of industrial repetition. The casting of Noomi Rapace, fresh from her uncompromising role in *The Girl with the Dragon Tattoo* trilogy (2009), might have given the impression that that this would be another kick-boxing female for the science fiction genre. Instead, Scott takes Rapace's Dr. Elizabeth Shaw away from current expectations and away from Ripley. The result is an understated and resilient character, played to great effect by Rapace. Charlize Theron's appearance as the nasty head of the corporation has a more familiar feel to it, sitting as it does alongside despotic heads of organizations in the likes of *Babylon A.D.* (2008), *Elysium* (2013) and *Divergent* (2014). Ridley Scott would return to very familiar territory with *Alien: Covenant* (2017) which is a re-tread of *Alien*—complete with Ripley clone.

Gravity
(Alfonso Cuarón, UK, 2013)

This was always destined to be a showcase movie: one of the genre's state-of-the-cinema-art pieces. And with Sandra Bullock's Hollywood clout giving her the pick of the project crop, this had the potential to offer the best female-in-science-fiction role since Dr. Arroway. It failed to deliver. Bullock is very good, but her hapless heroine, Dr. Ryan Stone, gets flung around from crisis to crisis with barely a clue about what to do—eventually escaping back to Earth by accident. Knowledge resides almost exclusively with George Clooney's Commander Matt Kowalski, who even re-appears post-mortem in a fantasy sequence to save Stone again after she has given up. The female may have more presence here than in other "showcase" films, but she has scarcely any more significance or point. Add all this to motherhood-related psychological demons that would have debarred Stone from going to space with NASA in the first place, and the result is a chaotic car-wreck of a character.

Under the Skin
(Jonathan Glazer, UK, 2013)

This feels like *Species* (1995) meets *The Man Who Fell to Earth* (1976). Indeed, the director is on record stating his debt to Nicolas Roeg, whose work can be detected in the detached nature of both the cinematography and the alien. This film joins *Devil Girl from Mars* (1954), *Unearthly Stranger* (1963), *Queen of Blood* (1966), *Spermula* (1976), *Lifeforce* (1985), *My Stepmother Is an Alien* (1988) and many other examples of tales in which female aliens arrive on Earth to prey on human men. Glazer's piece is more artistic than most; however, like so many of its forbears, it relies on its lead female, played by Scarlett Johansson, to be alluring and deadly—a *femme fatale*. This film does have more to say than others in its class, as the alien learns to respect her prey as people and discovers more about the human body she is inhabiting. Whether character arcs and cinematic art are enough to justify this film's voyeuristic love of the Johansson's naked body is open to debate.

Ex Machina
(Alex Garland, UK/USA, 2015)

There is a lingering feeling here that Alex Garland set out to secure his legacy by making a female robot as iconic as Maria in *Metropolis*. He may have come close, but he has leaned on a number of science fiction stereotypes along the way: a mad male scientist, a sexy female robot, naked young women, violence against the female body. Alex Garland argues that his film's use of these tropes is a comment on society's expectations about A.I. and a call for new ways of thinking; however, his lingering gaze at Alicia Vikander's naked body towards the end of the film, coupled with the prominence of her firm buttocks in the promotional material, does feel a lot like good old-fashioned, commercial scopophilia. *Ex Machina* is rescued by great cinematography, stylish visuals, intelligent dialogue and good acting. It is also notable for its condemnation of its central male characters, neither of whom is presented as particularly noble. In fact, the character who gains most audience sympathy, empathy and respect is the sexy robot, Ava.

Mad Max: Fury Road
(George Miller, Australia/USA, 2015)

This is an important development in the fighting female sub-genre that has emerged through the 21st century. Charlize Theron's Imperator Furiosa is tough, but crucially this element comes out of her character and is deployed in the service of her story—which is not always the case with the kick-boxing babes who now litter the genre. Women's issues are front-and-center in this film—especially the issue of sexual violence—but George Miller does not encourage his viewer to be a voyeur. Instead, he chooses to leave the graphic, visceral, and sexual elements implied. What is left is action, as Furiosa leads a group of sex slaves across the desert to the "land of many mothers"—elderly matriarchs on dirt bikes. Many politically correct bases are covered here: age, gender, disability, race, hair color, but it feels like a seamless whole. *Mad Max Beyond Thunderdome* (1985) had not been entirely successful with Tina Turner as Auntie Entity, a sort post-apocalyptic pantomime damenatrix, but here Max has found his match—and perhaps worthy successor.

Star Wars VII: The Force Awakens
(J.J. Abrams, USA, 2015)

This re-tread of the original 1977 *Star Wars* film presents Rey, Daisy Ridley's slightly rougher, slightly tougher Luke Skywalker clone. What it does not present is the patient, layered development that made Luke a much-loved and believable figure. In just three reels, Rey masters elements of the force that it took Luke three films to grasp. There is little room to breathe here, as *The Force Awakens* races through its plot points and in-joke gags. The result has little of the emotional development required for rounded characters—and this includes Rey. It is worth noting that the leader of the stormtroopers is female (Captain Phasma, played by a chrome-masked Gwendoline Christie) and Princess (General) Leia seems now to be in command of the new rebel army, but these are token roles. Rey's place at the head of a *Star Wars* film is an important development; however, key events of *The Force Awakens* confirm that this is still a saga about boys and their fathers—until, perhaps, the final scene.

Arrival
(Denis Villeneuve, USA, 2016)

This female-framed narrative deftly explores the cyclical nature of life and time; alongside this, its science fiction art reflects the cyclical nature of female representation. Much of this has been seen before: *The Day the Earth Stood Still* (1951), *Starman* (1984), *The Abyss* (1989), *Contact* (1997) and others all cast their shadow on this impressive effort, led by Amy Adams in a strong performance, as linguist, Dr. Louise Banks. This is one of the most satisfying, rounded 21st century female science fiction characters: she is attractive without being objectified, smart without being obnoxious, and flawed without being undermined. To achieve this, *Arrival* leans on some of the stalwarts of the genre: Dr. Banks is a mediator and a mother—two of science fiction cinema's default female positions. The difference between this grieving mother and the one presented in *Gravity* (2013) is that here she also drives the narrative—and seems to know what she is doing.

Rogue One
(Gareth Edwards, USA, 2016)

The original *Star Wars* (1977) was criticized for its lack of diversity on screen, offering little more than an Asian X-Wing pilot and the voice of Darth Vader (which has itself drawn criticism). Since then, the franchise has gradually become home to a range of identities, including black leaders, alien teachers, female generals, and pilots of all types. In *Rogue One*, the journey to the diverse side is just about complete. This is the second mainstream *Star Wars* film to feature a female lead, but Felicity Jones' journey as Jyn Erso is not as obvious a hack as Rey's re-tread of Luke Skywalker's for *The Force Awakens*. It is, however, familiar: an orphaned child initially refuses the call to fight the Empire, then saves the day after a reconciliation with the father. This is not surprising, as Luke's journey is itself a distillation of the traditional hero myths identified by Joseph Campbell and others. Women are now beginning the get a better swing at the old stories, but perhaps one day there will be room for their own.

The 2090s

Shortly after the aliens invaded Earth in 2091, they reviewed 196 years of cinema history to glean what information they could about humanity. Their analysis of the science fiction genre revealed a vast array of movies telling a deceptively small number of stories, none of which chimed with their own experience of the universe at large. They noted that central to these narratives were repeated efforts by one half of the human species to invent new ways make the other half look and act a particular way, again regardless of reality. The aliens saw little point in this endless recycling, and so cinema was banned altogether at Christmas—just before the next *Star Wars* release.

CHAPTER NOTES

Introduction

1. Phil Hardy's authoritative encyclopedia (see: Hardy 1991/1995) lists around 1,500 science fiction films, shorts and chapter-plays between 1895 and 1995. The Internet Movie Database offers 3,000 titles for the same period. Bringing the IMDb.com search up to date yields around 10,000 titles, tagged as "Released Sci-Fi/Feature Film/Short Film"; this figure does not include TV movies and straight-to-video releases, which take the tally much higher. These statistics alone indicate the difficulties inherent to attempting an historical survey. It cannot cover every title. Nor can it hope to propose a theory without the real danger of the reader coming up with a counter example supporting an opposing theory.

2. For a clear general survey of science fiction definitions, begin with Clute and Nicholls, 1993, 311–14. Then *cf.* Roberts, 2005 [2007], 1–20; James, 1994, esp. 2–11; Scholes and Rabkin, 1977; Amis, 1961; Aldiss and Wingrove, 1986; and for an emphasis on cinema, Cornea, 2007, esp. 2–22.

3. Armitt, 1991, 11.

4. "Foreword," in Barnes, 1998a [1976], *xi*.

5. Brosnan, 1991, *xiii*.

6. Clute and Nicholls, 1993, 314.

7. Andrew Tudor, quoted in Kuhn, 1995, 3 [with Kuhn's own inserted interpolation removed].

8. Peter Nicholls, in Clute and Nicholls 1993, 408.

9. See: Sternbach and Okuda, 1991, esp. 104.

10. James, 1994, 1.

11. See: Ash, 1977, Contents Page (5).

12. See: Gifford, 1991.

13. See: Kavanagh 1995 and Newton 1995, in Kuhn, 1995 [1990].

14. *Femspec* journal is available online at: www.femspec.org.

Chapter I

1. Taken from a handbill advertising the Cinématographe Lumière at *The Empire Theatre*, Cardiff, c.1895. Reproduced in Barnes, 1998a [1976], 103.

2. See: Introduction.

3. Hardy, 1991, 18.

4. *Warwick Trading Company Catalogue*, 1897. Quoted in Hardy, 1991, 19.

5. Cornea, 2007, 156.

Edison Catalog, 1901, quoted at www.IMDb.com/title/tt0352358/ [Accessed 12th January 2017].

6. Acker, 1991, 7.

7. Ramsaye, 1964 [1926], *xxxvii–lxx*.

8. Ramsaye, 1964 [1926], *lxx*.

9. Ramsaye, 1964 [1926], *xl*.

10. See: Jones, 1995 (at 109:24:23). There is a great deal of debate online and elsewhere about what Neil Armstrong did actually say from the surface of the Moon. Some argue that the "a" is audible in the recordings, but there is no doubt that he said "mankind," which probably meant "humankind."

11. The original *Star Trek* phrase, "where no man has gone before" was altered to "where no one has gone before" for *The Next Generation* television series (1987–94), spoken by

Patrick Stewart as Captain Picard. William Shatner, as Captain Kirk, alludes to the change in the closing voice over for the movie *Star Trek VI: The Undiscovered Country* (1991), when he says, "where no man—no one—has gone before."

12. Ramsaye, 1964 [1926], *xl*.

13. For a comprehensive survey of early cinema science and technology in Britain, see: Barnes, 1998a/b/c/d/e [1978].

14. Among the commentators who do mention the original four astronauts in *Planet of the Apes* (1968) are Menville and Reginald, 1977; and Gallardo and Smith, 2004. For more discussion about the significance of the Stewart role in *Planet of the Apes*, see: Conrad and Magowan, 2015.

15. Nama, 2008, 32.

16. Lathers, 2012 [2010], 199. See also: Greene, 1996, 36.

17. Penley, 1997, 90.

18. Cixous and Clément, 1986 [1975], 64.

19. Some texts refer to this as *The* (?) *Motorist* or *The* '?' *Motorist*, &c. (see: IMDb.com and Hardy, 1991, 27); this suggests that the original title included an adjective—now lost.

20. Ramsaye, 1964 [1926], 394.

21. Variations in running time can be due to alternative release versions, missing sections, wrongly assumed frame-rate, and so forth. Georges Méliès sometimes inserted a ballet mid-way though his films, a theatrical technique that took advantage of the background of many of his players (see: Robinson, 1993, 40). This is not there in the colorized version available on youtube.com at the time of writing [Accessed: 9th December 2016].

22. This French player is also listed in some sources as Bleinette Burnon. See: Robinson, 1993, 40.

23. See: Robinson, 1993, 39–41.

24. Gamman and Marshment, 1994 [1988], 1.

25. See Lacan, 1977; Bakhtin, 1981; Gatens, 1991; Mead, 1964; Garfinkel, 1967.

26. Sampson, 1993, 17/31. See also: Carrithers, 1985.

27. See: Sampson, 1993, 28, note.

28. See: Sampson, 1993, 4/5.

29. Sampson, 1993, 4.

30. Sampson, 1993, 16n4. See also: Morrison, 1992.

31. If the title *Freezing Auntie* refers to the act of freezing the woman, then "Auntie" is the object here; however, if "freezing" is taken as an adjective, then "Auntie" becomes the subject.

32. Hardy, 1991, 46 (image caption).

33. The term "suffragist" refers generally to a non-violent campaigner for women's votes from the late 19th century onwards. "Suffragette" is usually applied specifically to the more militant activists within the wider movement—especially in the UK. The term "suffragist" is preferred in this text as a catch-all term for those campaigning for female suffrage. It also avoids the pejorative and censorious attitude that was often applied to the suffragettes at the time. For much more on the difference between these terms, see: Robinson, 2018.

34. See: Ramsaye, 1964 [1926], 394–400.

35. Hardy, 1991, 45.

36. Hardy, 1991, 50.

37. It is worth noting that Edith Cavell's World War I clinic in Belgium treated injured soldiers from all sides of the conflict, a practical demonstration of her words, "Patriotism is not enough. I must have no hatred or bitterness for anyone." For more on Cavell, see: Clark-Kennedy, 1965; and Souhami, 2010.

38. See: Francke, 1994, 5.

39. Gregory 2002, *xi*.

40. Taking the films included in Hardy, 1991 as a guide (although care must be taken with this approach), during the period 1895–1914, most science fiction film were made in France: 42 percent. The British produced 27 percent, followed by the Americans at just under 26 percent. During World War I, with its large focus on mainland Europe, output shifted to: U.S.: 33 percent, France: 33 percent, UK: 24 percent. After the war, output shifted further in favor of America, which produced 68 percent of the genre movies for the period 1920–1929. The French produced 7 percent and the British, less than 1 percent. Germany produced 12 percent of the science fiction films of the 1920s listed in Hardy, 1991, more than half of them directed by Fritz Lang.

41. For a more nuanced discussion on Denmark's involvement in World War I, see: Sørensen, 2014.

42. Hardy, 1991, 57 (image caption).

43. Thomas in Armitt, 1991, 109. See also: Dadoun, 1986.

44. For a discussion of the "Alien Other" of science fiction literature, see Wolmark, 1993, esp.27–53.

45. Keller, 2008, 9/10.

46. *Cf.* Gamman and Marshment, 1994 [1988], 1.

Chapter II

1. "Fantastic Films" is used by Walt Lee to corral "Science Fiction, Fantasy & Horror" movies. See: Lee, 1972a/b/c.

2. *Just Imagine*'s elaborate set model of New York City c. 1980 reputedly cost $250,000 in 1930.

3. See: Introduction. See also: Clute and Nicholls 1993, 408.

4. Metz, 1982c, 120.

5. Cornea, 2007, 156.

6. H.G. Wells was referring specifically to the concept of machines enslaving humans (Tookey, 1994, 526). Pauline Kael begins her review of *Metropolis* (1927) with, "This is one of the greatest insanities ever perpetrated in the world of film—..." (Kael, 1970, 310). And Luis Buñuel made a distinction between the script and the visuals, writing that it is "two films glued together by their bellies" (Hardy, 1991, 74).

7. For an account of how Shakespeare's *The Tempest* is simplified, adapted and re-told as *Forbidden Planet* (1956), see: Pilkington, 2015.

8. Sinclair, 1933, 114.

9. Hardy, 1991, 82.

10. *Coriolanus*, Act 5, scene 5 (William Shakespeare).

11. Moorcock, 1993, 37.

12. Jason Gould, in correspondence with the author, February 2017.

13. On first seeing a mirror image of itself, the child, according to Lacan, is "captivated by his 'specular image' becoming forever alienated from his body, which from then on has less reality for him than his mirrored image" (Rycroft, 1995, 92. See also: Lacan, 1968, 161–67). For a detailed account of the application of Lacanian psychoanalysis to and for feminist theory, see Grosz 1990; for a discussion of the place of the female within the symbolic order, see esp. 50–81, in which Grosz highlights Lacan's adherence to the notion of instinctual language.

14. Lacan, 1968, 41.

15. Metz, 1982b, 72.

16. Mulvey, 1975, 9.

17. Mulvey, 1975, 10.

18. Gamman and Marshment, 1994 [1988], 1.

19. Mulvey, 1975, 10.

20. Ramsaye, 1964 [1926], *lxx.*

21. Paglia, 1992 [1990], 31.

22. See also: Stacey, 1994 [1987], 116.

23. Mulvey, 1989c [1981], 29.

24. Mulvey, 1975, 17.

25. In Hardy, 1991, 26, the pendulum is removed; in the IMDb.com entry the girl fiddles with the hands of the clock (www.IMDb.com/title/tt2063674 [Accessed 12th September 2016]).

26. Ramsaye, 1964 [1926], 397. Incidentally, the art of women climbing in trees is explored in the vintage photographic collections of Jochen Raiss, 2016 and 2017.

27. See Rich, 1987, esp. 38.

28. See Dworkin, 1990 [1981]; and Russell, 1993b.

29. John Streets, in conversation with the author, March 2017.

30. Mulvey, 1975, 8.

31. Sobchack, 1995, 103.

32. Sobchack, 1995, 111/2.

33. Hardy, 1991, 58.

34. Hardy, 1991, 73.

35. Sobchack, 1995, 108.

36. See: Chapter One, "The Origin of the Species: Mary Shelley," in Aldiss, 1975 [1973]. See also: Aldiss, 1995, 78.

37. Mary Shelley's name is not on the original 1818 edition of *Frankenstein*; instead, it includes a preface by her husband, Percy Shelley. Over the years, there have been suggestions that the work was edited, revised or even written by Percy, but there is not enough space here to enter that debate. Nor is there time to discuss whether Mary should be referred to as Mary Wollstonecraft Shelley, a title that incorporates the name of her mother, noted 18th century women's rights advocate, Mary Wollstonecraft.

38. Roberts, 2005 [2007], 2007, 42. For a fascinating interpretation of *Somnium*, see: Lear, 1965.

39. Roberts, 2005 [2007], 2007, 93.

40. Aldiss, 1975 [1973], 29.

41. Cranny-Francis, 1995, 220.

42. Susan Denberg also plays one of the beautiful sirens in the classic *Star Trek* episode, "Mudd's Women."

43. Telotte, 1995, 54–71 and 63.

44. These male robots appear respectively in *The Day the Earth Stood Still* (1951), *Forbidden Planet* (1956), *Silent Running* (1971), *Star Wars* (1977), *The Black Hole* (1979), *Short Circuit* (1986), and *RoboCop* (1987).

45. Kael, 1970, 310.

46. Roberts, 2007 [2005], 287.

47. Hardy, 1991, 82.

48. It is quite possible that some of these name variations combine the biblical Eve with the 18th century English mathematician, Ada Lovelace, who has been called the first computer programmer for her work on Charles Babbage's difference and analytical engines. See also: note 3, Chapter III.

49. Jenkins, 1985, 336.

50. See: Samuel Taylor Coleridge's *Biographia Literaria; or Biographical Sketches of My Literary Life and Opinions*, published 1817.

51. Paglia, 1990, 40.

52. Creed, in Kuhn, 1995, 216/7.

53. Hardy, 1991, 89/90.

54. A post on the website io9.com includes *It's Great to Be Alive* (1933) in its list of lost films. See: gordonmjackson, 2012. A discussion on nitrateville.com dated 2014 suggests that the only extant copy of *It's Great to Be Alive* (1933) as of 2008 was in the Museum of Modern Art (MoMA, in NYC) archive, awaiting transfer from its very flammable original nitrate stock. See: bradleyem, 2008.

55. Wajcman, 1993 [1991], 54. For related discussions, such as social obligations tied to biological motherhood, see: Chodorow, 1979, 83–106; and Firestone, 1979 [1971], 73. For "a survey of motherhood," see: De Beauvoir, 1988 [1949/53], 501–542.

Chapter III

1. See: Lee, 1972a/b/c.

2. The Paramount movie *When Worlds Collide* (1951) was filmed in 3-color Technicolor, as was the British film, *The Tales of Hoffman*, released in the same year. Paramount had used the format for *Dr. Cyclops* (1940) and MGM had experimented with a 2-color Technicolor process for *The Mysterious Island.* (1929). Before this, hand-tinting had been used for selected sequences of films as far back as the 19th century.

3. For a good insight into the workings of Charles Babbage's difference engine, see: Swade, 2000.

4. Jason Gould, in correspondence with the author, July 2017. For more on female roles as code-breakers and technicians during World War II from a British perspective, see: Smith, M., 2015.

5. Hardy, 1991, 83.

6. Penley, 1986, 75/6.

7. Clute and Nicholls, 1993, 924.

8. Baxter, 1970, 77.

9. It is not clear from the credits who plays the "stewardess" role in *When Worlds Collide* (1951). Kasey Rogers seems the most likely candidate from the IMDb.com listing for this movie.

10. For alternative readings about what is the "them" that threatens "us" in 1950s science fiction cinema, especially in America, see Jancovich, 1996, 18. Peter Biskind recognizes the importance of this configuration to the science fiction films of the 1950s, referring to "the idea of the alien as profoundly influenced by the Manichean Us/Them habit of thought that was an occupational hazard of the cold-war battle of ideas" (Biskind, 1984, 111). He further observes that in machine-loving America of the 1950s, the threat was often natural, a fact borne out by the proliferation of "revenge of nature" films, in which the social Self is in conflict with the natural Other. While this culture/nature dynamic is essential to Barbara Creed's notion of the male/female distinction in the horror film, in science fiction film, the female is part of the cultural "us" against the anti-cultural "them" (see: Chapter VI). Susan Sontag has linked the Other in 1950s science fiction film to the threat of radiation (Sontag, 1966b), and John Brosnan suggests that monsters and aliens in the 1950s are "commonly regarded as metaphors for the anxieties of the period ..." (Brosnan, 1991, 85).

11. See also: Wright, 1993: 104. Kathleen Hughes also features on the cover of the 2003 Universal Pictures DVD release of *It Came from Outer Space* (1953).

12. Nicholls, 1979, 537.

13. For more on the alien-as-communist allegory in *I Married a Monster from Outer Space*, see: Biskind, 1984, esp.123–44.

14. Smith, 1994, 227.

15. Sobchack, 1988, 112.

16. Grant, 1993, 33.

17. Smith, 1994, 226.

18. Barker, 1992, 14.

19. Firestone, 1979 [1971], 73.

20. Sheen, 1991, 140.

21. Noonan, 2005, 5.

22. Lewenhak, 1980, 228.

23. Lewenhak, 1980, 232.

24. Greer, 1972 [1970], 123.

25. Hardy, 1991, 65.

26. For further details on most of these films and their female journalists, see the "Filmography" in Noonan, 2005, 163–91.

27. Noonan, 2005, 49.

28. Noonan, 2005, 163. From the 1930s, a standard cinema program would generally consist of a news reel, cartoons, adverts, the main picture and the supporting B-picture, or B-movie. These were usually cheap, quickly made, and often science fiction. Many of these, as Noonan points out, have become genre classics. The "Science Fiction/Double Feature" is memorably evoked in the song that accompanies the opening titles to *The Rocky Horror Picture Show* (1975).

29. Patrick Luciano, quoted in Noonan, 2005, 49.

30. Lant, 1991, 15.

31. Lant, 1991, 15.

32. Biskind, 1984, 102.

33. Biskind, 1984, 135, footnote.

34. *The Thing from Another World* (1951) also includes Sally Creighton as Mrs. Chapman.

35. Scholes and Rabkin, 1977, 136. Examples of "hard" sciences proposed include: physics and astronomy, computers and thermodynamics; the "soft" sciences include: biology and psychology.

36. Wajcman, 1993 [1991], 137. In her text, Judy Wajcman examines many of the relationships between scientific knowledge and gender.

37. Wajcman, 1993 [1991], 141.

38. Biskind, 1984, 133.

39. Biskind, 1984, 133.

40. For more on Dr. Lindsey Brigman, and James Cameron's other leading female characters, see: Conrad, 2011.

41. Noonan, 2005, 2.

42. Brosnan, 1991, 40.

43. Lathers, 2012 [2010], 6.

44. For further details on most of these films and their female astronauts, plus a few from the early 1960s, see the "Filmography" in Noonan, 2005, 163–91.

45. Sobchack, 1995, 107.

46. Hardy, 1991, 181.

47. Wright, 1993, 34.

48. Booker, 2006, 43.

49. Kapell and Pilkington, 2015, 46.

50. Brosnan, 1976, 198.

51. Katz, 1994, 484.

52. De Beauvoir, 1988 [1949/53], 186.

53. For a discussion on patriarchal, and especially Christian, views on the power of virginity and its effect on early vernacular literature, see: Bloch 1991, 93–112.

54. Pallot, et al., 1994, 269.

55. *Cf.* Gamman and Marshment, 1994 [1988], 1.

56. Hardy, 1991, 461.

57. Neal, 1989, 161.

58. *Star Trek* fans will correct this statement by citing the 1990 episode of *Star Trek: The Next Generation*, "Yesterday's Enterprise," in which USS *Enterprise-C* is captained by Rachel Garrett, played by Tricia O'Neil. In addition, Kirsty Alley appears as a trainee starship captain in *Star Trek II: The Wrath of Khan* (1982) and Madge Sinclair is the unnamed captain of the USS *Saratoga* in *The Voyage Home* (1986); there are doubtless other examples. Captain Janeway represents the franchise's first full-time female captain as a central character.

59. Kate Mulgrew, quoted in *Radio Times*, 19–25 October 1996, vol.291#3795, 30.

60. Mulgrew's performance (especially vocally) also evokes Katharine Hepburn, who had already influenced the casting of Neal in *The Day the Earth Stood Still*—after Hepburn's regular screen partner, Spencer Tracey, was slated to play Klaatu.

61. Menville and Reginald, 1977, 87.

62. Greer, 1972 [1970], 123.

63. Oakley, 1974, 186.

64. Bradbury, 1981.

65. Neal, 1989, 161–2.

66. Baxter, 1970, 105.

67. Pallot et al., 1994, 182.

68. Chibnall, 1999, 62.

69. Christian elements underpinning *The Day the Earth Stood Still* (1951) have been recognized by a number of commentators, including: Baxter, 1970; John Brosnan, 1991, 61; Hardy, 1991, 127; Pallot et al., 1994, 182; Wright, 1993, 100; and Booker, 2006, 36. According to Steven M. Sanders, this Christ analogy "went right over the head of director Robert Wise, who has professed surprise that people read religious subtexts into the film" (Sanders, 2008, 4). Sanders cites Scalzi, 1997, 79; however, it seems unlikely that a director as perceptive and accomplished as Wise could have missed the overt allusions in North's screenplay.

70. Daly, 1973, 13. *Cf.* Hamerton-Kelly, 1979. See also: Paglia, 1992 [1990], 40–71.

71. Jancovich 1996, 45. *Cf.* Jancovich 1996, 28. See also: Brosnan, 1978, 83; Brosnan, 1991, 61; and Clute and Nicholls, 1993, 306.

72. Barker, 1992, 11.

73. John's Gospel, 19:25, Authorized Version.

74. Paglia, 1992 [1990], 40.

Chapter IV

1. Hardy, 1991, 196.
2. Booker, 2006, 75.
3. Alfred Hitchcock's first foray into science fiction was as one of the directors on the British *portmanteau* piece, *Elstree Calling* (1930).
4. Hardy, 1991, 196.
5. Elvis' first film was the black-and-white *Love Me Tender* (1956). *Loving You* (1957) was in color, but it is notable that there was a return to black and white for his final two pre-army movies, *Jailhouse Rock* (1957) and *King Creole* (1958).
6. Hardy, 1991, 121.
7. Care must be taken here. As noted before, color had been seen in science fiction cinema as far back as the silent period, with a number of Georges Méliès's films painstakingly hand-tinted frame-by-frame largely by female artists. Single-color experiments appeared sporadically and *Dr. Cyclops* (1940) was filmed using an early Technicolor process. For more on early Technicolor, see: Layton and Pierce, 2015.
8. There are examples of later films that used black and white alongside color, largely for artistic and atmospheric effect. These include the Soviet films, *Stalker* (1979) and *Pisma Myortvoi Chelovyeka* (*Letters form a Dead Man*, 1986), and Hilary Brougher's independent movie *The Sticky Fingers of Time* (1997).
9. Tannahill, 1992 [1980], esp. 402–22.
10. Douglas, 1995, 90.
11. Grant, 1993, 99/100.
12. Grant, 1993, 2.
13. Grant, 1993, 110.
14. Cornea, 2007, 79.
15. These tag-lines are taken from the poster reproduced in a series of "Sixties Design" postcards, produced by Taschen in 1996. It is interesting to note that this poster refers to Barbarella as "the girl of the 21st century," whereas the film is set in the 40th century. This may represent a mistake in translation from the French, which may also account for the poor literary quality of the tag lines cited. More importantly, the discrepancy highlights that the important element of the poster design was the projection of sexual imagery, not the accuracy of the written text.
16. *Barbarella* (1968) poster reproduced in Karney 1995, 582.
17. Jane Fonda had appeared on the covers of the July 1959 and January 1960 issues of *Vogue* magazine. She appears at least once more, on the Spring 1970 cover.
18. Bizony, 1994, 153.
19. Spigel, 1991, 223.
20. Jensen, 1996 [1993], 115.
21. Lathers, 2012 [2010], 9.
22. James, 1994, 1.
23. Clute and Nicholls, 1993, 222.
24. In addition to Cliff Robertson (*Charly*, 1968), the genre's acting Academy Awards have been won by Frederic March for *Dr. Jekyll and Mr. Hyde* (1931) and Don Ameche for his supporting role in *Cocoon* (1984). To date, no woman has won an Oscar for a performance in a science fiction movie.
25. To see how zombies and vampires might be considered as science fiction, read Richard Matheson's 1954 novel, *I am Legend*. For a discussion on this, see: Conrad, Spring 2014.
26. Peter Nicholls, in Clute and Nicholls, 1993, 222.
27. Brosnan, 1991, 153.
28. Davis, 2013, 254.
29. Nama, 2008, 127.
30. Telotte, 2001, 104.
31. Nama, 2008, 124. For more on the various readings of *Planet of the Apes*, racial and otherwise, see: Greene, 1996; Littman, 2013; and Conrad and Magowan, 2015.
32. Hardy, 1991, 276.
33. Milne, 1968, 53.
34. Francke, 1994, 93; see also: 86–97.
35. See: Glassy, 2001, 120.
36. Schiebinger, 2001, 61.
37. Boulle, 1975 [1963], 23.
38. APJAC Productions, 1967, 11.
39. Mulvey, 1989a, 11.
40. Champlin, quoted in Haddad-Garcia, 1981, 144.
41. Noonan, 2015, 63.
42. See: Haddad-Garcia, 1981 and Tookey, 1994.
43. Gravett, 2014.
44. Roger Vadim caused a sensation when he filmed Brigitte Bardot nude for his debut feature, *And God Created Woman* (1956). Annette Stroyberg was listed as Annette Vadim in the director's version of the erotic classic, *Les Liaisons Dangereuses* (1959) and in his elegant horror story, *Blood and Roses* (1960).
45. Baxter, 1970, 199–200.
46. Hall, 1968, 30.
47. Jane Fonda, quoted in Haddad-Garcia, 1981, 143.

48. Haddad-Garcia, 1981, 142.

49. Paco Rabanne, quoted in Finnegan, September 2016, 49.

50. Hardy, 1991, 260.

51. Ian Christie, quoted in Tookey, 52.

52. Pauline Kael, quoted in Haddad-Garcia, 1981, 145.

53. John Simon, *The New York Times*, quoted in Haddad-Garcia, 1981, 144.

54. J.I., June 1968, 88.

55. Hardy, 1991, 279.

56. Noonan, 2015, 3.

57. Bizony, 1994, 22.

58. Penley, 1997, 22.

59. Gallardo and Smith, 2004, 13.

60. Gallardo and Smith, 2004, 124.

61. Cixous and Clément, 1986 [1975], 64.

62. These names do not appear in cast listings, so they have been transcribed from dialogue in the movie itself.

63. See: Noonan, 2005, 2.

64. For a comprehensive survey of the female characters in *2001: A Space Odyssey*, and those who played them, see: Odino, 2013.

65. Bizony, 1994, 21.

66. Willmetts, 2015.

67. Kuhn, 1987, 126.

68. Hardy, 1991, 196.

69. Greer, 1972, 11.

70. Barr, 1987, *xii*. Barr's examples for this are Betty Friedan's 1963 criticism, *The Feminine Mystique*, followed four years later by Pamela Zoline's fiction, *The Heat Death of the Universe*.

71. Barr, 1987, *xx*.

72. Banks, 1993 [1981], 211. Here Olive Banks is developing the contemporary observations of Bernard, 1971 and Freeman, 1975.

73. See: Grant, 1993, esp.16.

74. Lewenhak, 1980, 270.

75. Odino, 2016, quoting Krämer, 2014, 87.

76. Pauline Kael, quoted in Tookey, 1994, 137.

77. Danny Peary, quoted in Tookey, 1994, 137.

78. Sobchack, 1988, 106.

79. The vending machine figures represent kneeling women with open crotches, their hands shackled behind their backs, and their breasts thrust forward; the tables consist of two female figures facing the ceiling, balanced on their hands and feet in "crab" positions, with their legs interlocked to the crotch.

80. See: Mulvey 1989b. Allen Jones's "Women as Furniture" sculpture was exhibited at Tooth's Gallery, London in 1970. Jones's publication *Projects* (1971) contains designs for the Korova Milk Bar. Mulvey also refers to a further publication, *Figures* (1969).

81. Mulvey, 1989b, 7, 8/9.

82. Haskell, 1975 [1974], 323.

83. See: Faraci, 2013.

84. Goldman, 1983, quoted in Brosnan, 1991, 228.

85. Greer, 1972 [1970], 59.

86. Lucas, 2015, 26.

87. Rosenbaum, 1975, 224.

88. Thomas, 1991, 111.

89. Telotte, 2001, 141. See also: 127–141.

90. Wajcman, 1993, 4.

91. Noonan, 2015, 77.

92. Clute and Nicholls, 1993, 1343.

93. Baxter, 1970, 10/11.

Chapter V

1. See: McClintick, 1984 [1983], 167.

2. Champlin, 1992, 45.

3. Aldiss and Wingrove, 1986, 274.

4. Champlin, 1992, 42

5. Princess Leia also owes much to the character of Princess Yuki Akizuki in Akira Kurosawa's *Kakushi-Toride no san-Akunin* (*The Hidden Fortress*, 1958)—a key inspiration for *Star Wars*. See: Conrad, 1996, 20–24.

6. See: "Women of Punk" in *Media Cited* (website reference).

7. Quindlen 1977, 13.

8. Pollock, 1983, 31.

9. *Cf.* Loomis, 1963, esp.13–22 and Bloch, 1991, esp.93–164.

10. See: Rinzler, 2008 [2007], 159–60.

11. Cowie, 1987 [1979], 164.

12. Kael, 1980, 394.

13. Brunsdon, 1987, 119.

14. Gallardo and Smith, 2004, 17.

15. Kael, 1980, 395.

16. Geraghty, 1987, 142.

17. Rohn, 2010, 552. Cited in Pilkington, [2019], Introduction. MS supplied to the author for the preparation of this text.

18. The movie *Coma* is included in the science fiction cinema studies of, amongst others: Meyers 1984; Hardy, 1991; Clute and Nicholls, 1993; Pringle, 1997; and Telotte, 2001.

19. Gordon, 1979, 132.

20. Brosnan, 1991, 209.

21. Pulleine, 1979, 191.

22. See: Hardy, 1991, 181 and 346.

23. Following the release of *Alien* (1979),

A.E. van Vogt took legal action, claiming that the work plagiarized his 1939 publication, *Discord in Scarlet*. He subsequently received fifty thousand dollars in an out-of-court settlement (see: Clute and Nicholls, 1993, 15).

24. Pulleine, 1979, 191.
25. Pulleine, 1979, 191.
26. See: Vogler, 1999 [1992], 14.
27. Campbell, 1993 [1949], 97.
28. See: Lawrence, 2006, esp.22–7. *Cf.* Conrad, 1996, esp.6/7, 44.
29. See: Conrad, 1996, esp.9, 22, 45.
30. Noonan, 2005, 2.
31. Booker, 2006, 188.
32. Campbell 1993 [1949], 33.
33. Booker, 2006, 192.
34. Pallot et al., 1994, 874.
35. Booker, 2006, 192.
36. Keegan, 2009, 44.
37. Keegan, 2009, 218.
38. Booker, 2006, 198.
39. *Empire* Magazine, 1997, 21.
40. Transcribed from BBC 2 television broadcast, 17th October 1993.
41. Stacey, 1994, 125/6.
42. Barker, 1992, 13.
43. Greer, 1972 [1970], 25–9.
44. Cixous and Clément, 1986 [1975], 63.
45. Nama, 2008, 29. The author is summarizing observations made by comedian Richard Pryor, soon after the release of *Star Wars*. See also: 28–35.
46. Cranny-Francis, 1995, 223.
47. Nama, 2008, 31.
48. Brackett, 1978, 25. Incidentally, Lando in this first draft is not specified as black (80). *Cf.* Brackett and Kasdan, 1994.
49. Enough of Brackett's writing work on *The Empire Strikes Back* remained for Lucas to insist that her estate should benefit from her contribution to the film and so her co-screenwriter credit was secured (See: Pollock 1983, 206/7).
50. Reproduced in Williams 1992, 186. See also: BL Editors, No date.
51. Greenberger, 1983, 34.
52. According to IMDb.com, *Alien* took over $60m at the box office in its first six months, against an estimated budget of $11m.
53. Barker, 1992, 14.
54. Pym, 1986, 263.
55. Ripley's development through *Aliens* is discussed further in Conrad, 2011, 133–6; and explored more fully in Gallardo and Smith, 2004, esp. 80–114.

56. IMDb-Editors, 2017.
57. Taubin, 1992, 9.
58. See: Cornea, 2007, Chapter 5, "Gender Blending and the Feminine Subject in Science Fiction Film," 146–74.
59. Keegan, 2009, 118.
60. Booker, 2006, 198.
61. Lynne Magowan, in conversation with the author, April 2017.
62. Rayns, 1991, 51.
63. It should also be noted that Linda Hamilton suffered illness for many years, which may have affected her availability to appear in *Terminator 3*. However, she did also make a number of other screen appearances between 1991 and 2003. She was married to James Cameron for much of this time, so his withdrawal from the *Terminator 3* project may also have been a factor.
64. Hardy, 1995, 477.
65. Mizejewski, 1995, 159.
66. Cornea, 2007, 167.
67. Mulvey, 1989c [1981], 30
68. Gallardo and Smith, 2004, 54.
69. In *Star Trek VI: The Undiscovered Country* (1991) Kirk is echoing, perhaps even mocking, Picard's voice over in the *Star Trek* spin-off television series, *The Next Generation*, which had begun its broadcast run in 1987.
70. Critics who applauded *The Motion Picture* include Philip Strick, whose BFI *Monthly Film Bulletin* review ranks the film alongside *2001* and *Solaris* as "one of the screen's finest science fiction achievements..." (Strick, 1980, 22).
71. See: Nichols, 1994, 220–5.
72. Jensen, 1996 [1993], 217.
73. The inspiration for *Star Trek II: The Wrath of Khan* (1982) was the original television series episode, "Space Seed" (1967).
74. Killick, 1992, 57.
75. Killick, 1992, 57. The episodes that she references are "Requiem for Methuselah" (1970) and "Turnabout Intruder" (1971).
76. Barker, 1992, 11/13.
77. Killick, 1992, 59.
78. See: Altman and Gross, 1998, 223; and Shatner 1994, 266/7.
79. Tookey, 1994, 803.
80. Nichols, 1994, 238/9. While Nichols' Uhura does eventually wear a "unisex" pant suit in *Star Trek: The Motion Picture* (1979) and *The Wrath of Khan* in 1982, she returns to wearing skirts in *The Search for Spock* (1984).

Chapter VI

1. For more on ILM's contribution to the development of CGI, see: Vaz and Duigan, 1996; and Smith, Thomas G., 1991, esp. Chapter 10.

2. Hardy, 1991, 378.

3. Thomas, 1991, 111.

4. See: "@YoriLives" on twitter.com.

5. Lynne Magowan, in conversation with the author, September 2016.

6. See: Sampson 1993, esp. 59–63; and Gardner, 1985.

7. Sampson, 1993, 59.

8. Cowie, 1987 [1979], 156.

9. It could be argued that Sampson is being disingenuous to a science which has, at its foundation, the aim of discovering a theory for the *human* mind. Applying social ideologies to the pure cognitive model introduces a variable which, as Sampson himself has stated, needs to be eliminated in order for the model to exist. Therefore, Sampson is arguing from a standpoint which cannot exist in the same environment as the pure cognitive model. What his argument does highlight, perhaps, is a need for a change in the manner in which society, treats theories of knowledge. Pure cognitive knowledge can only be viewed through "pure" eyes, leaving the fault with society, not with cognitive theory. Sampson addresses the conjoining of cognitive and social theories in Chapter 9, 132–34. Feminist applications of some of these theories are discussed in Code, 1991.

10. Westbrook, 1996, 26.

11. This line is taken from Morgan Freeman's closing narration in the movie *War of the Worlds* (2005).

12. See: Wajcman, 1993. See also: Keller, 1978; Irigaray, 19 87; Potter, 1988; and Young, 1990.

13. Sampson, 1993, 60. See also: Osherson and Smith, 1990.

14. For more on the "think/feel—male/female" dynamic, see: Bowers, 1991.

15. See: Wajcman, 1993, 141/2.

16. Cornea, 2007, 167.

17. Barr, 1991, 30.

18. Sammon, 1996, 5.

19. Barr, 1991, 25.

20. Cornea, 2007, 155. "Rachel" [*sic*].

21. Bruno, 1995, 191.

22. Cornea, 2007, 154.

23. Taubin, 1992, 10.

24. Creed, 1994, 52/3.

25. Hardy, 1995, 468.

26. Creed, 1994, 48.

27. Creed 1995a, 215.

28. Felperin, 1997, 49.

29. Creed 1995b [1994], 133.

30. Rucker, 2015, 6.

31. Creed, 1994, 53.

32. Eaton, 1997, 9.

33. For more on the "bra-burning feminists" myth, see: Johnson Lewis, 2017.

34. Eaton, 1997, 8.

35. Eaton, 1997, 6.

36. See: Firestone, 1979, esp. 73–102.

37. Wajcman, 1993, 59.

38. Sobchack, 1988, 246.

39. See: Irigaray, 1985 [1977], esp. 23–33.

40. Glennon, 1979, 138.

41. Frye, 1993, 493.

42. This conflict theme is developed in Kaveney, 2005, 189–204, where the author describes artistic clashes between *Alien: Resurrection's* director, Jeunet and its screenwriter, and Joss Whedon.

43. Felperin, 1997, 49.

44. Nama, 2008, 2.

45. Felperin, 1997, 49.

46. Newman, July 1997, 40.

47. Strick, 1997, 46

48. See: Schatz, 1981, esp. 37/8.

49. See: Gregory, 2002, 151–269 and 271–359.

50. Collin, 2016, 28.

51. Penley, 1986, 75/6.

52. According to IMDb.com, *Tank Girl* (1996) grossed $6.6m at the worldwide box office, against an estimated budget of $25m. [Accessed: 1st August 2017].

53. Cornea, 2007, 166.

Chapter VII

1. Some argue that the absence of the year "0" in the historic Western calendar means that the 3rd Millennium A.D. actually started on 1st January 2001. Following that method, centuries would start a year later too, i.e., the 20th century began on 1st January 1901. There is some merit to this argument, but for clarity and neatness, this text has adopted what appears to be the majority approach. For more information, visit: www.timeanddate.com/counters/mil2000.html.

2. For a generally balanced review of the

Star Wars Special Editions, see: Newman, April 1997.

3. Landon, 1999, 39.

4. Baxter, 1970, 107.

5. Garrett Stewart, quoted in Landon, 1999, 39.

6. Ramsaye, 1964 [1926], *lxx*.

7. From the author's interview with Glen Donnar, originally for Conrad, 2011. Reviewed and revised by Donnar for this text.

8. Cornea, 2007, 146.

9. Atkins, 2000, 28.

10. Atkins, 2000, 38.

11. Newman, March 2006, 48.

12. According to IMDb.com, the estimated budget for *Æon Flux* (2005) is $62 million [Accessed: 4th August 2017].

13. O'Hehir, 2001, 15.

14. *Planet of the Apes* (2001) does include a character called Nova, played by Lisa Marie; however, Estella Warren's Deanna is closer to the Nova of Pierre Boulle's original novel.

15. O'Hehir, 2001, 12.

16. *Zombie Strippers* (2008) is included as science fiction because its premise relies on a virus created by rogue government scientists. No judgment is offered regarding the quality of the movie or its underlying concepts.

17. Zoe Saldana's use of the umlaut in her first name seems to have been preferred, if not always used, at the beginning of her career. There are also examples of Zoë Saldaña in her IMDb.com listing. Spellings vary until 2013, after which the diacritics disappear completely.

18. Killick, 1992, 57.

19. According to www.the-numbers.com, as of 6th August 2017, the worldwide box office receipts *Avatar* (2009) are $2,783,918,982. [Accessed: 8th August 2017].

20. Osmond, 2010, 48.

21. Hewitt, 2010, 54.

22. Osmond, 2010, 49.

23. Brooke, 2012, 68.

24. Felperin, 1995, 55.

25. Conrad, 2009, 67.

26. Bell, 2015, 21. For more on the various versions of *Blade Runner*, see: Off-world Editors, No date.

27. Pinkerton, 2016, 34.

28. David Bordwell, quoted in Pinkerton, 2016, 34.

29. According to IMDb.com, the estimated budget for the 2008 remake of *The Day the Earth Stood Still* is $80 million [Accessed: 6th June 2017].

30. Ebert, 2008.

31. Newman, 2009, 57.

32. For a wider ranging discussion on the role of Helen Benson in the 2008 remake of *The Day the Earth Stood Still*, see Conrad, 2009.

33. Spencer, 2004, 85.

34. Kelly, 2016.

35. Bitel, 2015, 87.

36. Nayman, April 2015, 79.

37. Since 1963, twelve actors have played The Doctor in the BBC television series *Doctor Who*. Many others have played the character in TV specials and spin-offs, feature films, radio broadcasts and stage plays. While Jodie Whitaker is technically not the first woman to portray The Doctor, she is the first to take the lead role in the flagship television series.

38. For a short, early internet discussion on *Westworld* and "Rape Culture," see: Horn, 2016. For some of Gemma Chan's personal perspective on *Humans*, see Kelly, 2016.

39. Mulkerrins, 2016, 42.

40. Anil, 2015, 45.

41. Smith, D., 2015, 111.

42. See: "Alex Garland on *Ex Machina*" in *Media Cited*.

43. Collin, 2013, 33.

44. Clarey, 2015.

45. Newman, 2014, 74.

46. Newman, 2016, 73.

47. Newman, 2017, 73.

48. Sobchack, 1988, 151.

49. www.dorkly.com/static/about.

50. Staff, 2017.

51. A good place to begin a discussion on pornography's relationship with feminism is the collection of essays in Russell, 1993a.

52. Hunter, 2015, 32.

53. Hiscock, 2015.

54. www.imdb.com/name/nm0735442/ [Accessed 22nd August 2017].

55. Smurfs Wiki Editors, No date.

56. GWBB Editors, No date.

57. See: "Ridley Scott" in *Media Cited*.

58. Metz, 1982b, 3.

59. Pinkerton, 2016, 34.

60. Hayes, 2017, 87.

Conclusion

1. Turner, 1998, 195. The author changed his name in 2006.

2. See: Barr, 1987, *xii*. For "Statement of Problem," Barr cites Betty Friedan's 1963 crit-

icism, *The Feminine Mystique* and Pamela Zoline's 1967 fiction, *The Heat Death of the Universe*; "Radical Feminist Solutions" are exemplified by Shulamith Firestone's *The Dialectic of Sex* (1970) followed by Joanna Russ's *The Female Man* (1975). "Moderate Womanist Solutions" are forwarded by Alice Walker with *In Search of Our Mother's Gardens* (1984), and the fictional *Shadow Singer*, by Marcia Bennet (1984).

3. Sobchack, 1988, 63.

4. See: Nichols, 1994, 238/9.

5. Noonan, 2005, 2.

6. The following lists and comments are edited from e-mail submissions specifically for this section, received by the author from these contributors during August 2017. Further correspondents are recognized in the Acknowledgements.

7. Greer, 1972 [1970], 114.

8. James, 2014, 5.

9. Strimpel, 2017, 25. See also: the-numbers.com [Accessed: 4th September 2017].

10. 20th century Academy Award "Best Picture" nominations were received for *Dr. Strangelove or: How I Learned to Stop Worrying and Love the Bomb* (1964), *A Clockwork Orange* (1971) and *E.T. the Extra-Terrestrial* (1982).

11. Brunsdon, 1987, 119

12. Brunsdon, 1987, 51.

13. Clarey, 2015.

14. Casey Jaye's documentary, *The Red Pill*, does not feature Aaron Carey himself. Incidentally, the Men's Rights Movement takes the term "Red Pill" from *The Matrix* (1999). Neo is offered two pills: the blue one will return him to a state of blissful ignorance; the red pill will reveal the world as it really is. The Men's Rights Movement feels that its campaign is doing the latter.

15. Laffly, 2016.

16. See: Collin, 2016, 28.

Bibliography and Filmography

Books, Articles and Reviews

Acker, Ally. 1991. *Reel Women: Pioneers of the Cinema, 1896 to the Present*. London: Batsford.

Aldiss, Brian W. 1975. *Billion Year Spree: The History of Science Fiction*. London: Corgi. (Original edition, London: Weidenfeld and Nicolson, 1973. Expanded edition, Aldiss and Wingrove, 1986.)

_____. 1995. *The Detached Retina: Aspects of SF and Fantasy*. Liverpool: Liverpool University Press.

_____, and David Wingrove. 1986. *Trillion Year Spree: The History of Science Fiction*. London: Victor Gollancz. (Expanded version of Aldiss, 1973.)

Altman, Mark A., and Edward Gross. 1998. *Trek Navigator: The Ultimate Guide to the Entire "Star Trek" Saga*. London: Boxtree.

Amis, Kingsley. 1960. *New Maps of Hell: A Survey of Science Fiction*. New York: Harcourt, Brace and Co.

Anil, Seth. 2015, 24th January. "*Ex Machina*: Quest to Create an AI Takes No Prisoners," in *New Scientist*, no. 3005, 44/5.

APJAC Productions, 1967. *Preliminary Production Information Guide on the Arthur P. Jacobs Production of "Planet of the Apes."* Unpublished production document. PDF file available at http://pota.goatley.com/scripts.html. (Accessed 19th April 2017.)

Armitt, Lucie, ed. 1991. *Where No Man Has Gone Before: Women and Science Fiction*. London: Routledge.

Ash, Brian, ed. 1977. *The Visual Encyclopedia of Science Fiction*. New York: Harmony.

Atkins, Ian. 2000. "SF Babes," in *Starburst Yearbook 2000*, vol. 46, Summer Special, 28–39.

Atwood, Margaret. 1985. *The Handmaid's Tale*. Toronto: McClelland and Stewart.

Bakhtin, Mikhail Mikhailovich. 1981. *The Dialogic Imagination*. Edited by M. Holoquist. Austin: University of Texas Press.

Banks, Olive. 1993. *Faces of Feminism: A Study of Feminism as a Social Movement*. London: Basil Blackwell. (Original edition, Martin Robertson, 1981.)

Barker, Heather. 1992, July. "SFemale: Ladies First, Please!," in *Starburst* Summer Special 12, 9–14.

Barnes, John. 1998a. *The Beginnings of the Cinema in England 1894–1901, Vol.1: 1894–1896*. Exeter: University of Exeter Press. (Original edition, 1976.)

_____. 1998b. *The Beginnings of the Cinema in England 1894–1901, Vol. 2: 1897*. Exeter: University of Exeter Press. (Original edition, 1976.)

_____. 1998c. *The Beginnings of the Cinema in England 1894–1901, Vol.3: 1898*. Exeter: University of Exeter Press. (Original edition, 1976.)

_____. 1998d. *The Beginnings of the Cinema in England 1894–1901, Vol.4: 1899*. Exeter: University of Exeter Press. (Original edition, 1976.)

_____. 1998e. *The Beginnings of the Cinema in England 1894–1901, Vol.5: 1900*. Exeter: University of Exeter Press. (Original edition, 1976.)

Barr, Marleen S. 1987. *Alien to Femininity: Speculative Fiction and Feminist Theory (Contributions to the Study of Science Fiction and Fantasy Series #27)*. New York and London: Greenwood Press.

_____. 1991. "Metahuman 'Kipple' Or, Do Male Movie Makers Dream of Electric Women?," in Kerman, 1991, 25–31.

Bates, Harry. 1957. "Farewell to the Master," in Healy and McComas, 1957, 779–815. (First published in *Astounding Science Fiction*, edited by John W. Campbell, Jr., October 1940. Subsequently published in Raymond J. Healy and J. Francis McComas, eds. *Famous Science-Fiction Stories: Adventures in Time and Space*. Toronto: Random House, 1946).

Baxter, John. 1970. *Science Fiction in the Cinema*, from *The International Film Guide Series*. New York: A.S. Barnes and Co.

Bell, James. 2015, April. "Remake/Remodel: Director's Cuts & Alternative Versions," in *Sight & Sound*, vol. 25 no. 4, 18–30.

Biskind, Peter, 1984. *Seeing Is Believing: How Hollywood Taught Us to Stop Worrying About the Fifties*. London: Pluto Press.

Bitel, Anton. 2015, March. Review of *Predestination*, in *Sight & Sound*, vol. 25, no. 3, 86/7.

Bizony, Piers. 1994. *2001: Filming the Future*. London: Aurum Press. (Updated and included in the limited-edition box set *The Making of Stanley Kubrick's 2001: A Space Odyssey*. Berlin: Taschen, 2014.)

Bloch, R. Howard. 1991. *Medieval Misogyny and the Invention of Western Romantic Love*. London: University of Chicago Press.

Booker, M. Keith. 2006. *Alternate Americas: Science Fiction Film and American Culture*. Westport, CT: Praeger.

Borden, Lizzie. 1983. "Script to 'Born in Flames'" *Heresies*, #16, 12–6.

Boulle, Pierre. 1959. *The Bridge on the River Kwai*. London: Fontana Books. (Translated from the French by Xan Fielding. Original edition, *Le Pont de la Rivière Kwai*. Paris: René Julliard, 1952).

_____. 1968. *Planet of the Men*. Unpublished, unproduced screenplay. PDF file available at http://pota.goatley.com/scripts.html (accessed 3rd May 2017).

_____. 1975. *Planet of the Apes*. London: Penguin Books. (Translated from the French by Xan Fielding as *Monkey Planet*. Original edition, *La Planète des Singes*. Paris: René Julliard, 1963).

Bowers, J. M. 1991. "Time Representation and Power/Knowledge: Towards a Critique of Cognitive Science as a Knowledge Producing Practice," in *Theory and Psychology* vol. 1, 543–69.

Brackett, Leigh. 1978. *Star Wars Sequel*. Unpublished, unproduced screenplay; first draft of *The Empire Strikes Back*. PDF film available at http://scyfilove.com/wp-content/uploads/2010/05/. (Accessed 14th June 2017).

_____, and Lawrence Kasdan. 1994. *"The Empire Strikes Back": The Screenplay*. Monterey Park, CA: O.S.P. Publishing.

Bradbury, Ray. 10th March 1981. *The Evening of the Second Day*. Unpublished 45-page screenplay/outline, 20th Century–Fox. (Copyright status is unclear; however, versions of the text are readily available on the internet).

bradleyem. 2008, 2nd July. "Question about It's Great to Be Alive (1933)," online at: *Nitrate-Ville: Talking, collecting and preserving classic film*. http://www.nitrateville.com/viewtopic.php?f=4&t=17868 (Accessed: 26th August 2017).

British Library Editors. No date. "Elizabeth's Tilbury Speech," online at: *British Library Learning Timelines: Sources From History*. www.bl.uk/learning/timeline/item102878.html (Accessed: 13th June 2017).

Brooke, Michael. 2012, August. Review of *Prometheus*, in *Sight & Sound*, vol. 22, no. 8, 67/8.

Brosnan, John. 1976. *Movie Magic: The Story of Special Effects in the Cinema*. New York: Plume.

_____. 1991. *The Primal Screen: A History of Science Fiction Film*. London: Orbit. (An updated and expanded version of *Future Tense: The Cinema of Science Fiction*. New York: St. Martin's Press, 1978).

Bruno, Giuliana. 1995. "Ramble City: Postmodernism and 'Blade Runner,'" in Kuhn, 1995, 183–95.

Brunsdon, Charlotte, ed. 1987. *Films for Women*. London: BFI.

Campbell, Joseph. 1993. *The Hero with a Thousand Faces*. London: Fontana. (First edition, Princeton University Press, 1949).

Čapek, Karel. 1923. *R.U.R. (Rossum's Universal Robots)*. "A Play in Three Acts and an Epilogue." (Original English edition, 1923. First published in Czech, 1920).

Carrithers, Michael. 1985. "An Alternative Social History of the Self," in Carrithers, Collins, and Lukes, 1985, 234–56.

_____, Steven Collins, and Steven Lukes, eds. 1985. *The Category of the Person: Anthropology, Philosophy, History*. Cambridge: Cambridge University Press.

Carson, Diane, Linda Dittmar, and Janice R. Welsch, eds. 1994. *Multiple Voices in Feminist Film Criticism*. London: University of Minnesota Press.

Castaneda, Carlos. 1974. *Tales of Power*. New York: Penguin. (First UK edition, London: Hodder & Stoughton).

Champlin, Charles. 1992. *George Lucas: The Creative Impulse*. London: Virgin.

Chibnall, Steve. 1999. "Alien Women: The politics of Sexual Difference in British SF Pulp Cinema," in Hunter, 1999, 57–74.

Chodorow, Nancy. 1979. Mothering, Male Dominance, and Capitalism," in Eisenstein, 1979, 83–106.

Cixous, Hélène, and Catherine Clément. 1986. "Sorties," in *The Newly Born Woman*, vol. 24, Manchester: Manchester UP. (*Theory and History of Literature* series. Translated by Betsy Wing. Introduction by Sandra M. Gilbert. Original French edition, Paris: Union Générale d'Éditions, 1975).

Clarey, Aaron. 2015, 11th May. "Why You Should Not Go See 'Mad Max: Feminist Road'," online at: *Return of Kings*. www.returnofkings.com/63036/why-you-should-not-go-see-mad-max-feminist-road (Accessed: 26th August 2017).

Clark-Kennedy, A.E. 1965. *Edith Cavell: Pioneer & Patriot*. London: Faber & Faber.

Clute, John, and Peter Nicholls, eds. 1993. *The Encyclopedia of Science Fiction*. 2nd edition. London: Orbit.

Code, L. 1991. *What Can She Know? Feminist Theory and the Construction of Knowledge*. Ithaca, NY: Cornell University Press.

Collin, Robbie. 2013, 13th December. Review of *Gravity*, in *The Daily Telegraph*, London, 33.

_____. 2016, 15th December. "The Force is With Her," in *The Daily Telegraph*, London, 28.

Conrad, Dean. 1996. *Star Wars: The Genesis of a Legend*. London: Valis Books.

_____. 2009. "Where Have all the Ripleys Gone?," in *Foundation: The International Review of Science Fiction*, vol. 38, no. 105, 55–72.

_____. 2011, Spring. "Femmes Futures: 100 Years of Female Representation in Science Fiction Cinema," in *Science Fiction Film and Television*, vol. 4 no. 1, 79–99.

_____. 2011. "'So, what's your story?' Morphing Myths and Feminising Archetypes, from *The Terminator* to *Avatar*," in Kapell and McVeigh, 2011, 124–45.

_____. 2014. "In Search of Richard Matheson: Science Fiction Screenwriter," in *Foundation: The International Review of Science Fiction*, vol. 43, no. 117, 31–45.

_____, and Lynne Magowan. 2015. "Damn, Dirty Dames: Dissecting Difference in *Planet of the Apes*," in Kapell and Pilkington, 2015, 101–16.

Cook, Pam, and Philip Dodd, eds. No date. *Women and Film: A Sight and Sound Reader*. London: Scarlett Press.

Cornea, Christine. 2007. *Science Fiction Cinema: Between Fantasy and Reality*. Edinburgh: Edinburgh University Press.

Cowie, Elizabeth. 1987. "A Discussion of *Coma*," in Brunsdon, 1987, 155–65. (First published as part of "The Popular Film as a Progressive Text—A Discussion of *Coma*," in *m/f*, no. 3, 1979, 59–81).

Cranny-Francis, Anne. 1995. "Feminist Futures: A Generic Study," in Kuhn, 1995, 219–27.

Creed, Barbara. 1994. *The Monstrous Feminine: Film Feminism, Psychoanalysis*. London: Routledge.

_____. 1995a. "Gynesis, Postmodernism and the Science Fiction Horror Film," in Kuhn, 1995, 214–18.

_____. 1995b. "'Alien' and the Monstrous-Feminine," in Kuhn 1995, 128–41. (First published as Chapter 2, "Horror and the Archaic Mother," in Creed 1994, 16–30).

Dadoun, Roger. 1986. "'Metropolis': Mother-City—'Mittler'—Hitler," in *Camera Obscura*, #15, 136–63. (Translated by Arthur Goldhammer. Also in Penley et al., 1991, 132–59.)

Daly, Mary. 1973. *Beyond God the Father: Toward a Philosophy of Women's Liberation*. Boston: Beacon.

Davies, Margery. 1979. "Woman's Place Is at the Typewriter," in Eisenstein 1979a, 248–66.

Davis, Jason. 2013. "Aping Race, Racing Apes," in Huss, 2013, 245–54.

De Beauvoir, Simone. 1988. *The Second Sex*. London: Picador. (Translated from the French and edited by H.M. Parshley. Original edition, France: Gallimard, 1949. Original translation, London: Jonathan Cape, 1953).

Dick, Philip K. 1969. *Do Androids Dream of Electric Sheep?* London: Rapp and Whiting.

Donnar, Glen. 2013. "Terrified Men, Monstrous Masculinities: Representing & Recuperating American Masculinities in Contemporary Hollywood 'Terror Threat' Films." Doctoral thesis. Melbourne: RMIT University. (PDF copy supplied by author).

Dorkly.com staff. 2017, 27th July. "20 Honestly Unbelievable Cosplays from SDCC 2017," online at: *Dorkly*. www.dorkly.com/post/84726/san-diego-cosplay-time-cosplay-cosplay. (Accessed: 12th August 2017).

Douglas, Susan J. 1995. *Where the Girls Are:*

Growing up Female with Mass Media. Harmondsworth: Penguin.

Dworkin, Andrea. 1990. *Pornography: Men Possessing Women.* London: The Women's Press. (Original edition, New York: Perigree Books, 1981).

Dziech, Billie Wright, and Linda Weiner. 1993. "The Lecherous Professor," in Jaggar and Rothenberg, 1993, 323–27.

Eaton, Michael. 1997, December. "Born Again," in *Sight & Sound,* vol. 7 no. 12, 6–9.

Ebert, Roger. 2008, 10th December. "The Day the Earth Stood Still," online at: RogerEbert.com. www.rogerebert.com/reviews/the-day-the-earth-stood-still-2008. (Accessed: 24th August 2017).

Eisenstein, Zillah R., ed. 1979. *Capitalist Patriarchy and the Case for Socialist Feminism.* London: Monthly Review Press, 1979.

Empire Magazine. 1997, December. "The Ten Definitive Science Fiction Films of All Time," Special Insert in *Empire,* vol. 112.

Faraci, Devin. 2013, 1st August. "Why Stanley Kubrick Banned A CLOCKWORK ORANGE," online at: *Birth. Movies. Death.* http://birthmoviesdeath.com/2013/08/01/the-disappearance-of-a-clockwork-orange (Accessed: 23rd June 2017).

Felperin, Leslie. 1995, July. Review of *Tank Girl,* in *Sight & Sound,* vol. 5, no. 7, 54/5.

_____. 1997, January. Review of *Star Trek: First Contact,* in *Sight & Sound,* vol. 7, no. 1, 48/9.

Filmer, Alison J., and Andre Golay. 1989. *Harrap's Book of Film Directors and Their Films.* London: Harrap.

Finnegan, Kate. 2016, 10th September. "Reinventing Rabanne," in *Telegraph Magazine,* London, 46–51.

Firestone, Shulamith. 1979. *The Dialectic of Sex: The Case for Feminist Revolution.* London: The Women's Press. (Introduced by Rosalind Delmar. Original edition, London: Jonathan Cape, 1971).

Francke, Lizzie. 1994. *Script Girls: Women Screenwriters in Hollywood.* London: BFI.

Friedan, Betty. 1963. *The Feminine Mystique.* New York: Norton.

Frye, Marilyn. 1993. "Virgin Women," in Jaggar and Rothenberg, 492–6.

Gallardo, Ximena C., and C. Jason Smith. 2004. *Alien Woman: The Making of Lt. Ellen Ripley.* New York: Continuum.

Gamman, Lorraine, and Margaret Marshment, eds. 1994. *The Female Gaze: Women as Viewers of Popular Culture.* London: The Women's Press. (Original edition, 1988).

Gardner, Howard. 1985. *The Mind's New Science: A History of the Cognitive Revolution.* New York: Basic Books.

Garfinkel, Harold. 1967. *Studies in Ethnomethodology.* Englewood Cliffs, NJ: Prentice Hall.

Gatens, Moira. 1991. *Feminism and Philosophy: Perspectives on Difference and Equality.* Cambridge: Polity Press.

Geraghty, Christine. 1987. "Three Women's Films," in Brunsdon, 1987, 138–45.

Gifford, Denis. 1991. *Things, Its and Aliens: Lobby Card Posters from Sci-Fi Shockers!* London: Blossom.

Glassy, Mark C. 2001. *The Biology of Science Fiction Cinema.* Jefferson, NC: McFarland.

Glennon, Lynda M. 1979. *Women and Dualism: A Sociology of Knowledge Analysis.* London: Longman.

Goldman, William. 1983. *Adventures in the Screen Trade: A Personal View of Hollywood and Screenwriting.* New York: Warner Books.

Gordon, Linda. 1979. "The Struggle for Reproductive Freedom: Three Stages of Feminism," in Eisenstein, 1979, 107–32.

gordonmjackson. 2012, 25th January. "Weird and Wonderful Movies That You'll Never Get to See," online at: *io9.* http://io9.gizmodo.com/5877874/lost-films (Accessed: 12th June 2017).

Grant, Linda, 1993, *Sexing the Millennium: A Political History of the Sexual Revolution.* London: HarperCollins.

Gravett, Paul. 2014, 25th September. "Jean-Claude Forest's Barbarella: A Landmark in Adult French Comics," online at: *Paul Gravett.* www.paulgravett.com/articles/article/jean_claude_forests_barbarella (Accessed: 20th April 2017).

Greenberger, Robert. 1983, June. "Carrie Fisher," an interview, in *Starlog,* #71, 32–6.

Greene, Eric. 1996. Planet of the Apes *as American Myth: Race and Politics in Popular Culture.* Middletown, CT: Wesleyan University Press.

Greer, Germain, 1972. *The Female Eunuch.* London: Paladin. (Original edition, MacGibbon and Kee Ltd., 1970).

Gregory, Mollie. 2002. *Women Who Run the Show.* New York: St. Martin's Press.

Grosz, Elizabeth. 1990. *Jacques Lacan: A Feminist Introduction.* London: Routledge.

GWBB Editors. No date. "About Us," online at: GWBB: *Girls Will Be Boys.* www.gwbbclothing.com/about-us (Accessed: 8th May 2017).

Haddad-Garcia, George. 1981. *The Films of Jane Fonda.* Secaucus, NJ: Citadel Press.

Hall, William. 1968, February. "Barbarella," in *Photoplay Film Monthly*, vol. 19, no. 2, 30–1/63.

Hamerton-Kelly, Robert. 1979. *God the Father: Theology and Patriarchy in the Teaching of Jesus*. Philadelphia: Fortress Press.

Hardy, Phil, ed. 1991. *The Aurum Film Encyclopedia: Science Fiction*. London: Aurum Press. (First edition, 1984.)

———. 1995. *The Aurum Film Encyclopedia: Science Fiction*. London: Aurum Press.

Haskell, Molly. 1975. *From Reverence to Rape: The Treatment of Women in the Movies*. London: New English Library. (Original edition, New York: Holt, Rinehart and Winston, 1974).

Hayes, Tim. 2017, February. Review of *Rogue One*, in *Sight & Sound*, vol. 27, no. 2, 87.

Healy, Raymond J. and J. Francis McComas, eds. 1946. *Famous Science-Fiction Stories: Adventures in Time and Space*. Canada: Random House, 1946.

Heinlein, Robert A. 1959. *All You Zombies*. (First published in the March 1959 issue of *The Magazine of Fantasy & Science Fiction*. Available subsequently in various collections.)

Hewitt, Chris. 2010, February. Review of *Avatar*, in *Empire*, vol. 248, 54/5.

Hiscock, John. 2015, 15th May. "Charlize Theron: 'I'm not a fan of scrawny little girls pretending to kick butt'," online at: *The Telegraph*. www.telegraph.co.uk/film/mad-max-fury-road/charlize-theron-interview/ (Accessed: 20th August 2017).

Horn, Tina. 2016, 7th October. "What the Rape Scenes in *Westworld* Say About Rape Culture," online at: *Refinery29*. www.refinery29.com/2016/10/125731/westworld-sex-robot-rape-culture-hbo (Accessed: 10th October 2016).

Hunter, I.Q. 2015, September. "The Road to Excess," in *Sight & Sound*, vol. 25, no. 9, 32.

Hunter, I.Q., ed. 1999. *British Science Fiction Cinema*. London: Routledge.

Huss, John, ed. 2013. Planet of the Apes *and Philosophy: Great Apes Think Alike*. Chicago: Open Court.

Hutchinson, Pamela. 2015, October. "Primal Screen: The World of the Silent Cinema," in *Sight & Sound*, vol. 25, no. 10, 61.

IMDb-Editors. 2017. "10 Influential Sci-Fi Films That Inspire Tim Smit," online at: IMDb Picks. www.imdb.com/imdbpicks/tim-smit-sci-fi-films/ls068712040/ (Accessed: 16th June 2017).

Irigaray, Luce. 1985. *This Sex Which is Not One*.

Ithaca, NY: Cornell University Press. (Translated by Catherine Porter. Original French edition, 1977).

———. 1987. "Is the Subject of Science Sexed?," in *Hypatia*, vol. 2no. 3.

J.I. 1968, June. Review of *2001: A Space Odyssey*, in *Monthly Film Bulletin*, vol. 35 no. 413, 88. (Reviewer's identity not known).

Jaggar, Alison M., and Paula Rothenberg, eds. 1993. *Feminist Frameworks: Alternative Theoretical Accounts of the Relations Between Women and Men*, 3rd edition. London: McGraw-Hill.

James, Edward. 1994. *Science Fiction in the Twentieth Century*. Oxford and New York: Oxford University Press.

James, Nick. 2014, November. "The Equalizers," Editorial in *Sight & Sound*, vol. 21, no. 11, 5.

James, P.D. 1992. *The Children of Men*. New York: Alfred A. Knopf/London: Faber & Faber.

Jancovich, Mark. 1996. *Rational Fears: American Horror in the 1950s*. Manchester: Manchester University Press.

Jenkins, Steve. 1985, November. Review of *The Bride*, in *Monthly Film Bulletin*, vol. 52, no. 622, 336.

Jensen, Claus. 1996. *Contest for the Heavens: The Road to the Challenger Disaster*. London: Harvill Press. (Translated from the Danish by Barbara Haveland. Original edition, *Challenger—et Teknisk Uheld*. Copenhagen: Samlerens Forlag, 1993).

Johnson Lewis, Jone. 2017, 13th March. "Bra-Burning Feminists? Another Myth of Women's History," online at: *ThoughtCo*. www.thoughtco.com/bra-burning-feminists-3529832 (Accessed: 5th July 2017).

Jones, Eric M. 1995. "One Small Step," online at: *Apollo 11 Lunar Surface Journal*. www.hq.nasa.gov/alsj/a11/a11.step.html (Accessed: 1st November 2016).

Kael, Pauline. 1970. *Kiss Kiss, Bang Bang*. London: Calder and Boyars.

———. 1980. *When the Lights Go Down*. London: Marion Boyars.

Kapell, Matthew Wilhelm, and Ace G. Pilkington, eds. 2015. *The Fantastic Made Visible: Essays on the Adaptation of Science Fiction and Fantasy from Page to Screen*. Jefferson: McFarland.

———, and John Shelton Lawrence, eds. 2006. *Finding the Force of the Star Wars Franchise: Fans, Merchandise and Critics*. New York: Peter Lang.

———, and Stephen McVeigh, eds. 2011. *The*

Films of James Cameron: Critical Essays. Jefferson: McFarland.

Karney, Robyn, ed. 1995. *Chronicle of the Cinema.* London: Dorling Kindersley.

Katz, Ephraim. 1994. *The Film Encyclopedia,* 2nd edition. New York: HarperCollins.

Kavanagh, James H. "Feminism, Humanism and Science in *Alien,*" in Kuhn, 1995, 73–81.

Kaveney, Roz. 2005. *From Alien to The Matrix: Reading Science Fiction Film.* London and New York: I.B. Tauris.

Keegan, Rebecca. 2009. *The Futurist: The Life and Films of James Cameron.* New York: Crown Publishers.

Keller, Craig, ed. 2008. *Frau im Mond* (Booklet supplied with the DVD release, "Masters of Cinema" series no. 41). Germany: Eureka!

Keller, Evelyn Fox. 1978. "Gender and Science," in *Psychoanalysis and Contemporary Thought,* vol. 1, 409–33.

Kelly, Guy. 2016, 24th May. "A (nearly) complete glossary of gender identities for your next census," online at: *The Telegraph.* www.telegraph.co.uk/men/the-filter/a-nearly-complete-glossary-of-gender-identities-for-your-next-ce/ (Accessed: 3rd August 2017).

_____. 2016, 30th October. "Gemma: 100% Human," in *Stella* magazine, 26–32 (and cover).

Kerman, Judith B., ed. 1991. *Retrofitting "Blade Runner": Issues in Ridley Scott's "Blade Runner" and Philip K. Dick's "Do Androids Dream of Electric Sheep?"* Bowling Green, OH: Bowling Green State University Press.

Keyes, Daniel. 1959. *Flowers for Algernon.* (First published in the April 1959 issue of *The Magazine of Fantasy & Science Fiction.* Book edition, Harcourt, Brace and World, 1966).

Killick, Jane. 1992, July. "'Star Trek' Sex: The Female Frontier," in *Starburst* Summer Special 12, 57–60.

Klein, Amanda Ann. 2011. *American Film Cycles: Reframing Genres, Screening Social Problems, and Defining Subcultures.* Austin: University of Texas Press.

Krämer, Peter. 2014. *Dr. Strangelove or: How I Learned to Stop Worrying and Love the Bomb.* London: British Film Institute. (*BFI Classics* series).

Kristeva, Julia. 1982. *Powers of Horror: An Essay on Abjection.* New York: Columbia University Press. (Translated by Leon S. Roudiez. Original French edition, 1980).

Kuhn, Annette, ed. 1995. *Alien Zone: Cultural Theory and Contemporary Science Fiction Cinema.* London and New York: Verso. (Original edition, 1990).

Kuhn, Annette, ed. 1999. *Alien Zone II: The Spaces of Science Fiction Cinema.* London and New York: Verso.

Kuhn, Annette. 1987. *Hollywood and the New Women's Cinema.* In Brunsdon 1987, 125–30.

Lacan, Jacques. 1968. *The Language of the Self: The Function of Language in Psychoanalysis.* New York: Delta. (Translated by Antony Wilden).

_____. 1977. *The Four Fundamental Concepts of Psycho-Analysis.* International Psychoanalytical Library Edition, no. 106. London: Hogarth Press and the Institute of Psychoanalysis. (Edited by Jacques-Alain Miller. Translated by Alan Sheridan).

Laffly, Tomris. 2016, 19th December. "*Passengers* Is Sexist Nonsense," online at: *Film School Rejects.* https://filmschoolrejects.com/passengers-review-2016-7f42b6b38cdd/ (Accessed: 20th August 2017).

Landon, Brooks. 1999. "Diegetic or Digital? The Convergence of Science-Fiction Literature and Science-Fiction Film," in Kuhn, 1999, 31–49.

Lant, Antonia. 1991. *Blackout: Reinventing Women for Wartime British Cinema.* Princeton, NJ: Princeton University Press.

Lathers, Marie. 2012. *Space Oddities: Women and Culture in Popular Film and Culture, 1960–2000.* New York: Continuum. (First published, 2010).

Lawrence, John Shelton. 2006. "Joseph Campbell, George Lucas, and the Monomyth," in Kapell and Shelton, 2006, 21–34.

Layton, James, and David Pierce. 2015. *The Dawn of Technicolor 1915–1935.* Rochester, NY: George Eastman Museum.

Lear, John. 1965. *Kepler's Dream.* Berkeley: University of California Press. ("With the full text and notes of *Somnium, Sive Astronomia Lunaris,* Joannis Kepleri." Translated by Patricia Frueh Kirkwood.)

Lee, Walt. 1972a. *Reference Guide to Fantastic Films—Science Fiction, Fantasy & Horror: Volume 1 (A–F).* Los Angeles: Chelsea-Lee Books.

_____. 1972b. *Reference Guide to Fantastic Films—Science Fiction, Fantasy & Horror: Volume 2 (G–O).* Los Angeles: Chelsea-Lee Books.

_____. 1972c. *Reference Guide to Fantastic Films—Science Fiction, Fantasy & Horror: Volume 3 (P–Z).* Los Angeles: Chelsea-Lee Books.

Lewenhak, Sheila. 1980. *Women and Work.* N.p.: Fontana Paperbacks.

Littmann, Greg. 2013. "Banana Republic," in Huss, 2013. 125–42.

Loomis, Roger Sherman. 1963. *The Development of Arthurian Romance*. London: Hutchinson University Library.

Lucas, Tim. 2015, September. "Total Trash," in *Sight & Sound*, vol. 25, no. 9, 26–31.

McClintick, David. 1984. *Indecent Exposure: A True Story of Hollywood and Wall Street*. London: Corgi. (Original edition, Columbus, 1983).

Mead, George Herbert. 1964. *On Social Psychology*. Chicago: University of Chicago Press. (Edited by Anselm Strauss).

Menville, Douglas, and R. Reginald. 1977. *Things to Come: An Illustrated History of the Science Fiction Film*. New York: Times Books.

Metz, Christian. 1982a. *Psychoanalysis and the Cinema: The Imaginary Signifier*. London: Macmillan. (Translated by Celia Britton, Annwyl Williams, Ben Brewster and Alfred Guzzetti).

_____. 1982b. "The Imaginary Signifier," in Metz 1982a, 1–87. (Translated by Ben Brewster. Also published in *Screen* vol. 16, no. 2, Summer, 14–76.)

_____. 1982c. "The Fiction Film and its Spectator: A Metapsychological Study," in Metz 1982a, 99–147. (Translated by Alfred Guzzetti. Also published in *New Literary History* vol. VIII, no. 1, 1976, 75–105).

Meyers, Richard. 1984. *The Great Science Fiction Films: From "Rollerball" to "Return of the Jedi."* Secaucus, NJ: Citadel.

Millett, Kate. 1971. *Sexual Politics*. London: Rupert Hart-Davis.

Milne, Tom. 1968, April. Review of *Planet of the Apes*, in *Monthly Film Bulletin*, vol. 35, no. 411, 53/4.

Mitchell, Juliet. 1971. *Women's Estate*. Harmondsworth: Penguin.

Mizejewski, Linda. 1995. "Action Bodies in Futurist Spaces: Bodybuilder Stardom as Special Effect," in Kuhn, 1999, 147–72.

Moorcock, Michael. 1993, May. "Trouble Ahead," in *Sight & Sound*, vol. 5, no. 37, 37.

Morrison, Toni. 1992. *Playing in the Dark: Whiteness and the Literary Imagination*. London and Cambridge, MA: Harvard University Press.

Muir, Anne Ross. 1994. "The Status of Women Working in Film and Television," in Gamman and Marshment, 1994, 143–52.

Mulkerrins, Jane. 2nd October 2016. "It's MY BODY, MY CHOICE, MY TERMS," in *You* magazine, *Mail on Sunday*, UK, 40–5.

Mulvey, Laura. 1975. "Visual Pleasure and Narrative Cinema," in *Screen*, vol. 16, no. 3, 6–18. (Also in Mulvey 1989a, 14–26).

_____. 1989a. *Visual and Other Pleasures*. London: Macmillan.

_____. 1989b. "Fears, Fantasies and the Male Unconscious, *or* 'You Don't Know What's Happening, Do You Mr. Jones?,'" in Mulvey, 1989a, 6–13.

_____. 1989c. "Afterthoughts on 'Visual Pleasure and Narrative cinema' Inspired by King Vidor's 'Duel in the Sun' (1946)," in Mulvey 1989a, 29–38. (First published in *Framework* 15–17, 1981, 12–15).

Nama, Adilifu. 2008. *Black Space: Imagining Race in Science Fiction Film*. Austin: University of Texas Press.

Nayman, Adam. Review of *Jupiter Ascending*, in *Sight & Sound*, vol. 25, no. 4, April 2015, 79.

Neal, Patricia, with Richard Deneut. *As I Am*, 1989. London: Arrow.

Newman, Kim. 1997, April. Review of *Star Wars: Episode IV—A New Hope (Special Edition)*, in *Sight & Sound*, vol. 7, no. 4, 50/1.

_____. 1997, July. Review of *The Fifth Element*, in *Sight & Sound*, vol. 7, no. 7, 39/40.

_____. 2006, March. Review of *Aeonflux*, in *Sight & Sound*, vol. 16, no. 3, 48.

_____. 2009, February. Review of *The Day the Earth Stood Still*, in *Sight & Sound*, vol. 19, no. 2, 57/8.

_____. 2013, November. "Space, the Communist Frontier," in *Sight & Sound*, vol. 23, no. 11, 96/7.

_____. 2014, May. Review of *Escape from Planet Earth*, in *Sight & Sound*, vol. 24, no. 5, 74.

_____. 2016, April. Review of *Deadpool*, in *Sight & Sound*, vol. 26, no. 4, 73.

_____. 2017, September. Review of *Spider-Man: Homecoming*, in *Sight & Sound*, vol. 27, no. 9, 73/4.

Newton, Judith. 1995. "Feminism and Anxiety in 'Alien'," in Kuhn 1995, 82–90.

Nicholls, Peter, ed. *The SF Encyclopedia*. New York: Doubleday, 1979.

Nichols, Nichelle. 1994. *Beyond Uhura: "Star Trek" and Other Memories*. New York: G.P. Putnam's Sons.

Noonan, Bonnie. 2005. *Women Scientists in Fifties Science Fiction Films*. Jefferson: McFarland.

_____. 2015. *Gender in Science Fiction Films, 1964–1979: A Critical Study*. Jefferson: McFarland.

O'Hehir, Andrew. 2001, September. "Gorilla Warefare," in *Sight & Sound*, vol. 11, no. 9, 12–15.

Oakley, Ann. 1972. *Housewife*. London: Allen Lane.

Odino, Simone. "'God, it'll be hard topping the H-bomb': Fragments of Kubrickiana on the Path from Strangelove to 2001," paper presented at "Stanley Kubrick: A Retrospective," De Montfort University, Leicester (UK), 13th May 2016. (Text supplied by the author, July 2017).

_____. 2013, 27th August. "Who's that girl? (actress-spotting in '2001: a space odyssey')," online at: www.2001italia.it/2013/08/whos-that-girl-actress-spotting-in-2001.html (Accessed: 1st July 2017).

Off-world Editors. No date. "Blade Runner Versions," online at *Off-world: The Blade Runner Wiki*. http://bladerunner.wikia.com/wiki/Blade_Runner_versions (Accessed: 26th August 2017).

Osherson, Daniel N., and Edward E. Smith. 1990. *An Invitation to Cognitive Science, Vol. 1: Thinking*. Cambridge, MA: MIT Press.

Osmond, Andrew. 2010, March. Review of *Avatar*, in *Sight & Sound*, vol. 20, no. 3, 48–9.

Paglia, Camille. 1992. *Sexual Personae: Art and Decadence from Nefertiti to Emily Dickinson*. Harmondsworth: Penguin. (Original edition, New Haven: Connecticut: Yale UP, 1990).

Pallot, James, and the editors of CineBooks, eds. 1994. *The Virgin Film Guide*, 3rd edition. London: Virgin Books.

Penley, Constance. 1986, fall. "Time Travel, Primal Scene, and the Critical Dystopia," in *Camera Obscura*, no. 15, 66–85. (Also in Kuhn, 1995, 116–27. Also in Penley et al. 1991, 3–31).

_____. 1989. *The Future of an Illusion: Film, Feminism, and Psychoanalysis. A Camera Obscura Book*. Minneapolis: University of Minnesota Press.

_____. 1997. *NASA/Trek: Popular Science and Sex in America*. London: Verso.

_____, Elisabeth Lyon, Lynn Spigel, and Janet Bergstrom, eds. 1991. *Close Encounters: Film, Feminism and Science Fiction*. Minneapolis: University of Minnesota Press.

Petley, Julian. 1985, February. Review of *The Terminator*, in *Monthly Film Bulletin*, vol. 52, no. 613, 58/9.

Piercy, Marge. 1976. *Woman on the Edge of Time*. Original edition, New York: Fawcett Crest Books.

Pilkington, Ace G. 2015. "Forbidden Planet: Aliens, Monsters and Fictions Nuclear Disaster," in Kapell and Pilkington, 2015.

_____, and Olga Pilkington, eds. [2019]. *LabLit: Exploring Literary Fictions About Science*. Manuscript being prepared for publication. Lanham, MD: Lexington Books. (*Introduction* by Olga Pilkington quoted in this text.)

Pinkerton, Nick. 2016, March. "Rise of the Reboots," in *Sight & Sound*, vol. 26, no. 3, 32–5.

Pollock, Dale. 1983. *Skywalking: The Life and Times of George Lucas*. London: Elm Tree Books.

Potter, Elizabeth. 1988. "Modelling the Gender Politics of Science," in *Hypatia*. vol. 3, no. 1, 19–33.

Pringle, David. 1997. *The Ultimate Encyclopedia of Science Fiction*. Godalming, Surrey: Colour Library Direct.

Pulleine, Tim. 1979, September. Review of *Alien*, in *Monthly Film Bulletin*, vol. 46, no. 548, 191.

Pym, John. 1986, September. Review of *Aliens*, in *Monthly Film Bulletin*, vol. 53, no. 632, 263/4.

Quindlen, A. 1977, July 13th. "Carrie Didn't Get *Carrie*, But *Star Wars* Made Up for It," in *The New York Times*, section III, 13.

Raiss, Jochen. 2016. *Frauen auf Bäumen/Women in Trees*. Berlin: Hatje Cantz.

_____. 2017. *More Women in Trees: Climbing Up Again*. Berlin: Hatje Cantz.

Ramsaye, Terry. 1964. *A Million and One Nights: A History of the Motion Picture Through 1925*. New York: Simon & Schuster. (First published, 1926).

Rayns, Tony. 1991, September. Review of *Terminator 2: Judgment Day*, in *Sight & Sound*, vol. 5, no. 9, 50–1.

Rich, B. Ruby. 1987. "Anti-Porn: Soft Issue, Hard World," in Brunsdon, 1987, 31–43.

Rinzler, J.W. 2008. *The Making of Star Wars: The Definitive Story Behind the Making of the Original Film*. London: Ebury Press. (First published, 2007).

Roberts, Adam. 2007. *The History of Science Fiction*. Basingstoke: Palgrave Macmillan. (*Palgrave Histories of Literature* series. First published, 2005.)

Robinson, David. 1993. *Georges Melies: Father of Film Fantasy*. London: MoMI/BFI.

Robinson, Jane. 2018. *Hearts and Minds: Suffragettes, Suffragists and How Women Won the Vote*. London: Doubleday.

Rohn, Jennifer. 2010. "More Lab in the Library." *Nature*, no. 465, 552.

Rosenbaum, Jonathan. 1975, October. Review of *Rollerball*, in *Monthly Film Bulletin*, vol. 42, no. 501, 224.

Rucker, Lynda E. 2015, March-April. "Our Bodies, Ourselves," in *Black Static*, no. 45, 6/7.

Russ, Joanna. 1985. *The Female Man*. London: The Women's Press.

Russell, Diana H., ed. 1993a. *Making Violence Sexy: Feminist Views on Pornography*. Buckingham: Open University Press.

Russell, Diana H, ed. 1993b. "Testimony from Public Hearings on the Ordinance to Add Pornography as Discrimination Against Women," in Russell, 1993a, 48–62.

Rycroft, Charles. 1995. *A Critical Dictionary of Psychoanalysis*, 2nd edition. Harmondsworth: Penguin.

Sagan, Carl. 1985. *Contact*. New York: Simon & Schuster.

Sammon, Paul M. 1996. *Future Noir: The Making of Blade Runner*. New York: Harper/Prism.

Sampson Edward E. 1993. *Celebrating the Other: A Dialogic Account of Human Nature*. London: Harvester Wheatsheaf.

Sanders, Steven M. 2008. *The Philosophy of Science Fiction Film*. Lexington: University Press of Kentucky.

Scalzi, John. 1997. *The Rough Guide to Sci-Fi Movies*. London: Rough Guides.

Schatz, Thomas. 1981. *Hollywood Genres: Formulas, Filmmaking, and the Studio System*. New York: McGraw-Hill.

Schiebinger, Londa. 2001. *Has Feminism Changed Science?* Cambridge: Harvard University Press.

Scholes, Robert, and Eric S. Rabkin. 1977. *Science Fiction: History, Science, Vision*. New York: Oxford University Press.

Shatner, William (with Chris Kreski). 1994. *"Star Trek" Movie Memories: The Inside Story of the Classic Movies*. London: HarperCollins.

Sheen, Erica. 1991. "'I'm Not *In* the Business: I *Am* the Business': Women at Work in Hollywood Science Fiction," in Armitt, 1991, 139–161.

Shelley, Mary Wollstonecraft Godwin. *Frankenstein; or, The Modern Prometheus*. (Original edition, Hughes, Harding, Mavor & Jones, 1818.)

Sinclair, Upton. 1933. *Upton Sinclair Presents William Fox*. Los Angeles: Published by the author.

Smith, Dan. 2015, April. Review of *Ex Machina*, in *Sight & Sound*, vol. 25, no. 4, 111.

Smith, Judith E. 1994. "The Marrying Kind: Working-Class Courtship and Marriage in 1950s Hollywood," in Carson et al., 1994, 226–42.

Smith, Michael. 2015. *The Debs of Bletchley Park*. London: Aurum.

Smith, Thomas G. 1991. *ILM: The Art of Special Effects*. London: Virgin.

Smurfs Wiki Editors. No date. "Smurfstorm," online at: www.smurfs.wikia.com/wiki/Smurfstorm (Accessed: 22nd August 2017).

Sobchack, Vivian. 1980. *The Limits of Infinity*. London: Thomas Yoseloff. (Original edition, New York: A.S. Barnes and Co, 1980).

_____. 1988. *Screening Space: The American Science Fiction Film*. New York: Ungar. (Expanded version of Sobchack 1980).

_____. 1995. "The Virginity of Astronauts: Sex and the Science Fiction Film," in Kuhn, 1995, 103–15.

_____. 1999. "Cities on the Edge of Time: The Urban Science-Fiction Film," in Kuhn, 1999, 121–43.

Sontag, Susan. 1966a. *"Against Interpretation" and other essays*. London: Eyre and Spottiswoode. (First published, 1961).

_____. 1966b. "The Imagination of Disaster," in Sontag, 1966a, 209–25.

Sørensen, Nils Arne. 2014, 8th October. "Denmark Version 1.0," online at: *1914–1918 Online: International Encyclopedia of the First World War*. http://encyclopedia.1914-1918-online.net/article/denmark (Accessed: 30 January 2017).

Souhami, Diana. 2010. *Edith Cavell*. London: Quercus.

Spencer, Liese. 2004, September. Review of *The Stepford Wives*, in *Sight & Sound*, vol. 14, no. 9, 84/5.

Spigel, Lynn. 1991. "From Domestic Space to Outer Space: The 1960s Fantastic Family Sit-Com," in Penley, et al., 1991, 204–35.

Stacey, Jackie. 1994. "Desperately Seeking Difference," in Gamman and Marshment 1994, 112–29. (Also published in *Screen*, vol. 28, no. 1, Winter 1987, 48–61).

Sternbach, Rick, and Michael Okuda. 1991. *Star Trek: The Next Generation Technical Manual*. London: Boxtree.

Stevens, Isabel. 2015, October. "The Female Gaze: 100 Overlooked Films Directed by Women," in *Sight & Sound*, vol. 25, no. 10, 18–37.

Strick, Philip. 1980, February. Review of *Star Trek: The Motion Picture*, in *Monthly Film Bulletin*, vol. 47, no. 553, 29/30

_____. 1997, October. Review of *Contact*, in *Sight & Sound*, vol. 7, no. 10, 44–6.

Strimpel, Zoe. 2017, 27th August. "Even Feminists Shed Tears of Wonder at Gadot," in *The Sunday Telegraph*, London, 25.

Swade, Doron. 2000. *The Cogwheel Brain*. London: Little, Brown and Co.

Tannahill, Reay. 1992. *Sex in History*. Chelsea, MI: Scarborough House. (Updated and revised from first edition, New York: Stein and Day, 1980).

Taubin, Amy. 1992, July. "Invading Bodies: Aliens[3] and the Trilogy," in *Sight & Sound*, vol. 2, no. 3, 8–10. (Also reproduced as "The 'Alien' Trilogy: From Feminism to Aids," in Cook and Dodd, 93–100).

Telotte, J.P. 2001. *Science Fiction Film*. Cambridge: Cambridge University Press. (*Genres in American Cinema* series).

_____. 1995. *Replications: A Robotic History of the Science Fiction Film*. Urbana and Chicago: University of Illinois Press.

Thomas, Susan. 1991. "Between the Boys and Their Toys: The Science Fiction Film," in Armitt, 1991, 109–122.

Tookey, Christopher. 1994. *The Critics' Film Guide*. London: Boxtree.

Turner, Dean. 1998. "An Assessment of the Development of the Female in Commercial Science Fiction." PhD dissertation. Hull: University of Hull.

Vaz, Mark Cotta. and Patricia Rose Duigan. 1996. *Industrial Light and Magic: Into the Digital Realm*. London: Virgin.

Vogler, Christopher. *The Writer's Journey: Mythic Structure for Storytellers and Screenwriters*.

Basingstoke and Oxford: Pan Macmillan, 1999. (Original version, 1992).

Wajcman, Judy. 1993. *Feminism Confronts Technology*. Cambridge: Polity Press. (First published, 1991).

Walker, John. 2006. *Halliwell's Film, DVD & Video Guide 2007*. London: HarperCollins.

Westbrook, Caroline. 1996, November. "Incoherence Day?," in *Empire*, no. 89, 26.

Williams, Neville. 1992. *The Life and Times of Elizabeth I*. London: Weidenfeld and Nicolson.

Willmetts, Geoff. 2015, 10th December. "*The Fantastic Made Visible*, edited by Matthew Wilhelm Kapell and Ace G. Pilkington (book review)," online at: SFcrowsnest. http://sfcrowsnest.org.uk/the-fantastic-made-visible-edited-by-matthew-wilhelm-kapell-and-ace-g-pilkington-book-review/ (Accessed: 8th November 2016).

Wolmark, Jenny. 1993. *Aliens and Others: Science Fiction, Feminism and Postmodernism*. Hemel Hempstead: Harvester Wheatsheaf.

Wright, Bruce Lanier. 1993. *Yesterday's Tomorrows: The Golden Age of Science Fiction Movie Posters, 1950–1964*. Dallas: Taylor Publishing Company.

Young, Iris Marion. 1990. *Justice and the Politics of Difference*. Princeton, NJ: Princeton University Press.

Film, Television and Radio

Movies, television series and episodes, chapter serials and radio broadcasts are listed here in three sections: Science Fiction. Non-Science Fiction, Radio Broadcasts. They are listed alphabetically by title, ignoring articles (a, an, the, le, la, el, der, die, das, etc.). The names of any listed female contributors have been italicized in the science fiction movie data, following this format:

> *Title* (alt: *English Language Title/Original Language Title/Alternative Title*). General Release Date. Director. F/Pr: (*Female Producers*). F/Wr: (*Female Writers*). F/Pl: (*Selected Female Players*). Country of Origin: Production Company. (Additional information, formats, viewing sources, &c.).

Title: The film titles prioritized in this text are generally the original language titles. These are followed in this filmography by the English language title(s) or the original title if the English title has been used. Any alternative title by which the film may be better known, has also been included. Online sources now supply exhaustive release titles for many regions in many languages. These lists are made longer by name changes—which seems to be occurring more frequently. *Alien[3]* appears to have become *Alien 3*, although not everywhere, *Star Wars* gained "Episode IV—A New Hope" after the release of *The Empire Strikes Back* in 1980 and *Rogue One* lost "A Star Wars Story" shortly before its theatrical release. There are many other examples; it is not practical to reproduce them here, so for this extra information, the reader is referred to www.IMDb.com.

Date: These are release dates, which can differ according to territory and source. First general release dates are favored here, which usually means the year in which the title was widely available in the country where it was made. As with all data regarding films from the very early period, it is not always possible to be exact. Even modern films cause problems. *Ex Machina* was released in a single UK cinema in December 2014, before going on general release in January 2015. Data sources vary in the date given for this film. Dates given under these circumstances take a consensus from the sources listed below. (Dates in brackets) are for films cited by this text, but not released at the time of writing.

Director: All directors have been listed—both male and *female*. Where no director data is available, again usually from the very early period, "Not Known" has been entered.

Female Producers, Writers and other Creatives/Crew: For older films especially, it is not always possible to locate all production details. This is due partly to the fact that records have been lost, and partly to the fact that personnel titles and roles have changed over 120+ years of cinema production. In the early days, often the term "producer" was synonymous with "director," and writing was not generally recognized as a discrete art. Given the growing number of producers and production companies on modern films, it is not practical to list comprehensive data for these. It is also not necessary to this study. Therefore, only the women taking creative roles have been listed—although, again, this is not exhaustive. Where men have shared a role, this has been indicated with the additional number, for example: *"Flora M. Gordon +1"* under the entry for *Beginning of the End*, 1957.

Female Players: Selected female cast members, including everyone included in the main text, have been listed and italicized.

Country or Countries of Origin: Again, this number has risen since the days of the big studios, reflecting the growing number of production companies for each project. For example, *Valerian and the City of a Thousand Planets* (2017) has eight country affiliations. Origin may be useful for those looking for a link between nationality and content, although this is becoming harder to gauge.

A Note on Sources: Information here draws on a personal database, added to over 20+ years. It is tempting these days to reach for the internet, but this is not always ideal. For example, IMDb.com is not consistent in the way it lists character names: sometimes professional titles are given, as in Dr. Lisa van Horn (*Rocketship X-M*, 1950), sometimes they are missing, as with (Dr.) Louise Banks (*Arrival*, 2016). Data has been collected, corrected and augmented over time using a number of sources, including: Hardy, 1991/95; *Sight & Sound* magazine; *Monthly Film Bulletin*; Clute and Nicholls, 1993; www.sf-encyclopedia.com; www.imdb.com; Katz, 1994; Tookey, 1994; Walker, 2006; Pallot et al., 1994; Altman and Gross, 1998; Filmer and Golay, 1989; www.wikipedia. org; www.the-numbers.com; www.rottentomatoes.com; Noonan, 2005.

SCIENCE FICTION

The *"?" Motorist*. 1906. (See: *The Motorist*).

1,000 Years from Now. 1952. (See: *Captive Women*).

100 Years Hence. 1908. (See: *The Airship*).

1984. 1956. Michael Anderson. F/Pl: *Jan Sterling*. UK: Holiday Film Productions.

20,000 Leagues Under the Sea. 1954. Richard Fleischer. F/Pl: *none*. USA: Walt Disney.

2001: A Space Odyssey. 1968. Stanley Kubrick. F/Pl: *Margaret Tyzack, Edwina Carroll, Penny Brahms, Heather Downham, Chela Mathison, Ann Gills*. USA: MGM.

2010. 1984. Peter Hyams. F/Pl: *Helen Mirren, Madolyn Smith*. USA: MGM.

A 20th Century Surgeon. 1897. (See: *Chirugien Americain*).

The 27th Day. 1957. William Asher. F/Pr: *Helen Ainsworth*. F/Pl: *Valerie French, Marie Tsien*. USA: Romson Productions.

3,000 AD. 1952. (See: *Captive Women*).

The 30-Foot Bride of Candy Rock. 1959. Sidney Miller. F/Pl: *Dorothy Provine, Gale Gordon*. USA: Columbia.

400 Million Miles from the Earth. 1917. (See: *Himmelskibet*).

A.I. Artificial Intelligence. 2001. Steven Spielberg. F/Pr: *Bonnie Curtis, Kathleen Kennedy.* F/Pl: *Frances O'Connor, April Grace, Sabrina Grdevich.* USA: Warner Bros./DreamWorks/ Amblin/Stanley Kubrick Prod.

Abbott and Costello Go to Mars. 1953. Charles Lamont. F/Pl: *Mari Blanchard, Martha Hyer, Jean Willes, Anita Ekberg.* USA: Universal.

Abbott and Costello Meet Dr. Jekyll and Mr. Hyde. 1953. Charles Lamont. F/Pl: *Helen Westcott.* USA: Universal.

Abbott and Costello Meet Frankenstein. 1948. Charles T. Barton. F/Pl: *Leonore Aubert, Jane Randolph.* USA: Universal.

The Absent Minded Professor. 1961. Robert Stevenson. F/Pl: *Nancy Olson, Belle Montrose.* USA: Walt Disney.

The Abyss. 1989. James Cameron. F/Pr: *Gale Anne Hurd.* F/Pl: *Mary Elizabeth Mastrantonio, Kimberly Scott.* USA: 20th Century-Fox.

Advantageous (internet movie). 23rd June 2015. Jennifer Phang. F/Pr: *Sally Jo Fifer, Jacqueline Kim, Mina Kim, Qi Luo, Liz Ortiz Mackes, Theresa Navarro, Laura Priscilla Paule, Jayda Thompson* +13. F/Wr: *Jacqueline Kim, Jennifer Phang.* F/Pl: *Jacqueline Kim, Freya Adams, Jennifer Ehle, Samantha Kim, Troi Zee, Olivia Horton, Jennifer Ikeda, Mercedes Griffeth, Sameerah Luqmaan-Harris, Theresa Navarro, Jeanne Sakata.* USA: Good Neighbors Media/ D.K. Entertainment/I Ain't Playin' Films.

An Adventurous Automobile Trip. 1904. (See: *Le Raid Paris à Monte Carlo en deux heures).*

The Adventurous Voyage of the Arctic. 1903. (See: *The Voyage of the Arctic).*

Aelita: Queen of Mars (alt: *Aelita: The Revolt of the Robots).* 1924. Jakov Protazanov. F/Pl: *Yulia Solnetseva, Vera Orlova, Valentina Kuindzi, Aleksandra Peregonets, N. Tretyakova.* USSR: Mezrapbom.

Aelita: The Revolt of the Robots. 1924. (See: *Aelita: Queen of Mars).*

Æon Flux. 2005. Karyn Kusama. F/Pr: *Martha Griffin, Gale Anne Hurd* +7. F/Pl: *Charlize Theron, Sophie Okenedo, Frances McDormand, Amelia Warner, Caroline Chikezie, Yangsom Brauen. Aoibheann O'Hara, Weijian Liu.* USA: Paramount Pictures/Lakeshore Entertainment/Valhalla Motion Pictures/ MTV Films/MTV Productions/Colossal Pictures.

The Airship (alt: *100 Years Hence).* 1908. J. Stuart Blackton. USA: Vitagraph.

A.Li.Ce. 1999. Kenichi Maejima. F/Pl: (voices) *Mariko Kouda. Yûko Miyamura. Urara Takano. Shoko Kikuchi. Rei Igarashi.* Japan: GAGA Communications.

Alien. 1979. Ridley Scott. F/Pl: *Sigourney Weaver,* *Veronica Cartwright, Helen Horton* (voice of Mother). UK/USA: 20th Century-Fox/ Brandywine Productions.

Alien: Covenant. 2017. Ridley Scott. F/Pl: *Katherine Waterston, Carmen Ejogo, Callie Hernandez, Amy Seimetz, Tess Haubrich, Lorelei King.* USA: 20th Century-Fox/Scott Free Productions/TSG/Brandywine.

Alien: Resurrection. 1997. Jean-Pierre Jeunet. 1997. F/Pr: *Sigourney Weaver* (co-). F/Pl: *Sigourney Waever, Winona Ryder, Kim Flowers.* USA: 20th Century-Fox/Brandywine Productions.

Alien 3. 1992. (See: *Alien³,* 1992).

Alien³ (alt: *Alien 3).* 1992. David Fincher. F/Pl: *Sigourney Weaver.* USA: 20th Century-Fox/ Brandywine Productions.

Aliens. 1986. James Cameron. F/Pr: *Gale Ann Hurd.* F/Pl: *Sigourney Weaver, Jenette Goldstein, Carrie Henn, Colette Hiller, Cynthia Dale Scott.* USA/UK: 20th Century-Fox/ Brandywine Productions/SLM Production Group.

Alita: Battle Angel. (2018). Robert Rodriquez. F/Wr: *Laeta Kalogridis.* F/Pl: *Rosa Salazar, Jennifer Connelly, Eiza González, Michelle Rodriquez, Ella Lamont.* USA/Canada/ Argentina: 20th Century Fox/Lightstorm/ Troublemaker.*Alraune.* 1918. Eugen Illes. F/Pl: *Hilde Wolter.* Germany: Neutrat Film.

Alraune. 1918. Mihaly Kertesz (Michal Curtiz) and Fritz Odon. F/Pl: *Margrit Lux, Violetta Szlatenyi.* Austria/Hungary: Not Known.

Alraune (alt: *Daughter of Destiny).* 1928. Heinrich Galeen. F/Pl: *Brigitte Helm, Mia Pankau, Valeska Gert.* Germany: Ama Film.

Alraune (alt: *Daughter of Evil).* 1930. Richard Oswald. F/Pl: *Brigitte Helm, Agnes Straub, Kaethe Haack, Liselott Schaak.* Germany: UFA.

Alraune (alt: *Unnatural/Vengeance/Mandrigore).* 1952. Arthur Maria Rabenault. F/Pl: *Hildegard Knef, Jula Koschka, Trude Hesterberg.* West Germany: Carlton.

Andromeda (TV series). 2000–5. Various Directors. F/Pl: *Lisa Ryder, Laura Bertram, Lexa Doig.* USA: Fireworks/Tribune/BLT/ Global/MBR. (110 episodes).

The Andromeda Strain. 1970. Robert Wise. F/Pl: *Kate Reid, Paula Kelly.* USA: Universal/Robert Wise Productions.

An Animated Doll. 1908. Not Known. 1908. USA: Essanay.

Annihilation. 2018. Alex Garland. F/Pr: *Jo Burn, Dana Goldberg* +7; F/Pl: *Natalie Portman, Tessa Thompson, Jennifer Jason Leigh, Gina Rodriquez, Sonoya Mizuno, Tuva Novotny,*

Honey Holmes. UK/USA: DNA Films/Paramount/Scott Rudin Prod./Skydance.

Ant Man and the Wasp. (2018). Peyton Reid. F/Pr: *Victoria Alonso +7;* F/Pl: *Hannah John-Kamen, Michelle Pfeiffer, Evangeline Lilly, Judy Greer, Abby Ryder Forston.* USA: Marvel Studios.

Antinea, l'amante della città sepolta (alt: *Journey Beneath the Desert*). 1961. Edgar G. Ulmer and Giuseppe Masini. F/Pl: *Haya Harareet, Gabriella Tinti, Gianmaria Volonte.* France/Italy: CCM/Fides.

A.P.E.X. 1993. Philip J. Roth. 1994. F/Pl: *Lisa Ann Russell, Anna B. Choi, Kristin Norton, Kathleen Randazzo.* USA: Green Communications/Republic.

Appleseed. 2004. Shinji Aramaki and Steven Foster. F/Wr: *Haruka Handa +1.* F/Pl: (voices) *Ai Kobyashi, Mami Koyama, Miho Yamada, Yuki Matsuoka.* Japan: Appleseed Partners/Digital Frontier/Geneon Entertainment/MBS/Micott & Basara/TYO Productions/Toho/TBS.

Armageddon. 1998. Michael Bay. F/Pr: *Gale Anne Hurd +8.* F/Pl: *Liv Tyler, Jessica Steen, Grace Zabriskie.* USA: Touchstone, Jerry Bruckheimer, Valhalla, Digital Image Associates.

Around a Star. 1906. (See: *Voyage autour d'une etoile*).

Arrival. 2016. Denis Villeneuve. F/Pr: *Karen Lunder* (exec.) *+13.* F/Pl: *Amy Adams, Abigail Pniowsky, Julia Scarlett Dan, Jadyn Malone, Sonia Vigneault.* USA: Paramount/FilmNation Entertainment/Lava Bear Films/21 Laps Entertainment/Xenolinguistics.

The Astounding She-Monster (alt: *The Mysterious Invader*). 1958. Ronnie Ashcroft. F/Pl: *Marilyn Harvey, Jeanne Tatum, Shirley Kilpatrick.* USA: Hollywood International Productions.

The Astronaut's Wife. 1999. Rand Ravich. F/Pr: *Jody Hedien, Donna Langly, Diana Pokarny +3.* F/Pl: *Charlize Theron, Clea DuVall, Donna Murphy, Samantha Eggar, Blair Brown, Lucy Lin.* USA: New Line/Mad Chance.

L'Atlantide, 1932. (See: *Die Herrin von Atlantis*).

Atlantis. 1949. (See: *Siren of Atlantis*).

Atlantis, The Lost Continent. 1961. George Pal. F/Pl: *Joyce Taylor.* USA: Galaxy Productions/MGM.

Atom Man Versus Superman. 1950. Spencer Gordon Bennet. F/Pl: *Noel Neill.* USA: Columbia.

The Atomic Man. 1956. (See: *Timeslip*).

Attack of the 50 Foot Woman. 1958. Nathan Hertz (Juran). F/Pl: *Allison Hayes, Yvette Vickers.* USA: Woolner/Allied Artists.

Attack of the Killer Tomatoes! 1978. John De Bollo. F/Pl: *Sharon Taylor.* USA: Nai Entertainments.

Automated Hat-Maker and Sausage-Grinder. 1900. (See: *Chapellerie et charcuterie mécanique*).

The Automatic Motorist (alt: *The Clockwork Man*). 1911. Walter R. Booth. UK: Kineto.

Avatar. 2009. James Cameron. F/Pl: *Zoe Saldana, Sigourney Weaver, CCH Pounder, Michelle Rodriguez.* USA/UK: 20th Century–Fox/Dune Entertainment/Ingenious Film Partners/Lightstorm.

The Avengers. 2012. (See: *Avengers Assemble*).

Avengers Assemble (alt: *The Avengers*). 2012. Joss Whedon. F/Pr: *Victoria Alonso, Patricia Whitcher +6.* F/Pl: *Scarlett Johansson, Cobi Smulders, Gwyneth Paltrow.* USA: Marvel/Paramount.

Avengers: Age of Ultron. 2015. Joss Whedon. F/Pr: *Victoria Alonso, Patricia Whitcher +14.* F/Pl: *Scarlett Johansson, Cobi Smulders, Elizabeth Olsen, Hayley Atwell, Linda Cardellina, Claudia Kim, Julie Delpy.* USA: Marvel/Walt Disney.

Avengers: Infinity War. 2018. Anthony Russo and Joe Russo. F/Pr: *Victoria Alonso +8.* F/Pl: *Pom Klementieff, Karen Gillian, Scarlett Johansson, Zoe Saldana, Cobi Smulders, Elizabeth Olsen.* USA: Marvel.

Babylon A.D. 2008. Mathieu Kassovitz. F/Pl: *Michelle Yeoh, Mélanie Thierry, Charlotte Rampling.* France/UK/USA: Babylon/MNP Entreprise/StudioCanal/Babylon Films/M6 Films/M6/Canal+/CinéCinéma.

Babylon 5 (TV series). 1994–8. Various Directors. F/Pl: *Mira Furlan, Claudia Christian, Patricia Tallman.* USA: Babylonian/Warner Bros. Television. (110 episodes).

Back to the Future. 1985. Robert Zemekis. F/Pl: *Lea Thompson, Claudia Wells, Wendy Jo Sperber.* USA: Universal/Amblin Entertainment.

The Bamboo Saucer. 1968. Frank Telford. F/Pl: *Lois Nettleton.* USA: NTA/Harris Associates/Jerry Fairbanks.

Barb Wire. 1996. Hogan, David. F/Wr: *Ilene Chaiken +1.* F/Pl: *Pamela Anderson (Lee), Temuera Morrison, Victoria Powell.* USA: Dark Horse/Propaganda/PolyGram.

Barbarella. 1968. Roger Vadim. F/Pl: *Jane Fonda, Anita Pallenberg, Veronique Vendell, Catherine Chevallier, Marie Therese Chevallier.* France/Italy: Marianne Productions/Dino De Laurentiis.

Batgirl. (20??). Joss Whedon. USA: DC Entertainment. (Not yet released; full details not available).

Batman (chapter serial). 1943. Lambert Hillyer. F/Pl: *Shirley Patterson*. USA: Columbia. (15 chapters).

Batman and Robin (alt: *The Return of Batman*) (chapter serial). 1949. Spencer Gordon Bennet. F/Pl: *Jane Adams*. USA: Columbia. (15 chapters).

*batteries not included. 1987. Matthew Robbins. F/Pl: *Jessica Tandy, Elizabeth Peña, Jane Hoffman, Wendy Schaal*. USA: Amblin/Universal.

Battle Beyond the Stars. 1980. Jimmy T. Murakami. F/Pl: *Sybil Danning, Darlanne Fluegal, Lynn Carlin, Julia Duffy, Marta Kristen*. USA: New World.

Battle for the Planet of the Apes. 1973. J. Lee Thompson. F/Pl: *Natalie Trundy, France Nuyen, Heather Lowe*. USA: 20th Century–Fox/APJAC Productions.

Battlefield Earth (alt: *Battlefield Earth: A Saga of the Year 3000*). 2000. Roger Chritian. F/Pr: *Linda Favilla, Elie Samantha, Tracee Stanley +7*. F/Pl: *Sabine Karsenti, Kelly Preston, Marie-Josée Croze*. USA: Warner Bros./Morgan Creek/Franchise Pictures/JTP/Battlefield Prod./MELS.

Battlestar Galactica (TV series). 2004–9. Various Directors. F/Pl: *Mary McDonnell, Tricia Helfer, Grace Park, Katee Sackhoff, Kandyse McClure, Nicki Clyne*. USA: BSkyB/Dick Eike Prod./NBC/R&D TV/Stanford Pictures/UMS. (73 episodes).

Battlestar Galactica. 1978. Richard A. Colla. F/Pl: *Jane Seymour, Maren Jenson*. USA: Universal.

The Beast with a Million Eyes. 1956. David Kramarsky. F/Pl: *Lorna Thayer, Donna Cole*. USA: San Mateo Productions.

The Bees. 1978. Alfredo Zacharias. F/Pl: *Alicia Encinas*. USA: Bee One/Panorama Films.

Beginning of the End. 1957. Bert I. Gordon. F/Cr: *Flora M. Gordon +1*. F/Pl: *Peggie Castle*. USA: American Broadcast—Paramount Theatres Productions.

Beneath the Planet of the Apes. 1970. Ted Post. F/Pl: *Kim Hunter, Linda Harrison, Natalie Trundy*. USA: 20th Century–Fox/APJAC Productions.

Beneath the Sea. 1915. Sigmund Lubin. F/Pl: *Velma Whitman*. USA: Lubin.

The Big Broadcast of 1936. 1935. Norman Taurog. F/Pl: *Gracie Allen, Lyda Roberti, Wendy Barrie*. USA: Paramount.

The Big Broadcast of 1938. 1938. Mitchell Leisen. F/Pl: *Martha Raye, Dorothy Lamour, Shirley Ross, Lynn Overman, Harriette Had-*

don, Joyce Matthews, Lola Jensen, Alma Ross. USA: Paramount.

Bílá nemoc (alt: *The White Disease/Skeleton on Horseback*). 1937. F/Pl: *Karla Olicova*. Czechoslovakia: Moldavia C.L.

The Birds. 1963. Alfred Hitchcock. F/Pl: *Tippi Hedren, Jessica Tandy, Suzanne Pleshette, Ethel Griffies, Veronica Cartwright, Ruth McDevitt*. USA: Universal.

The Black Hole. 1979. Nelson, Gary. F/Pl: *Yvette Mimieux*. USA: Walt Disney.

Blade Runner. 1982. Ridley Scott. F/Pl: *Sean Young, Daryl Hannah, Joanna Cassidy*. USA/Hong Kong/UK: Warner Bros./Shaw Brothers/The Ladd Company/Blade Runner Partnership.

Blade Runner: The Director's Cut. 1992. (details as for *Blade Runner*).

Blade Runner 2049. 2017. Denis Villeneuve. F/Pr: *Dana Belcastro, Asa Greenberg, Val Hill, Cynthia Sikes +12*; F/Pl: *Robin Wright, Ana de Armas, Sylvia Hoeks, Sean Young, Loren Peta*. USA/UK/Hungary/Canada: Alcon/Columbia/Scott Free/16:14/Thunderbird/Torridon.

The Blob. 1958. Chuck Russell. F/Pl: *Candy Clark, Sharon Spelman*. USA: Tri-Star.

The Blood of Fu Manchu. 1968. Jess (Jesús) Franco. F/Pl: *Tsai Chin, Shirley Eaton*. UK: Udastex Films.

Boku no kanojo wa saibougu. 2008. (See: *Cyborg She*).

Born in Flames. 1983. *Lizzie Borden*. F/Pr: *Lizzie Borden*. F/Wr: *Lizzie Borden*. F/Pl: *Honey, Adele Bertei, Jeanne Satterfield, Flo Kennedy, Hillary Hurst, Pat Murphy, Katheryn Biblow, Becky Johnston*. USA: First Run Features.

Un bot lit (alt: *A Midnight Episode*). 1899. Georges Méliès. France: Star.

A Boy and His Dog. 1975. L.Q. Jones. F/Pl: *Susanne Benton, Helen Winston*. USA: Third LQ/JAF Productions.

Brain from Planet Arous. 1958. Nathan H. Juran. F/Pl: *Joyce Meadows*. USA: Marquette Productions.

Brazil. 1985. Terry Gilliam. F/Pl: *Kim Greist, Katherine Helmond, Barbara Hicks, Kathryn Pogson*. UK: Brazil Productions/Embassy International.

Break Free (Featuring Zedd) (music video). 2014. Chris Marrs Piliero. F/Pl: *Ariana Grande*. USA: Republic Records. (Available on youtube.com at the time of writing. Accessed: 1st January 2017).

The Bride. 1985. Franc Roddam. F/Pl: *Jennifer Beals, Clancy Brown, Geraldine Page*. USA: Columbia/Delphi II Productions.

Bride of Frankenstein. 1935. James Whale. F/Pl: *Elsa Lanchester, Valerie Hobson, Una O'Connor*. USA: Universal.

Bride of the Atom. 1956. (See: *Bride of the Monster*).

Bride of the Monster (alt: *Bride of the Atom*). 1956. Edward D. Wood Jnr. F/Pl: *Loretta King*. USA: Rolling M. Productions/Banner Films.

Buck Rogers (chapter serial). 1939. Ford Beebe and Saul A. Goodkind. F/Pl: *Constance Moore, Jackie Moran*. USA: Universal. (12 chapters).

Buck Rogers in the 25th Century. 1979. Daniel Haller. F/Pl: *Pamela Hensley, Erin Gray*. USA: Universal.

Bulldog Drummond at Bay. 1937. Norman Lee. F/Pl: *Dorothy Mackaill*. UK: BPI-Wardour.

Bumblebee. (2018). Travis Knight. F/Wr: *Christina Hodson*. USA: Allspark Pictures/Hasbro/Paramount Pictures/Platinum Dunes.

Burglary by Airship. 1910. Not Known. France: Gaumont.

By Rocket to the Moon. 1929. (See: *Frau im Mond*).

Capricorn One. 1977. Peter Hyams. F/Pl: *Brenda Vaccaro, Karen Black*. USA: Capricorn One Associates/Associated General Films.

Captain America (chapter serial). 1944. John English and Elmer Clifton. F/Pl: *Lorna Gray*. USA: Republic. (15 chapters).

Captain America: Civil War. 2016. Anthony Russo and Joe Russo. F/Pr: *Victoria Alonso, Trinh Tran, Patricia Whitcher* +11. F/Pl: *Scarlett Johansson, Elizabeth Olsen, Emily Vancamp, Marissa Tomei*. USA/Germany: Marvel/Vita-Ray Dutch Prod./Studio Babelsberg/Walt Disney.

Captain America: The First Avenger. 2011. Joe Johnston. F/Pr: *Victoria Alonso* +10. F/Pl: *Hayley Atwell, Natalie Dormer*. USA: Marvel/Paramount.

Captain America: Winter Soldier. 2014. Anthony Russo and Joe Russo. F/Pr: *Victoria Alonso* +8. F/Pl: *Scarlett Johansson, Cobi Smulders, Jenny Agutter, Hayley Atwell, Emily Vancamp*. USA: Marvel/Walt Disney.

Captain Midnight (chapter serial).1942. James W. Horne. F/Pl: *Dorothy Short, Luana Walters*. USA. Columbia. (15 chapters).

Captive Women (alt: *3,000 AD/1,000 Years from Now*). 1952. Stuart Gilmore. F/Pl: *Margaret Field, Gloria Saunders*. USA: Wisberg-Pollexfen Productions.

Capture the Flag. 2015. Enrique Gato. F/Pr: *Vic-*

toria Borrás +14. F/Pl: (voices) *Michelle Jenner, Marta Barbará, Margarita Cavero*. Spain: 4 Cats Pictures/Lightbox/Los Rockets La Película, Los/Telecina/Telfonica.

Cat Women of the Moon (alt: *Rocket to the Moon*). 1953. Arthur Hilton. F/Pl: *Marie Windsor, Susan Morrow*, Carol Brewster. USA: Astor/2-M Productions.

Catwoman. 2004. Pitof. F/Pr: *Denise Di Novi* +9. F/Wr: *Theresa Rebeck* +3. F/Pl: *Halle Berry, Sharon Stone, Frances Conroy, Alex Borstein, Kim Smith, Ona Grauer*. USA: Warner Bros./Village Roadshow/DiNovi Pictures/Frantic Films/Maple Shade Films/Catwoman Films.

Chapellerie et charcuterie mécanique (alt: *Mecanical Hat-Maker and Butcher/Automated Hat-Maker and Sausage-Grinder*). 1900. Dir./Pr./Wr., *Alice Guy-Blaché*. France: Gaumont.

Chappie. 2015. Neill Blomkamp. F/Pr: *Victoria Burkhart, Trishia Downie* +4. F/Wr: *Terri Tatchell* +Dir. F/Pl: *Yo-Landi Visser, Sigourney Weaver*. South Africa/USA: Columbia/MRC/LStar Capital/Simon Kinberg Prod./Genre Films/Alph Core/OllinVFX/Sony.

La Charcuterie mécanique (alt: *The Mechanical Butcher/The Mechanical Delicatessen*). 1895. A & L Lumière. France: Lumière.

Charleston Parade. 1927. (See: *Sur un Air Charleston*).

Charlie Chan at the Olympics. 1937. H. Bruce Humberstone. F/Wr: *Helen Logan* +2. F/Pl: *Katherine De Mille, Pauline Moore*. USA: Fox.

Charly. 1968. Ralph Nelson. F/Pl: *Claire Bloom, Lilia Skala*. USA: Selmur/Robertson Associates.

Cherry 2000. 1987. Steve de Jarnatt. F/Pl: *Melanie Griffith, Pamela Gidley*. USA: Orion/ERP.

Children of Men. 2006. Alfonso Cuarón. F/Pr: *Kristel Laiblin, Hilary Shor* +7. F/Wr: *P.D. James* (source novel). F/Pl: *Julianne Moore, Rita Davies, Mishal Husain*. USA/UK/Japan: Universal/Strike Entertainment/Hit & Run Prod./Ingenious Film Partners/Toho-Towa.

The China Syndrome. 1979. James Bridges. F/Pl: *Jane Fonda*. USA: IPC Films.

Chirugien Americain (alt: *A 20th Century Surgeon*). 1897. Georges Méliès. France: Star.

The Clockwork Man. 1911. (See: *The Automatic Motorist*).

A Clockwork Orange. 1971. Stanley Kubrick. F/Pl: *Adrienne Corri, Miriam Karlin*. UK: Polaris Productions/Warner Bros.

Clone. 2010. (See: *Womb*).

Close Encounters of the Third Kind. 1977. Steven

Spielberg. F/Pr: *Julia Phillips* +1. F/Pl: *Teri Garr, Melinda Dillon*. USA: Columbia/EMI.
Close Encounters of the Third Kind—The Special Edition. 1980. (details as for *Close Encounters of the Third Kind*).

The Clown and the Automaton. 1897. (See: *Gugusse et l'Automate*).

Code of the Air. 1928. James P. Hogan. F/Pl: *June Marlowe, Edna Mae Cooper*. USA: Bischoff Productions.

Codependent Lesbian Space Alien Seeks Same. 2011. Madeleine Olnek. F/Pr: *Melissa Finell, Cynthia Fredette, Madeleine Olnek, Lucy Sexton, Laura Terruso*. F/Wr: *Madeleine Olnek*. F/Pl: *Lisa Haas, Susan Ziegler, Jackie Monahan, Cynthia Kaplan, Rae C. Wright*. USA: Peccadillo Pictures.

Colossus: The Forbin Project (alt: *The Forbin Project*). 1970. Joseph Sargent. F/Pl: *Susan Clark, Marion Ross*. USA: Universal.

Coma. 1978. Michael Crichton. F/Pl: *Geneviève Bujold, Elizabeth Ashley, Lois Chiles*. USA: MGM.

The Comet's Comeback. 1916. William Bertram. F/Pl: *Carol Holloway*: USA: Beauty.

Conceiving Ada. 1997. Lynn Hershman-Leeson. F/Pr: *Lynn Hershman-Leeson* +1. F/Wr: *Lynn Hershman-Leeson, Eileen Jones, Sadie Plant, Betty A. Toole*. F/Pl: *Tilda Swinton, Francesca Faridany, Karen Black, Esther Mulligan*. USA/Germany: Hotwire Prod./Outpost Studios.

À la conquête de l'air (alt: *The Flying Machine*. 1901. Ferdinand Zecca. France: Pathé.

À la conquête du pôle (alt: *The Conquest of the Pole*). 1912. Georges Méliès. France: Star.

Conquest of the Planet of the Apes. 1972. J. Lee Thompson. F/Pl: *Natalie Trundy, Asa Maynor*. 20th Century–Fox/APJAC Productions.

The Conquest of the Pole. 1912. (See: *À la conquête du pôle*).

Consequences of Feminism. 1906. (See: *Les Résultats du féminisme*).

Contact. 1997. Robert. Zemeckis. F/Pl: *Jodie Foster, Angela Bassett*. USA: Warner Bros./Southside Amusement.

Coppélia: la poupée animée (alt: *Coppelia the Animated Doll*). 1900. Georges Méliès. France: Star.

Coppelia, the Animated Doll. 1900. (See: *Coppélia: la poupée animée*).

Cosmonauts on Venus. 1962. (See: *Planeta Bur*).

Countdown. 1967. Robert Altman. F/Pl: *Barbara Baxley*, Joanna Moore. USA: William Conrad Productions.

Counterattack of the Monster. 1955. (See: *Gojira no gyakushu*).

The Creature from the Black Lagoon. 1954. Jack Arnold. F/Pl: *Julia Adams*. USA: Universal.

The Creeping Unknown, 1955. (See: *The Quatermass Xperiment*).

Crimes of the Future. 1970. David Cronenberg. F/Pl: *Tania Zolty*. Canada: Emergent Films.

Croisières sidérales (alt: *Sideral Cruises*). 1941. André Zwoboda. F/Pl: *Madeleine Sologne, Suzanne Dehelly*. France (occupied): Industrie Cinématographique.

Cube. 1997. Vincenzo Natali. F/Pr: *Betty Orr*. F/Pl: *Nicole de Boer, Nicky Guadagni*. Canada: Cube Libre/Feature Film Project/Harold Greenberg Fund/Odeon Films/Ontario Film Development Corporation/Téléfilm Canada/Viacom Canada.

La cuisine magnétique. 1908. Segundo de Chamon. France: Pathé.

The Curious Dr. Humpp. 1967. (See: *La venganza del sexo*).

Curious Female. 1969. Paul Rapp. F/Pl: *Angélique Pettyjohn, Charlene Jones, Bunny Allister, Julie Connors, Elaine Edwards*. USA: Fanfare Films.

Cyborg Girl. 2008. (See: *Cyborg She*).

Cyborg She (alt: *Gamera the Invincible/Boku no kanojo wa saibougu/Cyborg Girl*). 2008. Jae-young Kwak. F/Pl: *Haruka Ayase*. Japan: Amuse Soft Entertainment/Dentsu/Fields Pictures/GAGA/MBS/Shogkukan/Suplex/TBS/Toshiba Entertainment/Tristone.

Daikaiju Gamera (alt: *Gamera the Invincible/Gammera*). 1966. Noriaki Yuasa. F/Wr: *Fumi Takahashi*. F/Pl: *Harumi Kiritachi, Michiko Sugata*. Japan: Daiei.

Danger: Diabolik (alt: *Diabolik*). 1967. Mario BavaDino De Laurentiis. F/Pl: *Marissa Mell, Claudio Gora*. Italy/France: Dino De Laurentiis/Marianne Productions.

Daredevil. 2003. Mark Steven Johnson. F/Pr: *Kathleen M. Courtney, Becki Cross Trujillo, Kim H. Winther*. F/Pl: *Jennifer Garner, Ellen Pompeo, Josie DiVincenzo*. USA: Marvel/20th Century–Fox/New Regency/Horseshoe Bat Prod./Epsilon/Regency Enterprises.

The Dark Knight Rises. 2012. Christopher Nolan. F/Pr: *Emma Thomas* +8. F/Pl: *Anne Hathaway, Marion Cotillard*. UK/USA: Warner Bros./Legendary Entertainment/DC/Syncopy.

D.A.R.Y.L. 1985. Simon Wincer. F/Pl: *Mary Beth Hurt, Kathryn Walker, Colleen Camp*. USA: Paramount.

Daughter of Destiny. 1928. (See: *Alraune*, 1928).

Daughter of Evil. 1930. (See: *Alraune*, 1930).

Dawn of the Planet of the Apes. 2014. Matt Reeves. F/Pr: *Amanda Silver, Jennifer Teves, Jenno Topping, Heather William* +5. F/Wr:

Amanda Silver +2. F/Pl: *Keri Russell, Karin Konoval, Judy Greer*. USA/UK/Canada: Chernin Entertainment/Ingenious Media/Soh VFX/TSG Entertainment.

The Day the Earth Caught Fire. 1961. Val Guest. F/Pl: *Janet Munro*. UK: British Lion/Paramount.

The Day the Earth Stood Still. 1951. Robert Wise. F/Pl: *Patricia Neal, Frances Bavier, Edith Evanson, Marjorie Crossland*. USA: 20th Century–Fox.

The Day the Earth Stood Still. 2008. Scott Derrickson. F/Pl: *Jennifer Connelly, Kathy Bates, Sunita Presad, Tanya Campoux*. USA/Canada: 20th Century–Fox/3 Arts Entertainment/Dune Entertainment III/Earth Canada Productions/Hammerhead Productions.

Dead Man's Letters. 1986. (See: *Pisma myortvogo cheloveka*).

The Deadly Mantis (alt: *The Incredible Praying Mantis*). 1957. Nathan Juran. F/Pl: *Alix Talton, Florenz Ames*. USA: Universal.

Deadpool. 2016. Tim Miller. F/Pr: *Lauren Shuler Donner +9*. F/Pl: *Brianna Hildebrand, Taylor Hickson, Morena Baccarin, Donna Yamamoto, Gina Dust*. USA: 20th Century–Fox/Marvel/Kinberg/Donners' Company/TSG.

Death Race 2000. 1975. Paul Bartel. F/Pl: *Simone Griffeth, Mary Woronov, Roberta Collins*. USA: New World/Columbia Associates.

Deathsport. 1978. Henry Suso and Allan Arkush. F/Pl: *Claudia Jennings, Brenda Venus*. USA: New World.

Debug. 2014. David Hewlett. F/Pr: *Jane Loughman +4*. F/Pl: *Tenika Davis, Jadyn Wong, Sidney Leeder, Jeananne Goossen, Jessica Phillips, Kate Hewlett*. Canada: Copperheart/Monkeys & Parrots.

Deep Impact. 1998. *Mimi Leder*. F/Pr: Joan Bradshaw +5. F/Pl: *Téa Leoni, Vanessa Redgrave, Laura Innes, Mary McCormack, Leelee Sobieski*. USA: Paramount/DreamWorks/Zanuck/Brown Prod./Manhattan Project.

Demon Seed. 1977. Donald Cammell Herb. F/Pl: *Julie Christie, Berry Kroeger, Lisa Lu*. USA: MGM.

Demons of the Swamp (alt: *The Giant Leeches*). 1959. Bernard L. Kowalski. F/Pl: *Yvette Vickers*. USA: Bilboa.

"Demon with a Glass Hand," *The Outer Limits* (TV episode). 17th October 1964, Season 2#5. Byron Haskin. Wr: Harlan Ellison. F/Pl: *Arline Martel*.

Desert Warrior. 1985. Ciro H. F/Pl: *Laura Banks, Lynda Weismeier, Linda Grovenor*. USA: Redeo Productions.

Destination Moon. 1950. Irving Pichel. F/Pl: *Erin O'Brien Moore*. USA: George Pal Productions.

Deux cent milles lieues sous les mers, ou Le cauchemar d'un pêcheur (alt: *Under the Seas*). 1907. Georges Méliès. F/Pl: *Corps de Ballet du Châtelet*. France: Star.

Devil Girl from Mars. 1954. David MacDonald. F/Pl: *Patricia Laffan, Hazel Court, Adrienne Corri*. UK: Danziger Productions.

Diabolik. 1967. (See: *Danger: Diabolik*).

Dick Tracy's G-Men (chapter serial). 1939. William Witney and John English. F/Pl: *Phyllis Isley (Jennifer Jones)*. USA: Republic. (15 chapters).

District 9. 2009. Neill Blomkamp. F/Wr: *Terri Tatchell +1*. F/Pl: *Nathalie Boltt, Sylvaine Strike*. NZ/USA/South Africa: TriStar/Block/Hanson/WingNut Films/Covert Media/District 9/Majority Entertainment.

Divergent. 2014. Neil Burger. F/Pr: *Lucy Fisher, Rachel Shane +5*. F/Wr: *Vanessa Taylor, Veronica Roth* (source novel). F/Pl: *Shailene Woodley, Ashley Judd, Zoë Kravitz, Maggie Q, Kate Winslett, Amy Newbold*. USA: Summit/Red Wagon/Soho VFX.

Dr. Breedlove. 1964. (See: *Kiss Me Quick!*).

Dr. Coppelius (alt: *El fantástico mundo del doctor Coppelius/Dr?? Coppelius!!!*). 1966. Ted Kneeland. F/Pl: *Claudia Corday, Eileen Elliott, Carman Rojas*. USA/Spain: Copelia/Frank J. Hale Productions.

Dr?? Coppelius!!!. 1966. (See: *Dr. Coppelius*).

Dr. Goldfoot and the Bikini Machine. 1965. Norman Taurog. F/Pl: *Susan Hart*. USA: AIP.

Dr. Goldfoot and the Girl Bombs (alt: *Le spie vengono dal semifreddo/I due mafiosi dell'FBI*). 1966. Mario Bava. F/Pl: *Laura Antonelli, Movana Tahi*. USA/Italy: Italian International Film/AIP.

Dr. Jekyll and Mr. Hyde. 1920. John S. Robertson. F/Wr: *Clara S. Beranger*. F/Pl: *Martha Mansfield, Nita Naldi*. USA: Famous Players Lasky.

Doctor Jekyll and Mr. Hyde. 1932. Rouben Mamoulian. F/Pl: *Miriam Hopkins, Rose Hobart*. USA: Paramount.

Dr. Skinum. 1907. Wallace McCutcheon. USA: American Mutoscope/Biograph Co.

Dr. Strangelove or: How I Learned to Stop Worrying and Love the Bomb. 1964. Stanley Kubrick. F/Pl: *Tracy Reed*. USA/UK: Columbia/Hawk Films.

Doctor Who (TV feature). 1996. Geoffrey Sax. F/Pr: *Jo Wright +4*. F/Pl: *Daphne Ashbrook, Catherine Lough Haggquist, Dolores Drake, Eliza Roberts*. USA/UK: Universal Television/BBC Worldwide/Fox Network.

Doctor Who (TV series). 1963–1989. Various Directors. UK: BBC. (696 episodes).

Doctor Who (TV series). 2005–. Various Directors. UK/Canada: BBC/CBC. (167+ episodes).

Dog Factory (alt: *Edison's Dog Factory*). 1904. Edwin S. Porter. USA: Edison.

The Doll Maker's Daughter. 1906. Lewin Fitzhamon. F/Pl: *Dolly Lupone.* UK: Hepworth.

The Doll. 1962. (See: *La poupée*).

Dollhouse (TV series). 2009–10. Various Directors. F/Pl: *Eliza Dushku, Dichen Lachman, Olivia Williams, Miracle Laurie, Amy Acker.* USA: 20th Century–Fox Television/ Boston Diva. (27 episodes).

Dos cosmonautas a la fuerza. 1967. Lucio Fulci. F/Pl: *Mónica Randall, Maria Silva, Linda Sini.* Spain/Italy: Aggata Films/IMA Films.

A Dream of Tomorrow. 1914. (See: *Wake Up!*).

Duel of the Space Monsters. 1965. (See: *Frankenstein Meets the Space Monster*).

Dune. 1984. David Lynch. F/Pr: *Raffaella De Laurentiis +2.* F/Pl: *Francesca Annis, Siân Phillips, Linda Hunt, Virginia Madsen, Silvana Mangano, Sean Young.* USA: Dino De Laurentiis Productions/Universal.

Earth Girls Are Easy. 1988. Julien Temple. F/ Wr: *Julie Brown +2.* F/Pl: *Geena Davis, Julie Brown.* USA: Kestrel/Odyssey.

Edison's Dog Factory. 1904. (See: *Dog Factory*).

Ein Unsichtbarer geht durch die Stadt (alt: *An Invisible Man Goes Through the City*). 1933. Harry Piel. F/Pl: *Lissy Arna, Annemarie Soerensen, Olga Limburg, Gina Falckenburg.* Germany: Ariel Film.

The Electric Leg. 1912. Percy Stow. UK: Clarendon.

The Electric Servant. 1909. Walter R. Booth. UK: Urban.

Electric Transformations. 1909. Percy Stow. UK: Clarendon.

The Electronic Monster. 1957. (See: *Escapement*).

The Elixir of Life. 1901. James A. Williamson. UK: Williamson.

The Elixir of Life. 1911. (See: *Vers l'Immortalitié*).

The Elixir of Strength. 1909. Not Known. France: Pathé.

Elstree Calling. 1930. Alfred Hitchcock, André Charlot, Jack Hulbert, Paul Murray. F/Pl: *Anna May Wong.* UK: British International Pictures.

Elysium. 2013. Neill Blomkamp. F/Pr: *Sue Bade-Powell, Victoria Burhart, Stacy Perskie +3.* F/Pl: *Jodie Foster, Alice Braga, Emma Tremblay, Catherine Lough Haggquist.* USA: TriStar/MRC/QED International/Alpha Core/ Simon Kinberg Prod./Genre Films/Sony.

The Empire Strikes Back. 1980. (See: *Star Wars: Episode V—The Empire Strikes Back*).

The End of All Things. 1897. (See: *Making Sausages*).

The End of the World. 1930. (See: *La Fin du monde*).

England's Menace. 1914. Harold Shaw. F/Pl: *Edna Flugrath.* UK: London.

An Englishman's Home. 1914. Ernest G. Batley. F/Pl: *Dorothy Batley.* UK: B. and C.

Escape from Planet Earth. 2013. Cal Brunker. F/Pr: *Tamara Boutcher, Jinko Gotoh, Catherine Winder +13.* F/Pl: (voices) *Jessica Alba, Sofia Vergara, Sarah Jessica Parker, Jane Lynch.* USA/Canada: Blue Yonder/GRF/Jon Shestack Prod./Protocol Pictures/Rainmaker.

Escape from the Planet of the Apes. 1971. Don Taylor. F/Pl: *Kim Hunter, Natalie Trundy.* USA: 20th Century–Fox/APJAC Productions.

Escapement (alt: *The Electronic Monster*). 1957. Montgomery Tully. F/Pl: *Mary Murphy, Meredith Edwards, Kay Callard.* UK: Alec C. Snowden Productions/Anglo-Amalgamated.

E.T. the Extra-Terrestrial. 1982. Steven Spielberg. F/Pr: *Kathleen Kennedy +1.* F/Wr: *Melissa Mathison.* F/Pl: *Dee Wallace, Drew Barrymore, Erika Eleniak.* USA: Universal/ Amblin Entertainment.

Event Horizon. 1997. Paul Anderson. F/Pr: *Sarah Isherwood.* F/Pl: *Kathleen Quinlan, Joely Richardson, Holley Chant.* UK/USA: Golar Prod./Impact Pictures/Paramount.

Ex Machina. 2015. Alex Garland. F/Pr: *Caroline Levy, Tessa Ross, Joanne Smith +6.* F/Pl: *Alicia Vikander, Sonoya Mizuno, Claire Selby, Symara Templeman, Gana Bayarsaikhan, Tiffany Pisani, Elina Alminas.* UK: UPI/Film4/ DNA Films.

Expedition Moon. 1950. (See: *Rocketship X-M*).

The Exploits of Elaine (chapter serial). 1914. L. Gasnier and J.A. Golden. F/Pl: *Pearl White.* USA: Wharton Prod. Co./Pathé Exchange. (14 chapters).

Extant (TV series), 2014–5. Various Directors. F/Pl: *Halle Berry, Grace Gagnon, Lynnanne Zager, Camryn Manheim, Kiersey Clemons.* USA: 22 Plates/Amblin Television/CBS. (26 episodes).

"Family Guy: Episode VI: It's a Trap!," *Family Guy* (TV episode). 17th July 2011 Season 9 #18. Peter Shin and James Perdum. F/Pr: *Cherry Chevapravatdumrong, Kim Fertman, Karin Perrotta, Shannon Smith, Kara Vallow +4.* F/Wr: *Cherry Chevapravatdumrong +3.* F/Pl: (voices) *Alex Borstein, Mila Kunis, Car-*

rie Fisher, Mary Hart, Anne Hathaway. USA:
20th Century–Fox TV/Fox TV Animation/
Fuzzy Door Prod.

Fantastic Voyage. 1966. Richard Fleischer. F/Pl:
Raquel Welch, Jean Del Val, Shelby Grant.
USA: 20th Century–Fox.

El fantástico mundo del doctor Coppelius. 1966.
(See: *Dr. Coppelius*).

The Fifth Element. 1997. Luc Besson. F/Pl:
*Milla Jovovich, Julie T. Wallace, Maïwenn Le
Besco.* France: Gaumont.

La Fin du monde (alt: *The End of the World*).
1930. Abel Gance. F/Pl: *Colette Darfeuil,
Sylvie Grenade, Wanda Vangen,* Jeanne Brin-
deau. France: L'Ecran D'Art.

Final Fantasy: The Spirits Within. 2001. F/Pr:
Deidre Morrison. F/Pl: (voices) *Min-Na Wen,
Peri Gilpin, Jean Simmons.* USA/Japan: Chris
Lee Prod./Square Company/Square USA.

Fire Maidens from Outer Space. 1956. Cy Roth.
F/Pl: *Susan Shaw, Jacqueline Curtis.* UK: Criterion.

The Fire Monster. 1955. (See: *Gojira No Gyakushu*).

Firefox. 1982. Clint Eastwood. F/Pl: *Dimitra
Arliss.* USA: Malpaso Company.

First Wave (TV series). 1998–2001. Various Di-
rectors. F/Pl: *Traci Lords, Stacy Grant, Dana
Brooks.* Canada: Sugar Entertainment/Vida-
tron Entertainment/Pearson Television/
American Zoetrope/Chum Television/First
Wave Productions. (66 episodes).

Flash Gordon (chapter serial). 1936. Frederick
Stephani, Ray Taylor. F/Wr: *Ella O'Neill +3.*
F/Pl: *Jean Rogers, Priscilla Lawson.* USA:
Universal. (13 chapters).

Flash Gordon Conquers the Universe (chapter se-
rial). 1940. Ford Beebe, Ray Taylor. F/Pl:
Carol Hughes, Beatrice Roberts, Anne Gwynne.
USA: Universal. (12 chapters).

Flash Gordon's Trip to Mars (chapter serial).
1938. Ford Beebe, Robert F. Hill. F/Wr: *Ella
O'Neill +4.* F/Pl: *Jean Rogers, Beatrice Rob -
erts.* USA: Universal. (15 chapters).

Flesh Gordon. 1974. Michael Benveniste and
Howard Ziehm. F/Pl: *Suzanne Fields, Mycle
Brandy.* USA: Graffiti Productions.

Flick (alt: *Frankenstein on Campus*). 1967. F/Pl:
Kathleen Sawyer. Canada: Agincourt/Glen
Warren Productions.

Flight to Mars. 1951. Lesley Selander. F/Pl: *Mar -
guerite Chapman, Virginia Huston.* USA-
Monogram Pictures.

The Fly. 1958. Kurt Neumann. 1958. F/Pl: *Patricia Owens.* USA: 20th Century–Fox.

The Fly. 1986. David Cronenberg. F/Pl: *Geena
Davis, Joy Boushel.* USA: 20th Century–Fox/
Brooksfilms.

The Flying Machine. 1901. (See: *À la conquête
de l'air*).

The Flying Saucer. 1950. Mikel Conrad. F/Pl:
Virginia Hewitt. USA: Colonial.

Forbidden Planet. 1956. Fred Wilcox. F/Pl:
Anne Francis. USA: MGM.

The Forbin Project. 1970. (See: *Colossus: The
Forbin Project*).

Frankenstein Created Woman. 1966. Terence
Fisher. Anthony Nelson Keys. F/Pl: *Susan
Denberg.* UK/USA: Hammer/Warner Bros.

Frankenstein Meets the Space Monster (alt: *Duel
of the Space Monsters*). 1965. Robert Gaffney.
F/Pl: *Nancy Marshall, Marilyn Hanold.* USA:
Vernon-Seneca Films.

Frankenstein on Campus. 1967. (See: *Flick*).

Frankenstein. 1910. J. Searle Dawley. F/Pl: *Mary
Fuller.* USA: Edison.

Frankenstein. 1931. James Whale. F/Pl: *Mae
Clark, Marilyn Harris.* USA: Universal.

Frau in Mond (alt: *Woman in the Moon/Girl in
the Moon/By Rocket to the Moon*). 1929. Dir./
F/Pr: Fritz Lang. F/Wr: *Thea von Harbou.*
F/Pl: *Gerda Maurus, Margarete Kupfer,
Tilla Durieux.* Germany: Fritz Lang Film/
UFA.

Freezing Auntie. 1912. Not Known. F/Pl: *Alice
Washburn, Marion Brooks, Bliss Milford.* USA:
Edison.

Freezing Mixture. 1910. Walter R. Booth. UK:
Kineto.

From Earth to the Moon. 1958. Byron Haskin.
F/Pl: *Debra Paget.* USA: Waverly.

Fun in a Butcher Shop. 1901. Edwin S. Porter.
USA: Edison.

Furankenshutain no kaijū: Sanda tai Gaira (alt:
The War of the Gargantuas). 1966. Inoshiro
Honda. F/Pl: *Kumi Mizuno.* Japan: Toho.

Futurama (TV series). 1999–2015. Various Directors. F/Pl: (voices) *Katey Segal, Tress
MacNeille, Lauren Torn, Kath Soucie, Sigourney Weaver.* USA: 20th Century–Fox/Fox
Animation/The Curiosity Company.

Galaxis. 1995. William Mesa. F/Pl: *Brigitte
Nielsen, Cindy Morgan. Kristin Bauer.* USA:
Interlight, Morphosis Prod./Prism Enter-
tainment.

Galaxy Quest. 1999. Dean Parisot. F/Pr: *Elizabeth Cantillon, Allegra Clegg, Suzann Ellis,
Janet Lewin, Sona Partayan +2.* F/Pl: *Sigourney Weaver, Missi Pyle, Kaitlin Callum.* USA:
DreamWorks/Gran Via Prod.

Galvanic Fluid (alt: *More Fun with Electricity*).
1908. J. Stuart Blackton. USA: Vitagraph.

Gamera the Invincible. 1966. (See: *Daikaiju
Gamera*).

Gammera. 1966. (See: *Daikaiju Gamera*).

The Gargon Terror. 1959. (See: *Teenagers from Outer Space*).

Gattaca. 1997. Andrew Niccol. F/Pr: *Gail Lyon, Stacey Sher, Georgia Kacandes* +3. F/Pl: *Uma Thurman, Jayne Brook, Maya Rudolph.* USA: Columbia/Jersey Films.

Ghost in the Shell. 1995. Mamoru Oshii. F/Pl: (voice) *Atsuko Tanaka, Mimi Woods.* Japan/UK: Kodansha/Bandai Visual/Manga Entertainment/Production I/G.

Ghost in the Shell. 2017. Rupert Sanders. F/Pr: *Holly Bario, Jane Nerlinger Evans, Maki Terashima-Furuta* +9. F/Pl: *Scarlett Johansson, Juliette Binoche, Danusia Samai, Anamarie Marinca.* USA/India/China/Japan/Hong Kong/UK/NZ/Canada/Australia: Paramount/DreamWorks/Reliance Entertainment/Shanghai Film Group/Huahua Media/Arad Productions/Steven Paul Production/Amblin Partners/Grosvenor Park Prod./Seaside Entertainment/Weying Galaxy Entertainment.

Ghost in the Shell 2: Innocence. 2004. Mamoru Oshii. F/Pr: *Maki Terashima-Furuta* +3. F/Wr: *Mary Claypool* +3. F/Pl: (voices) *Atsuko Tanaka.* Japan: Bandai Visual/Buena Vista/Dentsu/ITNDDTD/Koudansha/Production I.G./Studio Ghibli.

Ghost Patrol. 1936. Sam Newfield. F/Pl: *Claudia Dell.* USA: Puritan.

Ghostbusters. 1984. Ivan Reitman. F/Pl: *Sigourney Weaver, Annie Potts, Jennifer Runyon, Slavitza Jovan, Alice Drummond.* USA: Columbia/Delphi Film/Black Rhino.

Ghostbusters 2016. Paul Feig. P/Pr: *Ali Bell, Jessie Henderson, Michele Impertato, Amy Pascal* +8. F/Wr: *Katie Dippold* +1. F/Pl: *Kristen Wiig, Melissa McCarthy, Kate McKinnon, Bess Rous, Leslie Jones, Katie Dippold.* USA/Australia: Columbia/LStar/Village Roadshow/Pascal Pictures/Feigco Entertainment/Ghostcorps/Montecito.

The Giant Claw. 1957. Fred F. Sears. F/Pl: *Mara Corday.* USA: Clover.

The Giant Leeches. 1959. (See: *Demons of the Swamp*).

G.I. Joe: The Rise of Cobra. 2009. Stephen Sommers. F/Pr: *JoAnn Perritano* +13. F/Pl: *Karolina Kurkova, Sienna Miller, Rachel Nichols.* USA/Czech Republic: Paramount/Spyglass/Hasbro/Di Bonaventura Pictures/Digital Image Associates.

Gigantis. 1955. (See: *Gojira no gyakushu*).

Gill Women of Venus. 1966. (See: *Voyage to the Planet of Prehistoric Women*).

Gill Women. 1966. (See: *Voyage to the Planet of Prehistoric Women*).

The Girl from Monday. 2005. Hal Hartley. F/Pr: *Lisa Porter.* F/Pl: *Sabrina Lloyd, Tatiana Abracos, Juliana Francis, Edie Falco.* USA: Possible Films/The Monday Company.

The Girl from Scotland Yard. 1937. Robert Vignola. F/Wr: *Doris Anderson* +1. F/Pl: *Karen Morley, Katherine Alexander, Milli Monti.* USA: Paramount.

Girl in the Moon. 1929. (See: *Frau im Mond*).

The Girl That Made Time Fly. 1906. (See: *How to Make Time Fly*).

The Girl Who Leapt Through Time. 2006. Mamoru Hosoda. F/Wr: *Satoko Okudera.* F/Pr: *Jennifer Fairweather* +4. F/Pl: *Riisa Naka, Ayami Kakiuchi, Mitsuki Tanimura, Yuki Seko, Midori Ando.* Japan: Madhouse, Happinet, Kadokawa Pictures, Kadokawa Shoten, Memory Tech, Q-Tec.

The Giver. 2014. Phillip Noyce. F/Pr: *Genevieve Hofmeyr, Noga Isackson, Alison Owen, Nikki Silver, Janine van Assen* +8. F/Pl: *Meryl Streep, Odeya Rush, Katie Holmes, Taylor Swift, Emma Tremblay.* Canada/South Africa/USA: Asis Prod./Canada Film Capital/Tonik Prod./Walden Media/Weinstein Co.

Godzilla King of the Monsters. 1954. (See: *Gojira*).

Godzilla Raids Again. 1955. (See: *Gojira no gyakushu*).

Godzilla's Counterattack. 1955. (See: *Gojira no gyakushu*).

Gojira (alt: *Godzilla King of the Monsters*). 1954. Inoshiro Honda. F/Pl: *Momoko Koichi.* Japan: Toho.

Gojira no gyakushu (alt: *Gigantis/The Return of Godzilla/The Fire Monster/The Volcano Monster/Godzilla Raids Again/Godzilla's Counterattack/Counterattack of the Monster*). 1955. Motoyoshi Oda. F/Pl: *Setsuko Wakayama.* Japan: Toho.

Gojira. 1985. Dir., Kohji Hashimoto and R.J. Kizer. F/Wr: *Lisa Tomei* +1. F/Pl: *Yasuko Sawagachi.* Japan: Toho.

Golem (alt: *The Golem*). 1935. Piotr Szulkin. F/Pl: *Krystyna Janda, Joanna Zolkowska.* Poland: Zespoly Filmowe/Perspekty Unit.

Grave Robbers from Outer Space. 1959. (See: *Plan 9 from Outer Space*).

Gravity. 2013. Alfonso Cuarón. F/Pr: *Nikki Penny, Gabriela Rodriguez* +4. F/Pl: *Sandra Bullock, Amy Warren* (voice). USA/UK: Warner Bros./Esperanto Filmoj/Heyday Films.

Guardians of the Galaxy Vol. 2. 2017. James Gunn. F/Pr: *Victoria Alonso* +8. F/Pl: *Zoe Saldana, Karen Gillan, Pom Klementieff, Elizabeth Debicki, Laura Haddock.* USA/NZ/Canada: Walt Disney/Marvel.

Gugesse et l'Automate (alt: *The Clown and the*

Automaton). 1897. Georges Méliès. France: Star.

Hair Restorer. 1907. Not Known. USA: Williams Brown and Earle.

The Handmaid's Tale. 1990. Volker Schlöndorff. F/Wr: *Margaret Atwood* (source novel). F/Pl: *Natasha Richardson, Faye Dunaway, Elizabeth McGovern, Victoria Tennant, Blanche Baker, Traci Lind, Zoey Wilson, Kathryn Doby, Lucia Hartpeng, Karma Ibsen Riley.* USA/W. Germany: Cinecom-Bioscop/Cinecom Entertainment Group/Cinétudes Films/Daniel Wilson Productions/Master Partners/Odyssey.

The Handmaid's Tale (TV series). 2017–. Various Directors. F/Wr: *Margaret Atwood* (source novel). F/Pl: *Elisabeth Moss, Yvonne Strahovski, Amanda Brugel, Madeline Brewer, Ann Dowd, Samira Wiley, Nina Kiri, Tattiawna Jones.* USA: MGM Television. (11+ episodes).

The Hands of Orlac. 1924. (See: *Orlacs Hände*).

The Hands of Orlac. 1935. (See: *Mad Love*).

He, She or It. 1962. (See: *La poupée*).

Her. 2013. Spike Jonze. F/Pr: *Chelse Barnard, Megan Ellison, Natalie Farrey, Samantha Morton +4.* F/Pl: *Scarlett Johansson* (voice), *Amy Adams, Rooney Mara, Kristen Wiig, Lynne Adrianna, Lisa Renee Pitts, Olivia Wilde.* USA: Annapurna Pictures.

Hercules Against the Moon Men. 1965. (See: *Maciste e la regina di Samar*).

Die Herrin von Atlantis (alt: *L'Atlantide/Lost Atlantis/The Mistress of Atlantis/The Queen of Atlantis*). 1932. Georg Wilhelm Pabst. F/Pl: *Brigitte Helm, Odette Florelle* (German, French and English versions), *Florelle Tela-Tchai* (German and French versions). Germany: Nero Film.

High Treason. 1929. Maurice Elvey. F/Pl: *Benita Hume.* UK: Gaumont.

Himmelskibet (alt: *400 Million Miles from the Earth/A Trip to Mars*). 1917. Holger Madson. F/Pl: *Zanny Petersen, Lilly Jacobsson.* Denmark: Nordisk Film.

Hoffmanns Erzaehlungen (alt: *Tales of Hoffmann*). 1923. Max Neufeld. F/Pl: *Lola Urban-Kneidlinger.* Austria: Vita/Neufeld Film.

Hollow Man. 2000. Paul Verhoeven. F/Pr: *Stacy Lumbrezer, Marion Rosenberg +3.* F/Pl: *Elisabeth Shue, Kim Dickens, Mary Randle, Rhona Mitra.* USA/Germany: Columbia/Global Entertainment.

The Horror of Frankenstein. 1970. Jimmy Sangster. F/Pl: *Kate O'Mara, Veronica Carlson.* UK: Hammer/EMI.

Hotel Eléctrico, El. 1905. Segundo de Chomon. Spain: Hispanofilm.

How Patrick's Eyes Were Opened. 1912. Not Known. F/Pl: *Alice Washburn.* USA: Edison.

How to Make Time Fly (alt: *The Girl That Made Time Fly*). 1906. J. H. Martin. UK: Paul.

Howard the Duck. (alt: *Howard... A New Breed of Hero*). 1986. Willard Huyck. F/Pr: *Gloria Katz.* F/Wr: *Gloria Katz* +Dir. F/Pl: *Lea Thompson, Liz Sagal.* USA: Lucasfilm/Universal.

Howard... A New Breed of Hero. 1986. (See: *Howard the Duck*).

Hulk. 2003. Ang Lee. F/Pr: *Gale Anne Hurd, Cheryl A. Tkach.* F/Pl: *Jennifer Connelly, Cara Buono, Celia Weston, Regina McKee Redwing.* USA: Universal/Marvel/Valhalla/Good Machine.

Humans (TV series). 2015–. Various Directors. F/Pl: *Jennifer Chan, Katherine Parkinson, Lucy Carless, Pixie Davies, Emily Berrington, Ruth Bradley.* UK/Sweden/USA: Kudos Film and Television/Channel 4/AMC/Endemol Shine/Matador. (24+ episodes).

The Hunger Games. 2012. Gary Ross. F/Pr: *Diana Alvarez, Suzanne Collins, Chantal Ferghali, Nina Jacobson, Louise Rosner.* F/Wr: *Suzanne Collins* (screenplay and source novel) +2. F/Pl: *Jennifer Lawrence, Willow Shields, Elizabeth Banks, Paula Malcomson, Brooke Bundy, Amandla Steberg, Latarsha Rose.* USA: Lionsgate/Color Force.

The Hunger Games: Catching Fire (alt: *The Hunger Games 2*) 2013. Francis Lawrence. F/Pr: *Suzanne Collins, Nina Jacobson, Louise Rosner, Allison Shearmur +5.* F/Wr: *Suzanne Collins* (source novel). F/Pl: *Jennifer Lawrence, Taylor St. Clair, Sandra Ellis Lafferty, Willow Shields, Elizabeth Banks, Paula Malcomson, Brooke Bundy.* USA: Lionsgate/Color Force.

The Hunger Games: Mockingjay—Part 1. 2014. Francis Lawrence. F/Pr: *Suzanne Collins, Nina Jacobson, Allison Shearmur +5.* F/Wr: *Suzanne Collins* (source novel). F/Pl: *Jennifer Lawrence, Julianne Moore, Willow Shields, Elizabeth Banks, Jena Malone, Paula Malcomson, Natalie Dormer, Sarita Choudhury, Stef Dawson, Patina Miller.* USA: Lionsgate/Color Force.

The Hunger Games: Mockingjay—Part 2. 2015. Francis Lawrence. F/Pr: *Suzanne Collins, Nina Jacobson, Allison Shearmur +12.* F/Wr: *Suzanne Collins* (source novel). F/Pl: *Jennifer Lawrence, Julianne Moore, Willow Shields, Elizabeth Banks, Jena Malone, Paula Malcomson, Natalie Dormer, Sarita Choudhury, Stef Dawson, Patina Miller, Eugenie Bondurant,*

Michelle Forbes, Gwendoline Christie, April Grace. USA: Lionsgate/Color Force.

I due mafiosi dell'FBI. 1966. (See: *Dr. Goldfoot and the Girl Bombs*.)

I Married a Monster from Outer Space. 1958. Gene Fowler, Jr. F/Pl: *Gloria Talbott, Valeria Allen, Maxie Rosenbloom*. USA: Paramount.

I, Robot. 2004. Alex Proyas. F/Pl: *Bridget Moynahan, Fiona Hogan, Sharon Wilkins*. USA: 20th Century–Fox/Mediastream Vierte Film GmbH & Co. Vermarktungs KG/Mediastream IV/Entertainment Company/ Laurence Mark/Overbrook Films/Canlaws Prod.

I Was a Teenage Frankenstein. 1958. Herbert L. Strock. F/Pl: *Phyllis Coates*. USA: Santa Rosa Productions.

Iceman. 1984. Fred Schepisi. F/Pl: *Lindsey Crouse, Amelia Hall*. USA: Universal.

If England Were Invaded (alt: *The Raid of 1915*). 1914. Fred W. Durrant. 1914. F/Pl: *Diana Shaw*. UK: Gaumont.

I'll Follow You Down. 2013. Richie Mahta. F/Pl: *Gillian Anderson, Kiara Glasco, Catherine Bruhier, Susanna Fournier, Laura Miyata, Sherry Miller*. Canada: Resolute Films and Entertainment, Harold Greenberg Fund, Telefilm.

Immediate Disaster. 1954. (See: *The Stranger from Venus*.)

In the Year 2014. 1914. Not Known. USA: Joker.

Inception. 2010. Christopher Nolan. 2010. F/Pr: *Emma Thomas + 9*. F/Pl: *Ellen Page, Marion Cotillard*. USA/UK: Warner Bros./Syncopy/ Legendary Entertainment.

The Incredible Praying Mantis. 1957. (See: *Deadly Mantis*.)

Independence Day. 1996. Roland Emmerich. F/ Pl: *Mary McDonnell, Margaret Colin, Vivica A. Fox, Lisa Jakub*. USA: 20th Century–Fox/Centropolis.

InnerSpace. 1987. Joe Dante. F/Pl: *Meg Ryan, Fiona Lewis, Wendy Schaal*. USA: Amblin/ Warner Bros.

Interstellar. 2014. Christopher Nolan. F/Pr: *Kaari Autry, Jenny Basen, Stacey Douglas, Kim Goddard-Rains, Lynda Obst, Debbie Schwab, Inga Björk Sólnes, Emma Thomas +10*. F/Pl: *Jessica Chastain, Anne Hathaway, Ellen Burstyn, Mackenzie Foy, Colette Wolfe, Leah Cairns*. USA/UK/Canada/Iceland: Paramount/Warner Bros./Legendary Entertainment/Syncopy/Lynda Obst Prod.

The Intrigue. 1916. Frank Lloyd. F/Pr: *Julia Crawford Ivers*. F/Wr: *Julia Crawford Ivers*. F/Pl: *Lenore Ulric, Florence Vidor, Winifre Kingston*. USA: Pallas Pictures/Paramount.

Invaders from Mars. 1953. William Cameron Menzies. F/Pl: *Helena Carter, Hillary Brooke*. USA: National Pictures Corp.

The Invasion of Britain. 1918. (See: *Victory and Peace*.)

Invasion of the Body Snatchers. 1956. Don Siegel. F/Pl: *Dana Wynter, Carolyn Jones*. USA: Walter Wanger Productions.

Invasion of the Body Snatchers. 1978. Philip Kaufman. F/Pl: *Brooke Adams, Veronica Cartwright, Leila Goldini*. USA: Solofilm Co.

The Inventions of an Idiot. 1909. Sigmund Lubin. USA: Lubin.

The Inventor's Galvanic Fluid. 1907. (See: *Liquid Electricity*.)

The Inventor's Secret. 1911. D.W. Griffith. USA: Biograph.

Invisibility. 1909. Lewin Fitzhamon. UK: Hepworth.

An Invisible Man Goes Through the City. 1933. (See: *Ein Unsichtbarer geht durch die Stadt*.)

The Invisible Woman. 1940. A. Edward Sutherland. F/Wr: *Gertrude Purcell +2*. F/Pl: *Virginia Bruce, Maria Montez*. USA: Universal.

Iron Man 2. 2010. Jon Favreau. F/Pr: *Victoria Alonso, Susan Downey, Karen Gilchrist +12*. F/Pl: *Scarlett Johansson, Gwyneth Paltrow, Leslie Bibb, Kate Mara*. USA: Paramount/ Marvel/Fairview Entertainment.

The Island. 2005. Michael Bay. F/Pr: *Heidi Fugeman +8*. F/Pl: *Scarlett Johansson, Siobhan Flynn, Noa Tishby*. USA: Warner Bros./ DreamWorks/Parkes+MacDonald Image Nation/K/O Paper Products/Platinum Dunes.

It Came from Beneath the Sea. 1955. Robert Gordon. F/Pl: *Faith Domergue*. USA: Clover.

It Came from Outer Space. 1953. Arnold, Jack. F/Pl: *Barbara Rush*. USA: Universal.

It Conquered the World. 1956. Roger Corman. F/Pl: *Beverley Garland, Sally Fraser*. USA: Sunset Productions.

It! The Terror from Beyond Space (alt: *It! The Vampire from Beyond Space*). 1958. Edward L. Cahn. F/Pl: *Kim Spalding, Ann Doran*. USA: Vogue Pictures.

It! The Vampire from Beyond Space. 1958. (See: *It! The Terror from Beyond Space*.)

It's a Trap! 2011. (See: "Family Guy: Episode VI: It's a Trap!".)

It's Great to Be Alive. 1933. Alfred L. Werker. F/Pl: *Gloria Stuart, Edna May Oliver, Emma Dunn, Amy Burgess*. USA: Fox.

A Jersey Skeeter. 1900. Arthur Marvin. USA: American Mutoscope/Biograph Co.

Jesse James Meets Frankenstein's Daughter. 1966. William Beaudine. F/Pl: *Narda Onyx, Es-*

telita Rodriguez, Rosa Turich. USA: Circle Productions.

Johnny Mnemonic. 1995. Robert Longo. F/Pr: *Victoria Hamberg* +4. F/Pl: *Dina Meyer, Barbara Sukowa, Tracy Tweed, Sherry Miller*. Canada/USA: TriStar/Alliance/Peter Hoffman/Cinévision.

Journey Beneath the Desert. 1961. (See: *Antinéa, l'amante della citta sepolta*.)

Judge Dredd. 1995. Danny Cannon. F/Pl: *Diane Lane, Joanna Mills, Joan Chen*. USA: Cinergi.

Jupiter Ascending. 2015. Lana Wachowski and Lilly Wachowski (as The Wachowskis). F/Pr: *Lana Wachowski and Lilly Wachowski*. F/Wr: *Lana Wachowski and Lilly Wachowski*. F/Pl: *Mila Kunis, Tuppence Middleton, Nikki Amuka-Bird, Chistina Cole, Maria Dyle Kennedy, Frog Stone, Doona Bae, Gugu Mbatha-Raw, Larissa Kouznetsova, Amily Warren, Vanessa Kirby, Charlotte Beaumont*. USA/Australia: Warner Bros./Village Roadshow/Dune Ent./Anarchos Prod.

Jurassic Park. 1993. Steven Spielberg. F/Pr: *Kathleen Kennedy, Lata Ryan* +2. F/Pl: *Laura Dern, Ariana Richards*. USA: Universal/Amblin Entertainment.

Jurassic World. 2015. Colin Treorrow. F/Wr: *Amanda Silver* +3. F/Pl: *Bryce Dallas Howard, Judy Greer, Lauren Lapkus, Katie McGrath*, Anna Talakkottur. USA: Universal/Amblin Entertainment/Legendary/Dentsu/Fuji television network/Kennedy/Marshall.

Jurassic World: Fallen Kingdom. (2018). J.A. Bayona. F/Pr: *Belén Atienza* +6. F/Pl: *Bryce Dallas Howard, Daniella Pineda, Geraldine Chaplin*. USA: Amblin/Apaches/Legendary/Perfect World Pictures/Universal Pictures.

Just Imagine. 1930. David Butler. F/Pl: *Maureen O'Sullivan, Marjorie White, Joyzelle Joyner, Vera Lewis*. USA: Fox Pictures.

Kill Switch. 2017. Tim Smit. F/Pr: *Shanan Becker, Wendy van Veen* +13. F/Pl: *Bérénice Marlohe, Carity Wakefield, Chloe-May Cuthill*. Netherlands/Germany/USA: CTM Prod./FilmNation/RainMaker/SquareOne.

Killers from Space. 1954. W. Lee Wilder. F/Pl: *Barbara Bestar*. USA: Planet Filmways Inc.

King Kong. 1933. Merian C. Cooper and Ernest B. Schoedsack. F/Wr: *Ruth Rose* +2. F/Pl: *Fay Wray*. USA: RKO.

King of the Rocket Men (chapter serial). 1949. Fred C. Brannon. F/Pl: *Mae Clark*. USA: Republic. (12 chapters).

Kiss Me Quick! (alt: *Dr. Breedlove*). 1964. Russ Meyer. F/Pl: *Althea Currier, Claudia Banks*. USA: Fantasy Productions.)

The Land Unknown. 1957. Virgil Vogel. F/Pl: *Shirley Patterson*. USA: Universal International.

The Last Man on Earth. 1924. John. G. Blystone. F/Pl: *Grace Cunard, Gladys Tennyson, Derelys Perdue, Clarissa Selwynne, Faye Holderness, Marion Aye*. USA: 20th Century–Fox.

The Last Starfighter. 1984. Nick Castle. F/Pl: *Catherine Mary Stewart, Barbara Bosson*. USA: Lorimar/Universal.

The Last Will of Dr. Mabuse (French version of: *Das Testament des Dr. Mabuse*). 1933. Fritz Lang. F/Wr: *Thea von Harbou*. F/Pl: *Monique Rolland, Lily Rezillot, Ginette Gaubert*. Germany: Nero Film/Constantin/Deutsche Universal.

Letters from a Dead Man. 1986. (See: *Pisma myortvoi chelovyeka*.)

Lifeforce. 1985. Tobe Hooper. F/Pl: *Mathilda May*. UK: London Cannon Films.

Liquid Electricity (alt: *The Inventor's Galvanic Fluid*). 1907. J. Stuart Blackton. USA: Vitagraph.

Liquid Sky. 1982. Slava Tsukerman. F/Pl: *Nina Kerova, Anne Carlisle, Paula Sheppard, Susan Doukas*. USA: Z Films Inc.

Logan's Run. 1976. Michael Anderson. F/Pl: *Jenny Agutter, Farrah Fawcett-Majors*. USA: MGM.

Lost Atlantis. 1932. (See: *Die Herrin von Atlantis*.)

Lost in Space. 1998. Stephen Hopkins. F/Pr: *Carla Fry* +3. F/Pl: *Mimi Rogers, Heather Graham, Lacey Chabert, June Lockhart*. USA: Prelude Pictures/Irwin Allen Productions/New Line Cinema.

Lost Women of Zarpa. 1953. (See: *The Mesa of Lost Women*.)

Lucy. 2014. Luc Besson. F/Pr: *Virginie Besson-Silla* +1. F/Pl: *Scarlett Johansson, Analeigh-Tipton*. France: EuropaCorp/TF1 Films/Grive Prod./Canal+.

La Lune à un mètre (alt: *A Trip to the Moon*). 1898. Georges Méliès. France: Star/Lubin.

Maciste e la regina di Samar (alt: *Hercules Against the Moon Men*). 1965. Giacomo Gentilomo. F/Pl: *Jany Clair, Ann-Maria Polani, Delia D'Alberti*. Italy/France: Nike Cinematografica/Comptoir Francais du Film.

Mad Love (alt: *The Hands of Orlac*). 1935. Karl Freund. F/Pl: *Frances Drake, Sarah Haden*. USA: MGM.

Mad Max. 1979. George Miller. F/Pl: *Joanne Samuel*. Australia: Kennedy Miller/Crossroads/Mad Max Films.

Mad Max Beyond Thunderdome. 1985. George Miller and George Ogilvie. F/Pl: *Tina Turner,*

Helen Buday. Australia: Kennedy-Miller Productions.

Mad Max: Fury Road. 2015. George Miller. F/Pr: *Genevieve Hofmeyr, Courtenay Valenti, Holly Radcliffe* +8. F/Pl: *Charlize Theron, Zoë Kravitz, Abbey Lee, Courteney Eaton, Rosie-Huntington-Whiteley, Riley Keough, Meliss Jaffer, Melita Jurisic, Gillian Jones, Joy Smithers, Christina Koch, Antoinette Kellermann*. Australia/USA: Warner Bros./Villag Roadshow/Kennedy Miller Prod./RatPac-Dune/White Noise Factory.

Mad Max 2 (alt: *The Road Warrior*). (1981). George Miller. F/Pl: *Virginia Hey*. Australia: Kennedy Miller Productions.

The Magnetic Squirt. 1909. Georges Hatot. France: Le Lion.

Making Sausages (alt: *The End of all Things*). 1897. George A. Smith. UK: G.A.S.

The Man From Planet X. 1951. Edgar G. Ulmer. F/Pl: *Margaret Field*. USA: Mid-Century Films.

Man in the Moon. 1960. Basil Dearden. F/Pl: *Shirley Anne Field*. UK: Allied Film Makers/Excalibur Films.

The Man Who Fell to Earth. 1976. Nicolas Roeg. F/Pl: *Candy Clark, Linda Hutton, Adrienne Larussa*. UK: British Lion.

Mandrigore. 1952. (See: *Alraune*.)

Marooned. 1969. John Sturges. F/Pl: *Nancy Kovack, Mariette Hartley*. USA: Frankovich-Sturges Productions.

Mars Attacks! 1996. Tim Burton. F/Pl: *Glenn Close, Annette Bening, Sarah Jessica Parker, Natalie Portman*. USA: Warner Bros.

The Martian. 2015. Ridley Scott. F/Pr: *Teresa Kelly* +8. F/Pl: *Jessica Chastain, Kristen Wiig, Kate Mara*. USA/UK: 20th Century–Fox Film Corporation/TSG Entertainment/Scott Free/Kinberg Genre/International Traders/Mid Atlantic Films.

Mary Shelley's Frankenstein. 1994. Kenneth Branagh. F/Wr: *Steph Lady* +1. F/Pl: *Helena Bonham-Carter, Cherie Lunghi, Celia Imrie*. USA: American Zoetrope/TriStar/Japan Satelite Broadcasting/Indieprod.

The Matrix. 1999. The Wachowski Brothers. F/Pl: *Carrie-Anne Moss, Gloria Foster, Belinda McClory*. USA: Warner Bros./Village Roadshow Pictures/Groucho II Film Partnership/Silver Pictures.

The Matrix Reloaded. 2003. The Wachowski Brothes. F/Pl: *Carrie-Anne Moss, Gloria Foster, Nona Gaye, Jada Pinkett Smith, Christine Anu, Essie Davis, Gina Torres, Robyn Nevin, Monica Bellucci*. USA: Warner Bros./Village Roadshow Pictures/NPV Entertainment/

Silver Pictures/Heineken Branded Entertainment.

The Matrix Revolutions. 2003. The Wachowski Brothers. F/Pl: *Carrie-Anne Moss, Tanveer K. Atwal, Mary Alice, Nona Gaye, Jada Pinkett Smith, Rachel Blackman, Francine Bell, Essie Davis, Gina Torres, Robyn Nevin, Monica Bellucci*. USA: Warner Bros./Village Roadshow Pictures/NPV Entertainment/Silver Pictures.

Maze Runner: The Death Cure. (2018). Wes Ball. F/Pr: *Ellen Goldsmith-Vein, Lindsey Williams* +11. F/Pl: *Kaya Scodelario, Rosa Salazar, Patricia Clarkson, Katherine McNamara*. USA: Gotham Group/Temple Hill Ent./20th Century-Fox.

The Mechanical Butcher. 1895. (See: *Charcuterie mécanique*.)

The Mechanical Delicatessen. 1895. (See: *Charcuterie mécanique*.)

Mechanical Hat-Maker and Butcher. 1900. (See: *Chapellerie et charcuterie mécaniques*.)

The Mechanical Statue and the Ingenious Servant. 1907. Stuart Blackton. USA: Vitagraph.

Men in Black. 1997. Barry Sonnenfeld. F/Pr: *Laurie MacDonald* +4. F/Pl: *Linda Fiorentino, Siobhan Fallon, Becky Ann Baker*. USA: Columbia/Amblin Entertainment/Parkes +MacDonald Image Nation.

Men Just Fight. 1933. Edgar Selwyn. F/Pl: *Diana Wynyard, May Robson, Ruth Selwyn, Hedda Hopper*. USA: MGM.

The Mesa of Lost Women (alt: *Lost Women of Zarpa*). 1953. Herbert Tevos and Ron Ormon. F/Pl: *Mary Hill, Tandia Quinn*. USA: A.J. Frances White-Joy Houck Productions.

A Message from Mars. 1913. J. Wallett Waller. F/Pl: *Chrissie Bell, Kate Tyndale, Evelyn Beaumont, Eileen Temple, Tonie Reith*. UK: United Kingdom Films.

Meteor Monster. 1957. (See: *Teenage Monster*.)

Metropolis. 1927. Fritz Lang. F/Wr: *Thea von Harbou* +1. F/Pl: *Brigitte Helm, Grete Berger, Helene Weigel*. Germany: UFA

A Midnight Episode. 1899. (See: *Un Bot Lit*.)

Midstream. 1929. James Flood. F/Wr: *Bernice Boon* (story), *Frances Guihan* (scenario), *Fanny Hatton* (dialogue and titles) +1. F/Pl: *Claire Windsor, Helen Jerome Eddy, Florence Foyer, Geneveive Schrader*. USA: Tiffany-Stahl Productions.

Minority Report. 2002. Steven Spielberg. F/Pr: *Bonnie Curtis* +7. F/Pl: *Jessica Capshaw, Anna Maria Horsford, Klea Scott*. USA: DreamWorks/20th Century–Fox/Cruise/Wagner Prod./Blue Tulip/Ronald Shusett/Gary Goldman/Amblin Entertainment/Digital Image Associates.

Missile to the Moon. 1958. Richard Cuhna. F/Pl: *Cathy Downs, Nina Bara*. USA: Astor.

The Mistress of Atlantis. 1932. (See: *Die Herrin von Atlantis*.)

The Monitors. 1968. Jack Shea. F/Pl: *Susan Oliver, Sherry Jackson, Helen Malone*. USA: Bell & Howell /Wilding/Second City.

The Monster That Challenged the World. 1957. Arnold Laven. F/Wr: *Patricia Fielder* +1. F/Pl: *Audrey Dalton, Casey Adams*. USA: Gramercy Productions.

Moon. 2009. Duncan Jones. F/Pr: *Nicky Bentham, Trudie Styler, Julia Valentine* +10. F/Pl: *Dominique McElligott, Rosie Shaw, Adrienne Shaw, Kaya Scodelario*. UK: Liberty Films/ Xingu Films/Limelight Fund/Lunar Industries.

More Fun with Electricity. 1908. (See: *Galvanic Fluid*.)

Mortal Engines. (2018). Christian Rivers. F/Pr: *Fran Walsh, Philippa Boyens, Deborah Forte, Pamela Silverstein, Amanda Walker* +3. F/Wr: *Fran Walsh, Philippa Boyens* +1. F/Pl: *Frankie Adams, Hera Hilmer, Caren Pistorius*. NZ/ USA: MRC/Scholastic Productions/Silvertongue Films/Wingnut/Universal.

The Motor Car of the Future. 1911. Not Known. Germany: Messter.

The Motorist (alt: *The '?' Motorist/The (?) Motorist*). 1906. Walter R. Booth. UK: Paul.

"Mudd's Women," *Star Trek* (TV episode). 9th August 1969, Season 1#6. Harvey Hart. F/ Pl: *Nichelle Nichols, Karen Steele, Maggie Thrett, Susan Denberg*.

Mutiny in Outer Space. 1958. (See: *Space Master X-7*.)

My Stepmother Is an Alien. 1988. Richard Benjamin. F/Pl: *Kim Basinger, Alyson Hannigan, Amy Prentis*. USA: Columbia.

The Mysterious Invader. 1958. (See: *The Astounding She-Monster*.)

Mysterious Island. 1929. Spencer G. Bennet. F/Pl: *Karen Randal*. USA: Columbia.

Ne Le Criez Pas sur les Toits. 1943. Jaques Daniel-Norman. F/Pl: *Meg Lemonnier, Thérèse Dorny, Marie-José Mafféi, Madeleine Pagès*. France (occupied): SNEG.

The New Exploits of Elaine (chapter serial). 1915/J.A. Golden and L. Gasnier. F/Pl: *Pearl White*. USA: Wharton Prod. Co./Pathé Exchange. (10 chapters).

A New Hope. 1977. (See: *Star Wars: Episode IV—A New Hope*.)

The New Mutants. (2019). Josh Boone. F/Pr: *Karen Rosenfelt, Lauren Shuler Donner*. F/Pl: *Anna Taylor-Joy, Maisie Williams, Alice Braga, Blu Hunt*. USA: Marvel/20th Century-Fox.

A Novice at X-Rays. 1897. (See: *Les Rayons Roentgen*.)

Nuevo Viaje a la Luna. 1909. (See: *Le Voyage dans la Lune*.)

Okja. 2017. Bong Joon Ho. F/Pr: *Sarah Esberg, Pauline Fischer, Dede Gardner, Christina Oh, Tilda Swinton* +12. F/Pl: *Tilda Swinton, Sheena Kamal, Kathryn Kirkpatrick, Shirley Henderson*. South Korea/USA: Lewis Pictures, Plan B/Kate Street Picture Co.

The Omega Man. 1971. Boris Sagal. F/Wr: *Joyce Hooper Corrington* +1. F/Pl: *Rosalind Cash, Jill Giraldi*. USA: Walter Seltzer Productions.

One Hundred Years After. 1911. Not Known. France: Pathé.

Orlacs Haende (alt: *The Hands of Orlac*). 1924. Robert Wiene. F/Pl: *Carmen Cartellieri, Alexandra Sorina*. Austria: Pan Film.

Our Man Flint. 1965. Daniel Man. F/Pl: *Gila Golan, Shelby Grant*. USA: 20th Century–Fox.

Outbreak. 1995. Wolfgang Petersen. F/Pl: *Rene Russo, Susan Lee Hoffman*. USA: Warner Bros.

The Outer Limits (TV series.) 1963–5. Various Directors. USA: Villa Di Stefano/Daystar Productions/United Artists Television. (49 episodes).

Outland. 1981. Peter Hyams. F/Pl: *Frances Sternhagen, Kika Markham*. UK: Ladd Co.

An Over-Incubated Baby. 1901. Walter R. Booth. UK: Paul.

Pacific Rim: Uprising. (2018). Steven S. DeKnight. F/Pr: *Jennifer Conroy, Mary Parent, Brook Worley* +11. F/Wr: *Emily Carmichael, Kira Snyder* +2. F/Pl: *Cailee Spaeny, Tian Jing, Adria Arjona, Rinko Kickuchi*. USA/ China/UK: Clear Angle Studios/Dentsu/ DDY/Double Negative/Fuji Television Network/Perfect World Pictures/Twisted Media/ Universal Pictures/UpperRoom Productions.

Passengers. 2016. Morten Tyldum. F/Pl: *Jennifer Lawrence, Kara Flowers, Julee Cerda, Aurora Perrineau, Emma Clarke* (voice of the computer). USA: Columbia/LStar/Village Roadshow/Original Film/Company Films/Start Motion Pictures/Wanda Pictures.

Pawns of Mars. 1915. Theodore Marston. F/Pl: *Dorothy Kelly*. USA: Broadway Star.

Percy Pimpernickel, Soubrette. 1914. Albert Hale. USA: Kalem.

Perfect Lover. 2001. (See: *The Woman Every Man Wants*.)

The Perfect Woman. 1949. Bernard Knowles. F/Pl: *Patricia Roc, Irene Handl, Pamela Devis, Constance Smith*. UK: Two Cities.

The Perils of Pauline (chapter serial). 1914. F/Pl: *Pearl White, Eleanor Woodruff*. USA: General Film/Eclectic Film. (20 chapters).

The Phantom Empire (chapter serial). 1935. Otto Brower and B. Reeves Eason. F/Pl: *Betsy King Ross, Dorothy Christie*. USA: Mascot. (12 chapters).

The Pill Maker's Mistake. 1906. Lewin Fitzhamon. UK: Hepworth.

Pisma myortvogo cheloveka (alt: *Letters from a Dead Man/Dead Man's Letters*). 1986. Konstantin Lpoushansky. F/Pr: *Raisa Proskuryakova +1.* F/Pl: *Nora Gryakalova, Vera Mayorova. Svetlana Smirnova*. USSR: Lenfilm.

Plan 9 from Outer Space (alt: *Grave Robbers from Outer Space*). 1959. Edward D. Wood Jnr. F/Pl: *Maila Nurmi, Mona McKinnon, Joanna Lee, Norma McCarty*. USA: J. Edward Reynolds Productions.

Planet of Blood. 1966. (See: *Queen of Blood.*)

Planet of Storms. 1962. (See: *Planeta Bur.*)

Planet of the Apes. 1968. Franklin J. Schaffner. F/Pl: *Kim Hunter, Linda Harrison*. USA: APJAC Productions.

Planet of the Apes. 2001. Tim Burton. F/Pr: *Katterli Frauenfelder* (assoc.) +4. F/Pl: *Helena Bonham Carter, Estella Warren, Freda Foh Shen, Lisa Marie*. 20th Century–Fox, The Zanuck Company, Tim Burton Productions.

Planeta Bur (alt: *Storm Planet/Cosmonauts on Venus/Planet of Storms*). 1962. Pavel Klushantsev. F/Pl: *Kyunna Ignatova*. USSR: Leningrad Studio of Popular Science Films.

La poupée (alt: *The Doll/He, She or It*). 1962. Baratier, Jacques. F/Pl: *Catherine Milinaire, Sasha Pitoëff*. France: Films Franco-Africains.

The Predator. (2019). Shane Black. F/Pl: *Yvonne Strahovski, Olivia Munn*. USA: Davis Entertainment/TSG/Canada Film Capital/ Dark Castle/20th Century-Fox.

Predestination. 2014. The Sperig Brothers. F/Pl: *Sarah Snook, Sara El-Yafi, Cate Wolfe*. Australia: Screen Australia/Screen Queensland/Blacklab Entertainment/Wolfhound Pictures.

Project Almanac. 2015. Dean Israelite. F/Pr: *Vicki Dee Rock +6.* F/Pl: *Sofia Black-D'Elia, Virginia Gardner, Amy Landecker, Michelle DeFraites, Katie Garfield*. USA: Insurge Pictures/Platinum Dunes/MTV Films/Paramount.

Project Moonbase. 1953. Richard Talmadge. F/Pl: *Donna Martell*. USA: Galaxy Pictures.

Prometheus. 2012. Ridley Scott. F/Pr: *Teresa Kelly* (assoc.), *Mary Richards* (co.). F/Pl: *Noomi Rapace, Charlize Theron, Kate Dickie, Lucy Hutchinson*. USA/UK: 20th Century–

Fox/Dune Entertainment/Scott Free Productions/Brandywine Productions.

The Quatermass Xperiment (alt: *The Creeping Unknown*). 1955. Val Guest. F/Pl: *Margia Dean*. UK: Hammer Films.

Queen of Atlantis. 1932. (See: *Die Herrin von Atlantis.*)

Queen of Atlantis. 1949. (See: *Siren of Atlantis.*)

Queen of Blood (alt: *Planet of Blood*). 1966. Curtis Harington. F/Pl: *Judi Meredith, Florence Marley*. USA: George Edwards Productions/ AIP.

Queen of Outer Space. 1958. Edward Bernds. F/Pl: *Zsa Zsa Gabor, Barbara Darrow, Laurie Mitchell, Lisa Davis*. USA: Allied Artists.

The Raid of 1915. 1914. (See: *If England Were Invaded.*)

Le Raid Paris à Monte Carlo en deux heures (alt: *An Adventurous Automobile Trip*). 1904. Georges Méliès. F/Pl: *Stars of the Follies Bergères, Jane Ivon*. France: Star.

Les rayons Roentgen (alt: *A Novice at X-Rays*). 1897. Georges Méliès. France: Star.

The Red Pill (feature documentary). 2016, Casey Jaye. F/Pr: *Cassie Jaye, Nena Jaye, Anna Laclergue, Tanja Snodgrass +6.* USA: Jaye Bird Productions.

Repo Man. 1984. Alex Cox. F/Pl: *Tracey Walter, Susan Barnes, Olivia Barash*. USA: Edge City Productions.

"Requiem for Methuselah," *Star Trek* (TV episode). 30th December 1970, Season 3# 19. Murray Golden. F/Pl: *Nichelle Nichols, Madlyn Rhue*.

Rescued in Mid-Air. 1906. Percy Stow: UK: Clarendon.

Resident Evil. 2002. Paul W.S. Anderson. F/Pl: *Milla Jovovich, Indra Ové, Anna Bolt, Heike Makatsch, Fiona Glascott, Michelle Rodriguez*. UK/Germany/France/USA: Constantin Film, New Legacy, Davis Films, Impact Pictures.

Les Résultats du féminisme (alt: *Consequences of Feminism*). 1906. Alice Guy Blaché. France: Société des Etablissements L. Gaumont.

The Return of Batman. 1949. (See: *Batman and Robin.*)

The Return of Godzilla. 1955. (See: *Gojira no gyakushu.*)

Return of the Jedi. 1983. Richard Marquand. 1983. (See: *Star Wars: Episode VI—Return of the Jedi.*)

Revenge of the Creature. 1955. Jack Arnold. F/Pl: *Lori Nelson*. USA: Universal.

Rise of the Planet of the Apes. 2011. Rupert Wyatt. F/Pr: *Amanda Silver +6.* F/Wr: *Amanda Silver +1.* F/Pl: *Karin Konoval, Devyn Dal-*

ton, *Frieda Pinto*. USA/UK/Canada: 20th Century–Fox/Dune Entertainment/Chernin Entertainment/Ingenious Media/Big Screen Productions/Ingenious Film Partners/Dune Entertainment III.

The Road Warrior. 1981. (See: *Mad Max 2*.)

The Road. 2009. John Hillcoat. F/Pr: *Paula Mae Schwartz +8*. F/Pl: *Molly Parker, Charlize Theron*. USA: Dimension Films/2929 Prod./Nick Wenchsler Prod./Chockstone Pictures.

RoboCop. 1987. Paul Verhoeven. F/Pl: *Nancy Allen*. USA: Orion.

Rocket to the Moon. 1953. (See: *Cat Women of the Moon*.)

Rocketship X-M (alt: *Expedition Moon*). 1950. Kurt Neumann. F/Pl: *Osa Massen*. USA: Lippert.

The Rocky Horror Picture Show. 1975. Jim Sharman. F/Pl: *Susan Sarandon, Nell Campbell, Patricia Quinn, Hilary Labow* (Farr). UK/USA: 20th Century–Fox/Michael White Prod.

Rogue One. 2016. Gareth Edwards. F/Pr: *Kiri Hart, Kathleen Kennedy, Allison Shearmur, Susan Towner +6*. F/Pl: *Felicity Jones, Genevieve O'Reilly, Sharon Duncan-Brewster, Valene Kane* (*Carrie Fisher*). USA: Lucasfilm, Allison Shearmur Productions/Black Hangar Studios/Stereo D/Walt Disney.

Rollerball. 1975. Norman Jewison. F/Pl: *Maud Adams*. USA: Universal Artists.

The Romance of Elaine (chapter serial). 1915. George B. Seitz, Joseph A. Golden, Theodore Wharton, Leopold V. Wharton. F/Pl: *Pearl White*. USA: Wharton Prod. Co./Pathé Exchange. (12 chapters).

Sammy's Automaton. 1914. Not Known. France: Eclipse.

The Sausage Machine. 1897. Not Known. USA: American Mutoscope/Biograph Co.

The Screaming Shadow (chapter serial). 1920. Duke Worne. F/Pl: *Neva Gerber, Frances Terry, Pansy Porter, Claire Mille*. USA: Hallmark Pictures. (15 chapters).

Scroggins Goes in for Chemistry and Discovers a Marvellous Powder. 1911. A.E. Coleby. UK: Cricks and Martin.

Seksmisja (alt: *The Sex Mission*). 1984. Juliusz Machulski. F/Wr: *Jolanta Hartwig +2*. F/Pl: *Doreta Stalinska, Bozena Strjkowna, Hanna Stankowna, Zofia Plewinska*. Poland: Zespoly Filmowe/KADR.

Serenity. 2005. Joss Whedon. F/Pr: Alisa Tager. F/Pl: *Summer Glau, Gina Torres, Morena Baccarin, Jewel Staite, Sarah Paulson*. USA: Universal/Barry Mendel Prod.

The Sex Mission. 1984. (See: *Seksmisja*.)

She Devil. 1957. Kurt Neumann. F/Wr: *Caroll Young +1*. F/Pl: *Mari Blanchard, Fay Baker, Blossom Rock*. USA: Regal.

Shirley Thompson Versus the Aliens. 1972. Jim Sharman. F/Pl: *Jane Harders, June Collins*. Australia: Kolossal Films.

Short Circuit. 1986. John Badham. F/Pl: *Ally Sheedy, Penny Santon, Barbara Tarbuck*. USA: TriStar/PSO/Turman-Foster.

Sideral Cruises. 1941. (See: *Croisières sidérales*.)

Silent Running. 1971. Douglas Trumbull. F/Pl: *Cheryl Sparks* (as Maintenance Drone 2, Huey). USA: Universal/Michael Gruskoff Productions/Douglas Trumbull Productions.

Sinners in Silk. 1924. Hobart Henley. F/Pl: *Eleanor Boardman, Jean Hersholt, Hedda Hopper, Virginia Lee Corbin, Dorothy Dwan*. USA: MGM.

Sins of the Fleshapoids. 1965. Mike Kuchar. F/Pl: *Donna Kerness, Maren Thomas, Gina Zuckerman*. USA: Mike Kuchar.

Siren of Atlantis (alt: *Atlantis/Queen of Atlantis*). 1949. Gregg Tallas. F/Pl: *Maria Montez, Alexis Minotis*. USA: United Artists.

Skeleton on Horseback. 1937. (See: *Bílá nemoc*.)

Solaris (alt: *Solyaris*). 1971. Andrei Tarkovsky. F/Pl: *Natalya Bondarchuk, Olga Barnet, Olga Kizilova, Tatyana Malykh, Tamara Ogorodnikova*. USSR: Mosfilm/Unit Four/Creative Unit of Writers and Cinema Workers.

Solaris. 2002. Steven Soderbergh. F/Pr: *Rae Sanchini +5*. F/Pl: *Natasha McElhone, Viola Davies, Donna Kimball, Elpida Carrillo, Lauren Cohn*. USA: 20th Century–Fox/Lightstorm Entertainment.

"Soldier," *The Outer Limits* (TV episode). 19th September 1964, Season 2 #1. Gerd Oswald. Wr: Harlan Ellison. F/Pl: *Jill Hill, Catherine McLeod*.

Solo: A Star Wars Story. (2018). Ron Howard. F/Pr: Kathleen Kennedy, Kiri Hart, *Allison Shearmur, Susan Towner +6*; F/Pl: *Emilia Clarke*. USA: Lucasfilm/Walt Disney Pictures/Allison Shearmur Productions/Imagine Entertainment.

Solyaris. 1971. (See: *Solaris, 1971*.)

Some Girls Do. 1969. Ralph Thomas. F/Pr: *Betty E. Fox*. F/Wr: *Liz Charles-Williams +1*. F/Pl: *Daliah Lavi, Beba Loncar*. UK: Ashdown Film Productions.

Soylent Green. 1973. Richard Fleischer, Richard. F/Pl: *Leigh Taylor-Young, Paula Kelly*. USA: MGM.

The Space Between Us. 2017. Peter Chelsom. F/Pr: *Cherilyn Hawrysh, Gabrielle Jerou, Cathy Schulman +20*. F/Pl: *Janet Montgomery, Sarah Minnich, Laren Meyers, Beth Bailey*,

Carla Gugino, Britt Robertson. USA: LAMF/STX/Southpaw.

Space Master X-7 (alt: *Mutiny in Outer Space*). 1958. Edward Bernds. F/Pl: Lyn Thomas, Joan Barry. USA: Regal.

"Space Seed," *Star Trek* (TV episode). 16th February 1967, Season 1 #22. Marc Daniels. F/Pl: *Nichelle Nichols, Madlyn Rhue*.

Spaceballs. 1987. Mel Brooks. F/Pl: *Daphne Zuniga, Lorene Yarnell Jansson, Joan Rivers* (voice), *Leslie Bevis*. USA: Brooksfilms/MGM.

Species. 1995. Roger Donaldson. F/Pl: *Natasha Henstridge, Marg Helgenberger*. USA: MGM.

Spermula. 1976. Charles Matton, Charles. F/Pl: *Dayle Haddon, Ginnette Leclerc, Joycelyne Boisseau, Isabelle Mercanton*. France: Film and Co./Parlafrance.

Sphere. 1998. Barry Levinson, Barry. F/Pl: *Sharon Stone, Marga Gómez*. USA: Baltimore Pictures/Constant c productions/Punch Productions.

Spider-Man: Homecoming. 2017. Jon Watts. F/Pr: *Victoria Alonso, Rachel O'Connor, Amy Pascal, Patricia Witcher*. F/Pl: *Marisa Tomei, Gwyneth Paltrow, Zendaya, Laura Harrier, Tyne Daly, Angourie Rice*. USA: Columbia/Marvel/Pascal Picture.

Le spie vengono dal semifreddo. 1966. (See: *Dr. Goldfoot and the Girl Bombs*.)

Splice. 2009. Vincenzo Natali. F/Pr: *Sidone Dumas, Susan Montford +7*. F/Wr: *Antoinette Terry Bryant +2*. F/Pl: *Delphine Chanéac, Sarah Polley, Simone Maicanescu, Abigail Chu*. Canada/France/USA: Gaumont/Copperhart Entertainment/Dark Castle Entertainment/Senator.

Stalker. 1979. Andrei Tarkovsky. F/Pl: *Alisa Freindlikh, Natasha Abramova*. USSR: Mosfilm.

Star Trek (TV series). 1966–9. Various Directors. F/Pl: *Nichelle Nichols, Majel Barrett, Grace Lee Whitney*. USA: Paramount Television. (79 episodes).

Star Trek: The Next Generation (TV series). 1987–1994. Various Directors. F/Pl: *Marina Sirtis, Gates McFadden, Denise Crosby, Whoopie Goldberg, Majel Barrett*. USA: Paramount Television. (178 episodes.)

Star Trek: Voyager (TV series). 1995–2001. Various Directors. F/Pl: *Kate Mulgrew, Roxann Dawson, Majel Barrett, Jeri Ryan, Jennifer Lien*. USA: Paramount Television/UPN. USA. (172 episodes).

Star Trek: The Motion Picture. 1979. Robert Wise. F/Pl: *Nichelle Nichols, Persis Khambatta, Jeri Ryan, Jennifer Lien, Majel Barrett*.

USA: Paramount Pictures/Century Associates.

Star Trek II: The Wrath of Khan. 1982. Nicholas Meyer. F/Pl: *Nichelle Nichols, Bibi Besch, Kirstie Alley*. USA: Paramount.

Star Trek III: The Search for Spock. 1984. Leonard Nimoy, Leonard. F/Pl: *Nichelle Nichols, Judith Anderson, Robin Curtis, Cathie Sherriff, Grace Lee Whitney*. USA: Paramount/Cinema Group Ventures.

Star Trek IV: The Voyage Home. 1986. Leonard Nimoy. 1986. F/Pl: *Nichelle Nichols, Catherine Hicks, Jane Wyatt, Madge Sinclair* (as Captain of the USS *Saratoga*). USA: Paramount/ILM.

Star Trek V: The Final Frontier. 1989. William Shatner. 1989. F/Pl: *Nichelle Nichols, Cynthia Gouw, Spice Williams, Beverly Hart*. USA: Paramount.

Star Trek VI: The Undiscovered Country. 1991. Nicholas Meyer. F/Pl: *Nichelle Nichols, Kim Catrall, Grace Lee Whitney, Rosanna DeSoto, Iman, Darryl Henriques*. USA: Paramount.

Star Trek: Generations. 1994. David Carson, David. F/Pl: *Whoopi Goldberg, Marina Sirtis, Gates McFadden, Jacqueline Kim*. USA: Paramount.

Star Trek: First Contact. 1996. Jonathan Frakes. F/Pl: *Alice Krige, Alfre Woodard, Marina Sirtis, Gates McFadden*. USA: Digital Image Associates.

Star Trek: Insurrection. 1998. Jonathan Frakes. F/Pl: *Gates McFadden, Marina Sirtis, Donna Murphy, Stephanie Niznik*. USA: Paramount/Digital Image Associates.

Star Trek: Nemesis. 2002. Stuart Baird. F/Pl: *Gates McFadden, Marina Sirtis, Shannon Cochran, Dina Meyer, Kate Mulgrew*. USA: Paramount/Digital Image Associates.

Star Trek. 2009. J.J. Abrams. F/Pl: *Zoe Saldana, Winona Ryder, Jennifer Morrison, Rachel Nichols*. USA/Germany: Paramount/Spyglass/Bad Robot/Mavrocine.

Star Trek into Darkness. 2013. J.J. Abrams. F/Pr: *Dana Goldberg/Michelle Rejwan +11*. F/Pl: *Zoe Saldana, Alice Eve, Nazeen Contractor, Amanda Foreman*. USA: Paramount/Skydance Media/Bad Robot.

Star Trek Beyond. 2016. Justin Lin. F/Pr: *Dana Goldberg, Helen Pollak, Lindsey Weber +8*. F/Pl: *Zoe Saldana, Sofia Boutella, Lydia Wilson, Melissa Roxburgh, Anita Brown*. USA/Hong Kong/China: Paramount/Skydance Media/Alibaba Pictures/Huahua Media/Bad Robot/Sneaky Shark/Perfect Storm.

Star Trek: Discovery (TV series). 2017–. Various

Directors. F/Pl: *Sonequa Martin-Green, Michelle Yeoh, Mary Wiseman, Emily Coutts.* USA: CBS/Living Dead Guy/Roddenberry Entertainment/Secret Hideout. [15+ episodes].

Star Wars. 1977. (See: *Star Wars: Episode IV—A New Hope.*)

Star Wars Special Editions. 1997. (digitally remastered and enhanced versions of *Star Wars: Episode IV, V* and *VI*).

Star Wars: Episode I—The Phantom Menace. 1999. George Lucas. F/Pl: *Natalie Portman, Pernilla August.* USA: Lucasfilm.

Star Wars: Episode II—Attack of the Clones. 2002. George Lucas. F/Pl: *Natalie Portman, Pernilla August, Leeanna Walsman, Rose Byrne.* USA: Lucasfilm.

Star Wars: Episode III—Revenge of the Sith. 2005. George Lucas. F/Pl: *Natalie Portman, Keisha Castle-Hughes, Rebecca Jackson Mendoza, Bonnie Piesse.* USA: Lucasfilm.

Star Wars: Episode IV—A New Hope (alt: *Star Wars/A New Hope*). 1977. Lucas, George. 1977. F/Pl: *Carrie Fisher, Shelagh Fraser.* USA: Lucasfilm/20th Century–Fox.

Star Wars: Episode V—The Empire Strikes Back (alt: *The Empire Strikes Back*). 1980. Kershner, Irvin. 1980. F/Wr: *Leigh Brackett* +1. F/Pl: *Carrie Fisher, Marjorie Eaton.* USA: Lucasfilm Ltd./20th Century–Fox.

Star Wars: Episode VI—Return of the Jedi (alt: *Return of the Jedi*) 1983. F/Pl: *Carrie Fisher, Caroline Blakiston.* USA: Lucasfilm Ltd./20th Century–Fox.

Star Wars: Episode VII—The Force Awakens. 2015. J.J. Abrams. F/Pr: *Pippa Anderson, Kathleen Kennedy, Michelle Rejwan, Susan Towner* +11. F/Pl: *Daisy Ridley, Carrie Fisher, Gwendoline Christie, Lupito Nyong'o.* USA: Lucasfilm/Bad Robot.

Star Wars: Episode VIII—The Last Jedi. 2017. Rian Johnson. F/Pr: *Kathleen Kennedy* +6. F/Pl: *Daisy Ridley, Gwendoline Christie, Laura Dern, Billie Lourd, Carrie Fisher, Lupito Nyong'o, Kelly Marie Tran.* USA: Lucasfilm/Ram Bergman/Walt Disney.

Star Wars: Episode IX. (2019). J.J. Abrams. F/Pr: *Kathleen Kennedy, Michelle Rejwan.* F/Pl: *Daisy Ridley.* USA: Lucasfilm/Walt Disney Pictures/Bad Robot.

Stargate. 1994. Roland Emmerich. F/Pl: *Viveca Lindfors, Alexis Cruz.* USA: Le Studio Canal +/Centropolis/Carolco.

Stargate SG-1 (TV series), 1997–2007. Various Directors. F/Pl: *Amanda Tapping, Teryl Rothery, Claudia Black.* USA/Canada: Double Secret/Gekko Film/Kawoosh!/MGM Worldwide TV/Sony/Stargate SG-1 Production. (213 episodes).

Starman. 1984. John Carpenter. F/Pl: *Karen Allen.* USA: Columbia/ILM/Delphi II Productions.

Starship Troopers. 1998. Paul Verhoeven. F/Pl: *Dina Meyer, Denise Richards.* USA: TriStar/Touchstone/Jon Davison.

Stealth. 2005. Rob Cohen. F/Pr: *Michelle Purple, Sasisupa Sungvaribud, Laura Ziskin.* F/Pl: *Jessica Biel.* USA: Columbia/Original Film/Phoenix Pictures/Laura Ziskin Prod./AFG.

The Stepford Wives. 1974. Bryan Forbes. F/Pl: *Katherine Ross, Paula Prentiss, Nanette Newman, Tina Louise.* USA: Fadsin Cinema Associates.

The Stepford Wives. 2004. Frank Oz. F/Pl: *Nicole Kidman, Bette Midler, Glenn Close, Fallon Brooking, Faith Hill, Kate Shindle, Lorri Bagley.* USA: Paramount/Dreamworks/Scott Rudin Prod./De Line Pictures.

The Sticky Fingers of Time. 1997. Hilary Brougher. F/Pr: *Jean Castilli, Susan A. Stover* +5. F/Wr: *Hilary Brougher.* F/Pl: *Terumi Matthews, Nicole Zaray, Belinda Becker, Samantha Buck, Julie Anderson, Amanda Vogel, Amanda Cole, Alana Jerins, Rebeka Milkis.* USA: Crystal Pictures/Good Machine/Isen Robbins Prod.

Storm Planet. 1962. (See: *Planeta Bur.*)

Strange Days. 1995. Kathryn Bigelow. F/Pr: *Rae Sanchini.* F/Pl: *Angela Bassett, Juliette Lewis, Brigitte Bako.* USA: Lightstorm Entertainment.

The Stranger from Venus (alt: *Immediate Disaster/The Venutian*). 1954. Burt Balaban. F/Pl: *Patricia Neal, Marigold Russell.* UK. (A British remake of *The Day the Earth Stood Still,* 1951.)

Superman (chapter serial). 1948. Spencer Gordon Bennet and Thomas Carr. F/Pl: *Carol Forman, Noel Neill.* USA: Columbia. (15 chapters).

Superman. 1978. Richard Donner. F/Pl: *Margot Kidder, Valerie Perrine, Susannah York.* UK: Dovemead/Film Export AG/International Film Production.

El Supersabio. 1948. Miguel M. Delgado. F/Pl: *Perla Aguiar, Aurora Walker, Carmen Novelty.* Mexico: Posa Films.

Sur un air de Charleston (alt: *Charleston Parade*). 1927. Jean Renoir. F/Pl: *Catherine Hessling.* France: Films Jean Renoir.

Tales of Hoffmann. 1923. (See: *Hoffmanns Erzählungen.*)

Tank Girl. 1995. Rachel Talalay. F/Pl: *Lori Petty,*

Naomi Watts, Ann Cusack. USA: United Artists/Trilogy Entertainment.

Tarantula. 1955. Jack Arnold. F/Pl: *Mara Corday.* USA: Universal.

Teenage Monster (alt: *Meteor Monster*). 1957. Jacques Marquette, F/Pl: *Anne Gwynne, Gloria Castillo.* USA: Marquette Productions.

Teenagers from Outer Space (alt: *The Gargon Terror*). 1959. Tom Graeff. F/Pl: *Dawn Anderson.* USA: Tapor Corp.

The Terminator. 1984. James Cameron. F/Pr: *Gale Ann Hurd.* F/Wr: *Gale Ann Hurd* +1. F/Pl: *Linda Hamilton, Bess Mota.* USA: Hemdale/Pacific Western/Euro Film Funding/Cinema '84/Greenberg Brothers Partnership.

Terminator 2: Judgment Day. 1991. Cameron, James. F/Pr: *Stephanie Austin, Gale Anne Hurd* +3. F/Pl: *Linda Hamilton, S. Epatha Merkerson, Jenette Goldstein.* USA: Carolco/Pacific Western/Lightstorm.

Terminator 3: Rise of the Machines. 2003. Jonathan Mostow. F/Pr: *Gale Anne Hurd* +13. F/Pl: *Kristanna Loken, Claire Danes, Moira Sinise, Carolyn Hennesy.* USA/Germany/UK: C-2 Pictures/Intermedia/IMF/Mostow Lieberman/Columbia/Warner Bros.

Terminator Genisys. 2015. Alan Taylor. F/Pr: *Megan Ellison, Dana Goldberg, Shari Hanson, Laeta Kalogridis* +4. F/Wr: *Laeta Kalogridis* +1. F/Pl: *Emilia Clarke, Sandrine Holt.* USA: Paramount/Sydance.

Terminator Salvation. 2009. McG. Jeanne Allgood, Chantal Feghali, April Janow, Anjalika Mathur Nigam +16. F/Pl: *Moon Bloodgood, Helena Bonham Carter, Jadagrace, Bryce Dallas Howard, Jane Alexander, Beth Bailey.* USA/Germany/UK/Italy: Warner Bros./Columbia/Halcyon/Wonderland Sound and Vision.

Terminator: The Sarah Connor Chronicles (TV series). 2008–9. Various Directors. F/Pl: *Lena Headey, Summer Glau, Shirley Manson.* USA: Bartleby/C-2 Pictures/Warner Bros. Television/Halcyon/Sarah Connor Pictures/Syfy. (31 episodes).

Das Testament des Dr. Mabuse (German version of: *The Last Will of Dr. Mabuse*). 1933. Fritz Lang. F/Wr: *Thea von Harbou.* F/Pl: *Wera Liessem, Camilla Spira.* Germany: Nero Film/Constantin/Deutsche Universal.

Them! 1954. Gordon Douglas. F/Pl: *Joan Weldon, Sandy Descher, Mary Ann Hokanson.* USA: Warner Bros.

The Thing from Another World! (alt: *The Thing*). 1951. Christian Nyby. F/Pl: *Margaret Sheridan, Sally Creighton.* USA: RKO/Winchester.

The Thing. 1951. (See: *The Thing from Another World!*)

The Thing. 1982. John Carpenter. F/Pl: *Adrienne Barbeau* (voice). USA: Universal/Turman-Foster.

Things to Come. 1936. William Cameron Menzies. F/Pl: *Margaretta Scott.* UK: London.

This Island Earth. 1955. Joseph Newman, Joseph. F/Pl: *Faith Domergue.* USA: Universal.

THX 1138. 1970. George Lucas. F/Pl: *Maggie McOmie.* USA: American Zoetrope.

The Time Machine. 1960. George Pal. F/Pl: *Yvette Mimieux.* USA: Galaxy Films/MGM.

The Time Traveler's Wife (alt: *The Time Traveller's Wife*). 2009. Robert Schwentke. F/Wr: *Audrey Niffenegger* (source novel). F/Pl: *Michelle Nolden, Katherine Trowell, Esther Jun, Rachel McAdams, Carly Street, Brooklynn Proulx, Jane McLean.* USA: New Line, Plan B Entertainment, Nick Wechsler Prod.

Timeslip (alt: *The Atomic Man*). 1956. Ken Hughes. F/Pl: *Faith Domergue.* UK: Merton Park Productions.

Titan A.E. 2000. Don Bluth, Gary Goldman and Art Vitello. F/Pl: (voices) *Janeane Garofalo, Drew Barrymore, Tsai Chin, Crystal Scales.* USA: 20th Century–Fox, Fox Animation, David Kirschner Prod.

Total Recall. 1990. Paul Verhoeven. F/Pl: *Rachel Ticotin, Sharon Stone.* USA: Carolco.

Transcendence. 2014. Wally Pfister. F/Pr: *Yolanda T. Cochran, Kate Cohen, Annie Marter, Marisa Polvino, Mary Regency Boies, Emma Thomas* +9. F/Pl: *Rebecca Hall, Cillian Murphy, Kate Mara.* UK/China/USA: Alcon Entertainment/DMG/Straight Up Films.

Transformers. 2007. Michael Bay. F/Pr: *Allegra Clegg, Michelle McGonagle* +12. F/Pl: *Megan Fox, Rachael Taylor, Julie White.* USA: Paramount/DreamWorks/Hasbro/Di Bonaventura Pictures/Amblin Entertainment/Platinum Dunes/SprocketHeads/thinkfilm.

A Trip to Mars. 1902. (See: *Le Voyage dans la Lune*.)

A Trip to Mars. 1917. (See: *Himmelskibet*.)

A Trip to the Moon. 1898. (See: *La Lune à un mètre*.)

A Trip to the Moon. 1902. (See: *Le Voyage dans la Lune*.)

The Triton. 1917. (See: *A Tryton*.)

TRON. 1982. Steven Lisberger. F/Pl: *Cindy Morgan.* USA: Walt Disney/Lisberger-Kushner Prod.

TRON: Legacy. 2010. Joseph Kosinski. F/Pl: *Olivia Wilde, Beau Garrett, Serinda Swan, Elizabeth Mathis, Yaya DeCosta, Belinda*

Montgomery. USA: Walt Disney/Sean Bailey Productions/LivePlanet/Prana Studios.

"Turnabout Intruder," *Star Trek* (TV episode). 15th December 1971, Season 3 #24. Herb Wallerstein. F/Pl: *Nichelle Nichols, Sandra Smith, Majel Barrett.*

A Tryton (alt: *The Triton*). 1917. Alfred Deesy. F/Pl: *Annie Goth.* Austria: Star.

Under the Seas. 1907. (See: *Deux Cent Milles Lieues sous les Mers ou le Cauchemar d'un Pêcheur.*)

Under the Skin. 2013. Jonathan Glazer. F/Pr: *Gillian Berrie, Claudia Bluemhauber, Tessa Ross +7.* F/Pl: *Scarlett Johansson, Lynsey Taylor Mackay, Alison Chand.* UK/Switzerland/USA: Film4/BFI/Silver Reel/Creative Scotland/Sigma Films/FilmNation/Nick Wechsler Productions/JW Films/Canal+/Scottish Screen/UK Film Council.

Unearthly Stranger. 1963. John Krish. F/Pl: *Gabriella Licudi, Jean Marsh.* UK: Independent Artists. A Julian Wintel-Leslie Parkyn Prod.

Unnatural. 1952. (See: *Alraune.*)

Untamed Women. 1952. W. Merle Connell. F/Pl: *Doris Merrick.* USA: Jewell Enterprise Productions.

Valerian and the City of a Thousand Planets. 2017. Luc Besson. F/Pr: *Camille Courau, Virginie Besson-Silla +1.* F/Pl: *Cara Delevingne, Rihanna.* France/China/Belgium/United Arab Emirates/USA/Germany/UK/Canada: EuropaCorp/Fundamental Films/Grive Productions/Gulf Film/Novo Pictures/Orange Studio/River Road/TF1 Films/UFA.

La venganza del sexo (alt: *The Curious Dr. Humpp*). 1967. Emilio Vieyra. F/Pl: *Gloria Prat, Susan Beltrán, Mary Albano.* Argentina: Productores Argentinos Asociados.

Vengeance. 1952. (See: *Alraune.*)

The Venutian. 1954. (See: *The Stranger from Venus.*)

Vers l'Immortalitié (alt: *The Elixir of Life*). 1911. Not Known. France: Gaumont.

Victory and Peace (alt: *The Invasion of Britain*). 1918. Herbert Brenon. F/Pl: *Marie Lohr, Ellen Terry.* UK: National War Aims Committee.

Videodrome. 1983. David Cronenberg. F/Pl: *Deborah Harry, Sonja Smits.* Canada: Filmplan Int.

The Volcano Monster. 1955. (See: *Gojira no gyakushu.*)

Voyage autour d'une etoile (alt: *Around a Star*). 1906. Gaston Velle. France: Pathé.

Le Voyage dans la Lune (alt: *A Trip to the Moon/A Trip to Mars*). 1902. Georges Méliès. F/Pl:

Bleinette Bernon, Corps de Ballet du Châtelet, Acrobats from the Folies-Bergère. France: Star.

Le Voyage dans la Lune (alt: *Nuevo viaje a la Luna*). 1909. Segundo de Chomon. France: Pathé.

The Voyage of the Arctic (alt: *The Adventurous Voyage of the Arctic*). 1903. Walter R. Booth. UK: Paul.

Voyage to the Planet of Prehistoric Women (alt: *Gill Women/Gill Women of Venus*). 1966. Derek Thomas. F/Pl: *Mamie Van Doren, Mary Mark, Paige Lee.* USA: Filmgroup.

Voyage to the Prehistoric Planet. 1965. John Sebastian (Curtis Harington). F/Pl: *Faith Domergue.* USA: Filmgroup.

Wake Up! (alt: *A Dream of Tomorrow*). 1914. Laurence Cowan. 1914. UK.

WALL-E. 2008. Andrew Stanton. F/Pr: *Lindsey Collins +4.* F/Pl: (voices) *Elissa Knight* (as Eve), *Kathy Najimy, Sigourney Weaver.* USA: Walt Disney/Pixar/FortyFour Studios.

War for the Planet of the Apes. 2017. Matt Reeves. F/Pr: *Mary McLaglen, Amanda Silver, Jenno Topping +5.* F/Pl: *Karin Konoval, Amiah Miller, Judy Greer, Sara Canning, Devyn Dalton, Mercedes de la Zerda.* USA/Canada/New Zealand: Chernin Entertainment/TSG Entertainment.

The War of the Gargantuas. 1966. (See: *Furankenshutain no kaijū: Sanda tai Gaira.*)

War of the Worlds. 1953. Byron Haskin, Byron. F/Pl: *Ann Robinson, Sandro Giglio.* USA: George Pal Productions/Paramount.

WarGames. 1983. John Badham. F/Pl: *Ally Sheedy, Susan Davis.* USA: MGM/United Artists/Sherwood Productions.

Waterworld. 1995. Kevin Reynolds. F/Pl: *Jeanne Tripplehorn.* USA: Universal.

Way...Way Out. 1966. Gordon Douglas. F/Pl: *Connie Stevens, Anita Ekberg.* USA: Coldwater/Jerry Lewis/20th Century–Fox.

Weird Science. 1985. John Hughes. F/Pl: *Kelly Le Brock, Suzanne Snyder, Judie Aronson.* USA: Universal.

Westworld (TV series). 2016–. Various Directors. F/Pl: *Evan Rachel Wood, Thandie Newton, Talulah Riley.* USA: Bad Robot/Jerry Weintraub Productions/Kilter Films/Warner Bros. Television. (20+ episodes).

Westworld. 1973. Michael Crichton. F/Pl: *Victoria Shaw, Linda Gaye Scott, Majel Barrett, Anne Randall.* USA: MGM

When the Man in the Moon Seeks a Wife. 1908. Percy Stow. UK: Clarendon.

When Worlds Collide. 1951. Rudolphe Mate. F/Pl: *Barbara Rush, Judith Ames.* USA: George Pal Productions/Paramount.

The White Disease. 1937. (See: *Bílá nemoc.*)

Without a Soul (alt: *Lola*). 1916. James Young. F/Pl: *Clara Kimball Young, Irene Tams, Mary Moore, Naomi Childers.* USA: World/Clara Kimball Young Co.

The Woman Every Man Wants (alt: *Perfect Lover*). 2001. Gabriela Tagliavini. F/Pr: *Lauren Moews, Gabriela Tagliavini* +2. F/Wr: *Gabriela Tagliavini.* F/Pl: *Daniela Amavia, Alexis Arquette, Michelle Anne Johnson, Pat Craword Brown.* USA/Argentina: Tonic Films/Venus Films.

Woman in the Moon. 1929. (See: *Frau im Mond.*)

Womb (alt: *Clone*). 2010. Benedek Fliegauf. F/Pl: *Mónika Mécs, Verona Meier, Daniela Meixner* +9. F/Pl: *Eva Green, Lesley Manville, Hannah Murray, Natalia Tena, Ella Smith, Wunmi Mosaku, Gina Stiebitz, Jennifer Lim.* Germany/Hungary/France: Razor Film Produktion/Inforg Stúdió/Asap Films/Arte France Cinéma/ZDF/Arte/Boje Buck Produktion.

The World, the Flesh and the Devil. 1959. Ranald MacDougall. F/Pl: *Inger Stevens.* USA: Sol C. Siegel/Harbel Productions.

World Without End. 1956. Edward Bernds. F/Pl: *Nancy Gates, Lisa Montell.* USA: Allied Artists.

*The X Files.*1998. Rob Bowman. F/Pr: *Mary Astadourian, Lata Ryan* +3. F/Pl: *Gillian Anderson, Blythe Danner.* USA: 20th Century–Fox/Ten Thirteen Productions.

Xenogenesis. 1978. James Cameron and Randall Frakes. F/Pl: *Margaret Umbel.* USA: Xenogen Production. (12-minute short).

The X-Files (TV Series). 1993–2003. Various Directors. F/Pl: *Gillian Anderson, Annabeth Gish, Sheila Larken.* Canada: Ten Thirteen Production/20th Century–Fox Television/ X-F Productions. (210 episodes).

The X-Files: I Want to Believe. 2008. Chris Carter. F/Pl: *Gillian Anderson, Amanda Peet, Nicki Aycox, Carrie Ruscheinsky.* USA: 20th Century–Fox/Ten Thirteen Productions/ Dune Entertainment III/Crying Box Productions.

The X-Ray Fiend. 1897. (See: *X-Rays.*)

The X-Ray Mirror. 1899. Wallace McCutcheon. USA: American Mutoscope/Biograph Co.

X-Rays (alt: *The X-Ray Fiend*). 1897. George A. Smith. USA: G.A.S.

"Yesterday's Enterprise," *Star Trek: The Next Generation* (TV episode). 29th January 1990, Season 3 #15. David Carson. F/Pl: *Tricia O'Neil* (as Capt. Rachel Garrett), *Marina Sirtis, Gates McFadden, Denise Crosby, Whoopie Goldberg, Majel Barrett.*

The Young Diana. 1922. A. Capellani and R.G. Vignola. F/Pr: *Marion Davies.* F/Pl: *Marion Davies, Gypsy O'Brien.* USA: Cosmopolitan.

Zeta One. 1969. Michael Cort. F/Pl: *Yutte Stensgaard, Dawn Addams.* UK: Tigon British.

Zombie Strippers. 2008. Jay Lee. F/Pr: *Laura Bach, Angela Lee* +5. F/Pl: *Jenna Jameson, Roxy Saint, Penny Vital, Whitney Anderson, Jennifer Holland, Samron Moore, Jeannette Sousa, Carmit Levité.* USA: Stage 6 Films, Larande Productions, Scream HQ.

Zombies of the Statosphere. 1952. Fred C. Brannon. F/Pl: *Aline Towne, Lane Bradford.* USA: Republic.

FILM AND TELEVISION: NON–SCIENCE FICTION

Amélie. 2001. Jean-Pierre Jeunet. France/Germany: Claudie Ossard Productions/Union Générale Cinématographique/Victoires Productions/Tapioca Films/France 3 Cinéma/ MMC Independent/Sofica Sofinergie 5/ Filmstiftung Nordrhein-Westfalen/Canal+.

American Graffiti. 1973. George Lucas. USA: Universal/Lucasfilm Ltd./Coppola Co.

And God Created Woman (alt: *Et Dieu Créa la Femme/And Woman…Was Created*). 1956. Roger Vadim, Roger. France: lena/UCIL/ Cocinor.

Apocalypse Now. 1979. Francis Ford Coppola. USA: Zoetrope Studios.

Apollo 13. 1995. Ron Howard. USA: Universal/Imagine Entertainment.

Après le bal (alt: *After the Ball, the Bath*). 1897. Georges Méliès. France: Star.

The Artist. 2011. Michel Hazanavicius. France/ USA/Belgium: Studio 37/La Petite Reine/ La Classe Américaine/JD Prod/France 3 Cinéma/Jouror Productions/uFilm.

Atomic Blonde. 2017. David Leitch. F/Pl: *Charlize Theron.* Germany/Sweden/USA: 87 Eleven/Close on Mondays Entertainment/ Denver and Delilah Prod./Film i Väst/ TGIM.

Beauty and the Beast. Bill Condon. USA/UK: Walt Disney/Mandeville Films.

Blood and Roses. 1960. Roger Vadim. France/ Italy: Documento Film/Films EGE.

Bridge on the River Kwai. 1957. David Lean. UK/USA: Columbia/Horizon.

Broken Arrow. 1950. Delmer Daves. USA: 20th Century–Fox.

Buffy the Vampire Slayer. 1992. Fran Rubel Kuzai. USA: 20th Century–Fox/Kuzai Enterprises/Sandollar.

Das Kabinett des Dr. Caligari (alt: *The Cabinet of Dr. Caligari*). 1919. Robert Weine. Germany: Decla-Bioskop.

Casablanca. 1942. Michael Curtiz. USA: Warner Bros.

Cinderella and the Glass Slipper (alt: *Cedrillon*). 1899. Georges Méliès. France: Star.

Citizen Kane. 1941. Orson Welles. USA: RKO/ Mercury Productions.

Dances with Wolves. 1990. Kevin Costner. USA: Tig Prod./Majestic Films/Allied Filmmakers.

La Decima Vittima (alt: *The Tenth Victim*). 1965. Elio Petri. Italy/France: Compagnia Cinematografica Champion/Les Films Concordia.

Delicatessen. 1991. Marc Caro and Jean-Pierre Jeunet. France: Constellation/UGC/Hachette Première/Sofinergie Films/Sofinergie 2/Investimage 2/Investimage 3/La Fondation Gan pour le Cinéma/Victoires Productions.

Desperately Seeking Susan. 1985. Susan Seidelman. USA: Orion Pictures.

Friends (TV series). 1994–2004. Various Directors. USA: Warner Bros. Television/ Bright/Kauffman/Crane Productions. (236 episodes.)

G.I. Blues. 1960. Norman Taurog. USA: Hal Wallis Productions.

The Girl Who Kicked the Hornets' Nest (alt: *Luftslottet som Sprängdes*). 2009. Daniel Alfredson. F/Pl: *Noomi Rapace.* Sweden/Denmark/Germany: Yellow Bird/STV/Nordisk Film/ZDF Film i Väst.

The Girl Who Played with Fire (alt: *Flickan som Lekte med Elden*). 2009. Daniel Alfredson. F/Pl: *Noomi Rapace.* Sweden/Denmark/ Germany: Yellow Bird/STV/Nordisk Film/ ZDF/Filmpool Stockholm Mälardalen/Film i Väst/Spiltan Underhållning/SFI.

The Girl with the Dragon Tattoo (alt: *Män som Hatar Kvinnor*). 2009. Niels Arden Oplev. F/Pl: *Noomi Rapace.* Sweden/Denmark/ Germany/Norway: Yellow Bird/STV/Nordisk Film/ZDF/Filmpool Stockholm Mälardalen/Film i Väst/Spiltan Underhållning/ SFI/Nordisk Film-& TV-Fond/Det Danske Filminstitut.

Girlfight. 2000. *Karyn Kusama.* USA: Green/ Renzi/IFC.

Groundhog Day. 1993. Harold Ramis. USA: Columbia.

Halloween. 1978. John Carpenter. USA: Compass/Falcon.

The Hidden Fortress (alt: *Kakushi Toride no San Akunin/Three Men in a Hidden Fortress*). 1958. Akira Kurosawa. Japan: Toho.

High Noon. 1952. Fred Zinnemann. USA: Universal Artists.

His Girl Friday. 1940. Howard Hawks. USA: Columbia Pictures.

Howl's Moving Castle. 2004. Hayao Miyazaki. Japan: Buena Vista/DENTSU/Mitsubishi/ NTV/Studio Ghibli/TFC/Tokuma Shoten/ d-rights.

Hud. 1963. Martin Ritt. F/Pl: *Patricia Neal.* USA: Paramount/Salem-Dover Prod.

The Jazz Singer. 1927. Alan Crossland. USA: Warner Bros.

King Creole. 1958. Michael Curtiz. USA: Wallis-Hazen.

King Kong. 1933. Merian C. Cooper and Ernest B. Schoedsack. F/Pl: *Fay Wray.* USA: RKO.

Klute. 1971. Alan J. Pakula 1971. F/Pl: *Jane Fonda.* USA: Warner Brothers.

La La Land. 2016. Damien Chazelle. USA: Black Label Media/Gilbert Films/Impostor Pictures/Marc Platt Productions/Summit Entertainment.

Les Liaisons dangereuses. 1959. Roger Vadim. France/Italy: Les Films Marceau-Cocinor.

The Lion in Winter. 1968. Antony Harvey. UK: Haworth.

M. 1931. Fritz Lang. Germany: Nero-Film AG.

The Magnificent Seven. 1960. John Sturges. USA: Mirisch/Alpha.

My Fair Lady. 1964. George Cukor. USA: Warner Bros.

Night of the Living Dead. 1968. George A. Romero. USA: Image Ten/Laurel Group/ Market Square/Off Color Films.

One Million Years B.C. 1966. Don Chaffey. F/Pl: Raquel Welch. UK: Hammer Films/Associated British-Pathé/Seven Arts.

"The One with the Princess Leia Fantasy." *Friends* (TV episode). 16th September 1996, Season 3 #1. Gail Mancuso. USA: Warner Bros. Television/Bright/Kauffman/Crane Productions.

Peggy Sue Got Married. 1986. Francis Ford Coppola. USA: TriStar/Rastar/Zoetrope/Delphi V Prod.

Pocahontas. 1995. Mike Gabriel and Eric Goldberg. USA: Walt Disney.

Pride and Prejudice. 1940. Robert Z. Leonard. F/Pl: *Maureen O'Sullivan.* USA: MGM.

Rambo: First Blood, Part II. 1985. George P. Cosmatos. USA: Anabasis NV.

Red Sonja. 1985. Richard Fleischer. F/Pl: *Brigitte Neilsen.* USA/Netherlands: Dino Di Laurentiis Co./Famous Films.

Le Royaume des fées (alt: *Fairyland: A Kingdom of Fairies*). 1903. Georges Méliès. France: Star.

The Seven Samurai. 1954. Akira Kurosawa. Japan: Toho.

Smurfs: Lost Village. 2017. Kelly Asbury. F/Pl: *Michelle Rodriguez.* USA/Hong Kong: Columbia Pictures/Kerner Entertainment Company/LStar Capital/Sony Pictures Animation/Wanda Pictures.

The Sound of Music. 1965. Robert Wise. USA: Robert Wise Productions/Argyle Enterprises.

Spinal Tap. 1984. (See: *This Is Spinal Tap.*)

Spirited Away. 2001. Hayao Miyazaki. Japan: Tokuma Shotem/Studio Ghibli/NTV/Dentsu/Buena Vista/TFC/Mitsubishi.

A Streetcar Named Desire. 1951. Elia Kazan. F/Pl: *Kim Hunter.* USA: Warner Bros./Charles K. Feldman.

This Is Spinal Tap (alt: *Spinal Tap*) 1984. Rob Reiner. UK: Spinal Tap Productions.

A Touch of Class. 1973. Melvin Frank. 1973. UK: Brut.

Toy Story. 1995. John Lasseter. USA: Pixar/Walt Disney.

Twilight. 2008. Catherine Hardwicke. USA: Summit/Temple Hill/Maverick/Imprint/Goldcrest/Twilight Productions.

The Twilight Saga: New Moon. 2009. Chris Weitz. USA: Summit/Temple Hill/Maverick/Imprint/Sunswept.

The Twilight Saga: Breaking Dawn—Part 1. 2011. Bill Condon. USA: Summit/Sunswept/TSBD/Temple Hill/Total Entertainment/Zohar.

The Twilight Saga: Breaking Dawn—Part 2. 2012. Bill Condon. USA: Summit/Temple Hill/Sunswept.

The Twilight Saga: Eclipse. 2010. Davis Slade. USA: Summit/Temple Hill/Maverick/Imprint/Sunswept.

Viva Las Vegas. 1964. George Sidney. USA: MGM.

West Side Story. 1961. Jerome Robbins and Robert Wise. USA: Mirisch Corp./Seven Arts Prod.

The Wizard of Oz. 1939. Victor Fleming. USA: MGM.

Wonder Woman. 2017. Patty Jenkins. USA/China/Hong Kong/UK/Italy/Canada/New Zealand: Warner Bros./Atlas Entertainment/Cruel & Unusual Films/DC Entertainment/Rat-Pac Dune/Tencent Pictures/Wanda Pictures.

RADIO BROADCASTS

"Alex Garland on *Ex Machina*," on *The Film Programme, with Francine Stock.* (Radio broadcast.) 22nd January 2015. UK: BBC Radio 4. (Available online at: www.bbc.co.uk/programmes/b04ykk5b [Accessed: 13th August 2017].)

"Ridley Scott," on *The Film Programme, with Francine Stock.* (Radio broadcast). 11th May 2017. UK: BBC Radio 4. (Available online at: www.bbc.co.uk/programmes/b08pgbvb [Accessed 20th August 2017]).

"Women of Punk," on *The Reunion, with Sue MacGregor* (Radio broadcast). 21st April 2017. Contributors: Gaye Advert, Toyah Willcox, Gina Birch, Tessa Pollitt and Vivien Goldman. UK: BBC Radio 4. (Available online at: www.bbc.co.uk/programmes/b08m98q2 [Accessed 21st April 2017].)

INDEX

Numbers in **bold italics** indicate pages with illustrations